UNTY, M

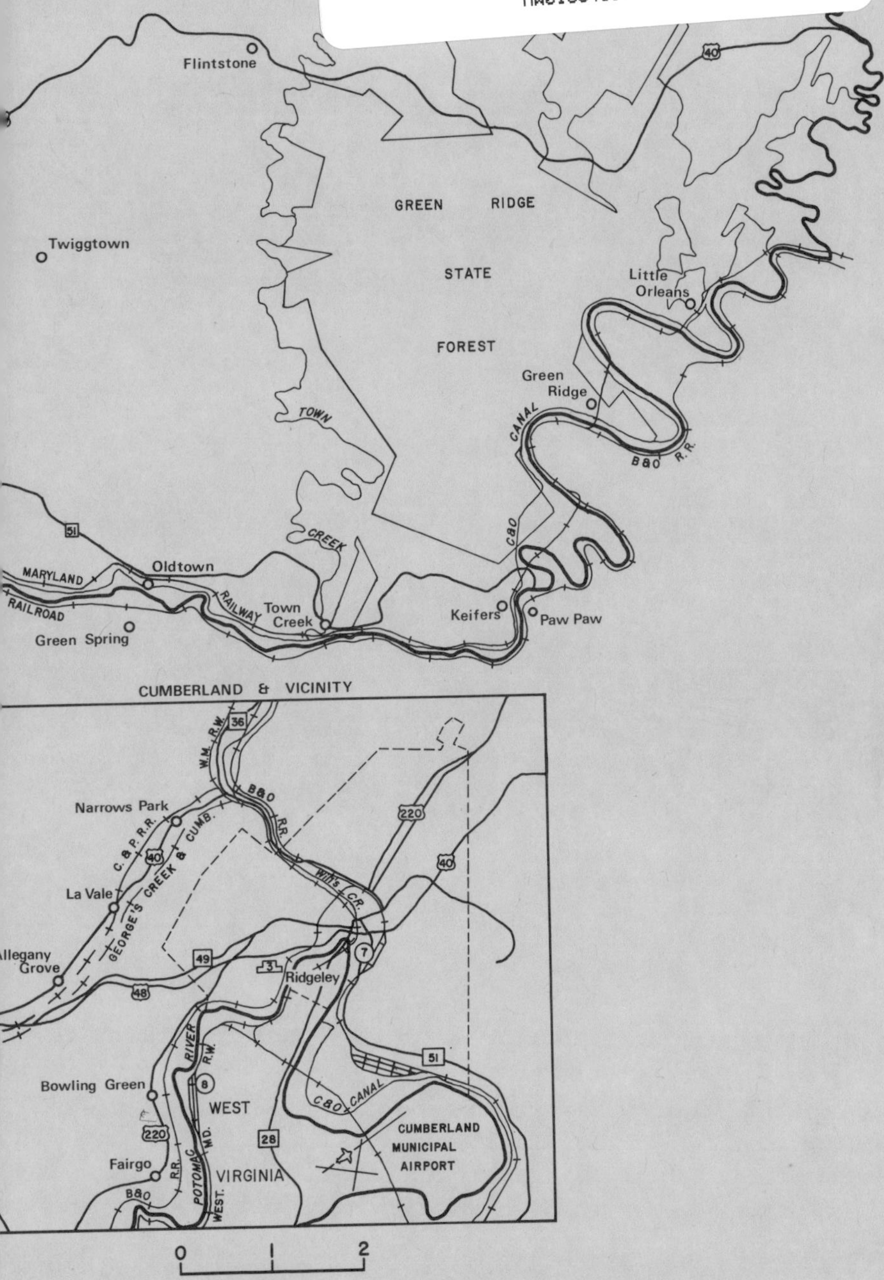
Flintstone
40
GREEN RIDGE
STATE
FOREST
Twiggtown
Little
Orleans
Green
Ridge
TOWN
CANAL
B&O R.R.
51
CREEK
C&O
MARYLAND
Oldtown
RAILROAD
RAILWAY
Town
Creek
Keifers
Paw Paw
Green Spring
CUMBERLAND & VICINITY
36
W.M. R.W.
B&O
R.R.
Narrows Park
C. & P. R.R.
40
CUMB.
GEORGE'S CREEK &
220
40
Will's CR.
La Vale
Allegany
Grove
49
48
7
3
Ridgeley
RIVER
R.W.
51
8
WEST
C&O
CANAL
Bowling Green
220
28
MD.
POTOMAC
CUMBERLAND
MUNICIPAL
AIRPORT
Fairgo
R.R.
VIRGINIA
B&O
WEST.
0
1
2
MILES

ALLEGANY COUNTY

A HISTORY

By: Harry I. Stegmaier, Jr.

David M. Dean

Gordon E. Kershaw

John B. Wiseman

Map By: Russell Berry

William Nizinski

McClain Printing Company

Parsons, West Virginia

1976

Standard Book Number 87012-257-6
Library of Congress Card Number 76-23983
Printed in the United States of America

SECOND PRINTING 1983

Dedicated to
the past, present, and future citizens
of Allegany County, Maryland

CONTENTS

PREFACE

In the historical research concerning the migrations of men, there are definite patterns and basic reasons why certain peoples migrated to a particular region. In Allegany County, Maryland, the junction of the Potomac River and Wills Creek, the spectacular geological formation known as the Narrows, which made the natural break in the Appalachian Mountains as a route west, and the abundance of wood, coal, water, and sand—all were the significant factors which led to the development of the entire Western Maryland region.

With these natural inducements, peoples with skills and knowledge for developing these assets gave impetus to the growth of the area. The ability to extract these native resources and the accompanying need for the distribution of them, which in turn led to the development of the National Road, the building of the great railroad lines, and the construction of the Chesapeake and Ohio Canal, brought our forefathers here. Perhaps those with the most marketable skills came first; others followed. Predominately they came from England, Scotland, Wales, Ireland, and Germany: coal miners, ironworkers, woodsmen, construction workers, brickmakers, and most importantly, the mining and construction engineers.

Above all, as in the settlement of the entire nation from the earliest days to the present era, there was always that deep feeling and need for religious freedom. The valley of the Potomac offered haven for all religious groups. Those of us as descendants of these people have this fervor deeply ingrained in our minds and hearts so that there is scarcely a native in these hills who does not feel instinctively the Biblical words:

I shall lift up mine eyes unto the mountains,
From whence cometh my help.

For we are truly a Mountain People.

In this Bicentennial Year, in order that "men's actions may not in time be forgotten," this book has been written. It is a tribute to and for the people of Allegany County. A people who understands its roots, who is proud of its heritage, grows confident and optimistic of its future. May the readers of this volume develop a love and appreciation for Allegany County.

We are grateful for the funding of this project by the Allegany County Commissioners: President John J. Coyle, Richard Mappin, and Arthur Bond. To members of the History Department of Frostburg State College, Dr. Harry I. Stegmaier, Jr., chairman of the project, Dr. David M. Dean, Dr. Gordon E. Kershaw, and Dr. John B. Wiseman, who gave so willingly of their time, knowledge, and research, as their contribution to the Bicentennial celebration in the county, we are most grateful.

Miriam Klawan Mirkin
Chairman
Allegany County Bicentennial
Committee, 1972-1976

We wish to thank the present Board of Commissioners of Allegany County, Maryland: Arthur T. Bond, President; Linda A. Golden; Francis G. Philpot; and their tourism and public relations director, Josephine L. Beynon, for making possible this second printing of *Allegany County: A History*.

March 1983

INTRODUCTION

Allegany County, one of the westernmost as well as one of the youngest of Maryland's counties, has a history which is both typical and atypical of the experience of the more eastern portions of the state. It shares a common origin, the same intermixture of races and nationalities, and many of the same interests and attitudes of the downstate area. Today its inhabitants live the same sort of lives, dress similarly, and perhaps think the same as their neighbors to the east, although their dialect is somewhat unique. But Allegany County is, above all, a mountain county; it must properly be considered more a northern extension of Appalachia than an integral part of lowland Maryland. Even during the colonial period its settlers, often migrants from more easterly counties, engaged in mixed farming on its rolling meadows and in its fertile valleys rather than in the traditional tidewater planting of tobacco. The excellent transportational facilities developed in the county by the mid-nineteenth century, successively the National Road, the Baltimore and Ohio Railroad, and the Chesapeake and Ohio Canal, tightened its bonds with the East, but also increasingly linked it with westward expansion. By the Civil War era, Cumberland had become one of the nation's great rail centers. Its connections made possible the development of the massive coal deposits at Georges Creek and elsewhere by the Consolidation Coal Company, an organization which, like others of its kind, was financed by outside capital. Development, however, has too often meant exploitation of both the land and its people. Slag heaps, denuded hillsides, victims of black lung disease, and undernourished children have frequently been the legacy of the past to the present in a region where corporate profits have drained from the county rather than having been invested in its future. This future has in recent years appeared increasingly bleak. The decades of the late nineteenth and early twentieth centuries were punctuated by labor unrest, repression, and periodic depression, and the post-1945 period has been characterized by declining and vanishing industry, misused natural resources, persistent unemployment, the flight of the younger generation, and a new, subtle form of isolation which is remarkable in this age of mass communications. In this year of the Bicentennial, 1976, the people of this county face the same kinds of challenges as did their ancestors of two hundred years ago.

This book is a history of Allegany County, but a history quite different from those written in the past. The authors respect these earlier works, and have in some instances relied heavily upon them, but they regard their present task as one of supplementing and updating their contents. It is a commonplace that each generation writes its own history. This is an absolute necessity, for each generation sees in the past what is reflected in its own experience. This book is not a work of filial piety or of hagiography, and its aim is not to repeat the earlier efforts of others. Its story is an account of the lives of the people of Allegany County—all of them—and it is to these people that this book is dedicated.

The idea for a history of Allegany County originated with Mrs. Miriam Mirkin, chairman of the County Bicentennial Committee, in the summer of 1974. Mrs. Mirkin believed that a new county history, sorely needed in recent years as older works became increasingly obsolete, would serve as a most appropriate complement to the many activities then being planned for the Bicentennial Year. She encouraged the county commissioners, John J. Coyle, chairman, Arthur T. Bond, and Richard C. Mappin, to fund the project. Drs. Harry I. Stegmaier, Jr., David M. Dean, Gordon E. Kershaw, and John B. Wiseman, all members of the Department of History at Frostburg State College, agreed to write the history, with Dr. Stegmaier serving as chairman. A Sales and Promotion Committee, headed by James E. Coyle and composed of volunteers from throughout Allegany County, devised and executed plans for publicity and sale of the book.

That the work has become a truly countywide project is evident in the large number of residents who have contributed in some way to its contents. We take this opportunity to thank those who have been especially generous in providing assistance: Harris W. LeFew, William M. Thompson, Gerald Hess, James E. Midgarden, M. Paul Thompson, George E. Yockey, Buford L. Saville, Dan Folk, Phyllis Feaga, Charles Nuzum, Clarence Dyche, Jerry Goodwin, Gerald McDonald, Raymond A. Walker, William L. Wilson, Thomas B. Finan III, Ralph Race, Matt Skidmore, James Klippstein, Frances D. Greaves, William E. Crooks, James G. Conway, James W. Bishop, Mrs. Frank Birmingham, Mary Margaret Birmingham, Virginia Birmingham, Mr. and Mrs. Harry I. Stegmaier, Sr., Robert C. Petersen, John E. Byrd, Leo Cave, William P. Price, Howard Parnes, Karen C. Messina, Elizabeth H. VanNewkirk, William Nizinski, and Russell Berry. Special recognition must go to Herman J. and Stacia B. Miller, who not only made their collection of historical scrapbooks available for research and answered many difficult questions, but also provided photographs from their invaluable collection. Westvaco Corporation and the Allegany County Historical Society also generously contributed photographs for the book.

Others who were helpful in innumerable ways we also thank: Wallace G. Ullery, Thomas Cope, Thomas Lankford, Richard Ross, Delores Waites, Nelson P. Guild, W. Ardell Haines, Susan Eisel, Audrey Wolford, John N. Bambacus, William R. Harvey, James Morris, Roger A. Dietsch, Stanley E. Zorick, F. Patrick Allender, Charles Bramble, Alva C. Lewis, Alvin H. Ternent, William F. Baker, Donald W. Duckson, Dorothy Van Scoy, Patricia Ward, Ruth M. Shaw Patterson, Katherine Stangel, Frederick Morton, the Reverend George Wehler, Blaine Willetts, Anne Everline, Edgar M. Lewis, George A. Smith, Jr., Anna Good, Carol Bland, and Olive Simpson.

The authors were especially fortunate in having the help of several research assistants, most of whom are students at Frostburg State College: Mary K. Snyder, Joan H. Baldwin, Mark A. Jacobson, Frank T. Mahew, Linda M. Bleasing, Savino Saraceni, Cynthia Crippen, Diana Allee, Daniel Gaver, and Terrance Ruppert.

Early drafts of the manuscript were typed by Anna Mae Alexander and Shelley B. Drees; we owe the final version, and much more, to Mary Margaret Birmingham. Grace Moore provided the Index. Martha Dean edited and harmonized the writing of four authors, a most unenviable and exacting task, with her usual skill, fortitude, and good humor. Finally, we thank Miriam K. Mirkin, who as chairman of the Bicentennial Committee for Allegany County, not only gave unsparingly of every assistance, but inspired us all by her energy and enthusiasm. Without the kind contributions of all of those listed above and many more, this history could not have been possible. Errors, omissions, and interpretations are, of course, the responsibility of the authors alone.

Frostburg, Maryland
June 1, 1976

Harry I. Stegmaier, Jr.
David M. Dean
Gordon E. Kershaw
John B. Wiseman

PART I

Allegany County: The Frontier Years

By

Gordon E. Kershaw

I

BEGINNINGS

Colonel George Washington had long been familiar with the mountain wilderness of western Maryland, but in the summer of 1755 he once again found himself in the region, this time as a member of the staff of General Edward Braddock. The general, commander of an army of British regulars and colonial militia, was then at Fort Cumberland, preparing his forces for an assault upon the French stronghold at the Forks of the Ohio. The summer was unbearably hot, frustrating, and fraught with danger for Washington, but even in this crisis he found time to assess the potentialities of the area. He found much to his liking. Writing to Governor Horatio Sharpe of Maryland on June 13, shortly before joining Braddock on the road to Fort Duquesne, Washington assumed the enthusiastic tones of a professional real estate salesman as he commented that:

> This wonderful country impresses me more and more each time I go through it. I am sure, Hon'd Sir, that it is destined to out-rival some day and outgrow His Most Christ'n Majesty's home country—England. These mighty forests of soft and hard woods will furnish the ships of the world, and with the native stones build the residences of future generations. . . . Again, what is beneath the soil? There may be stored mineral wealth which will astonish the countries of the Old World, while the fuel of the future may also be found therein. . . . To the right of our camp [Fort Cumberland] on the slightly sloping plateau between the Savage mountain and Will's Creek mtn., is a wondrous site for a city and as I muse by the campfire, I imagine that here will be the metropolis of His Excellency's Lord Baltimore's Colony.

Washington's words were prophetic, both in regard to the yet unexplored coal deposits and to the later city of Cumberland.

This would be by no means his last visit to western Maryland, a frontier whose future growth would remarkably parallel his own rise to fame, and which in the 1790s would witness his last appearance as commanding general. Washington's interests in the undeveloped but highly promising backcountry were speculative, strategic, and commercial. His *Journal* speaks of opportunities for profit, but not of scenic wonders. Probably he did not pause to admire, as would a more sensitive and aesthetic traveler, the natural and rugged beauties of Green Ridge, Warrior Mountain, Dans Mountain, and other prominent features of Allegany County. Washington last rode by their summits in 1794 while journeying to the little town of Cumberland for a review of the troops summoned to quell the insurgents of the Whiskey Rebellion. Throughout the history of this area, the beauty of these mountains has been the one unchanging theme.[1]

The boundaries which separate Allegany County from eastern Maryland are for the most part natural ones—boundaries which reflect the salient features of its geography as well as its history. It was by way of the upper reaches of the broad Potomac that the earliest pioneers first reached the county; today the Potomac forms much of its borderline. Flanking the county along much of its northeastern circumference, the great river bisects Sideling Hill, which ranges northward to the Pennsylvania line. From Lineburg the Potomac rushes southwestward, snakelike in its progress past Little Orleans; Fairplay; Town Creek; Oldtown, the site of Thomas Cresap's old trading post; paralleling the now-abandoned Chesapeake and Ohio Canal; pushing along the North Branch to Cumberland; then to Bowling Green, Cresaptown, and Rawlings. Turning northwestward at Keyser, West Virginia, the Potomac, diminished now, swirls on to skirt around Westernport, Maryland's westernmost "port" on the river, to move even farther westward, well beyond county boundaries. Here natural features lose their significance as landmarks, for the Garrett County border is artificial—a symmetrical, man-made projection canting southwestward in a line which roughly flanks Big Savage Mountain.

Within Allegany County, which encompasses an area of

some five hundred square miles, the topography is dominated from east to west by a series of irregular mountain ridges running down from the north towards the southwest. Their names are commonplace for the local inhabitants, but are poignant reminders of the early history of the region. The immigrant heading westward had good reason to remember Town Hill, Green Ridge, Stratford Ridge, Polish Mountain, Warrior Mountain, Martins Mountain, Evitts Mountain, Shriver Ridge, Wills Mountain, Allegany Mountain, and Dans Mountain. Even today the cautious motorist flinches when rounding the tortuous curves of Sideling Hill or Martins Mountain. For the traveler of the early nineteenth century the journey along the National Road westward through Allegany County, whether made on foot, by oxcart, or by stagecoach, was an arduous one. His well-deserved rests at the inns scattered along the famous road or his fireside encampments beside an upland meadow furnished him an opportunity to savor the attractions of the valleys between the many rolling mountains, and perhaps to speculate about the destinations of the many streams which impeded his progress as they flowed off to the south.

Like Fifteen Mile Creek, Town Creek, Georges Creek, and Wills Creek, most of these waterways rush downward to join the Potomac and swell its crest at flood tide. In the course of their advance they water the deep, fertile valleys they so long ago created, occasionally with a glint or reflection of light revealing the Oriskany or Pottsville sandstone riverbed which has yielded to their incessant attack. In turn, these great creeks are strengthened by the innumerable smaller tributaries which spill down the mountains to meet them. The contrast between these deep-cutting creeks and the mountains which tower beside them is striking. Dans Mountain rises to an average crest line of 2,913 feet, and Big Savage Mountain is 2,717 feet above sea level. The gorges which lie at their feet are wild, convoluted, and picturesque. An aerial perspective of this western plateau district, where Dans and Big Savage mountains command the landscape, reveals a stretch of relatively symmetrical ranges which once, ages past, formed the flat lands, not the crests, of this mountain plateau.[2]

Farther to the east rises the region which geologists have described as the "Ridge District" of Allegany County. Here pronounced, sharp-crested ridges intersected by narrow valleys cut across the county northeast to southeast. They include Wills, Martins, Warrior, and Polish mountains, and Town Hill, which range in height between 1,800 and 2,000 feet. These ridges are distinctive features in Allegany County, but in fact they are continuations of ranges which originate across the line in Pennsylvania, decline quickly as they cross the county, and taper to minor elevations as they near the Potomac River to the south. These mountains furnished sustenance in abundance as well as shelter for the varied animal life of the area in George Washington's time, as indeed they still do today.[3]

Even though the opossum and the rattlesnake, both of which inhabit the mountains, were objects of fascination, early settlers in the region were far more interested in slaying the white-tailed deer which coursed the ridges and the black bear of the deep forests, or in trapping the beaver, otter, and muskrat of the isolated river valleys. Peltry was the lure which drew adventurous men like Thomas Cresap to Shawanese Old Town and points west, there to trade with the Indians for the valuable skins they were unable to procure for themselves. Woodchucks, red and gray squirrels, gray foxes, and cottontail and snowshoe rabbits lent color and movement to the upland areas, and were useful additions to the cookpot. The songbirds of Allegany County—magnolia warbler, Canadian warbler, red-breasted nuthatch, and hermit thrush—added their charm. Yet far more useful to several generations of settlers were the passenger pigeons, now long extinct, but which in the eighteenth and early nineteenth centuries, if not numerous enough to "darken the sky," could still be easily knocked down by the hundreds from their evening roosts. These pigeons, whether roasted over the coals or baked into a pie, made good eating and formed a staple in the diet of the poor frontiersman. The passenger pigeons today are gone. However, much of the wildlife of Allegany County now lives a precarious existence, and some

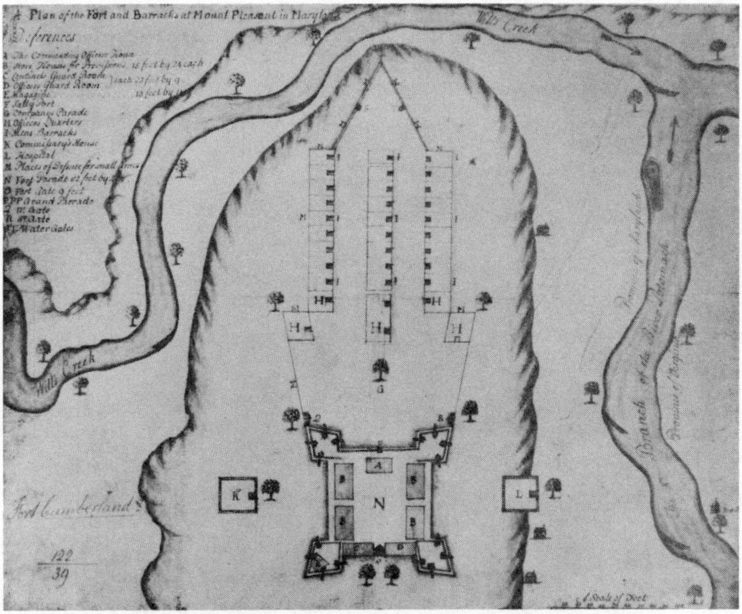

Plan for barracks and stockade, Fort Cumberland, at the time of the French and Indian War.

Governor Horatio Sharpe (1718-1790).
Private collection

George Washington in the uniform of a colonel in the Virginia militia. The portrait is by Charles Willson Peale and was painted in 1772. Courtesy Washington and Lee University

George Washington reviewing the troops of the Western Army at Fort Cumberland during the Whiskey Rebellion, October 18, 1794, by Frederick Kimmelmeyer. Courtesy the Henry Francis duPont Winterthur Museum

may be numbered among the endangered species. Others, surprisingly, appear to be making a strong comeback.

The vast forests of the region, covering hill and dale then as now, further contributed to the economic well-being of the early settlers and provided cover and subsistence for animal life as well. As is true of mountainous western Maryland generally, the county's flora is more typical of that found in the boreal area of northern North America than in that of the austral, to which the eastern portions of the state belong. Heavy snowfalls and invigoratingly cool summer temperatures exert an inevitable effect upon the plant forms of the region. Thus the north-facing ridge lines abound in northern hardwoods, and in the higher elevations generally, hard pine, red oak, white oak, chestnut oak, and cherry flourish. Here also teem a variety of shrubs and woody vines: blackberries, blueberries, elderberries, dewberries, wild grapes, witch hazel, greenbrier, hydrangea, rhododendron, azalea, and the inevitable poison ivy. In the valleys the county's flora changes. Encouraged by higher temperatures, here the red spruce, yellow birch, red maple, and hemlock grow.[4]

The eighteenth-century settler thus found himself surrounded by much that was beautiful and more that was useful. His life was primitive in the extreme on the frontier, but it was free. Land was plentiful, the forests supplied timber for building and fuel, and game furnished both meat and prime skins for trading. Nuts and berries in season provided additional supplement to the frontiersman's diet. The valley streams still flashed with white perch, trout, and salmon. If the white settler's life at best was idyllic, so it must have been for the aborigine who had preceded him in the wilds of Allegany County.

The original inhabitants of Maryland were the Algonquins—a not entirely exclusive designation, because this basic stock ranged along the east coast from Hudson Bay to Virginia, and westward as far as the Mississippi. But the Algonquins could be subdivided in turn into many smaller branches, tribes, and confederacies. The Piscataway tribe, for example, occupied that area of Maryland north of the Potomac and of the powerful Powhatan Confederacy of Virginia. The Piscataway welcomed the first white arrivals at Saint Mary's City as allies in their struggle to maintain themselves against the fiercer and more numerous Virginia Indians. To the north of the Piscataways lay the domain of the equally warlike Susquehannocks. In the early years of the eighteenth century, the upper reaches of the Potomac were the temporary home of the Shawanese, or Shawnees. As settlement advanced westward, however, the Shawnees, like their northern neighbors, the Delawares, were displaced from their traditional hunting grounds in Pennsylvania and Maryland, and forced westward towards the Ohio Valley.[5]

The Shawnees of western Maryland appear to have fled even in anticipation of white encroachments, for the vanguard of traders and trappers found only abandoned campsites in the vicinity of Wills Creek. The earliest map of the region, dated 1751 and still extant, characterizes the area simply as "Abandoned Shawnee Lands." The handful of Indians who remained after that date were probably from roving bands, or individuals who were not members of the original tribe. A few of these, lingering for years near the future site of Cumberland, gave their names to local landmarks.[6]

In spite of their abrupt flight, the Shawnees left their mark upon Allegany County. Their principal town was located on the North Branch, called by the Indians the Cohongaronta, or Upper Potomac. It was the custom of the Algonquin group to give descriptive names to each section of a great river; so it was with the North Branch. Here, at the point where modern-day Wills Creek enters the Potomac, the Shawnees erected their town of Caiuctucuc. Other towns were established along the Potomac nearby, such as the one at Oldtown (Shawanese Old Town), another at Braddocks Run, and a third at Cash Valley in LaVale. Will H. Lowdermilk, the early Cumberland historian, speculated that Caiuctucuc was composed of tent-shaped lodges, simply constructed. Two forked saplings stuck in the ground supported a ridgepole; branches laid at an angle on each side supported coverings of skin or bark. The interiors of these primitive dwellings were made comfortable by fur floor coverings. If the Allegany County Shawnees conformed to the governmental systems of other tribes of the Algonquin branch root, they must have been ruled by a sachem and a group of sub-chieftains, but little can be stated with certainty because of the early departure of these Indians from the area.[7]

More evidence is available, however, concerning the burial habits of the local Shawnees, for their graves have been uncovered over a period of many years. These appear to be of two types: occasional, isolated graves which mark the resting places of tribal members who died on the march, and settled, well-established graveyards situated near the Indian towns. The scattered burial mounds are distinctive: piles of stones several feet high covering a body which was simply laid upon the bare ground. Graves which have been examined reveal assorted weapons and evidence of food carefully packed in clay jars for use in the spirit world. In contrast, Lowdermilk described a graveyard uncovered in his own lifetime at Bradys Mills which contained bodies buried in the traditional sitting position. Especially impressive was ". . . a beautiful serpentine pipe, of green tinted stone . . ." which was found in a field about fourteen miles from Cumberland. Arrowheads, tomahawks, and the remnants of longbows recovered from Indian graves in Allegany County long ago found their way to the display cases of the Smithsonian Institution, but during the late 1940s a new group of graves was located. J. William Hunt reported these findings in a series of articles written for the Cumberland *Sunday Times,* concentrating his attention upon a burial ground located on the Dolly estate at Mexico Farms, about seven miles from Cumberland. At this site fronting on the Potomac River, W. R. Shaner discovered an ancient camping ground and burial mound twelve feet in diameter containing five skeletons. Three of these were the so-called "bundle burials," used for interring the remains of warriors killed in the field. According to Hunt, the flesh was hastily stripped from the bodies and the bones packed in deerskin robes for burial at the tribal encampment. Although the mound contained the usual arrowheads, bits of pottery, and stone weapons, there were no traces of European trade goods, indicating that these graves probably predated white penetration into the area. In any case, the main body of the

Shawnees had moved westward long before the first colonial settlers reached the future Allegany County.[8]

The eastern sections of Maryland had been well settled by the beginning of the eighteenth century, but the occupation of the backcountry largely depended upon forces beyond the control of the proprietary government in Annapolis. The backcountry, a region extending southward from the Mason and Dixon line for more than six hundred miles to inland Georgia, had scarcely an inhabitant as late as 1730. The impetus for settlement of the rich Shenandoah Valley came not from the Calvert proprietors, but from the land-hungry hordes of Scotch-Irish and Germans of southwestern Pennsylvania. The industrious Germans in particular poured across the Pennsylvania border to settle the new Frederick County. Soon they would be followed by thousands of others heading farther south. By 1776 they would push the population of the backcountry, Maryland to Georgia, to over 250,000 inhabitants, with more than 40,000 alone living in western Maryland. This massive migration southward was popular and spontaneous; probably it could not have been discouraged. Nor was it in the interest of the Maryland proprietorship to do so.[9]

Lord Baltimore was keenly aware of the potential value of his western lands, shrewdly advised as he was by his loyal supporter, Daniel Dulany the elder. Dulany, who emigrated from Ireland to Maryland in 1703, was a graduate of the University of Dublin, but he arrived in the colony as a penniless redemptioner. Fortunately for him, he accepted an indentureship with Colonel George Plater, the attorney general, and in time began the practice of law, soon becoming the most skillful lawyer in the Province. By 1721, Dulany had succeeded to his former master's position of attorney general. By virtue of his new position and as agent for Lord Baltimore, Daniel Dulany became watchdog in Maryland of the proprietary interests, and especially of the Calverts' landed affairs.[10]

In the early 1730s Dulany became especially concerned about the quarrel then developing between the Penn family and the Calverts regarding the exact boundary line between their respective provinces. The controversy became violent when in November 1732 mobs of Pennsylvanians began raids on disputed areas of Baltimore County. In January 1733 they returned to abduct a local settler, Thomas Cresap, whom they hoped to put on trial for trespass in the Lancaster County, Pennsylvania, courts. With the spirited aid of his wife and three children, however, Cresap fought back ferociously, killing one of his attackers and thwarting his abduction. Cresap began conducting his own guerrilla warfare, and soon earned notoriety as the "Maryland Monster." He won the attention of Daniel Dulany as well. "Captain Cresap," with Dulany's connivance and approval, conducted a series of retaliatory raids across the Pennsylvania border which became known collectively as the "Conjacular War." The hostilities ended with Cresap's temporary imprisonment in Pennsylvania in 1736; at this time Dulany arranged his release, for he had decided that the fierce fighter could be of use to him in his plans for the development of the proprietor's western lands.[11]

Daniel Dulany had begun to view the settlement of western Maryland not only as a way of strengthening the proprietary interest, but also as a means of lining his own pockets. He bought up thousands of acres of undeveloped lands in the valley of the Monocacy River, and as the Pennsylvania Germans surged down across the border in their trek southward, offered his holdings for sale at easy rates. Dulany's agent, Thomas Cresap, was already on the spot to greet the new settlers and sell them the rich farming lands which he had previously surveyed. As early as 1737, Cresap had purchased the rights to a 500-acre tract on Antietam Creek which he named "Long Meadow" and on which Dulany held a mortgage of £500. As the years passed, the pair continued their profitable relationship, with Cresap surveying and selling the loamy soil to thrifty Germans, who soon converted it into productive farms. In 1744 Dulany personally visited the lands of the Monocacy for the first time, and was so impressed that he invested more heavily than ever before, purchasing the "Tasker's Choice" tract from a group of speculators. The attorney general's new lands extended along the Monocacy for more than five miles. This was just the beginning. During the next two years he bought a total of 19,400 acres in the region. Cresap continued to survey his employer's lands, and in 1745 he laid out the future "Frederick Town." In this new development and elsewhere Daniel Dulany sold some lots and retained even more valuable ones, holding them for the time when land values would skyrocket. Meanwhile, he began to turn his eyes even farther westward, ever conscious of his responsibilities as agent to the lord proprietor.[12]

Lord Baltimore's claim to the lands of the west was somewhat obscure. The dividing line between his territory and that of neighboring Virginia rested, according to charter, at the "first Fountain of the River Pottowmack." The exact location of this "first Fountain," however, was a mystery. It was probably with assistance from Thomas Cresap that Dulany learned that in the west, the Potomac separated into two streams, one of the North Branch, and the other the South. The South Branch, he declared, was the largest and strongest, and it was on this river that he proposed to rest his proprietor's claim, thus adding many thousands of acres to his domain. But was the South Branch truly located at the "first Fountain" of the Potomac? Because the maps available to Dulany did not make this distinction, he decided to explore the region himself, although he was nearly sixty. Thus, the fall of 1744 found Dulany in a westward search not only for likely lands to add to his own holdings, but also for the elusive "first Fountain." Approaching winter prevented the completion of his mission, but he saw enough to arouse his admiration during a journey in which he must have penetrated deep into Washington if not the fringes of Allegany County. Dulany informed his patron, Lord Baltimore, that:

> I have not been long return'd from a journey into the back woods, as far as to the Temporary line between this province and Pennsylvania, where I had the pleasure of seeing a most delightfull Country, a Country My Lord, that Equals (if it does not exceed) any in America for natural Advantages, such as a rich & fertil Soil, well furnished with timber of all sorts abounding with lime stone, and stone fit for building, good slate and some Marble, and to Crown all, very healthy.
>
> The season of the year was so far advanced towards Winter, that I

> cou'd not possibly go to the Neck of land in the fork of Potomack, which I mentioned in former letter to your Lordship, the possession whereof I conceive to be of great Importance, and therefore beg leave to assure your Lordship that no Endeavours of mine shall be wanting to secure it for you.

Dulany's glowing account must have been something more than a press agent's dream; after all, he was reporting to his patron concerning lands he hoped to add to the proprietorship. His interest did much to encourage the settlement of western Maryland.[13]

It is especially regrettable that Dulany never saw the Potomac's two great western branches, for his agent, Thomas Cresap, was even then living in the region. Two years earlier Cresap had left his "Long Meadow" property on Antietam Creek to push westward himself to the forks of the Potomac. Upon its banks, at the now-abandoned site of "King Opessa's Town," a former Indian village, he erected a combined home, fortress, and trading post which was prudently surrounded by a strong stockade. He named his outpost Skipton, recalling his birthplace in Yorkshire, England, but the name never quite took hold. The settlers who soon joined him on the frontier could never forget that "Cresap's" had once been Indian, and spoke of the place as "Shawanese Old Town." In time they shortened this designation to Oldtown. Thomas Cresap moved his family out to Oldtown and established himself as feudal lord of the region. He continued to serve Daniel Dulany on occasion, and in 1745 he was employed by Governor Thomas Bladen of Maryland to survey an area a few miles down the Potomac then known as "Walnut Bottom," the present city of Cumberland. But Thomas Cresap took root in Oldtown after a wandering life. Here his youngest son, Michael, was born on June 29, 1742, the first white child born in the county. Daniel, Cresap's oldest son, gave his name to Dans Mountain, as well as to Dans Rock. The Cresaps, however, were not the first to be commemorated by place-names in the area. That honor probably belongs to an Englishman named Evart. According to legend, Evart, thwarted in love, moved west and built a cabin at Rocky Gap, where he lived as a hermit until his death in 1749. Evitts Mountain and Evitts Creek were named for him.

For many years the senior Cresap's home served as tavern to travelers passing through the area; the most famous, and one of the earliest, was George Washington. According to Washington's diary he stopped at Cresap's for the first time in 1748, when at the age of sixteen he accompanied a surveying party hired to lay out the newly acquired lands of his neighbor, Lord Fairfax, in the Shenandoah Valley. In the course of his work in the field, Washington went as far westward as the South Branch of the Potomac. He swam horses across the broad river, shot at wild turkeys, and was entertained by Cresap, who offered whatever rude hospitality that his estate could afford. This was by no means to be the last of Washington's visits to the home of Thomas Cresap, for both men would soon be linked together in a vast business enterprise which would precipitate a great war.[14]

A major reason for old Daniel Dulany's concern about the western boundaries of Lord Baltimore's proprietorship had been the fear that his patron's claims might soon be preempted by some rival agency. In 1744, when he moved to the western mountains, it could not have been clear whether the rival might be France, with whom Great Britain was then at war, or perhaps even Virginia, which was not likely to stand by while Lord Baltimore annexed the Potomac region north of the South Branch. Dulany's decision to press for this extreme southern boundary was well-timed if inconclusive. When the challenge came, it proved to be from the south.

Thomas, the sixth Baron Fairfax, had first ordered the surveying of his family land grant in 1736, one year after he arrived in America to assert his claim. Eventually he moved to Winchester, Virginia, where he lived in suitable baronial splendor at Greenway Court. The surveying party of 1736 had concluded that the source of the North Branch marked the northernmost boundary of his holdings, thereby establishing a line which was soon challenged by Daniel Dulany on behalf of the Calvert family. Because the survey of 1736 was never officially approved, and the wild lands not occupied in any case, the claims of the contending parties remained unresolved. But in 1746 a new threat to Lord Baltimore's interest arose when Lord Fairfax sent a second surveying party into the area. The party was a distinguished one, numbering over forty men, including Peter Jefferson, the father of Thomas Jefferson, and Joshua Fry, the surveyor of Albemarle County, Virginia. After enduring many hardships, the group reached the point they judged to be the "headspring" of the Potomac, a point not far from present-day Harpers Ferry, West Virginia. Here, on October 23, 1746, they erected the Fairfax Stone, marking the western boundary between Virginia and Maryland. Jefferson and Fry followed up their achievement in 1751 by publishing a map of the region—a map which not only designated the "official" boundary line, but indicated the "Abandoned Shawnee Lands" in the vicinity of Wills Creek, as well as the presence of a "Coal Mine" near Georges Creek. The availability of coal in western Maryland in 1746 was interesting, but there was no way in which it could be put to good use. That task would remain for future generations to accomplish. A final settlement of the Virginia-Maryland boundary line would not be made for many years. When it was decided, it was in Virginia's favor, and the demarcation commemorated by the Fairfax Stone prevailed.[15]

The success of the Fairfax surveying expedition was quickly followed by further initiative on the part of Virginians in the development of western Maryland, and this new thrust would result in war with France. The Ohio Company of Virginia was organized in 1747, not so much to develop the lands to the westward as to exploit the lucrative Indian fur trade which until this point had been enjoyed almost exclusively by the French and the more enterprising Pennsylvanians. At stake, ultimately, was the Ohio Valley, an immense prize to which both Great Britain and France laid claim, but which neither had deeply penetrated. The founders of the Ohio Company of Virginia were prepared to form the vanguard of the British advance, but for personal profit, not for king and country.[16]

The shareholders of the Ohio Company were a varied lot,

but collectively they represented substantial power and influence both in the colonies and in the mother country. Many were scions of the first families of Virginia, and Governor Robert Dinwiddie was himself a member. The company included Lees, Nelsons, Fairfaxes, Tayloes, and three Washingtons—Lawrence, Augustine, and George. The Duke of Bedford and four members of the famous London merchant house of Hanbury and Company purchased shares, thus providing influence where it counted the most. Thomas Cresap and his son Daniel were undoubtedly the least wealthy members of this august group, but their personal familiarity with the area of most immediate concern to the new company made them valuable additions to its ranks.[17]

Once the Ohio Company was organized, its most pressing business was to obtain a land grant in the Ohio Country. Influence peddling and lobbying in Virginia and back in England made this step relatively easy. Lieutenant Governor William Gooch, who preceded Dinwiddie in office, wrote to the Board of Trade on November 6, 1747, requesting that the newly formed Ohio Company of Virginia be granted a tract of land west of the Alleghenies. Gooch himself had the power to make the grant, but feared to take the step without prior approval from the British government. His letter was quickly followed by a petition to the Board of Trade from the rich Quaker merchant, John Hanbury, who advanced the persuasive argument that the Ohio Company would open the territory Great Britain coveted to a fur trade which might prove immensely valuable to the empire. Further justification for the action was provided by the famous Lancaster, Pennsylvania, conference of 1744, at which the Iroquois had ceded their Ohio lands to the British. Hanbury's reasoning was so convincing that the King in Council, upon advice from the Board of Trade, approved the grant in principle on September 2, 1748. Further consideration followed, and on March 16, 1749, the Council advised Governor Gooch to make the grant to the Ohio Company. Accordingly, on July 13, 1749, Gooch proceeded as directed, allotting the Company ". . . two hundred thousand acres of land lying betwixt Romanettos and Buffalo's creek on the south side of the river Alligane otherwise the Ohio, and betwixt the two creeks and the Yellow creek on the north side of the river. . . ." Furthermore, the company would receive title to 300,000 additional acres if the special conditions imposed by the King in Council were met: the building of a fort in the Ohio Country and the settling of at least two hundred families there. These requirements made the future of the enterprise seem highly questionable in 1749; nevertheless the proprietors resolved to proceed with the venture. They decided that this fort would be most effectively constructed at the junction of the Ohio, Monongahela, and Allegheny rivers—the fabled "Forks of the Ohio." By 1749, Great Britain was at peace with France, but the French were alert to the danger the company's plans presented to them in an area which was highly vital to their own expansion. The shareholders of the Ohio Company were realistic. In order to prevent a renewal of the war which had been concluded only a year before, they decided to postpone the building of the fort temporarily, and to construct a trading post at some point east of the Forks instead.[18]

The proprietors chose a convenient site upon the south bank of the Potomac River as a location for their trading post, only a few miles to the west of Thomas Cresap's dwelling at Shawanese Old Town and directly opposite a stream which was even then known as Wills Creek. The Shawnees who had once inhabited a village nearby had long since departed for the Ohio, but a few friendly Indians still lived in the area. One of these was "Chief Will," whose name was applied by the first settlers not only to the former Caiuctucuc Creek, but also to Wills Mountain and Wills Knob, which lay about three miles from the mouth of the creek. Here old Will lived out his days beside a small cove, finally dying during the American Revolution. Will and an Indian woman, appropriately enough named Eve, were thus on hand to greet the first representatives of the Ohio Company when they arrived to establish their trading post.[19]

The proprietors lost no time in developing the Wills Creek area. In 1750 they erected a small warehouse on the Virginia side of the creek at a point a few hundred feet from its conjunction with the Potomac. The next year they hired Thomas Cresap and a friendly Indian, Nemacolin, to survey a route leading from Wills Creek to the mouth of the Monongahela River at its juncture with the Allegheny. To the members of the Ohio Company all roads led to the Ohio Country. Probably they were premature, however, in sending several families to settle at the Forks in 1752; they had as yet made no attempt to build a fort for the settlers' protection. Before doing so the shareholders decided to further improve the facilities of their Wills Creek base. At a meeting in Williamsburg on November 2, 1753, the proprietors:

> Resolved that the Company's Storehouse at Wills Creek be repaired and put into good Order, that the Treasurer write to Col. Cresap to furnish plank and Scantlin from his Saw Mill for that purpose and that Col. George Mercer be desired and empowered to agree with Workmen to undertake the same taking Bond and Security for the performance and that the charge thereof be paid by the Treasurer on the Company's Account.

The storehouse was constructed on the south bank of the Potomac in what is now the town of Ridgeley, West Virginia. It stood on the riverbank beneath a high bluff near the site where the old Cumberland-Ridgeley bridge was located in the 1950s. The building was stoutly constructed, and was large enough so that it not only provided space for the accommodation of trade goods and precious furs, but also served as the residence of the agent and his family. As the years passed, the proprietors continued to improve their holdings. At the close of the French and Indian War, when they decided to lease these facilities, they consisted of:

> Two very good Store-Houses, opposite to Fort Cumberland, in Virginia, one 45 by 25 [feet], with a Counting-Room and Lodging-Room at one End, the other 44 by 20 [feet], with proper Conveniences for a Family to live in, two Stories high each, besides Garrets, with good dry Cellars fit for storing Skins, the whole Size of the Houses; and a Kitchen, Stable for 12 Horses, Meat House and the Dairy there are Two good Battoes, which will be given to the Person who Rents the Houses. The whole entirely new, and will be compleatly finished, and fit to enter upon immediately; and the Person who takes the Storehouses, may also have a Lease, for a term of years, of so much Land adjacent to them as he Chooses.

In 1753, however, the future of the Ohio Company was still in doubt, and was in fact becoming more precarious with the passing months. Although the British government supported the ambitious schemes of the company as complementary to its own plans for the annexation of the Ohio Country, it had its own game to play in the West, and that game was going badly.[20]

To counteract the increasing British influence on the fringes of the Ohio Valley, the French began in 1753 to construct a chain of forts from Lake Erie, their base of operations in western Pennsylvania, towards the Ohio River. The lilies of France now waved above Fort Presque Isle (Erie) on the lake; at Fort Le Boeuf on French Creek, a tributary of the Allegheny River; and at Venango, on the Allegheny itself. Logically, their next move would be towards the Forks of the Ohio, a step which would result in the ouster of the settlers placed there by the Ohio Company. To make matters worse, the company's opportunity to fortify the Forks would be lost, placing its royal charter in jeopardy.

Robert Dinwiddie, royal governor of Virginia, was not only the servant of the king, but an important stockholder of the Ohio Company who recognized the occasion to serve both public and private interests. He immediately informed the home government of the French threat. The War Office authorized him to use force if necessary to secure the Forks of the Ohio for the Crown, and Dinwiddie prepared for action. It may have appeared inappropriate for a governor of Virginia to assume responsibility for the protection of what was clearly the Pennsylvania frontier, but much of the Ohio Valley was claimed by both colonies. In addition, the Quaker-dominated Pennsylvania Assembly was notoriously unwilling to defend its own western border. Dinwiddie decided to try diplomacy rather than aggression, at least in the beginning, and elected to send a messenger to the French. His selection rather naturally fell upon George Washington, then only twenty-one, but with years of practical experience on the frontier and personal familiarity with much of the wilderness to be traversed.[21]

Washington's mission was a difficult and dangerous one.

He was to make his way across the wilderness of western Maryland, seek out friendly Indians who might be able to inform him of the whereabouts of the French, and finally establish contact with the commanders of the enemy garrisons in the Ohio Country. He would then deliver to the French governor Dinwiddie's ultimatum that they withdraw from the region, meanwhile spying out their defenses for future reference.[22]

Washington's feat in accomplishing the governor's design was both courageous and resourceful. The young Washington, now a major in the Virginia militia, was not without valuable assistance, for he was accompanied on his journey by Jacob van Braam, a Dutchman with an excellent command of French, and the renowned Christopher Gist, a wilderness scout who had previously been employed by the Ohio Company. In October 1753, the trio, well supplied with equipment loaded on packhorses, left Winchester and proceeded across the Alleghenies, passing the company's trading post at Wills Creek, pushing across the Great Meadows, and fording the Youghiogheny. In mid-November they reached the trading post of John Frazier, which was located at the junction of Turtle Creek and the Monongahela. Washington's party was now almost at the Forks of the Ohio. After a three-day conference with the legendary Half-King of the Iroquois, Washington, now accompanied by Indian guides, rode on to the French fort at Venango and from there proceeded to Fort Le Boeuf, where he delivered Dinwiddie's message to the French commandant, Legerdeur de St. Pierre. As might have been expected, St. Pierre refused to remove his troops from the Ohio Country. There was nothing to do but leave French territory. Washington's return trip, in the dead of winter, was torturous. If the stormy mountain weather were not bad enough, Washington's little party had to outrun the Indians, who had been sent by the French to pursue and slaughter them. It was not until January 7, 1754, that Washington reached the relative safety of Wills Creek after brief stopovers at the Frazier outpost and Christopher Gist's house on the Monongahela.[23]

Once back in Williamsburg, Washington made his report to

the governor and delivered St. Pierre's reply. His exploit was well worth publicizing, and Dinwiddie ordered the young man's *Journal* printed at Williamsburg within the year, including with it his own letter to the French commander and St. Pierre's answer. Washington's mission had been a failure in terms of any positive results, but the shareholders of the Ohio Company must at least have been satisfied to obtain official confirmation of their worst fears concerning French encroachments. They were further encouraged by Dinwiddie's decision to mount an expedition of Virginia militia to drive out the interlopers. In the absence of support from neighboring colonies, Virginia would have to supply the troops as well as bear the expense of the expedition.

The sequel to this story of George Washington's errand into the wilderness is better told in other works and too well known to require more than a cursory treatment here. Following Washington's adventure, Captain William Trent, who was sent out by Dinwiddie with a small force to construct the Ohio Company's long-awaited fort at the Forks of the Ohio, was driven off by a much larger French detachment, which proceeded to occupy the site and build Fort Duquesne. Washington, now promoted to lieutenant colonel, was dispatched with 159 Virginia militia to join Trent and reinforce the Forks, with orders that he was ". . . to act on the defensive, but in case any attempts are made to obstruct the works or interrupt our settlements by any persons whatsoever, [he was] to restrain all such offenders and in case of resistance to make prisoners of, or kill and destroy them." Washington, however, met Trent's defeated and dejected garrison trudging back along the path from the Forks. He also learned that the French ahead outnumbered his men at least four to one, and probably more. Nevertheless, knowing that Colonel Joshua Fry was somewhere in his rear, proceeding up from Virginia with reinforcements, Washington decided to march on towards Fort Duquesne. The process was slow and tedious. His little army, cutting a road as it advanced, could make no better progress than four miles per day. At the Great Meadows his force defeated a small French contingent, killed its commander, the Sieur de Jumonville, and took twenty-two prisoners, in what was undoubtedly the first, although unofficial, battle of the French and Indian War. The "Jumonville Affair" was a personal victory for Washington; its impact was blunted, however, by the news he received that Colonel Fry, on his way to join his sub-commander, had been killed in a fall from his horse at Wills Creek. His death left Washington in sole command of the expedition, and one which was not to remain victorious for long. On July 3, 1754, Washington was defeated by a much superior force of French and Indians at Great Meadows. The next day he led his survivors out of the hastily constructed Fort Necessity to surrender. The French terms were generous, and the Virginia militia was allowed to return to the eastward, baggage intact, but with its cannon forfeited as the spoils of war.[24]

The implications of Virginia's major defeat at the hands of the French were serious for the Ohio Company. The proprietors had lost their partially constructed fort at the Forks of the Ohio, on whose maintenance lay the validity of their claim to the royal grant. The capitulation of Fort Necessity represented another setback, since with it was lost so much more territory to the French. Even the wilderness road which Washington's men had cut with so much effort had fallen to the enemy, and the company's storehouse back at Wills Creek was endangered. Powerful and influential though it may have been, the Ohio Company was now at the end of its resources, as was the government of Virginia. At this juncture neither Maryland nor Pennsylvania could be expected to offer aid. That Great Britain and France were now at war after the little battle at Great Meadows was a foregone conclusion. Such a war could affect the fortunes of the Ohio Company either positively or adversely. Either the British government, by its commitment of the regular army, would win the company's battle for it on the Ohio, or the British Army and colonials alike would be run out of western Maryland. The next stage of what was to become the greatest of all intercolonial wars would involve the Maryland proprietorship as well as the armies of the king, and the outcome of this struggle would have great significance for the future of Allegany County.[25]

CHAPTER I NOTES

1. James W. Thomas and T. J. C. Williams, *History of Allegany County, Maryland* (Philadelphia: L. R. Titsworth and Co., 1923), I, p. 81.

2. Cleveland Abbe, Jr., *The Physiography of Allegany County* (Baltimore: The Johns Hopkins Press, 1900), p. 30.

3. Ibid., pp. 34-49.

4. C. Hart Merriam, "The Flora and Fauna: The Life Zones of Allegany County," *Maryland Geographical Survey: Allegany County* (Baltimore: The Johns Hopkins Press, 1900), p. 291; and Ian McHaig and Nicholas Muhlenberg, "Flora," *George's Creek* (University of Pennsylvania Department of Landscape, Architecture, and Regional Planning, 1966), pp. 142, 146-48.

5. James T. Flexner, *George Washington: The Forge of Experience, 1732-1775* (Boston: Little, Brown & Co., 1965), p. 53 (hereafter cited as Flexner, *Washington*).

6. Will H. Lowdermilk, *History of Cumberland* (Reprint of 1878 edition) (Baltimore: Regional Publishing Company, 1971), p. 20 (hereafter cited as Lowdermilk, *Cumberland*).

7. Ibid., pp. 18, 20.

8. Ibid., p. 17; and J. William Hunt, "Across the Desk," in the Cumberland *Sunday Times*, October 4, 1949 (hereafter cited as Hunt).

9. Carl Bridenbaugh, *Myths and Realities: Societies of the Colonial South* (New York: Atheneum Press, 1971), pp. 120-21.

10. Aubrey C. Land, *The Dulanys of Maryland* (Baltimore: The Johns Hopkins Press, 1968), p. 56.

11. Ibid., p. 143.

12. Ibid., p. 175.

13. Ibid., p. 171; Daniel Dulany to Lord Baltimore, Nov. 24, 1744, *The Calvert Papers*, II (Baltimore: Maryland Historical Society, 1894), Fund Publication No. 34, p. 172.

14. Flexner, *Washington*, pp. 37-38.

15. Mary Holmes Jones, "The Fairfax Stone," *State of West Virginia*, Vol. 39, No. 11 (January 1976): 18-19; Dumas Malone, *Jefferson the Virginian* (Boston: Little, Brown & Co., 1948), pp. 23-25; and Katherine A. Harvey, *Best Dressed Miners: Life and Labor in the Maryland Coal Region, 1835-1910* (Ithaca: Cornell University Press, 1969), p. 4.

16. Kenneth P. Bailey, *The Ohio Company of Virginia* (Glendale, Calif.: The Arthur H. Clark Company, 1939), p. 17.

17. Ibid., pp. 35-36.

18. Ibid., pp. 25, 27, 29-30; and Flexner, *Washington*, p. 48.

19. Lowdermilk, *Cumberland*, pp. 21-22.

20. Ibid., pp. 29-30; George Mercer Papers, 180, The Darlington Memorial Library, West Chester State College, West Chester, Pennsylvania; and Lois Mulkearn, ed., *George Mercer Papers Relating to the*

Ohio Company of Virginia (Pittsburgh: University of Pittsburgh Press, 1954).

21. Francis Parkman, *Montcalm and Wolfe* (New York: Collier Books, 1966), p. 63.

22. Flexner, *Washington*, pp. 55-56.

23. George Washington, *The Journal of Major George Washington* (Williamsburg, Va.: Institute of Early American History and Culture, 1959) (Facsimile edition of original edition, Williamsburg, 1754), pp. 21, 22.

24. Colonel Fry, with Peter Jefferson, published the map of western Virginia and Maryland referred to earlier in this chapter, in 1751. Fry died at Wills Creek on May 31, 1754, and "was buried on the slope between the fort and Wills Creek." J. William Hunt speculated that Fry was buried "somewhere near the bridge on Cumberland street and Spruce alley." Hunt, April 2, 1951; and Flexner, *Washington*, pp. 81-82, 106.

25. Frederick Gutheim, *The Potomac* (New York: Grosset & Dunlap, Inc., 1968), p. 97.

II

THE DEFENSE OF WESTERN MARYLAND

The governorship of Maryland held more than its usual share of frustrations for Horatio Sharpe, especially during the last years of the uneasy peace between Great Britain and France which followed the signing of the Treaty of Aix-la-Chapelle in 1748. That his responsibilities were threefold no doubt increased his problems. First, Sharpe was a proprietary governor. His primary loyalties inevitably lay with Lord Baltimore, for the proprietor, and he alone, controlled Sharpe's livelihood. Frederick Calvert, the sixth Lord Baltimore, must be kept contented at all costs; he valued his province solely in proportion to the income it brought him. Any diminution of that revenue, for whatever reason, would be cause for angry letters dispatched by Calvert to his placeman at Annapolis. Sharpe, however, was answerable not only to his patron, but to the people of Maryland as well, or at least to their representatives. The council, packed by the proprietor with members of the planting gentry, might have been expected to sympathize with Lord Baltimore, but, in view of its own interests, it was not consistently reliable. Advancement of the proprietary prerogative could be expected to meet with obstinacy. But if the council was unpredictable, the lower house, or assembly, was unmanageable. Part of the problem, which Governor Sharpe himself often expressed, lay in the unpleasant fact that ". . . there are too many instances of the lowest persons, at least, men of small fortunes, no soul, and very mean Capacities, appearing as Representatives of their respective counties." These democratic impulses, however, had to be met with fortitude and apparent good humor, for in the crisis of the 1750s it was the assembly which was the source of funds for the defense of the western frontier, not the proprietor, who absolutely refused to diminish his income through "unnecessary" expense. Horatio Sharpe continued to court the legislature with as good a grace as he could muster. Moreover, in addition to his loyalty to the proprietor and his concern for the well-being of the province, the governor owed a substantial allegiance to the British government as well. Like the governors of royal provinces, he was required to report regularly to the secretary of state of the Southern Department, the secretary at war, the president of the board of trade, and lesser agencies, and to correspond frequently with the other colonial governors. Finally, by virtue of his position he was expected to lead the province in time of war, if necessary even into battle.[1]

By training and temperament Governor Horatio Sharpe was far better equipped than most men to accomplish the many difficult tasks which his office demanded of him. Sharpe was a worthy member of a large and illustrious British family. Like his friend Thomas Cresap, Sharpe was a native of Yorkshire, England, but his connections were better and his antecedents more outstanding than Cresap's. Horatio Sharpe was one of six brothers. The eldest, Dr. Gregory Sharpe, was prebendary of Salisbury Cathedral and successively chaplain to Frederick, prince of Wales, and George III. Joshua was an attorney who was occasionally called in to comment upon the legal affairs of Maryland. Brother William became keeper of the Maryland Council Records. But Horatio Sharpe probably owed his position as governor of Maryland to his brother John, who had been one of the guardians of the present Lord Baltimore during his minority. Nevertheless, Horatio's qualifications were more than respectable. After entering the British Army as a professional he had served both as captain of marines and as lieutenant colonel of foot in the West Indies. Family influence had helped to secure him the governorship in 1753, but it had also been argued that in such trying times a man of military experience was needed to organize the defense of Maryland, so vulnerable with its exposed western frontier. Sharpe admired Maryland and its people, and in time his feelings were reciprocated. A visiting Englishman,

William Eddis, commented upon the goodwill which the governor retained after his retirement in 1769, stating that "Colonel Sharpe has resided many years in this country; where he has established a reputation which reflects the highest honour on his public capacity and on his private virtues." Sharpe easily assimilated into the planter class, establishing a country estate, Whitehall, which is still outstanding for its distinctive Georgian architecture and the formal gardens he himself laid out. In spite of his excellent qualities, a fine record, and a reputation for friendliness and hospitality, however, his role was not an easy one.[2]

From his first actions as governor, Sharpe closely identified with the interests of the proprietor. Building upon the foundations laid by Daniel Dulany a decade earlier, he worked towards the recognition by Lord Fairfax of the South Branch of the Potomac as Maryland's southern boundary in the west. Rather surprisingly, Fairfax agreed with him, and Sharpe took the initiative in hiring Thomas Cresap to survey a preliminary northern line. By June 6, 1754, the governor was able to report that "I have this Instant received a Letter from Col. Cresap with the Plan & Certificate concerning the North Branch of Potowmack & the Temporary Line as run by him." Cresap not only traced the boundaries of the two branches of the Potomac, but produced an accurate map showing their locations as well. Had the matter been pursued further Sharpe might well have been able to press his lordship's claim to the South Branch; unfortunately the commencement of the French and Indian War postponed the final settlement of the Virginia-Maryland boundary.[3]

While not directly involved at first, Governor Sharpe kept a keen eye on the actions of the Ohio Company of Virginia in extending its claims westward. From his central vantage point at Annapolis and using the latest information supplied him by his frontier correspondent, Thomas Cresap, he was able to act as an intermediary for the governors of Pennsylvania and Virginia. Robert Dinwiddie, governor of Virginia, not only respected Sharpe as a soldier, but also relied upon the military aid which he might contribute to a joint campaign in the west. Thus Dinwiddie wrote to Sharpe on January 29, 1754, informing him of French expansion in the Ohio Country and requesting his assistance in an expedition to be led by Washington to drive the French from the Forks of the Ohio. As we have seen, Washington's expedition terminated in surrender to the French at Fort Necessity. It is noteworthy, however, that Dinwiddie requested Sharpe to assemble his forces in March ". . . at a Place called Wills Creek, on the Head of Potowmack, which [Sharpe had] chosen for the Rendezvous. . . ." This location was already the westernmost trading center for the Ohio Company, which would be the chief beneficiary of the military venture planned by Dinwiddie. Still, the effort was in a cause common to both Virginia and Maryland, and Sharpe dutifully requested his assembly to furnish men and supplies. The assembly, however, proved intransigent, not only refusing to supply troops for Washington, but also voting only after much persuasion to provide Indian gifts for the Six Nations soon to meet with their British allies at the Albany Conference.[4]

Dinwiddie's next appeal to Sharpe elicited a far better response. Informing Sharpe of a projected expedition to be led by Colonel James Innes, a South Carolinian, against the French at Fort Duquesne, the Virginia governor asked him to assist in solving certain logistical problems. Sharpe was to ". . . order the building a Magazine for Provisions, any where near Will's Creek, large enough to receive provisions for 1500 Men for one year. . . ." Furthermore, he was to order the construction of a new road from Rock Creek to Wills Creek to facilitate the later movement of Innes's troops, and to contribute 100 Maryland militiamen as well. Dinwiddie estimated that with the Maryland company, his Virginia regiment, and a company each from New York, North Carolina, and South Carolina, Colonel Innes should have no less than 1,000 men under arms by late August.[5]

Governor Sharpe did his best to comply with Dinwiddie's appeal. Nevertheless, by September 2, he had been able to assemble but half of the soldiers requested, although he had already appointed a Captain John Dagworthy to lead the men westward. Dagworthy, a native of New Jersey, had seen service in Canada during King George's War and was certainly an experienced campaigner. Sharpe's efforts, incomplete as they were, exceeded those of Robert Dinwiddie. The Virginia governor was soon forced to explain that, in light of the failure of the Virginia House of Burgesses to fund his expedition, he would have to be content to send Colonel Innes with only 100 men to Wills Creek, there to fortify the warehouse of the Ohio Company. As Dinwiddie explained, the building "... will make a very good Magazine, & we had better pay rent than begin to build, have directed a Breast Work & the great Guns to be mounted for Defence; & if they can build a Shed round it [it] may be proper for the Soldiers to lodge in. ..." In the meantime, Dinwiddie had sensibly postponed his ambitious scheme to attack the French at the Forks pending additional support from the British Army.[6]

Sharpe not only sent his fifty militiamen out to Wills Creek, but in late November 1754 decided to conduct a personal on-the-spot reconnaissance. His own stake in the venture had now increased; he had recently been commissioned by King George II to take command of all operations against the French in the Ohio Country until the arrival of a general officer and several regiments from England in the spring. He assumed the position of commander in chief with enthusiasm, and once at Wills Creek, directed the construction of a new fort. Colonel Innes had arrived at the site on September 1, and had already begun building fortifications which were much more ambitious than the mere palisaded warehouse originally planned. Even so, the new fort, which Innes had named Mount Pleasant, did not meet with Sharpe's approval. As he explained to Dinwiddie,

> ... I found the Independents [the independent companies] preparing for themselves Barracks, having already compleated the small Stoccado Fort about which you were advised they were employed; but as the Fort they have finished is exceedingly small its Exterior Side not exceeding 120 feet, I conceived it requisite or rather absolutely necessary to have another much larger raised on an adjacent & more elevated piece of Ground which I have ordered the Maryland Company to proceed on & I hope they will be able to finish it this winter. The Eminence on which it will be situated gives it an entire Command of that already compleated & will defend a Face of that small Fort to which an Enemy might at present approach without

> being much annoyed or hardly seen from within. However That on which the Troops have been employed may be useful at present & will serve to enclose Store Houses or a Magazine after the other is compleated, which I think by an advanced Out Work or two will be easily defended against a considerable number of Troops that may presume to attack it with only a light Train.

The governor's delight in once more being about the business of his profession is evident in his letter, but building a fort, in spite of constructional problems, was one matter; keeping it and its garrison supplied was quite another.[7]

Horatio Sharpe was dismayed to learn that "At my Arrival at the Camp I . . . [found] there was no more Provision in the Fort than would suffice the Troops for one Day. . . ." As commander in chief at this formative early stage of the campaign it was his duty to furnish supplies for the expected army as well as to provide for its housing. He immediately recommended the appointment of a commissary to take charge of the situation, to be assisted by a clerk, ". . . always & himself for the most part to be resident in the Magazine at Wills Creek to receive Cure & deliver the Provisions. . . ." Meanwhile, Sharpe sent Dinwiddie his estimates of the cost of keeping 3,000 men provisioned for eight months at Wills Creek. He stressed the urgency of obtaining a large quantity of salt for curing meat at the fort in order that cattle already there might be butchered and preserved. Additional cattle could be purchased through the services of Sharpe's friend Thomas Cresap at nearby Oldtown. Finally, the governor furnished a tally of the troops already stationed at the fort: 12 officers, 25 non-commissioned officers, 7 drummers, and 295 privates. By the time he left Wills Creek for the return to Annapolis, Horatio Sharpe had all necessary preparations well in hand.[8]

Governor Dinwiddie's reaction to these arrangements was on the whole encouraging. He approved of Sharpe's improvements to the fort, and advised him that he was supervising the construction of a new road from Winchester to Wills Creek which would shorten the distance between by thirty miles. He also announced that he expected the arrival of 1,000 British regulars within six weeks. But, like Sharpe, Dinwiddie had to contend with a hostile legislature which was not inclined to grant money for supplies. Unless the Pennsylvania Assembly, still under the domination of the Quaker pacifists, could be induced to vote a sizeable grant, both he and Sharpe were in for trouble with the royal government. Consequently, he worried about the mounting expenses of the campaign, commenting that

> Your Calculations of Provisions for 3000 Men I think just; but how to supply the Salt & Cask I know not; for the carrying these two Articles to Wills Creek will be near three Times the first Cost. I can purchase Barrell'd Pork & Beef, but the same extraordinary Carriage will attend them. . . .[9]

Back in Annapolis, Governor Sharpe was contending with the same lack of cooperation from his own assembly. He feared that the ". . . conduct of the neighboring province [Pennsylvania] had a great influence upon its actions." The Maryland legislators would consent to vote money "for the King's use" only if they were permitted to finance the amount by issuing an additional amount of paper money, an action which even the council disapproved. Checkmated for the moment, Sharpe decided to return to Wills Creek, where he might at least be helpful in readying the fort for the expected regiments.[10]

By the end of April 1755, the prospects for the success of the proposed assault upon Fort Duquesne, using Wills Creek as a base, appeared much brighter to Horatio Sharpe than upon his first visit to Wills Creek. First, the Maryland Assembly had unexpectedly voted support for the expedition. Next, on his second trip to Wills Creek he had found the fort's construction well on its way to completion. Here he had held a pleasant meeting with Sir John St. Clair, deputy quartermaster general of the new army sent to America for the campaign. St. Clair had forged ahead of the main force to investigate conditions at the fort. Sharpe accompanied him back to Williamsburg, but unfortunately missed meeting the new commander in chief, General Edward Braddock. Braddock did not arrive in Virginia until February 25; with him on his first campaign in America came several troop transports and his artillery train. Upon receiving the news of the general's arrival, Governor Sharpe hurried back to Williamsburg from Annapolis to officially transfer his command, but this formal ceremony by no means marked the end of his responsibilities for the expedition.[11]

Sharpe continued to be involved in the details of logistics, supply, and transportation, and to facilitate these matters he was host to the general at Annapolis in April. In addition to Braddock, the party included Commodore William Keppel of the British Navy, Governor Dinwiddie, and Braddock's aide, William Shirley, Jr., the son of the Massachusetts governor, who was now second in command of British troops in the colonies. The chief purpose of Braddock's visit was to consult with the governors of Pennsylvania, New York, and Massachusetts, but they were held up on the road by a sudden spring snowstorm. At the end of what should have been a productive weekend in Annapolis, he returned in disgust to his troops at Alexandria.

To Braddock, impatient to begin his trek to the Forks of the Ohio, the delays seemed endless. Reluctant to entirely postpone the march, he compromised by dispatching units of the army westward as soon as they were equipped. Six companies of Sir Peter Halkett's Forty-Fourth Regiment left for Winchester on April 10, to be followed a few days later by Colonel Thomas Dunbar's regiment, the Forty-Eighth. Braddock himself was detained by the three northern governors, who finally arrived at Alexandria on April 15. His conference over, the general left for western Maryland, reaching Frederick on April 21. Waiting to greet him were his quartermaster general, St. Clair, Governor Sharpe, and Benjamin Franklin, who had ridden down from Pennsylvania. This last-minute conference was occasioned by a mounting crisis: a shortage of the horses, wagons, and provisions necessary to undertake the march to Fort Duquesne. Franklin willingly volunteered to solve the problem, advertising for wagons, teams, and drivers by handbill in Lancaster, Pennsylvania, at the rate of fifteen shillings per day. He even underwrote the costs of these necessities pending later payment by the British Army. By May 1, Braddock was again on his way westward, riding in style in a chariot loaned by Sharpe. On

May 10, after an exhausting journey overland, he reached Wills Creek and entered the fort to the booming of cannon. One of his first actions upon arrival was to rename the structure for the Duke of Cumberland, soldier-son of George II and Captain General of the British Army. Undoubtedly the gesture was politically sound, but even in his own time the duke was controversial. He had earned the sobriquet of "Bloody Butcher" for his relentless extermination of the Highland rebels defeated at the Battle of Culloden in 1745. General Edward Braddock was the first to use the title "Fort Cumberland" in a letter written to Governor Sharpe on May 22, 1755, less than two weeks after his arrival at Wills Creek.[12]

Braddock could hardly have been impressed by the fort, which had all of the rawness of the surrounding countryside. Still, Horatio Sharpe's addition, although makeshift, made the structure militarily defensible. Lieutenant Robert Orme, who accompanied Braddock up from Frederick, described Fort Cumberland as it looked on his arrival:

> Fort Cumberland is situated within 200 yards of Will's Creek, on a hill, and about 400 from the Potomack; its length from east to west is about 200 yards, and breadth 46 yards, and is built by logs driven into the ground, and about 12 feet above it, with embrasures for 12 guns, and 10 mounted, 4 pounders, besides stocks for swivels, and loop holes for small arms.

It is difficult today to visualize exactly what the fort looked like and where it stood. The hill on which it was located was later graded to make way for Emmanuel Episcopal Church and the right-of-way for Washington Street, as well as for residential construction. What is today a gently sloping hill was in 1755 a high bluff along the banks of Wills Creek. The fort was in ruins by the late eighteenth century, and completely obliterated by the early 1800s. Today it is impossible to state exactly where the fort's boundaries began, but its situation can at least be described in a general way.[13]

The bluff on which Fort Cumberland was erected sloped upward toward a more level area where the county courthouse and the public library now stand. The palisade surrounding the fort was constructed, as Robert Orme observed, of eighteen-foot logs planted six feet deep, thus providing a wall twelve feet high. Inside the fort the logs composing the palisade were held together by strips and pins. The entire fort was approximately 400 feet long and 160 feet wide; its most distinctive feature was a bastion constructed at its western end. This bastion and other features of the fort are clearly delineated upon a contemporary map of the area (see illustration) whose key identifies individual buildings within the structure. The eastern extension of the fort was obviously an afterthought, and was the section built by Governor Sharpe. It was irregularly shaped and narrowed to a peak overlooking Wills Creek. The fort's northern wall was probably located parallel to present-day Washington Street, and its south wall must have been very close to the eastern sidewalk of today's Prospect Square. Fort Cumberland, while irregular, was generally rectangular with the exception of the pointed section nearest to Wills Creek. The pointed palisade sloped back about 25 feet, broadening until it reached a width of about 140 feet. Here, in Fort Cumberland's center, lay the parade ground (G). In the bastion erected by Colonel Innes, the parapets constructed at opposing angles at the western end were matched by two others to the east. Governor Sharpe's addition of the western section of the fort obscured and partly destroyed their original function.

Small gates (S and T) were incorporated into the northern and southern walls of the fort at the eastern point. From each of these gates a trench led down to the creek, providing some protection for the inhabitants in their daily forays for water. After Braddock's defeat, however, the emboldened Indians came so close to the walls of Fort Cumberland that the trenches became useless. To counteract this threat, the garrison dug a well eighty feet deep within the fort near the main south gate (R). In his *History of Cumberland* Lowdermilk reports that this well still existed in 1870 on what was then the property of one Hopewell Hebb. There are persons now living who can locate the site of the well. The well-established legend that the fort's "tunnels," or trenches, remain in the foundations of Emmanuel Episcopal Church appears to be nothing more than tradition. Probably these "tunnels" were built for much more recent utilitarian use.

The parade ground (G) was the natural center of activity within Fort Cumberland, and the buildings erected within the fort ranged around its perimeter. Sharpe's militia had built the enlisted men's barracks along the northeastern and southeastern walls, with an additional row of quarters extending down the center of the quadrangle. The officers' quarters (H) were centrally located near the parade ground. The western side of the parade ground was actually the eastern wall of Colonel Innes's bastion; from it four cannon looked down upon the fort's western extension. Twelve other cannon were mounted on the three remaining sides of the bastion, situated so as to control flanking fire and discourage marauders from advancing too close to the fort. When Braddock arrived, four twelve-pounders and twelve four-pounders were already in place upon the bastion walls. Inside the bastion itself, four provision storehouses (B), each fifteen by twenty-four feet, had been raised near the walls, leaving space in the center for a small parade ground (N). Here also was located the commandant's house (A), although, probably to inspire his men, Braddock had ordered his own tent pitched beside the parade ground of the center fort. The west wall of the bastion contained a gate, or sally port, nine feet wide (O), which led to a large cleared area used for additional parade-ground space, or as a campsite when large numbers of troops were present. Finally, the bastion end of Fort Cumberland was flanked by a commissary building (K) to the north and a hospital (L) to the south, each of which was surrounded by a small palisade.[14]

Fort Cumberland was primitive, but probably no more so than most other British fortifications of the period in the American colonies. The construction of these forts was by design, not accident. British Army policy decreed that costly stone forts were not to be erected without official approval, which was sparingly given—a policy enforced by the Duke of Cumberland, who believed that ". . . stockaded forts, with pallisadres and a good ditch, capable of containing 200 men or 400 upon an emergency," should prove substantial enough for semitemporary, campaign purposes. A contemporary officer commented that:

> These American forts are in general no such formidable things; they are for the most part no more than a fort of retrenchment of Trees and Earth & even when they have a facing of stone they are generally too small to sustain a regular siege and may be reached by bombardments.

Fort Cumberland was probably no better and no worse than the average, but it certainly was not admired by Braddock's army. The Widow Browne, sister of the commissary, had accompanied her brother with the general's party up from Frederick, and her first impression of the fort was not favorable. Assigned to quarters within the bastion, she snorted: "I was put into a hole that I could see daylight through every log and a port hole for a window, which was as good as any in the fort." George Croghan, the Indian agent, had been assigned to Braddock's army to supervise its Indian allies. He, well accustomed to frontier conditions, described Fort Cumberland only as "a large, crude fortress." The fort was undoubtedly a hardship post, and its conveniences did not improve during its brief span of existence.[15]

Perhaps General Braddock did not care that the fort's accommodations were crude, for the structure was, after all, merely the advance base for his campaign to dislodge the French from the Forks of the Ohio. His only concern was to provision and equip his troops for the coming assault on Fort Duquesne. In fact, the general had even made plans for the disposition of the French fort once it fell into his possession. Writing to Horatio Sharpe on May 22, he explained that:

> If I take the Fort in its present condition I shall make additions to it, as I shall judge necessary & shall leave the Guns Ammunition & Stores belonging to the Fort with a Garrison of Virginia and Maryland forces. But should they as I have reason to apprehend they should abandon & destroy the Fortification with its Guns &c I will repair or construct some place of defence & leave a Garrison as before.

But if Braddock was overconfident regarding his coming encounter with the French, he was realistic enough about his continuing need for supplies, stressing that ". . . you [Governor Sharpe] must have all those things in readiness to be forwarded to the Fort escorted by your Militia." If the provisions were not delivered promptly, "... the men must starve & his Majesty's Arms be dishonour'd...." This was a refrain already thoroughly familiar to Horatio Sharpe, and one which he himself would repeat in the following years. Sharpe exerted himself as best he could, but his own assembly continued uncooperative, as did the Pennsylvania legislature. The Virginia House of Burgesses was of no assistance; it was in adjournment. Actually, Braddock was better supplied on May 22 than he indicated to Sharpe, for only two days before, William Franklin had appeared at Fort Cumberland leading ninety-one farm wagons with teams, of which eleven were loaded with provisions of butter, cheese, wine, and liquor, these niceties intended by the senior Franklin for Braddock's officers.[16]

Among Braddock's other problems was that posed by his Indian allies, whose presence as scouts on the expedition was vital to its success. Among their leaders was Captain Andrew Montour, the interpreter, a half-breed whose grandfather had been French, but who favored the English rather than his own ancestors. Officially, however, the Indians in camp were under the direction of the Indian agent, George Croghan, whom they affectionately named "our brother, the Buck." But even Croghan was unable to keep his charges in line. These Pennsylvania Indians had brought along many of their women, and the sight of these exotic and unfamiliar creatures parading around the fort was more than the British, both officers and men, could endure. The squaws were more than willing, and a girl named Bright Lightning became especially popular, to the extent of being "... in a fair way to become the mistress of a regiment." The increasing jealousy of the husbands of these squaws and the fights in which they and the troopers engaged finally compelled the general to order the Indian women from the fort. Their warrior-husbands were no less of a problem to Braddock, for they had come to the fort not as full-fledged allies, but to allow themselves to be courted into assistance by suitable promises and gifts. In the end, after several lengthy conferences, they did commit their aid, climaxing their pledge with a horrifying nightlong war dance which chilled the hearts of the British soldiers, most of whom were beginning their first frontier campaign in America.[17]

By late May, General Braddock and his staff decided that their preparations were complete and that the expedition could at last get under way. The general had initially planned that the line of march should be directly across the nearest mountain, but a careful reconnaissance by Lieutenant Charles Spendlove, a naval officer attached to Braddock's forces, convinced him that a much easier approach would be to follow the present-day Route 40 through the Narrows and the valley beyond (LaVale). Braddock promptly ordered out a substantial force under Sir John St. Clair to clear the road. As Horatio Sharpe reviewed the action in a letter to the earl of Albemarle, British ambassador to France,

> The 28th of May a Detachment of 600 was ordered to march & fling a Bridge over a Stream that flows 14 or 15 miles from Fort Cumberland westward & the General with the Rest of the Troops followed the 10th Inst. & had on the 17th with a great deal of Difficulty on Account of the Hills and Mountains that occurred marched about 25 or 30 Miles . . . The Army consists of about 2300 Men fifty of whom are left under the command of Colo. Innes at Fort Cumberland.

General Braddock did not finally leave Wills Creek with his main army until June 10. His force included 1,300 men in the Forty-Fourth and Forty-Eighth regiments, 260 men enrolled in "independent" companies, 350 Virginians, 60 Marylanders, and 80 North Carolinians, as well as additional soldiers attached to the baggage train. Also traveling with the army were ten Pennsylvania Indian scouts under the command of Croghan; the others were all ordered home with their wives. The general and his council of war ordered that an advance party of 600 men led by Colonel St. Clair should lead the line of march on May 29. They would carry provisions for eight days for 3,200 men loaded in fifty wagons, which would be deposited at a storage point about thirty miles beyond Fort Cumberland. Since there was a shortage of wagons, they would then return for more supplies. On

May 30, the main body of the army started out, organized into three divisions. The first division, led by Sir Peter Halkett, was composed mainly of the baggage train, which included nearly one hundred wagons loaded with powder and additional supplies. Here also was placed the army's treasury—a chest containing somewhere between £3000 and £4000 in gold coins which Braddock intended to use to pay his troops after the capture of Fort Duquesne. Lieutenant Colonel Burton, commanding the second division, followed with most of the army and the artillery. The final force was under the leadership of Colonel Thomas Dunbar; to it were assigned the remaining wagons and provisions. The general and his staff traveled with this group. Braddock had abandoned his handsome carriage at Fort Cumberland, and now proceeded on horseback. As to the wives of the enlisted men and the single women who had been hired as "laundresses," most of these remained behind at Fort Cumberland, but upon Braddock's orders, some were allowed to proceed:

> No more than two women per company are to be allowed to march from this camp, a list of the names of those that are to be sent back to be given into Capt. Morris that there may be an order sent to Col. Innes at Fort Cumberland to victual them. A list of the names of the women that are allowed to stay with the troops to be given into the Major of Brigade, & any woman that is found in camp & whose name is not in that list will for the first time be severely punished & for the second suffer Death!

In spite of the general's harsh restrictions, it is known that some brave women not on the "approved" list persisted in accompanying the expedition.[18]

The roster of Braddock's army was swelled by the inclusion of a number of colonials who either were already famous or would achieve distinction in later life. First among these was George Washington. Because of his familiarity with the Ohio Country his presence with the army was indispensable, but owing to British Army restrictions Braddock was able to offer him only a commission as brevet captain assigned to his staff. In spite of this slight Washington would prove to be the most valuable member of the expedition. Captain Horatio Gates, the future victor at the Battle of Saratoga during the

American Revolution, was attached to an independent company from New York. Lieutenant Colonel Thomas Gage was an officer of Sir Peter Halkett's Forty-Fourth Regiment; in time he would become the last royal governor of Massachusetts. Among the doctors were James Craik, the friend of Washington, and Hugh Mercer of Revolutionary War fame. Christopher Gist had been hired as a scout. There was also Daniel Boone, then only twenty-one, who was hired as a wagon driver.

In spite of the efforts made by Braddock's advance party to clear a road for the main army, his men made incredibly slow progress in their march towards Fort Duquesne. By the third night, they had reached only the future site of the old National Road tollhouse at LaVale. On they marched up the mountain, passing Martin's Plantation on its crest. June 15 found the little army hacking its way through the thick forest of the "Shades of Death," several miles beyond the present city of Frostburg. Ahead lay another encampment at Little Meadows, the location of the storage warehouse erected by St. Clair's men. On June 23, Braddock reached the Bear Camp, which was reputed to be the halfway point to Fort Duquesne. The army toiled onward, sometimes covering only four miles per day, crossing and recrossing the Youghiogheny River and marching past the ruins of Fort Necessity, the scene of Washington's defeat only a year before. Braddock's Road, the fruit of their labor, was impressive, perhaps overly so; Washington later commented that "instead of pushing on with vigor, without regarding a little rough road, they were halting to level every mole-hill and erect bridges over every brook." Meanwhile, the order of march had been changed. General Braddock himself now led the procession, accompanied by the fighting men of two regiments to the number of 1,400 soldiers. The slower elements of the army straggled behind; last of all Colonel Dunbar's baggage limped along, far to the rear. It was not until Saturday, July 5, when the expedition was within twenty miles of the Forks of the Ohio, that it encountered the first enemy resistance. On that date, an Indian scalping party waylaid, killed, and took the scalps of three stragglers from the advance guard. The army forged ahead, but with more caution now. By July 8, it was only a few miles from Fort Duquesne.[19]

Back in Annapolis, Governor Horatio Sharpe followed Braddock's progress with understandable interest. Not only was Maryland militia a part of the expedition, but the western defense of the province was dependent upon its success as well. Sharpe had his own military problems to cope with during this trying period, but he nevertheless wrote to Braddock as often as he could find a carrier, and waited eagerly for the general's latest dispatches. Writing to Governor Dinwiddie on June 22, 1755, he commented that:

> I received a Letter this morning from General Braddock dated the 17th Inst. at the Little Meadows (between 20 & 30 Miles from Fort Cumberland). Mr. Shirley tells me they were got so far with much Difficulty & Distress but were preparing to go on with more speed by lessening the Number of waggons to those necessary for the Artillery & reducing the provision &c to such a quantity as may be carried on Horses. A Detachment of 1000 of the best Troops were to go forward to the great Crossing & the Rest were to follow more slowly with the remaining waggons & provisions.

By June 28, when Sharpe next heard from Braddock, he learned that his army had advanced "40 Miles westward from Fort Cumberland. . . ." Now, for the first time, the general reported the presence of a small party of French operating ahead of the line of march. The news from Colonel Innes at the fort was much more threatening; his letter advised Sharpe that:

> . . . on last Monday morning a party of French Indians fell upon some of the distant inhabitants of Frederick Cty of which they killed three with the Loss of only one of their own party & carried Eight away prisoners.

It was clear that the Indian allies of the French were infiltrating behind Braddock's army to attack the settlers of the backcountry near Fort Cumberland. The prospect of a general Indian attack was frightening, but the information which Sharpe relayed to the assembly at last alarmed it to the point of action. As the governor disclosed to Lord Baltimore, the legislature:

> Resolved that this House will make suitable provisions for the paying & maintaining 80 Men including Officers for 4 months (if Occasion) for ranging on the Frontiers of this Province to protect the same against the Incursions & Depredations that may be attempted or made by the French or their Indian Allies—Resolved further that this House will defray the reasonable Expense of Conveying Intelligence from Wills Creek to Annapolis & back thither for four months. . . .

This was at least a beginning, but Horatio Sharpe would have preferred more immediate action in the crisis. Also, the governor was piqued that the assembly failed to make any further grants either for Braddock's assistance, for supplying its own militia with the army, or for providing for the ranging company by the time of its adjournment early in July.[20]

The Indian raids upon the frontier continued. On July 9, 1755, Sharpe wrote to Captain Robert Orme, with Braddock's army, informing him that ". . . some Parties of Indians have made Incursions & killed or carried away 26 of the inhabitants who dwelt a few miles from Fort Cumberland. . . ." In the absence of even token support from the assembly, there was nothing that Sharpe as governor could do to assist the people of the backcountry. Until some even greater outrage aroused the legislature, the frontier inhabitants would have to fend for themselves.[21]

Bad news was not long in coming. Colonel Innes received the first fragmentary news of General Braddock's defeat at the Monongahela as early as July 11; he immediately notified Governor Sharpe by special messenger from Fort Cumberland. The message reached Sharpe on the fifteenth, although he was at first reluctant to believe the full extent of the disaster. By July 18, however, Captain Robert Orme, wounded in the thigh, had made his way back from the Forks of the Ohio to Fort Cumberland, and from there wrote a more complete account of the massacre. Orme informed Sharpe of the death of Edward Braddock, who had ". . . had five horses shot under him and also receiv'd a wound through his right arm into his Lungs of which he died the 18th Inst." Braddock's aide, William Shirley, Jr., had been shot through the head, and had died immediately. Sir Peter Halkett was also killed, and Sir John St. Clair, Colonel Burton, and Captain

Roger Morris were wounded. Washington, however, had performed with commendable bravery: "Mr. Washington had two horses shot under him and his cloaths shot thro in several places behaved the whole time with the greatest courage and resolution." Furthermore, even after Colonel Dunbar arrived with reinforcements, he had been unable to retrieve victory, and was forced to destroy provisions and ammunition as well, their wagons being urgently needed to transport the wounded back to Fort Cumberland. Of a total of fifteen hundred regulars and militia who were engaged in the battle, nearly one thousand had been killed or wounded. Dunbar's men had hurriedly buried Braddock's treasure chest somewhere along the road during the retreat. Future generations of western Marylanders would exhaust themselves searching for this elusive hoard.[22]

Horatio Sharpe received Captain Orme's letter on July 23 at Bladensburg; at that time he was already on his way to Fort Cumberland to assess the gravity of the situation. Upon learning the full extent of the defeat he delayed his plans, and stopped to judiciously expend a small fund raised by the council and concerned gentlemen of the province upon supplies for the now-beleaguered Fort Cumberland. His frustration must have been overwhelming. As he complained to Lord Albemarle, "It grieves me to see near 20,000 Men in this Province fit to bear Arms & yet for want of an effectual Militia Law which has been frequently recommended to our Assembly in vain not 100 are obliged or to be prevailed upon to Exort some Provisions out or even to act in their own Defence." On his arrival at Fort Cumberland in late July, Sharpe was relieved to find that the situation there was not quite as hopeless as he had expected. Colonel Dunbar had sufficient food supplies to tide over his badly mauled troops, but on the other hand, nearly all of his ammunition and artillery had been abandoned to the enemy on the long road back from the Monongahela. Sharpe noted that "This is a Loss that cannot be repaired in these Colonies where there is scarcely any military Stores not even Musquets but what have been lately sent to Virginia by his Majesty's gracious Order." Dunbar had very properly decided not to renew the attack on

Fort Duquesne, and was in fact planning to march his surviving troops to Philadelphia. This exodus would leave only the Maryland, Virginia, and North Carolina companies to defend Fort Cumberland in the face of almost certain attack. The number of those who were to remain was steadily dwindling. Sharpe reported to William Shirley on August 29 that "The Provincial Troops that were left to Garrison Fort Cumberland I hear desert daily. Near a fortnight since they had reduced themselves to 160. . . ."[23]

The western settlers were naturally alarmed at these desertions, and many took what seemed to be the only appropriate action. As Sharpe observed, "Our People too, have many of them fled to the more populous Parts of the Country tho' no Enemy has lately appeared on this side Potowmack River. . . ." By September 15, the governor had learned that many of the country people had simply abandoned their property and fled at least thirty miles east of Oldtown. Even Thomas Cresap, that redoubtable and experienced frontiersman, had joined their flight, retreating to his son's home at Conococheague. Those who remained had to face the Indians with diminished strength and resources. The raids began again in October. Sharpe informed a correspondent that

> . . . the Indians have . . . cut off a great many Families who dwelt near Fort Cumberland & on both sides Potowmack some Miles Eastward of the Fort. It is supposed that near 100 Persons have been murthered or carried away Prisoners by these Barbarians who have burnt the Houses & ravaged all the Plantations in that part of the Country. Parties of the Enemy appear within sight of Fort Cumberland every Day & frequently in greater Numbers than the Garrison consists of.[24]

Among those captured in the raids described by Governor Sharpe was Jane Frazier, who lived with her family near the mouth of Evitts Creek. The *Maryland Gazette* for October 9, 1755, reported the event:

> By a person who arrived in town [Annapolis] last Monday from Col. Cresap's we are told that Indians had taken a man prisoner who was going from Frazier's to Fort Cumberland, and had also carried off a woman from Frazier's Plantation which is four miles this side of Fort Cumberland.

Unlike most of the prisoners taken in western Maryland at this time, Jane Frazier not only returned from her Indian captivity but wrote a narrative of her experiences. Jane was only twenty years old and pregnant at the time of her capture, which occurred within sight of her home. A male servant, one Bradley, was killed on the spot, but Jane was taken westward by braves of the Miami tribe to their village on the Miami River in the Illinois Country. Here she was adopted by an Indian family and here her child died at the age of three months. After more than a year of captivity, Jane Frazier and several prisoners from Pennsylvania escaped, taking advantage of the absence of the warriors of the tribe. She eventually separated from the rest of her party and found her way back to Wills Creek alone after an absence of thirteen months. Her terrible experience was not yet over, however. Upon her return she learned that her husband, John Frazier, believing her dead, had married again. Nevertheless, the ending was a happy one, at least for Jane. As she related the story,

> . . . we all went into the house and I met his second wife. She seemed a very nice woman, but he told her that he could not give me up again, that as I was living their marriage was illegal, but he would still support her as he had promised, but she would have to go back to her father and consider herself the same as before they were married, and she being a woman of good sense took it all in good part, wished me much joy and said she would come some time and hear me tell all about my captivity.

Life was informal in frontier Maryland, especially during the horrors of the French and Indian War, when unintentional bigamy was a small matter compared to the struggle for survival. Jane Frazier raised three children to maturity and apparently lived out her life in contentment. The experiences of other settlers were not so fortunate. Naturally they looked to nearby Fort Cumberland for both protection and direction during those unsettled times. There was little leadership at the fort, however. The command there was a divided one, a fact which affected the overall defense of western Maryland.[25]

Colonel Innes had left Fort Cumberland when his North Carolina troops were withdrawn during the summer of 1755;

thus control of the military establishment had passed by default to Captain John Dagworthy, the New Jersey resident who commanded the thirty Maryland militiamen still at the fort. On August 14, 1755, George Washington, the hero of Braddock's unfortunate expedition, had been commissioned "Colonel of the Virginia Regiment and Commander in Chief of all forces now raised in the defence of his Majesty's Colony." When his inspection tour of the western defenses took him to Fort Cumberland, Washington was astonished to learn that Colonel Dagworthy not only had assumed charge of the fort, but had the presumption to give direct orders to the Virginian. Dagworthy's authority was a captain's commission in the British Army; regular officers were always assumed to outrank colonial militiamen. The confusion over the command of Fort Cumberland precipitated what might have been "a tempest in a teapot," but Washington was determined to make the most of it. The quarrel involved the governors of Maryland and Virginia, as well as William Shirley of Massachusetts, who had succeeded to Braddock's position of commander in chief of British and colonial forces in America. Washington appealed to Shirley for support, but the commander's response was long delayed. Dinwiddie not only supported Washington, but advised Shirley to give brevet regular army commissions to all of his high-ranking Virginia officers, a suggestion which would have solved the immediate problem as well as future conflicts between regulars and militiamen. In the end, William Shirley supported Washington, as he was bound to do, commenting that:

> I . . . cannot think that Capt. Dagworthy, who now acts under a Provincial Commission, had any right to the Command as there are no Regular Troops join'd with those Troops now at Fort Cumberland, which would be the only Circumstance, that could occasion a Dispute concerning the right of Provincial Field officers to Command, in preference to Captains bearing Commissions from his Majesty.

Instead of undertaking the unpleasant task himself, Shirley notified Sharpe to inform Captain Dagworthy accordingly.[26]

However, Horatio Sharpe rather understandably took the side of the captain of Maryland militia. According to the governor's reasoning, Fort Cumberland was, after all, within Maryland territory, not that of Virginia. For this reason alone he was likely to back Dagworthy's cause, but he also respected the man as a soldier. The captain remained in command. When Governor Dinwiddie wrote to Shirley on January 23, 1756, he complained that "Governor Sharpe has not answer'd your Excellency's Intentions in removing the Dispute between Col. Washington & Capt. Dagworthy; he has order'd him to keep the Command of the Fort, which he does in an absolute manner. . . ." The house of burgesses was next drawn into the quarrel, and became so aroused that it vowed to cut off all further military aid unless Washington succeeded to the command of Fort Cumberland. Washington himself threatened to resign over the issue, but decided instead to go directly to Boston to appeal to Shirley personally. William Shirley responded by again confirming Washington as commander of the fort. This time, Sharpe reluctantly ordered Captain Dagworthy to relinquish his control.[27]

Once the question of his authority had been settled, it might have been expected that Washington would immediately transfer the headquarters of his command from Winchester to Fort Cumberland. This, however, he declined to do, for Washington saw his duty elsewhere. Fort Cumberland was rent by quarrels, and desperately needed forceful leadership; its garrison had dwindled to under two hundred officers and men. But Fort Cumberland was located so far westward that it was isolated; occasionally it was even under siege. It could well be argued that it was too far out of the mainstream to provide a suitable headquarters for the commander in chief of all Virginia forces on the frontier. At any rate, Washington considered the matter in that light. It was far more sensible for him to remain at Winchester, where society was genteel, the ladies kind, and life agreeable. The famous "Washington's Headquarters," a well-documented and accurately restored log cabin now preserved in downtown Cumberland, was probably more often neglected than occupied by the Virginian during his years as commander. Washington inconvenienced himself with few inspection tours of Fort Cumberland, in spite of continued charges of dissension and misconduct among the officers there.

Meanwhile, Governor Sharpe was busy with his own preparations for the defense of western Maryland. He had persuaded the backcountry residents to return to their homes only by "... promising them that some effectual measures should be instantly taken for their Protection & security." Now he had to deliver on his promise, and he had every intention of keeping it. He immediately ordered the construction of several small forts, garrison houses really, which were manned by volunteers and used as defense centers in isolated areas of the frontier. The money to maintain these forts came, not from the recalcitrant assembly, but from the subscription of wealthy men in the province. Like Washington, Sharpe decided that Fort Cumberland was too vulnerable and remote to serve as a suitable defense center for the west. After due consideration, he selected a much more appropriate site: "... an Eminence about 16 miles lower down the River just at the Forks of Potowmack both which it commands that is the best if not the only place in that part of the Country, which would be easily rendered strong & defensible." The cost of this project, however, would be far above any amount which Sharpe and his gentlemen were capable of raising. In the absence of support from the legislature he could do little but send out Captain Dagworthy to garrison a fort at Conococheague and to keep several parties of rangers in the field. Not until May 15, 1756, did the assembly approve a bill granting £40,000 for defense, part of which was to be used for building and maintaining a fort on the frontier at North Mountain, the location earlier recommended by Sharpe. By August, the new Fort Frederick was well on its way to completion. The governor had insisted that Fort Frederick, unlike Fort Cumberland, be built of stone. As he described it, "We face the Bastions & Curtains with Stone & shall mount on each of the Bastions a Six pounder. The Barracks will receive & lodge very commodiously 200 Men beside Officers & on Occasion near twice that number." The construction of Fort Frederick completed the chain of new forts which extended across Pennsylvania and Maryland, thus furnishing an interlocking, intercolonial defensive system.[28]

With the completion of the new fortifications at the Forks of the Potomac, Fort Cumberland, outflanked as it was, became even more of a liability. Dinwiddie and Sharpe fell to quarreling over who should be required to maintain it. After the Virginia governor removed most of its stores to Winchester, he then requested that Sharpe send Maryland militia to garrison the outpost. Sharpe demurred, accurately stating that the move was not within his power. Nevertheless, he was forced to take responsibility for the place over his own objections and those of his assembly. When Colonel Washington ordered the 200 South Carolina militiamen then at Fort Cumberland to Fredericksburg, Virginia, their places were taken by 150 Maryland soldiers. Governor Sharpe had perhaps a modicum of revenge over the Virginians in that the commander he appointed was the despised Captain Dagworthy, but this time the captain was clearly subject to Washington. Characteristically, the Maryland Assembly looked with a jaundiced eye at the idea of continuing the maintenance of Fort Cumberland, even refusing to supply the militia recently posted there. By October 1756, the garrison was desperately in need of supplies; Sharpe had no alternative but to pay the bills himself. The assembly later grudgingly voted money for the provisions, but absolutely refused to again assist in the maintenance of Maryland troops stationed beyond Fort Frederick. Under the circumstances Sharpe was forced to withdraw Dagworthy's men to the eastward. Fort Cumberland thereafter was commanded by Colonel John Stanwix, in charge of the Southern District in the operations against the French.

In the summer of 1758 the British Army prepared to mount a new campaign against Fort Duquesne, and General John Forbes was chosen to command the expedition. At the onset, Colonel George Washington advised that Forbes's army follow the route which had led Braddock to defeat, but a road, nevertheless, which offered an easy passage. Forbes, however, elected to cut his own road across western Pennsylvania. In July he began his advance upon the Forks of the

Ohio with a force of no less than 7,000 men, including 500 Marylanders. Horatio Sharpe's role in the campaign was to again assume responsibility for the defense of Fort Cumberland. Since his assembly was still as obstinate as ever, Sharpe energetically rounded up two hundred members of the militia from five counties and marched them westward himself. He remained at Fort Cumberland for several weeks; his mission, as he explained it, was supportive: "General Forbes . . . has desired me to garrison Fort Cumberland for three or four Weeks with Militia, which will leave him at Liberty to strengthen the Rear of his Army with the Virginia Troops that are at present there." Thus it was that Horatio Sharpe paid his last visit to the outpost. While he was in command the smaller powder magazine exploded, causing the deaths of two men and the loss of important supplies. The governor took the accident in stride; he was much more concerned with the state of the defenses at Wills Creek for, as he stated to Forbes: "I think it my Duty to acquaint you that Lieut. Hays of the Virginia Forces (to whom I shall leave the Command of this place) has 20 men fit for Duty 47 upon the Recovery & 49 sick." Fort Cumberland to be henceforth commanded by a mere lieutenant, and a garrison composed of invalids! It is clear that Fort Cumberland, even three years after its completion, was no longer considered of strategic value. If Forbes's campaign succeeded, Fort Cumberland might safely be abandoned.[29]

Although debilitated "by the Flux . . . and a total Decay of his Constitution," General Forbes persevered in pushing his famous road through to Fort Duquesne, and took that stronghold without a struggle on November 25, 1758, after it was deserted by its garrison. Exhausted by his labors, Forbes died soon afterwards, but his efforts had effectively secured the western Maryland frontier from French and Indian raids.

The reasons for Fort Cumberland's existence continued to decline; nevertheless, the Crown maintained a garrison there until 1765, two years after the conclusion of the French and Indian War. It was in the year of the Stamp Act crisis that General Thomas Gage, writing from his command in New York City, advised Governor Sharpe that:

> As I shall soon find it necessary to withdraw the Troops which are now in Garrison in Fort Cumberland in your Province; I think it proper to acquaint you of it; that you may give such Directions concerning the Fort, or any stores which then may be belonging to your Province as you shall judge necessary.

Fort Cumberland had finally outlived its usefulness; indeed, conditions in the future Allegany County had so improved that the proprietor, Lord Baltimore, deemed the area to be at last ripe for economic exploitation. His loyal steward, Horatio Sharpe, laid the groundwork for his lordship's gain by ordering the surveying of much of the region. On July 18, 1768, Hugh Hammersley, secretary to Lord Baltimore, instructed Sharpe concerning the disposition of these lands, stating that:

> . . . the Survey of the New Tract of Land laid out by your Excellency beyond Fort Cumberland, Estimated at 96,610 Acres, which his Lordship will be glad to see Disposed of as proper opportunitys offer in such a manner as shall appear to his Board of Officers most Advantageous to his Interest, & to their Consideration and advice he desires it may be referred at the same time not seeing himself any good end that so great a reserve can answer & rather wishing only 10,000 or 12,000 Acres at most to be withheld, and the rest to be taken up by Patent upon Payment of Quit Rent.

The survey of the western lands was one of the last acts which Horatio Sharpe would perform for his proprietor, for to Lord Baltimore, family ties were far more important than the loyalty of his retainers. In 1769, Sharpe was dismissed from his post to make way for a new governor, Robert Eden, the brother-in-law of the proprietor. Sharpe lingered on at his country estate, Whitehall, until 1773, when he was called back to England by family business. He never returned to Maryland, but retained an interest in the new state after the American Revolution and died in London in 1790.[30]

As governor of Maryland during the long, troubled years of the French and Indian War, Horatio Sharpe had performed conscientiously, efficiently, and at times nobly. It was only with great difficulty that he had been able to please the proprietor while keeping relations as harmonious as possible with the consistently balky assembly. Furthermore, he had kept his pledge to protect the people of Maryland, especially those on the western frontier. The assemblymen who opposed Sharpe were not villains, of course, nor were they necessarily unpatriotic in a critical era. They operated, as Sharpe did, through principle. The assembly had bitterly resented being taxed to defend a frontier when the proprietor refused under any circumstances to allow the taxation of his own lands for the same purpose. The defense of such principles would soon bring on a revolution. Nevertheless, the harassed inhabitants of western Maryland had much reason for gratitude to Governor Sharpe. The conclusion of the French and Indian War in 1763 signaled the beginning of a period of broad expansion, prosperity, and development for the western part of the colony, and Horatio Sharpe had done more than his share to make it possible.

CHAPTER II NOTES

1. Lady Edgar, *A Colonial Governor in Maryland* (London and New York: Longmans, Green, and Co., 1912), p. 43.

2. Ibid., pp. 14, 248; and Allen Johnson and Dumas Malone, eds., *The Dictionary of American Biography* (New York: Charles Scribner's Sons, 1931), XVII, p. 26.

3. Horatio Sharpe to Lord Fairfax, Sept. 14, 1753, and Sharpe to Cecilius Calvert, Nov. 29, 1753, and June 6, 1754, in William Hand Browne, ed., *Archives of Maryland: The Correspondence of Governor Sharpe, 1753-1767* (Baltimore: Maryland Historical Society, 1888), I, pp. 6-7, 14, 72 (hereafter cited as *Correspondence of Governor Sharpe*).

4. Robert Dinwiddie to Sharpe, Jan. 29, 1754, and Sharpe to Calvert, June 6, 1754, ibid., pp. 33, 69.

5. Dinwiddie to Sharpe, July 31, 1754, ibid., p. 76.

6. Sharpe to Calvert, Sept. 2, 1754, ibid., p. 94.

7. Sharpe to Dinwiddie, Dec. 10, 1754, ibid., p. 136.

8. Ibid., pp. 136-37.

9. Dinwiddie to Sharpe, Dec. 17, 1754, ibid., pp. 143-47.

10. Sharpe to Sir Thomas Robinson, Jan. 12, 1754, ibid., p. 165.

11. Sharpe to William Sharpe, n.d., but probably February 1755, ibid., pp. 173-75.

12. Lee McCardell, *Ill-Starred General: Braddock of the Coldstream Guards* (Pittsburgh: University of Pittsburgh Press, 1958), pp. 166, 177 (hereafter cited as McCardell, *Ill-Starred General*).

13. Lois Mulkearn, ed., *George Mercer Papers Relating to the Ohio*

Company of Virginia (Pittsburgh: University of Pittsburgh Press, 1954), p. 373; and Will H. Lowdermilk, *History of Cumberland* (reprint of 1878 edition) (Baltimore: Regional Publishing Company, 1971), pp. 89-92 (hereafter cited as Lowdermilk, *Cumberland*).

14. Lowdermilk, *Cumberland*, pp. 89-92.

15. Alfred P. James and Charles M. Stotz, *Drums in the Forest* (Pittsburgh: Historical Society of Western Pennsylvania, 1958), p. 58; McCardell, *Ill-Starred General*, p. 185; and Nicholas Wainwright, *George Croghan: Wilderness Diplomat* (Chapel Hill: University of North Carolina Press, 1959), p. 85.

16. Edward Braddock to Sharpe, May 22, 1755, *Correspondence of Governor Sharpe*, I, p. 210; and McCardell, *Ill-Starred General*, pp. 197-98.

17. McCardell, *Ill-Starred General*, pp. 186-87, 191.

18. J. William Hunt, "Across the Desk," in the Cumberland *Sunday Times*, Aug. 21, 1955, and Feb. 1, 1948 (hereafter cited as Hunt); Sharpe to Lord Albemarle, June 22, 1755, and Sharpe to Calvert, May 22, 1755, *Correspondence of Governor Sharpe*, I, pp. 230, 308; and McCardell, *Ill-Starred General*, p. 207.

19. John T. Scharf, *History of Western Maryland* (Hatboro, Pa.: Tradition Press, 1967), Vol. I, pp. 84, 85; and McCardell, *Ill-Starred General*, p. 236.

20. Sharpe to Dinwiddie, June 22, 1755; Sharpe to Lord Baltimore, June 28, 1755; and Sharpe to Braddock, July 9, 1755, *Correspondence of Governor Sharpe*, I, pp. 227, 232-33, 242-43.

21. Sharpe to Robert Orme, July 9, 1755, ibid., p. 243.

22. Orme to Sharpe, July 18, 1755, ibid., p. 253; and Hunt, Jan. 2, 1966, and Jan. 13, 1967.

23. Sharpe to Albemarle, July 23, 1755; Sharpe to Robinson, Aug. 11, 1755; and Sharpe to Sir William Shirley, Aug. 29, 1755, *Correspondence of Governor Sharpe*, I, pp. 257, 264, 273.

24. Sharpe to Morris, Oct. 11, 1755, ibid., p. 292.

25. The *Maryland Gazette*, Oct. 9, 1755; and James W. Thomas and T. J. C. Williams, *History of Allegany County, Maryland*, I (Philadelphia: L. R. Titsworth and Co., 1923), pp. 84-87.

26. James T. Flexner, *George Washington: The Forge of Experience, 1732-1775* (Boston: Little, Brown, and Co., 1965), p. 138; and Shirley to Sharpe, March 5, 1756, *Correspondence of Governor Sharpe*, I, p. 348.

27. Dinwiddie to Shirley, Jan. 23, 1756, *Correspondence of Governor Sharpe*, I, pp. 348-49.

28. Sharpe to Dinwiddie, Aug. 11, 1755, and Aug. 23, 1756, ibid., pp. 265, 469.

29. Sharpe to William Sharpe, Aug. 27, 1758; and Sharpe to John Forbes, Sept. 20, 1758, in William Hand Browne, ed., *Archives of Mary-*

land: The Correspondence of Governor Sharpe, 1757-1761 (Baltimore: Maryland Historical Society, 1890), II, pp. 252, 270.

30. Thomas Gage to Sharpe, May 12, 1765, in William Hand Browne, ed., *Archives of Maryland: The Correspondence of Governor Sharpe, 1761-1771* (Baltimore: Maryland Historical Society, 1895), III, p. 197.

III

REVOLUTION AND EXPANSION

The hard-pressed settlers on the frontier of western Maryland had survived the terrors of the French and Indian War, but had little to show for their years of effort. During the early period of the war many had fled eastward, abandoning their possessions in the panic. In many cases their homes had been burned to the ground and their fields laid waste by marauding Indian bands. Only a few scattered dwellings such as the log house of John and Jane Frazier remained untouched. Fort Cumberland, the undermanned citadel of the west, remained alert to Indian alarms until as late as 1758. Nor did the Peace of Paris of 1763 entirely restore harmony to the region. The French and Indian War was quickly followed by Pontiac's War. The old French stronghold of Fort Duquesne, now renamed Fort Pitt, was besieged by Pontiac's warriors, and several other forts in the Ohio Valley fell to the Indians. Fort Cumberland was garrisoned until the conclusion of these troubles, but offered little protection to farmers in isolated areas. After 1765, however, conditions rapidly improved. The horrors of Indian warfare receded, and the region soon to become Allegany County experienced a rapid expansion which was uninterrupted even by the years of the American Revolution. During the last days of that war new towns began to appear, including the local market center, Cumberland. Coincident with the adoption of the United States Constitution, Allegany County also came into being. The last decade of the eighteenth century would mark the coming of age of the new county; it would be punctuated by a final visit of George Washington, now president of the United States, who appeared for the last time in a military role.

By the early 1760s, the former residents, their confidence restored, returned to the western mountains. They were joined by new settlers, drawn by the availability of land. It was just such a group who laid the foundations for the town of Flintstone. Like others who moved westward, the migrants selected a promising valley for their homes, in this case one situated between Martins Mountain and Warrior Ridge. Many of these first settlers came from Frederick County; their names are still extant in Flintstone: Robinette, Moore, Roberts, Twigg, Willison, Chaney, Wilson, McElfish, Read, Murley, Roberts, Bishop, Tatman, Perrin, and Leasure. These families were of English, Scotch-Irish, Scottish, and French descent. Narrow Indian trails had led them into the valley; in time these would be widened to accommodate packhorses, but the luxury of wagon roads would be postponed until the early days of the republic.[1]

The first settlers arrived towards the close of the French and Indian War. The town of Flintstone was founded by Joseph Flint, who obtained a patent for a tract which he called "Grassy Bottom" along Town Creek in 1752. He soon established a trading post on Flintstone Creek, but sold a part of his holding, "Morgan's Chance," to Griffin Johnson in 1774. The Perrin brothers, John and Joseph, were also early residents of this area, but they, after selling some of their property in Flintstone, moved on to Pennsylvania, leaving family representatives behind them. Twiggtown, once known as "Sink Hole Bottom," had its origins in a tract of land conveyed by deed from John Perrin to Robert Twigg in September 1760. Two members of the Twigg family were still in possession of farms there as late as 1908. According to local legend, the first Twiggs in the area had Indian blood, and were descended from such colorful ancestors as "Flat Foot" John Twigg, who raised twelve sons and a daughter in the upland valley. The Twiggs were soon rivaled by the Willisons, a family of Scottish origin which moved up from Lancaster County, Virginia. Cornelius Willison settled upon land called "The Two Springs" in 1775; here originated the once-famous "Willison Apple." These families were typical of the early pioneers of Flintstone; their scions were men of character, some of them eccentrics, who were long remembered in the locality.[2]

Life was simple and rugged in the western mountains at the end of the eighteenth century. Virtually the entire population lived in Spartan but serviceable log cabins. Even the local inn and general store were of log construction. Privacy was an unknown luxury; most families lived, cooked, worked, and slept within the confines of a single room. The men and boys boxed, wrestled, and ran footraces for amusement when they were not hunting and fishing. Most of their daylight hours, however, were spent in the endless farm tasks which were all the more onerous for the lack of proper equipment. The daily routine of farm wives involved, if that were possible, even more drudgery: cooking over open fires; boiling the laundry; spinning, dyeing, and weaving linsey-woolsey on handwrought looms. If the family hunter had been successful, supper might be fresh venison, but on other less fortunate nights it was more likely cornmeal mush. Hog-butchering time brought the promise of smoked or salted meat for winter use, but also a laborious process which sometimes occupied as much as three days, for as the aged Hilleary Willison, an early resident of Flintstone, recalled:

> They had no sausage grinders, lard presses, or anything of that kind to expedite the work. To heat the stones used in scalding, they set fire to long heaps filled with sand stones—and when the sandstone became hot, they were dropped into the scalding tubs. The sausage meat was put upon a heavy table or sausage block, and chipped into little cubes with the sausage chopper, the operator beating a tattoo all over the meat, right and left, forward and backward, up through the middle with a swing-around circle. . . . When finished, it was pushed to one side and another fresh batch put upon the block. . . . The "stuffer" was a tin horn about the size of a quart can as long again, with a spout at one end to hold the sausage, and a wooden socket to fit the large end. When all was ready, a strong man, if possible, put on a large apron, seated himself astride a bench, placed the end of the stuffer filled with the meat against the "solar plexus," drew in a deep breath, and pushed until the children standing around would think his eyes would surely pop out of his head. This was hard work and slow, but any one that ever tasted sausage [made] that way will say that it was the best ever eaten.

Frontier life in western Maryland was certainly severe, but some of the cares were lightened by cooperative activities such as that described above. Barn raisings, harvestings, and threshings, like hog-killing time, were all occasions for frolicking as well as for hard work. Country weddings, church services, and even funerals provided other opportunities for socializing. The simple pleasures of life at Flintstone were reflected in the lives of hundreds of other inhabitants of upland Maryland.[3]

Until long after the American Revolution, however, the settlers lived lonely, isolated lives for the most part, as tiny pockets of humanity scattered through the hills. They enjoyed few contacts with the outside world aside, perhaps, from the infrequent but welcome visits of a particularly aggressive tinker or trader. There would, however, be occasional trips across the mountains to Thomas Cresap's trading post at Oldtown, where the trapper's beaver skins could be bartered for salt, powder, and treasured yard goods. Thomas Cresap, full of years, had returned to his fortress on the Potomac after the Indian alarms ended, and around him settled members of his numerous family.

Daniel Cresap, the eldest, lived nearby with his wife and five children. A venturesome sort, he spent much of his time exploring the neighboring mountains, often accompanied by the Indians who frequented the Oldtown trading post. A favorite hunting companion was the old Nemacolin. One of Cresap's exploits in the hills achieved the status of legend. Dan and Nemacolin, on the trail of elusive bear cubs, tracked them to the crest of a mountain close-by. Finally they treed the bears. As the cubs ascended, Dan, right behind them, climbed hand over hand:

> . . . he pursued until the limbs of the tree broke, and down came Cresap and cubs to the ground—or rather to the stones—for it happened on a rough, stony piece of ground. This fall from such a height, and among stones, broke his bones, and nearly took his life. He lay on the ground motionless and senseless until the old Indian, who not finding him at the time and place agreed upon, and supposing that something had befallen him, had the good fortune to find him, after diligent search, in the situation above described; but his wounds and bruises were such that he could not be moved.

> Nemacolin, moved with compassion, went to his house and informed his wife, and between them with the aid of a horse and litter they took him to his home.

From that time until the present the ridge where Daniel Cresap suffered his fall has been known as Dans Mountain.[4]

Daniel Cresap was a transplanted mountain man; in contrast, Thomas Cresap's youngest son, Michael, was born and bred on western Maryland's frontier. By the end of the French and Indian War he had reached maturity, had married a Miss Whitehead from Philadelphia, and in 1764, constructed his own home near his father's trading post at Oldtown. Michael Cresap's house still stands—a narrow fieldstone building rearing up for more than two and a half stories with more of the air of a fort than a dwelling. The lines of this historic building where George Washington was once entertained have been somewhat obscured by a later brick addition, but the house has a rough dignity even in its present dilapidation. The basement, which was once used as a jail as well as a kitchen, was supplied with its own fresh spring water. Several of the rooms above were heated by fireplaces branching from the massive stone chimney built at one end of the structure. Even in its heyday the Michael Cresap house was plain and utilitarian, not luxurious; nevertheless, it was the most elaborate home of its time in the region.

Michael Cresap lived in his stone house for but a few years; the unexplored west beckoned to him as it had to his father, and his tangled financial affairs at Oldtown made migration necessary. In 1774, leaving his family behind, he led a party of similarly energetic young men out to the present site of Wheeling, West Virginia, where they began to clear the land. Here Cresap, who had selected some of the finest lands available, hoped to recoup his earlier losses through land speculation. His efforts, however, were interrupted by the outbreak of Indian attacks in what has been called Lord Dunmore's War by some historians, and Cresap's War by others. The spark which ignited the whole Ohio frontier was the Yellow Creek Massacre of April 30, 1774, in which a number of Indians, including the mother, sister, and brother of the renowned Mingo chieftain, Logan, were killed. By October, the uprising had been quelled by the Battle of Point Pleasant, in which Michael Cresap served as a captain. After the battle one John Gibson, who interviewed the vanquished Chief Logan, accused Cresap of the earlier slaughter.

The charges persisted even after Cresap's death the next year. No less a statesman than Thomas Jefferson repeated the accusations, and in the introduction to his *Notes on Virginia,* printed in 1782, he commented that Cresap was "... a man infamous for the many murders he had committed on those much injured people [the Indians]." Luther Martin of Maryland, Cresap's son-in-law, spoke out in his defense; nevertheless, Jefferson's 1800 edition of the *Notes* not only repeated his original indictment, but produced additional "evidence" supporting Cresap's guilt. The controversy continued, but in 1826, in his *A Biographical Sketch of the Life of the Late Captain Michael Cresap,* printed in Cumberland, John J. Jacob refuted Jefferson's charges, emphasizing that Cresap's purpose in moving to Ohio had been "... to secure and improve some lands on that river; and consequently, that an Indian war would be to him, above all men, most disastrous. ..." Modern historians have sustained Jacob's interpretation, although with more tangible evidence, including a letter of 1798 in which George Rogers Clark, the western hero, absolved Cresap of guilt in the Yellow Creek Massacre. Michael Cresap did not remain in the Ohio Country for long after the Battle of Point Pleasant. Overtaken by illness, he began the journey homeward to recuperate, and here was caught up in the revolutionary fervor which had gripped Frederick County since 1765.[5]

As might be expected, the center of resistance to British restrictive policies in western Maryland occurred at Frederick, rather than farther westward, where the population was sparse, scattered, and largely uninformed. Nevertheless, residents of the Fort Cumberland area played an important role in these anti-British demonstrations, as did representatives of some Frederick-Town families who would later settle in the Allegany County of the future. It was the Stamp Act which aroused much of the colony. Zachariah Hood of Annapolis had been chosen as the official stamp distributor for the Province of Maryland, and upon him fell the wrath of the outraged inhabitants of Frederick County. On August 29, 1765, Hood was burned in effigy by the citizens of Frederick-Town. This expression of public fury, repeated in similar actions throughout the colony, so alarmed Governor Eden that he called a special meeting of the assembly to consider the situation. Among the four representatives from Frederick County was Thomas Cresap, now well over sixty. Cresap had served in the legislature during the chaotic years of the French and Indian War; as one of Frederick County's most prominent citizens he was the natural choice of his neighbors to speak for them in the present upheaval. The assembly, stirred by the volume of public protest, not only appointed delegates to the Stamp Act Congress soon to meet in New York City, but adopted resolutions condemning the act—both proceedings which the governor must have deplored. The defiance continued. When the Frederick County Court assembled for its fall session on November 15, 1765, one of the first actions of its justices was to adopt resolutions to the effect that:

> It is the unanimous resolution and opinion of this Court that all the business thereof shall and ought to be transacted in the usual and accustomed manner, without any inconvenience or delay to be occasioned from the want of *Stamped Paper, Parchment, or Vellum, and that all proceedings shall be valid and effectual without the use of Stamps,* and they enjoin and order all Sheriffs, Clerks, Counsellors, Attorneys, and all officers of the Court to proceed in their several avocations as usual. . . .

The rebellious inhabitants of Frederick-Town supported the decision of their county court by staging a public parade on November 30 at which the Stamp Act ". . . expired of a mortal stab received from the genius of liberty in Frederick County Court . . ." was carried through the streets in a coffin, and buried with mock honors beneath the town gallows.[6]

Even before the events of November 1765, the people of Frederick County had formed their own Sons of Liberty organization, headed by Thomas Cresap, which in October even threatened to march to Annapolis in protest against the Stamp Act. In time their pressures, reinforced by those of other communities, had the desired effect. Somewhat belatedly, on March 31, 1766, the Maryland Provincial Court followed Frederick County's lead, and ordered that legal proceedings throughout the colony be processed without the use of stamped paper. At that juncture the courts had been closed in Maryland since November 1, 1765, but now protests throughout the American colonies were forcing their opening everywhere. Parliament repealed the unenforceable Stamp Act on March 18, 1766; Maryland received the news in late May. The Provincial Court's decision to defy the act lagged far behind that of other colonies. In its opposition to later parliamentary acts, however, Maryland soon fell into line behind the actions of more radical colonies such as Massachusetts and Virginia. Frederick County, capably led by the tightly organized Sons of Liberty, kept the revolutionary movement alive in the backcountry.

Extreme western Maryland, however, played a subordinate part in these proceedings. The region, thinly populated and without a single town worthy of the name to bolster public sentiment, could do little but follow the lead of the better organized communities to the eastward. Nevertheless, the people of the area continued to look to the aging Thomas Cresap of Oldtown for leadership. Insofar as his capabilities allowed, he did not disappoint them. On November 18, 1774, at a meeting of voters held at the Frederick-Town Courthouse, Cresap, then seventy-two, was elected one of 114 members of a committee to enforce the Non-Importation Agreements recently adopted by the First Continental Congress meeting at Philadelphia. Presumably the old gentleman was expected to prevent the inhabitants of his district from purchasing goods of British manufacture. Since he was almost the only trader in that district, the responsibility must almost have amounted to a charge upon himself. His loyalty could not have been questioned. Cresap was elected in January 1775 to a similar but even larger committee formed to compel obedience to the latest resolves of the congress. At the same meeting the delegates voted to raise "... the sum of $1313.00, being the County's proportion of the $10,000 which the provincial convention has appointed to be raised for the purchase of arms and ammunition. . . ." Subscriptions were to be solicited throughout the county in every town and "hundred." In the Skipton, or Oldtown, area, Thomas Cresap, Moses Rawlings, and Richard Davis, Jr., were appointed as collectors, and for Cumberland Hundred, Charles Clinton. Certainly it was expected that these men would set the example for giving in their local areas, as well as ". . . apply personally, or by Deputy, to every freeman in their respective Districts, and to solicit a generous contribution." That coercion was their ultimate weapon is evident in the fact that upon delivering their collections to the Committee of Correspondence at Frederick-Town, they were to report the names of those who refused donations. And so matters went in western Maryland as the American colonies increasingly stiffened their resistance to British policies during the last days before the outbreak of revolution.[7]

At this time, Michael Cresap had returned to Maryland from the Ohio Country. The fame of his exploits against the Mingoes had traveled before him, and it was a foregone conclusion that he would furnish leadership in the struggle against Great Britain. Hostilities began in Massachusetts on April 19, 1775, when a large British force searching for powder and other military supplies was defeated by militiamen at the Battle of Lexington-Concord. The colonies did not become generally aroused, however, until the Battle of Bunker Hill in Charlestown, Massachusetts, on June 17, when the British Army captured a strategic location overlooking the town of Boston only at the cost of heavy casualties. Two days before this encounter the Second Continental Congress, upon the nomination of Thomas Johnson, delegate from Frederick, had selected George Washington as commander in chief of the new Continental Army already gathered at Cambridge, Massachusetts. The Congress further decreed that each colony should raise a certain quota of rifle companies to join Washington at Cambridge. Frederick County's apportionment was two companies. On June 21, 1775, the Committee of Observation of Frederick-Town resolved ". . . that, agreeable to the resolution of the Congress, two companies of expert riflemen be forthwith raised and officered by the following gentlemen: Of the first company–Michael Cresap, Captain; Thomas Warren, Joseph Cresap, Richard Davis, Jr., lieutenants." Cresap would receive $20 per month as company commander, a small sum, but ample in proportion to a private's pay of $6 2/3. In addition to the captain and three lieutenants, each company was to consist of four sergeants, four corporals, a drummer, and sixty-eight privates. It was expected that those named as officers of the new companies would be responsible for the recruiting of their units, largely from the ranks of their own friends and neighbors.[8]

Immediately upon his return to Oldtown, Michael Cresap was contacted by a friend who relayed the news of his nomination, and urged him to accept. But Cresap was reluctant. His health was precarious, and there were other considerations:

> "When I communicated my business," says the messenger, "and announced his appointment, instead of becoming elated, he became pensive and solemn, as if his spirits were really depressed, or as if he had a presentiment that this was his death-warrant. He said he was in bad health and his affairs in a deranged state, but that, nevertheless, as the committee had selected him, and as he understood from me his father [Thomas Cresap] had pledged himself that he should accept of this appointment, he would go, let the consequences be what they might. He then directed me to proceed to the west side of the mountains, and publish to his old Companions in arms this his intention. This I did, and in a very short time collected and brought to him, at his residence in Old Town, about twenty-two as fine fellows as ever handled a rifle, and most, if not all, of them completely equipped."

In spite of his forebodings, Michael Cresap continued his recruiting and made swift preparations for the march northward.[9]

The Cresap company, much oversubscribed, was probably the first contingent from the southern colonies to reach Cambridge; in achieving this distinction the riflemen set a record for endurance which has had few equals in the annals of American history. The rifle company left Frederick on July 18, 1775, less than one month after its commissioning, and reached Cambridge on August 9. It had marched nearly

550 miles over bad roads in only twenty-two days. Cresap's men made a brief stopover in Lancaster, Pennsylvania; the marksmanship they displayed there was admiringly reported in the *Virginia Gazette:*

> On Friday last there arrived at Lancaster, Pa., Captain Cresap's Company of riflemen consisting of 130 active and brave young fellows, many of whom were in the late expedition under Lord Dunmore against the Indians. These men have been bred in the woods to hardships and danger from their infancy. . . . Two brothers in Cresap's Company took a piece of board five inches by seven inches with a bit of white paper nailed in the center. While one held the board between his knees, the other at 60 yards (without any kind of rest) shot eight balls through the paper. . . . The spectators were told that upwards of 50 men in the company could do the same.

Michael Cresap delivered his company to General Washington in triumph, without the loss of a single man. The general stationed the detachment with other troops at the town of Roxbury. Beyond lay Boston, where the British Army was now besieged. Here also, the mountain men of western Maryland made a fast reputation for their prowess. One Thatcher, a New Englander, confided in his journal that:

> They are remarkably stout and hardy men, many of them exceeding six feet in height. They are dressed in white frocks, or rifle shirts, and round hats. These men are remarkable for the accuracy of their aim, striking a mark with great certainty at two hundred yard's distance. At a review, a company of them, while on a quick advance, fired their balls into objects of seven inches diameter at the distance of two hundred and fifty yards. They are now stationed on our lines, and their shot have frequently proved fatal to British officers and soldiers, who expose themselves to view, even at more than double the distance of common musket-shot.[10]

Cresap's Western Maryland Rifles performed with distinction during the American Revolution, after 1776 being incorporated into a Virginia rifle regiment of which Moses Rawlings of Oldtown served as lieutenant colonel. This regiment was stationed at Fort Washington in New York, with the particular assignment of guarding Fort Tryon, located several miles away. Both forts were captured by the British under Lord Howe on November 16, 1776. The western Marylanders fought bravely, but they with nearly 2,000 others were forced to surrender. Most found their way into British prison ships and camps in New York City. Captain Cresap himself had long since met his own end.[11]

Michael Cresap's health had markedly deteriorated during the exhausting trek northward to Cambridge; he continued to decline after his arrival. After two months of active duty under Washington he was forced to request a leave of absence, and began his return to Maryland in an attempt to recover his strength. The trip was too much for Cresap, and in New York City he collapsed. Here he died of fever on October 18, 1775, thus fulfilling his earlier premonitions. Cresap was only thirty-three years old, and left a widow and four children in nearly destitute circumstances back in western Maryland. Captain Michael Cresap was buried in the graveyard of Trinity Church, New York City, with full military honors. The New York *Gazette* for October 23, 1775, printed his obituary, which included the order of the funeral procession:

> Led by a Sergeant Major walked the Grenadiers of the First Battalion with their flintlocks reversed. Behind two Lieutenants marched a fife and drum corps. Next came a Captain of Grenadiers, flanked by two sergeant aides. Two Adjutants appointed to conduct the funeral came next and were followed by a military band. Immediately preceding the casket walked the clergymen and alongside the Caisson bearing the body of Capt. Cresap walked eight pallbearers, all captains.

The Captain's coffin was followed by the mourners, probably army friends of the deceased. The rear of this funeral cortege was composed of no less than three infantry battalions, an entire battalion made up of officers, and a large assemblage of civilians. Cresap's sandstone monument can still be seen in Trinity chruchyard, bearing the inscription:

> In memory of Michael Cresap, First
> Captain of the Rifle Battalions, and son
> to Col. Thomas Cresap, who departed
> this life October the 18th, 1775

Michael Cresap has never been forgotten in Allegany County; his death provided not only an example to his contemporaries during the revolutionary era, but also a legend for present-day residents of the region. His youth and the manner of his death lent a special poignancy to his brief career.[12]

Gradually the Revolutionary War wound down to a close. In terms of troops raised, taxes collected, and requisitions made, western Maryland had done its share. It had furnished its heroes, such as Captain Michael Cresap and Colonel Moses Rawlings, the hero of Fort Tryon. For the most part its leadership, however, was provided by men from the Frederick area. The western section of Frederick County was set off as Washington County in 1775. The future Allegany County met its military quotas, but the individuals who appeared on the rosters are difficult to trace, their names and fortunes having merged with those from the eastern section of what was then Washington County. In spite of frequent alarms, western Maryland never experienced the shock and devastation of British invasion forces. Its inhabitants for the most part simply waited out the war, secure for once in their remoteness. After the defeat of Lord Cornwallis at Yorktown, Virginia, in 1781, there was not even the danger of attack. Revolutionary America experienced substantial development along all of its frontiers; western Maryland was no exception. The postwar years would witness even more spectacular growth.

During this period the foundations were being laid for the establishment of a settlement around the walls of the now-sagging Fort Cumberland. "Walnut Bottom" had been surveyed by Thomas Cresap in June 1745, but this initiative had not led to the movement of settlers into the area. It was natural, however, that Fort Cumberland, constructed in 1755, would serve as a nucleus for a future town. It functioned importantly as the local defense point, it was admirably suited for trade and transportation on the Potomac River, and its presence stimulated the production of foodstuffs for consumption by the garrison, thereby attracting farmers to the region. Soldiers' families, camp followers, small traders, and innkeepers all found their way to the outpost, for here was money to spend, entertainment, conviviality, and sometimes, important visitors to dazzle the unsophisticated. Thus a small civilian population gathered about Fort Cumberland almost from its inception. This population, however, was a temporary one whose continued existence depended upon the maintenance of the fort.

Meanwhile, the lands about Fort Cumberland changed hands. It was on March 25, 1756, only a year after Braddock's defeat, that Bladen, no longer governor of Maryland, sold his "Walnut Bottom" tract to George Mason, an important shareholder in the Ohio Company of Virginia. Mason kept the land for nearly twenty-seven years without developing it to any great extent, finally selling "Walnut Bottom," together with another tract called "Limestone Rock," to Thomas Beall of Samuel on October 25, 1783. "Limestone Rock" had formerly belonged to Thomas Cresap. The price for the two holdings, totaling several hundred acres, was £1,407.10.[13]

Thomas Beall was far more ambitious than the previous owners. He immediately set his workmen to clearing the land, and in 1785, laid out the village which he called "Washington Town." Settlers began to purchase the town lots he offered for sale. The village was soon a going concern, but it was not authorized by act of the state legislature. To achieve legitimacy and secure the advantages of incorporation, therefore, Thomas Beall of Samuel and thirty-four other heads of families then resident in the town petitioned the Maryland legislature in 1787 for incorporation. The assembly responded on January 20, 1787, by passing "An act for erecting a town at or near the mouth of Will's Creek, in Washington County." The town was to be called "Cumberland," a name which was certainly as appropriate as the previous "Washington Town," and as indicative of the history of the region. The legislative act provided that five residents of the area—Andrew Bruce, George Dent, John Lynn, Evan Gwynn, and Daniel Cresap—were to serve as commissioners for the new town, with the task of surveying and laying out additional acreage. All but Cresap were residents of the town.[14]

The act further provided for a local government, for the commissioners were authorized to make important decisions concerning the town's welfare, to hire a clerk, to appoint a successor if one of their number died (thus perpetuating their control), and were:

> ... empowered to levy, assess and take, by way of distress, if needful, from the inhabitants of the town, by even and equal proportion, a sum not exceeding ten pounds current money yearly, to be paid to their clerk; and [had] power to remove or displace their clerk as often as they [thought] fit.

According to the terms of incorporation, the commissioners were to construct the town's main streets so that they were not less than eighty feet wide; the side streets branching from these major thoroughfares were to measure not less than sixty feet wide. It is doubtful that these stipulations were ever observed; in fact, the surveys, boundaries, and first map of the town were never filed as the act directed.[15]

The thirty-five heads of families who petitioned for incorporation were in many cases so important in the early history of Cumberland that it seems appropriate to name them. They were, in addition to Thomas Beall of Samuel and the four commissioners: George Lowdermilk, Michael Kershner, David Lynn, George Calmes, Benjamin Wiley, Peter Devecmon, Dickenson Simpkins, William Hoye, Charles F. Broadhag, John Graham, Charles Clinton, George Hoffman, David Watkins, James McCoy, Jacob Lowry, Jonathan Cox, Thomas Stewart, David Hoffman, John S. Hook, George Payne, Robert Clark, Jeremiah Wilson, John C. Beatty, George Simmons, James Slicer, David Harvey, Eli Williams, John Mustard, George Blocher, and Henry Wineow. It is evident that nearly all of the first settlers were of English, Irish, and Scotch-Irish extraction. A few, such as Michael Kershner, were German. Charles Clinton had been living in the vicinity of Fort Cumberland since at least 1774, when he had been appointed to raise funds for ammunition at "Cumberland Hundred." Thomas Beall, Andrew Bruce, and the Lynns had moved to Cumberland from Frederick, as was probably true of others in the group.

Of the thirty-five petitioners, Thomas Beall probably holds the most interest. The Bealls were a prolific tribe, both at Frederick and elsewhere in Maryland. They were so numerous, in fact, that Thomas Beall had added the phrase "of

Samuel" to his surname to distinguish himself from the many other Thomas Bealls of the period. His father, Colonel Samuel Beall, was a resident of Frederick-Town, and must have been a man of distinction there. He was an inhabitant of Prince George's Parish, Frederick County, as early as June 9, 1760, when he, with others, contributed to a fund raised for sufferers of the great fire in Boston, Massachusetts, that year. In January 1775, he was elected one of fifteen representatives in Frederick County who were authorized to attend any provincial congress to be held in Annapolis during the following year, a nomination which clearly established him as a member of the radical party. Thomas, born in 1744, was the youngest of Samuel's five sons, and served as a captain in Colonel Rawlings' regiment during the American Revolution, seeing action in the New York campaign of 1776. By the end of the war he had sufficient resources to move westward to Fort Cumberland, and as we have seen, purchase two large tracts in 1783 for close to seven thousand dollars. Considering his military background, it is not surprising that Beall named several of the streets he laid out for colonial and Revolutionary War heroes: Washington, Fayette, Greene, Lee, Paca, Smallwood, and Beall (no false modesty here). Thomas Beall of Samuel lived on until 1823, and during his life span helped bring about many of the changes in the town that he founded.[16]

Beall also accumulated a sizeable fortune during his long years. Probably a part of this estate was acquired through his canny practice of attaching "ground rents" or "rents seck" to the sale of his lands. Beall's deeds often contained the stipulation that he be paid an annual fee of one Spanish milled dollar on January 1 of each year. For example, on January 1, 1791, Beall sold Captain Jonathan Morris a lot on Washington Street for the very reasonable sum of ten dollars plus the annual ground rent. Quitrents had been known and imposed for centuries in Great Britain; the Penns of Pennsylvania and the Calverts of Maryland had continued them in America, but quitrents, not so very different from ground rents, had been abolished in the new states during the American Revolution. That Thomas Beall saw fit to continue the practice in the

1790s appeared illegal to most residents of the town. Actually, many of those who purchased land from Beall had refused to pay the ground rents by as early as 1806, when he petitioned the Maryland Assembly for recovery of what he believed to be his due. After his death in 1823 the remaining purchasers defaulted, and eventually his heirs abandoned their attempts to collect the highly unpopular ground rents.[17]

Among the most prominent of Cumberland's early settlers were the Lynn brothers, David and John, who signed the 1787 petition. Like Thomas Beall of Samuel, the Lynns relocated in Cumberland from Frederick-Town. Their father, the first David Lynn, left Ireland for America in 1717, and settled in Frederick County. As Judge Lynn, he had been one of the twelve justices who declared the Stamp Act null and void in 1765; earlier, he had served as one of the commissioners who surveyed Georgetown (now in the District of Columbia) in 1751. Of his two sons, John was one of the five commissioners named to lay out Cumberland in 1787, and one of the commissioners later appointed to construct the first Allegany Courthouse and jail. John Lynn served as clerk of court during the period 1790-1801. David Lynn, born at Frederick in 1758, enlisted in the Continental Army at the age of eighteen and eventually earned the rank of captain in the Seventh Maryland Regulars. He was present with this regiment at the Battle of Yorktown. Once settled in Cumberland, David became a real estate speculator, probably one reason why he was appointed as a commissioner to mediate disputes arising from the disposition of the well-known "Soldier Lands." In 1801, David Lynn constructed a mansion at his Rose Hill estate. This house eventually passed to the Avirett family, and was for many years both a landmark and a showplace in Cumberland.[18]

Andrew Bruce, another of the five commissioners appointed in 1787, also moved to Cumberland from Frederick County, where his father, John Bruce, was a landowner at Big Pike Creek. Andrew, who arrived in the Fort Cumberland area after the Revolution, purchased the Mount Pleasant tract from his brother Normand, who never actually lived in the region. The holding was extensive, and included six "military lots"; altogether the estate comprised some 1,191 acres. Here Andrew Bruce built Bruce House, a handsome stone mansion which was destroyed by fire in the twentieth century. The Bruces were well connected with important families in eastern Maryland; Normand Bruce's wife was the aunt of Francis Scott Key. Eventually her son, Upton Key Bruce, moved to Cumberland and established his own family there. His uncle, Andrew Bruce, soon became one of the town's most influential citizens, serving as judge of the court established in 1791 and as a member of the Maryland General Assembly.[19]

In contrast to other members of the local gentry, Peter Devecmon was not a native Marylander, but surprisingly, a member of the French aristocracy. Pierre Duvaucel d'Evequemont, born in 1759, was a cousin of Louis XVI; his sister was a lady-in-waiting to Marie Antoinette. Tragedy struck when young Pierre killed another cousin in a duel; in remorse and disgrace he left France for America. After landing in Baltimore in 1783, he lived in Wilmington, Delaware, for a few months before moving to Cumberland in 1784. For convenience he shortened his name to Peter Devecmon. The young Frenchman may have wished to bury his past in a frontier backwater, but he did not do so in poverty. Until the beginning of the French Revolution his income in Cumberland was handsomely supplemented by profits from the family estates in France, which were forwarded to him by his sister. With this subsidy Devecmon was able to build gristmills at Oldtown, Cumberland, and Westernport and to open a general store at Clarksburg, West Virginia. Peter Devecmon lived in style in Cumberland, even maintaining his own carriage, and at the time of his death in 1803, was planning to take his family to Paris in an effort to persuade Napoleon I to restore the ancestral estates, which had been confiscated during the revolution.[20]

Men like Devecmon, Andrew Bruce, the Lynns, and Thomas Beall of Samuel were typical of the new breed who settled in Cumberland in the 1780s. The characteristics they shared—ambition, vision, aggressiveness—were peculiar to the qualities of those who pioneer the wilderness. But they had other distinguishing features: All of these men were the scions of families which were already well established elsewhere. They came to Cumberland at a time of great opportunity, true enough, but it was opportunity best suited for the well-heeled man with money to invest, not for the penniless. Under the influence of this new gentry, and with the talents and resources they brought to the region, the town of Cumberland grew rapidly.

What was initially a straggling village soon took on the aspects of a busy town, the thriving center of an increasingly prosperous farming district. In spite of its growing population, however, the appearance of the place was less than impressive. Nearly all of the houses were built along the old Braddock Road, which the older residents were now learning to call Greene Street. A few buildings also wound up the hill towards old Fort Cumberland along what was now Washington Street. Wagons moved slowly through the muddy, unpaved streets and with great effort up the hills everywhere, which were, if possible, even steeper than those of today. Nearly all of the houses were constructed of logs; frame houses were few and far between, and brick dwellings even scarcer. Washington's old headquarters, a stout log house, still stood near the former parade ground of the fort, but it had now been converted into a residence. Some idea of the quality of housing generally can be gained from the fact that this house was occupied successively by some of the first families of the town, including those of David Lynn and George Bruce. Still, the headquarters building compared very favorably with George Lowdermilk's log cabin on Washington Street or the log huts of Thomas Beall and John Miller, both located on Liberty Street. Of superior construction, evidently, was the large frame "rough-coated" house built on Greene Street in 1786 by George Dent. Here his son, Frederick Dent, was born in the fall of 1796, the first white child born within town limits, according to tradition. Frederick Dent would grow to maturity, move westward to Saint Louis, Missouri, prosper, and become the father of Julia Dent, the wife of General and later President Ulysses S. Grant. The Dent house was eventually purchased by Peter Devecmon. The grandest early home in town, however, was the Greene Street house of the William McMahon family, built in 1792. Apparently this was a frame house, for its chief claim to fame lay in the fact that it included a brick addition, probably the first such construction in town.[21]

Cumberland's early public buildings were much the same as its private homes: sturdy and functional, but entirely lacking in grace and charm. One of these was the first jail, or "Guard House," which may have served that function as a part of Fort Cumberland. It was natural that the first settlers would adapt portions of an existing structure to their own purposes. The Guard House was described by Thomas and Williams in their *History of Allegany County, Maryland,* as "built without windows, and had but one door, which was studded with heavy rod-iron nails." It was used as the Allegany County Jail until as late as 1799. The taverns of the day must also be counted as public buildings; they offered accommodations for the traveler as well as food and drink, and served important social functions in the town as well. Early Cumberland appears to have possessed more than its share. Simpkins' Tavern—Dickenson Simpkins, proprietor—stood on North Mechanic Street. George Shipley constructed a rival tavern nearby on the same street in 1790. Then there was Faw's Tavern, owned and operated by Abraham Faw on Greene Street. Although only a double, two-story log cabin, it was commodious enough to serve as the county courthouse until 1799. The Drovers' Tavern, a large, two-story frame building, was also a popular resort on Greene Street. These taverns were undoubtedly brawling, lawless places at times, the natural expressions of a cruder age. Controls and regulations were difficult either to formulate or to enforce in an isolated area like Cumberland. It would have been impossible for the five-man commission to maintain law and order in the situation.[22]

As the population of Cumberland and the outlying villages grew, pressures mounted for the separation of westernmost Maryland from Washington County, its center of government since late in 1775. The advantages of partition were obvious. The creation of a new county would provide an effective local court system, presided over by local judges, with decisions rendered by local juries. The people of western Maryland would elect their own senators and representatives to guard their interests at Annapolis. If Cumberland became the new county seat it would gain in prestige and prosperity; its central position would attract business and real estate prices would rise. As the largest and best located town in western Maryland, it was inevitable that Cumberland would become the new shiretown.

The Maryland Assembly easily gave way before the determined petitions of the western residents, and on December 25, 1789, it approved an "... Act for the division of Washington county and for erecting a new one by the name of Allegany." The preamble to this act clearly specified the reasons for the separation:

> Whereas, A number of the inhabitants of Washington county, by their petition to the General Assembly, have prayed that an act may pass for a division of said county by Sideling Hill Creek, and for erecting a new one out of the Western part thereof; and it appearing to this General Assembly that the erecting such a new county will conduce greatly to the due administration of justice, and the speedy settling and improving the western part thereof, and the ease and convenience of the inhabitants thereof. . . .

The act further stipulated that the county court, as well as the orphans' court, should be located in Cumberland, and that a new courthouse should be constructed with all due speed. These courts were to become operative on April 25, 1791, by which time their justices and other officials would have been appointed by the governor of Maryland. The transition to county government was smooth. On the day appointed, Associate Justice Andrew Bruce presided over the first Allegany County Court session in the home of John Graham of Cumberland, with John Beatty acting as sheriff and John Lynn serving as clerk of court.[23]

The next step was to provide the new county with a courthouse worthy of its dignity. With remarkable foresight, Thomas Beall had set aside four lots for a future courthouse when he first surveyed the town. These lots lay on the north side of Washington Street next to the present public library.

By an act of the Maryland Assembly passed in 1793, Thomas Beall of Samuel, John Lynn, William McMahon, George Dent, and Benjamin Tomlinson were appointed commissioners to supervise the construction of the county courthouse and jail. The building was to be financed by the levying of a special county tax of £600, one third of which was to be raised in each of the years 1794, 1795, and 1796. This sum proved inadequate to complete the structure; in 1796, the commissioners imposed an additional tax of £137.10-, and in 1799, £75 more. Little is known about the appearance of the finished building; probably it had no particular architectural significance. However, it was substantial, a one-story brick structure with a high stone basement that furnished courtroom space above, with the jail and jailer's quarters in the lower floor.

The creation of Allegany County with Cumberland as its seat seemed to impart a new vigor to the town during the 1790s. Facilities and services of all kinds expanded. For the first time, organized religion made its appearance in Cumberland. Even during this last decade of the eighteenth century the town's population was polyglot enough in origins to support several churches; what is remarkable is the degree of cooperation and harmony which prevailed among the different denominations during their early years in Cumberland. The first to organize was the "Roman Catholic Society." There had been a few Catholics living in the area from the last days of the French and Indian War, when John Mattingly settled in the vicinity of Cumberland. After the war he was joined by Patrick Burns, Peter Dugan, and Gabriel McKenzie, and later by Joseph Frost and the Arnold, Porter, and Logiston families. The Reverend Dennis Cahill was the first to minister to this little flock, but only in the capacity of a missionary who made occasional visits to the area. Nevertheless, it was Father Cahill whose initiative led to the society's purchase of Lot No. 5 in Cumberland in 1791, and to the erection of Saint Mary's Church, a log structure, the following year. Saint Mary's stood on the lot adjacent to present-day Saint Patrick's Church on North Centre Street. Despite this solid beginning, during the years 1795-1799 Saint Mary's had no resident priest, but relied on the pastoral visits of the Reverend Demetrius Augustine Galitzin, a circuit rider. Father Galitzin, born at The Hague in 1770, was the son of Prince Galitzin, the Russian Ambassador to the Netherlands. Converted to Catholicism in his youth, the younger Galitzin came to the United States in 1792, and became a priest in 1795. In 1799, however, Father Galitzin founded a religious colony in Cambria County, Pennsylvania, and when he left Cumberland the Burns and Dugan families followed him. Allegany County would remain without a resident priest for many years to come.[24]

It is rather surprising that the next to found a church society were the German Lutherans, since they do not appear to have settled in Cumberland in any numbers until after the American Revolution. Nevertheless, the Lutheran Church of Cumberland was the direct descendant of similar churches established in leapfrog fashion across western Maryland at Frederick, Monocacy, and Conococheague. As the German settlers spread farther and farther westward, they carried their religion with them. Other Germans moved directly to Allegany County from across the Pennsylvania line. By the 1790s such families as the Rizers and Shucks in Cumberland, and the Brotemarkles, Leybergers, Valentines, and Rices, who lived beyond town limits, began to press for their own church building, although they were already holding services in their homes under the guidance of the Reverend Friedrich Wilhelm Lange. On June 20, 1794, the Lutherans purchased Lot No. 240 from Thomas Beall of Samuel for £15 (current money). This lot was located at the corner of the streets then called Bedford and Mill (present-day Baltimore and Centre streets). Here they erected their first church, which was modest in the extreme: a log building about sixty feet long by forty feet wide containing a main floor with galleries built around three sides. John Rice, the contractor, also provided two long beams at one gable end of the church which supported a bell used to summon the congregation. This simple log church, improved by the addition of a vestibule and steeple in 1821, served the parish until as late as 1844.[25]

Methodist revivalism and the missionary activities of the

famous circuit riders in the 1780s account for the formation of a Methodist society in Cumberland by the end of the century. Earlier historians of the region disagree as to the exact date of the founding of the church, but the Reverend Hixon T. Bowersox's estimate that the formal organization of the Methodist society took place in 1797 seems reasonable. During their early years in Cumberland the Methodists borrowed the Lutheran Church for worship; the Lutherans made their building available for any denomination that wished to use it. In 1799 or 1800, however, the Methodists completed their own log church at Smallwood and Fayette streets.[26]

During the 1790s, Cumberland assumed many of the responsibilities and concerns of the older, better established municipalities farther east. Life in the town became easier and more orderly, but better facilities and services also meant increased regulation of the lives of its inhabitants. This was especially true in regard to the marketing of foodstuffs. The first market house was established by legislative act in 1795, and was located in a temporary shed on Mechanic Street. According to the terms of this act, after May 1, 1796, fruit, grain, and other foodstuffs could be offered for sale only on Wednesday and Saturday mornings. Furthermore, anyone who sold provisions elsewhere during these market hours was subject to a fine of fifteen shillings. Regulation of the taverns soon followed. In April 1798, the quarterly court set official "Innkeepers' Rates" which were to be carefully observed by taverns throughout the county:

	s.	p.
A Hot Dinner for a Gentleman, with Beer or Cider	3	
A Supper or Breakfast	2	
French Brandy, per ½ pint	1	10
Peach Brandy, per ½ pint	1	3
Lodging in clean sheets	1	10
ditto double ditto		9
Ditto in sheets before used		6
Hay per night for Horse	1	6
Ditto for 24 hours	2	6
Madeira and Claret Wine per quart	10	
Port, Sherry, or Lisbon Wine	7	6
Whiskey per gill		5½

Other Wine per quart	5	
Corn and Oats, per quart		3
Lodging for Servants		6
Cold Dinner, per Gentleman	1	10½
Supper and Breakfast per servant	1	6
Dinner per Servant	1	10

Fodder must have been scarce in the area; the cost of feeding a horse for twenty-four hours was nearly as high as a "gentleman's" dinner, and considerably higher than the cost of feeding a "servant," probably a slave. The menus offered at these taverns are not specified, but the chances are that pork, the universal staple of the period, appeared in some form at every meal, washed down with liberal quantities of the locally produced peach brandy and corn whiskey.[27]

If the tavern was a time-honored local institution, the school also became a fixture by the end of the 1790s. In 1799, the first "Allegany County School" was established by the state legislature, on the convincing grounds that it was ". . . reasonable that education should be extended to the several parts of this State, and that there should be a public school in Allegany County. . . ." Under the terms of this act the county was provided with a school budget of $200 per year, and a board of visitors comprising nine prominent citizens of Allegany County was empowered to purchase land in Cumberland, construct a school, and supervise that school. The act said nothing about who should attend, or whether fees should be charged; we must assume that this legislation did not by any means bring free public education to Allegany County. Nevertheless, the schoolhouse, a one-story brick building called the "Academy," was constructed on Fayette Street; its early "professors" included one Mr. Pierce and a Benjamin Brown. The Academy was the first semipublic school, but before it was established some small private schools flourished within the county. Two of these were for girls; the site of one was a log hut on Mechanic Street, and the other was located in a building close to "The Dingle." In 1947, J. William Hunt unearthed the copybook of Jonathan Arnold, who attended school in the county, probably in Cumberland, between 1787 and 1795, long before the official school was established. Because of the shortage of textbooks, young Arnold had to copy "... more than one hundred pages of arithmetic, legal forms, geometry, and bookkeeping . . . ," but he also cluttered up his pages with drawings of birds and the traditional schoolboy verses:

> Jonathan Arnold's hand and pen
> —He will be good but God knows when.
> and
> Jonathan Arnold is my name
> and with my pen I wrote the same.[28]

The population of Cumberland was growing so fast that, in 1798, Thomas Beall of Samuel decided that the time had come to expand the town. By 1797, according to historian Will Lowdermilk, the place contained no less than 125 families and at least 100 houses. Two physicians, Dr. Murray and Dr. John M. Reid, administered to the medical needs of the community, and there was even a drugstore, operated by one Wyatt on Bedford Street. The town's first post office had been established two years before, for on January 1, 1795, Cumberland had been officially designated a "Post Town" by the federal government. Charles F. Broadhag, one of the original petitioners for town status in 1787, was named postmaster, but the position could not have been a full-time one, as he operated the post office in one corner of his Mechanic Street store. The town also boasted at least one blacksmith shop, operated by Thomas Dowden; other trades were represented by Captain Thomas Blair, hatter; A. Rogers, butcher; Michael Fisher, cooper; and Henry Wineow, brickmason. Shryer's tannery was situated on Bedford Street, and Peter Devecmon's gristmill lay near the mouth of the millrace. The pride of the town, it had cost more than $8,000 to build, and was said to be the finest in the state. Keenly aware of all of this business development, Thomas Beall felt justified in increasing the boundaries of his town. Most of his earlier real estate venture lay to the west of Wills Creek; "Beall's Addition," surveyed in 1798, was on the eastern side. With the creation of this "Addition," much of modern-day Cumberland came into being; it included Bedford (Baltimore) Street, Mill (Centre) Street, and Mechanic Street. According to local tradition, the latter was laid out as a special residence and business district for the town's increasing number of tradesmen and artisans. Although "Beall's Addition" dates from 1798, it is evident that some homes and shops had been established in the area even before that time.[29]

Cumberland was now well on the way to becoming the "metropolis" George Washington had predicted back in 1755, but Allegany County was growing as well. The census of 1782 had set the population of Washington County, which then included all lands to the westward, at 11,488 whites. Allegany County, however, was separated from its parent in 1789, just in time to be recorded in the first federal census of 1790. That census listed a total population for Allegany County of 4,809 persons, of whom 1,068 were males over sixteen and 1,283 males under sixteen, with "all females" totaling 2,188. County residents owned 258 slaves; there were in addition twelve "free persons of color" living within its borders. Because the same census gave Washington County a total of 15,822 persons, it is clear that the populations of these two westernmost counties of Maryland had nearly doubled within the short space of eight years. Obviously, then, the country districts around Cumberland were growing as fast as the town itself.[30]

One reason for this expansion lay in Maryland's postwar land policies. It had been customary even during the colonial period for war veterans to be rewarded for their military service by the allocation of western lands. In this way, not only were the deserving compensated, but the individual colonies were able to grow at little cost to themselves. Maryland, like several of the new states, took similar action towards the end of the American Revolution. At its November 1781 session, the general assembly confiscated the holdings of the former proprietor, Lord Baltimore, which lay to the west of Fort Cumberland, and created two land offices to supervise the distribution of these lands. Next, in 1787, the assembly resolved that the western lands should be surveyed and divided into lots comprising fifty acres each. Francis Deakins, an experienced surveyor who in 1768 had measured out Lord Baltimore's Oakland lands, was hired to do the work with the aid of ten assistants. The Deakins crew laid out no less than 4,165 lots, mostly along the line of the old Braddock Road. The first of these was located near the mouth of Savage River near Bloomington Lake, but much of the land lay in what is now Garrett County. Veteran officers received four lots, or 200 acres apiece, while enlisted men were assigned one lot each. Actually, few of the veterans who were assigned the lands ever settled on them, or even took the trouble to inspect them. Not everyone in eastern Maryland was interested in moving to the frontier, or would have found it convenient to do so. It was far easier to sell the land to speculators, some of whom lived in the Cumberland area. A few of the recipients, however, took advantage of their opportunities and settled west of Cumberland.[31]

Among these settlers was Abraham Loar. He arrived in America from Germany on the ship *Union* in 1774, and subsequently fought in the Revolution. In return for his services Loar received Lot No. 3682, and his brother Jacob, Lot No. 3681. Later, Abraham Loar also purchased Lot No. 3684 from one William Rediford. The Loars settled about ten miles from Fort Cumberland in a district which soon became known as Eckhart, for Jacob Loar's wife was the former Sarah Eckhart. Her brother, George Adam Eckhart, had been a fellow passenger with Loar on the *Union.* He, like Loar, planted in Eckhart, which they laid out in 1789. Jacob and Sarah Loar were the parents of eleven children, and their descendants are legion.[32]

Westernport had its origins in the Potomac Company, whose leading stockholder, George Washington, had extensive real estate interests in western Virginia. Washington's Bullskin Plantation in the Shenandoah alone contained 550 acres, and he also received 15,000 acres of land in the Ohio Country for his services to Virginia during the French and Indian War. He continued to speculate in western lands throughout his lifetime. It was much to his advantage to wish to improve transportation along the Potomac River, and Washington was quick to realize this pressing need. Nevertheless, it was Thomas Johnson of Maryland who wrote to the Virginian in June 1770 requesting his assistance in securing his colony's support for improvements to the Potomac. Washington was even more ambitious than Johnson, replying that the great river must be made fully navigable well beyond Fort Cumberland, where a connection with the Ohio River should be possible. He urged that those interested in the project form a stock company and apply to the Maryland and Virginia legislatures for charters. The newly formed Potomac Company easily obtained its Virginia charter, but merchants in Baltimore who feared the loss of their interior trade defeated the charter in the Maryland Assembly. There matters stood at the beginning of the American Revolution.[33]

The question of the improvement of the Potomac was aired again at the Mount Vernon conference in 1785, a meeting which is considered an important forerunner of the Constitutional Convention. Commissioners representing Maryland and Virginia devised two plans: (1) a navigation company to remove obstacles, cut new channels, and build a canal around the Great Falls; (2) construction of a road which would join the headwaters of the Potomac and the Ohio. The plan was daring and costly, but if completed, would effectively connect the Potomac with the entire Mississippi Valley. To some extent the proposal was achieved. The Potomac Company hired James Rumsey, an engineer, to build the Great Falls Canal, which was completed in 1802; he also supervised the removal of huge boulders from the Potomac riverbed. What is more important here, however, is that the western junction with tributaries of the Ohio was fixed at the point where the Savage River joins the Potomac. The flurry of activity at that site was instrumental in the creation of a new town, Western Port (later contracted to Westernport).[34]

Actually, the area had been known to Indians and fur traders during the colonial era, long before a town was established there. It was a natural stopping place for them, as well as for hunters, in their passage to and from Fort Duquesne (later Fort Pitt), and subsequently, in their trips to Wheeling. For the first permanent settlers, however, waterpower was the attraction. It was Peter Devecmon, the Cumberland business entrepreneur, who bought up the land in the 1780s and built a prosperous, stone gristmill. Devecmon never lived in

Westernport, but his daughter, Anne, was born there in 1794. In time Devecmon's holdings were bought out by James Morrison and Adam Sigler, who surveyed and laid out a town. By the turn of the century, representatives of the following well-known local families had settled there: Wilt, Ravenscroft, Foss, Powers, Poland, Michael, Clark, Broadwater, Dayton, Coleman, Hight, Kooken, Grove, Duckworth, Hixenbaugh, Fazenbaker, Paxton, Murray, Murphy, and Jameson. Their life in early Westernport must have been filled with difficulties, as is indicated in the nickname they applied to their town: "Hardscrabble."[35]

On the whole, though, the first decade of the existence of Allegany County was one of boom, expansion, and general prosperity, which was only slightly interrupted by the specter of insurrection in 1794. The cause of this rebellion lay in what was probably the most controversial part of Secretary of the Treasury Alexander Hamilton's financial program: a tax on whiskey. His duty upon hard liquors produced within the continental United States hit the frontier farmers especially hard, because they viewed it as a tax on money. Indeed, liquor circulated as money in the frontier settlements, and in those days of almost impassable roads, where roads even existed, the conversion of grain into corn liquor, easily transported on packhorses, was almost the only means by which the farmers could get their produce to market. Discontent was general in the backcountry, but the opposition to the collection of the excise was strongest in Allegheny, Washington, Fayette, and Westmoreland counties in Pennsylvania. Western Maryland, however, was also in a turmoil.

President Washington was determined to enforce the act, and on August 7, 1794, he issued a proclamation calling upon the militia of New Jersey, Pennsylvania, Maryland, and Virginia, a total of 15,000 men, to quell the rebellion. By September, riots in opposition to the draft of these troops had reached alarming proportions at Frederick, Middletown, and Hagerstown in western Maryland. At Cumberland, whiskey rebels attempted to force tax collector Selby to surrender his papers of office; only the support of a local militia company prevented his unwilling compliance.[36]

On September 25, 1794, Washington published a second proclamation, ordering that the Pennsylvania and New Jersey troops assemble at Bedford, Pennsylvania, and that Maryland and Virginia militia gather at Cumberland. The president decided to himself lead the troops in the field, and attack the rebels mobilizing near Pittsburgh. General Alexander Hamilton accompanied him. On Tuesday, September 30, Washington's party left Philadelphia. He arrived at Harrisburg on October 3, consulted with his generals and the governors of Pennsylvania and New Jersey at Carlisle, and reviewed the troops of those states before they marched westward. On October 12, Washington headed south from Carlisle, passing through Chambersburg and Williamsport. On the night of the fifteenth he lodged at Oldtown, but not with his old friend Thomas Cresap, who had died in 1790. Washington observed that the road to Oldtown was as terrible as ever, commenting in his diary that "... from the extreme badness of the Road, more than half of it stoney, was a severe days journey for the carriage horses; they performed it however well." At eleven o'clock on October 16, he arrived in Cumberland.[37]

In spite of the emergency, Washington's final visit to Cumberland had all of the pomp and ceremony of a state visit. As he approached a point three miles from the town, the president was met by a troop of horses led by his nephew, Major George Lewis, and Brigadier General Samuel Smith of Maryland, who escorted him to the encampment of Virginia and Maryland militia, 3,200 strong, which was located close to the ruins of old Fort Cumberland. Washington then "... passed along the lines of the Army; was conducted to a house the residence of Major [David] Lynn of the Maryland line (an old Continental Officer) where [he] was well lodged, and civily entertained." Thus Washington returned to Cumberland, which he had last visited in 1784. He remained in the town for two more days, readying his troops for the battle he believed to be imminent. Finally, accompanying the Virginia and Maryland contingents, he headed for Bedford and reunion with the balance of his army. He did not lead these forces westward to Pittsburgh, there to see the rebels scatter in every direction, but returned to Philadelphia after delivering a farewell address to the army.[38]

Washington's last visit was long remembered in Cumberland. For generations, elders would recount to their children and grandchildren their recollections of what the first president had said, what he had worn, how he had looked. His appearance was commemorated by at least one artist, Frederick Kimmelmeyer of Baltimore, who had made the difficult journey to Cumberland for just that purpose. Kimmelmeyer was a primitive artist, without formal academic training, yet his "Washington Reviewing the Western Army at Fort Cumberland" has a charm and dignity. The general is depicted as an aging man, dressed in blue and buff Continentals, astride a high-stepping, spirited horse. His troops are lined up in the middle ground of the picture, their tents also in military precision behind. In the background lies a long, earthen mound, all that remained of Fort Cumberland in 1794. General Daniel Morgan, a comrade-in-arms of the Revolutionary era who participated in the review that day, bought the painting on the spot. It subsequently passed through several hands and is now on view at the Henry Francis duPont Winterthur Museum.

Today one tends to recall Washington's review of his forces at Cumberland without remembering the circumstances that brought it about. A rebellion was crushed and the power of the federal government asserted in 1794, but the grievances which caused the revolt were not redressed. The excise tax remained in effect, causing genuine hardship on the frontier, until the inauguration of President Thomas Jefferson in 1801. There must have been those at Cumberland who remembered Washington's final review with bitterness, not nostalgia, but history has not recorded the feelings of those discontents. In any case, a different spirit was in the air in the Allegany County of the late 1790s. Its inhabitants were like Americans everywhere; life seemed full of promise to them. The county's resources seemed inexhaustible and its potential illimitable. The people of Allegany County looked ahead to the nineteenth century with hope and anticipation.

CHAPTER III NOTES

1. Hilleary F. Willison, "History of the Pioneer Settlers of Flintstone, District #3, and Their Descendants" (unpublished typescript, 1910), p. 1.

2. Ibid., pp. 9, 22.

3. Ibid., p. 14.

4. John J. Jacob, *A Biographical Sketch of the Life of the Late Captain Michael Cresap* (Cincinnati: J. F. Uhlhorn, 1866), pp. 41-42 (hereafter cited as Jacobs, *Michael Cresap*).

5. Allen Johnson and Dumas Malone, eds., *The Dictionary of American Biography* (New York: Charles Scribner's Sons, 1931), IV, p. 538; and Jacobs, *Michael Cresap*, p. 50.

6. John T. Scharf, *History of Western Maryland* (Philadelphia: Louis Everts Company, 1882), pp. 121-22 (hereafter cited as Scharf, *Western Maryland*).

7. Ibid., p. 129.

8. Ibid., p. 130.

9. Ibid., pp. 130-31.

10. J. William Hunt, "Across the Desk," in the Cumberland *Sunday Times*, February 9, 1958 (hereafter cited as Hunt); and Scharf, *Western Maryland*, p. 131.

11. Michael Pearson, *The Revolutionary War* (New York: Capricorn Books, 1973), pp. 206-9; and Mark M. Boatner III, *Encyclopedia of the American Revolution* (New York: David McKay Co., Inc., 1966), pp. 386-87.

12. The New York *Gazette*, Oct. 25, 1775; and Hunt, Aug. 3, 1947.

13. Will H. Lowdermilk, *History of Cumberland* (reprint of 1878 edition) (Baltimore: Regional Publishing Company, 1971), p. 259 (hereafter cited as Lowdermilk, *Cumberland*).

14. Ibid., pp. 259-62.

15. Ibid., p. 261.

16. Scharf, *Western Maryland*, p. 129; *Calendar of Maryland State Papers: The Black Books* (Baltimore: The Genealogical Company, 1967), p. 151; and Mary G. Walsh, "Thomas Beall of Samuel, 1744-1823. Backward, Turn Backward!" in *Fort Cumberland Bicentennial, 1755-1955* (Cumberland: Fort Cumberland Bicentennial Committee, 1955), pp. 11-17.

17. Hunt, April 15, 1951.

18. Ibid., July 17, 1955, and June 17, 1951.

19. Ibid., Oct. 28, 1956.

20. Ibid., Jan. 20, 1957.

21. Lowdermilk, *Cumberland*, pp. 262, 281; and James W. Thomas and T. J. C. Williams, *History of Allegany County, Maryland* (Philadelphia: L. R. Titsworth and Co., 1923), I, p. 98 (hereafter cited as Thomas and Williams, *Allegany County*).

22. Thomas and Williams, *Allegany County*, I, p. 98.

23. Lowdermilk, *Cumberland*, pp. 267-69. Although the county court met on April 25, 1791, as the act directed, the Allegany County Orphans' Court met for the first time on April 4, 1791, before it was legally constituted.

24. Thomas and Williams, *Allegany County*, I, p. 99; and Thomas J. Stanton, *A Century of Growth or the History of the Church in Western Maryland* (Baltimore: John Murphy Co., 1900), I, pp. 8-16.

25. Hixon T. Bowersox, *History of St. Paul's English Lutheran Church of Cumberland, Maryland, 1794-1944* (Cumberland: Monarch Printing Company, 1944), pp. 13-41.

26. Ibid., pp. 43-44.

27. Hunt, April 16, 1950; and Lowdermilk, *Cumberland*, p. 277.

28. Lowdermilk, *Cumberland*, pp. 279-80; and Hunt, Aug. 10, 1947.

29. Thomas and Williams, *Allegany County*, I, pp. 100-101; and Lowdermilk, *Cumberland*, p. 97.

30. Evarts B. Greene and Virginia D. Harrington, *American Population Before the Federal Census of 1790* (Gloucester, Mass.: Peter Smith Press, 1966), pp. 132-33.

31. Scharf, *Western Maryland*, p. 145; and Hunt, May 25, 1952.

32. Hunt, Jan. 8, 1950, and Jan. 15, 1950.

33. Frederick Gutheim, *The Potomac* (New York: Grosset & Dunlap, Inc., 1968), p. 192 (hereafter cited as Gutheim, *The Potomac*); and James T. Flexner, *George Washington: The Forge of Experience, 1732-1775* (Boston: Little, Brown & Co., 1965), pp. 304-7.

34. Gutheim, *The Potomac*, p. 192.

35. Special thanks to Mrs. Frances D. Greaves of Westernport, Maryland, for material relating to the early history of that town.

36. Lowdermilk, *Cumberland*, pp. 273-74; and Leland D. Baldwin, *Whiskey Rebels: The Story of a Frontier Uprising* (Pittsburgh: University of Pittsburgh Press, 1968), pp. 207-8.

37. John C. Fitzpatrick, ed., *The Diaries of George Washington, 1748-1799* (Boston: Houghton Mifflin Company, 1971), IV, pp. 209-20.

38. Ibid.

PART II

New Directions, 1800-1865

By

David M. Dean

IV

GATEWAY TO THE WEST, 1800-1828

At the dawn of the nineteenth century the Baltimore-Cumberland Pike, a boulder-strewn, heavily rutted path, carried increasingly heavy traffic toward the mountains. Many people had left their older, worn farms on the eastern shore or in the south of Maryland to make a fresh start in the newer areas to the west.

The United States census of 1800 listed 6,303 residents in Allegany County, about 80 percent of whom lived within its current boundaries; the others resided in that part which broke off in 1872 to form Garrett County. By 1810, the census revealed a gain of only 606 people. Increased growth had been largely offset by the departure of many original citizens—families enticed still farther west by tales of richer and flatter land for the taking. Mountain homesteads with names like "Dung Hill" or "Will's Disappointment" had been abandoned. But newcomers filled the vacuum. Many of them, especially those who scratched out a livelihood in the Georges Creek valley, lived on the edge of poverty. There was not yet a demand for coal nor a market for the valuable timber of the unbroken forest in the valley, and the land was rough and poor for crops. But the creeks teemed with native trout, bass, and perch and the woods were alive with mountain hares, deer, bobcats, bears, squirrels, grouse, woodcocks, passenger pigeons, and turkeys so fat that, if one believes local legend, the birds burst upon hitting the ground.[1]

The largest center of population in the county was the village of Cumberland. It served as a convenient rest stop where a weary traveler on his way to the Ohio Country could put up in a local inn, eat a hot dinner with beer or cider, sleep on clean sheets, have his horse tended, and be fed breakfast, all for under nine shillings—a rate fixed by county law. And under these standard tariffs he could save a bit more than a shilling by sleeping on "sheets before used." Some travelers stayed on; by 1800, Cumberland boasted over 125 families and Methodist, Catholic, and German Lutheran religious congregations. The main commercial thoroughfare, Mechanic Street, was wide enough to allow a wagon to turn around. The street's composition, then and for half the nineteenth century, was packed dirt with slush, mud, and dust in season and horse manure at all times. In 1805, the state legislature authorized a town lottery to raise funds in order to erect a stronger bridge over Wills Creek and to conduct a survey of the town. The next year George Dent completed the survey and a bridge was built, only to be washed away in severe flooding in 1810. A wooden replacement subsequently gave way to a more modern single-lane suspension chain bridge in 1820. Some citizens believed the new bridge to be unsafe; in 1837, as if to prove them right, it collapsed into Wills Creek. A log courthouse, erected where the main branch of the county library now stands, remained in use until 1840, when a new building on the site of the present courthouse was constructed. Cumberland, incorporated by an act of the legislature in 1815, was blossoming from primitive outpost into a sedate town of log, frame, and brick houses, including the beautiful Rose Hill Mansion of David Lynn. In addition to its courthouse, Cumberland boasted a solid jail and two weekly newspapers. And the pungent smell from four tanneries indicated economic progress to most residents.[2]

In January 1808, citizens of the county were first able to read their own newspaper, the Cumberland *Impartialist*, published by G. P. W. Butler. The paper, like those in other frontier areas, had great appeal. It brought national and foreign news, no matter how stale, to western Maryland. And even if items of local interest were dated by printing time, subscribers could read about births, marriages, and deaths, the damage done by spring flooding, or the fact that a certain politician of state or even national reputation had stopped over in Cumberland or Flintstone for the night. Butler's first effort gave way to his new publication, the *American Eagle,* but when he moved to Pennsylvania in July 1809, the county was temporarily without a newspaper. On November 20, 1813, Samuel Magill issued the first copy of the *Allegany Freeman,* a paper which "vigorously" supported the presidential administration of James Madison. This paper was printed until 1818, when Magill was rewarded for his political loyalty to Madison's successor, James Monroe, and appointed postmaster of Cumberland. To counter the *Allegany Freeman,* William Brown, a successful publisher from Hagerstown, started an opposition, pro-Federalist paper, the Cumberland *Gazette,* in January 1814. William Magruder purchased the *Gazette* in 1815 and renamed it the *Allegany Federalist.* In late 1817, Joseph Smith bought Magruder's press and began a three-year run of a paper he called the *Western Herald,* a name he changed to the *Alleganian* in 1820. Apparently Editor Smith exhibited what one citizen called "a great want of punctuality on his part in the printing of the paper," allowing months to elapse between issues. Finally John Buchanan bought the press of the defunct *Alleganian* and produced on September 17, 1823, the first edition of the *Maryland Advocate.* Since that date, newspapers, as many as four different ones operating concurrently before the Civil War and over half a dozen by the 1890s, have been continuously published in Allegany County. Cumberland was the only town in the area to have a paper until 1857, when the Frostburg *Gazette and Miners Record* appeared.[3]

People in the region, while they relished stories about politics in their newspapers, were stubbornly independent in their allegiance. The county did not follow the typical frontier attitude in favoring the Madison administration's decision to fight Great Britain in the War of 1812. In other wilderness areas the flamboyant rhetoric of politicians like Henry Clay and Andrew Jackson convinced their half-literate constituents that a war with the opportunity to seize land in Canada was in the West's best interest. But in Allegany County in 1812, antiwar Federalist presidential electors won and in a hotly disputed contest, complete with claims of illegal voting by non-naturalized foreigners and countercharges of results "founded in iniquity," candidates committed to peace secured three of the area's four seats in the state legislature. Obviously, a sizeable portion of the voters, especially the German-Americans, remained dubious about the conflict.[4]

The threat in summer, 1814, against Washington and Baltimore led President Madison to call for help from state militia. Two companies were formed in the county, one in Cumberland of 123 men commanded by Captain Thomas Blair and another of 104 soldiers from outside the city under the direction of Captain William McLaughlin of Town Creek. Both companies served in the defense of Baltimore for slightly more than two months before being discharged. An earlier historian of the region noted that the "well-drilled and fully equipped" companies participated "gallantly." This may well have been true. A contemporary observer, however, considered the most exciting part of the trip east to have been when two volunteers from Flintstone, most likely fortified with camp whiskey, almost drowned when they rushed into the water to fire their muskets at British ships.[5]

At home, the two Cumberland papers fought their own battle over justification for the war. The *Allegany Freeman* zealously supported the conflict and praised in "high-flown patriotic sentences" every move of President Madison. On the other hand the Cumberland *Gazette,* the paper of the "Friends of Peace," castigated the war and the country's militarily inept president. But everyone loves a party and when word arrived on September 27, 1814, that a great victory had been won on Lake Champlain in upstate New York, the whole town exploded with excitement. No matter that many who paraded that night by torchlight had no idea where Lake Champlain was or of what strategic importance the battle had been, celebrating was fun. Streets were jammed, whiskey flowed freely, and singing, shouting, and overblown oratory were the order of the evening. When the war ended early in 1815, sentiment in this region reflected little of the bitterness found in other parts of the country against antiwar Federalists. Members of that party still sought election in Allegany County and occasionally won, long after their party was dead at the national level.[6]

Although the passing of each decade saw an increase in Cumberland's population, over 85 percent of the county's citizens still lived on farms well into the century. Even those who were active in the infant coal industry were farmers who filled idle time in the winter by working surface coal deposits with no other tools than those they used in the fields. As yet, the true wealth of the area was in farm products. In 1835, a visitor to the region reported to a Baltimore newspaper of the "hundreds of thousands of acres of the finest land in Maryland" where wheat, rye, Indian corn, oats "double the size of the common product," peas, beans, and potatoes were grown. Apple, cherry, and plum orchards were commonplace and even tobacco flourished on the very tops of mountains. Hundreds of horses, cows, both "milch" and "other cattle," sheep, and swine could be seen. The census of 1840 recorded 2,192 persons employed in agriculture compared to 648 in manufacturing and trade, and only 140 engaged in mining.[7]

Farm families worked together as units, and often married children settled down on lands about the original homestead. Neighbors helped each other in erecting cabins, smokehouses, and barns, and harvesting was often a community endeavor. As nearly every household distilled its own whiskey, ample quantities of locally made "tangle-foot" helped the job along. The larger the area to harvest, the fuller the whiskey barrel sitting in the field. Nevertheless the writer of one reminiscence of local farm life recalled that "no one ever became intoxicated." Another communal chore was hog butchering, which could become a three-day social event. Although they lacked sausage grinders or lard presses to expedite the work, people made do with the help of "lively" music and "lots of" whiskey.[8]

At all gatherings of men and boys there was fighting for amusement or as a test of manhood. Often there might be as many as three hard-fought battles between the same opponents before one would surrender. All games were tests of strength and endurance. Participants ran footraces, boxed, played yard games, wrestled, and pole-vaulted. Horse races were a popular attraction; an owner took great pride in his animal's speed and stamina and considered the loss of a race as a blow to his self-esteem. Formal races which drew participants from all over the county were held on a racecourse in Cumberland as early as 1796, and continued into the nineteenth century. Chicken fighting also proved a lively pastime for many men. A cockfight usually drew large crowds, with much money changing hands. Many farmers diligently bred these fighters and "a local battle ground" could be found outside each village.[9]

Hunting was often necessary to supplement the diet but for many it had become a sport by the 1820s. The area's most famous hunter, Meshach Browning, moved from Frederick to Flintstone before finally settling in the mountains of western Allegany County (now Garrett County). Browning's autobiography, *Forty-Four Years of the Life of a Hunter,* narrates his adventures between 1795 and 1839. He describes twenty-inch native trout caught by the hundreds, 400-pound bears, and twelve-point bucks. During his career as a professional hunter he killed nearly 400 bears, 50 panthers, 2,000 deer, and countless wild turkeys, otters, coons, and wolves, the latter for their eight-dollar bounty. Game remained plentiful into the 1840s. In 1834, a Cumberland paper headlined a "Bear Alert," reporting that "almost every day in the week we can hear of them being seen and killed, even in the vicinity of towns." Another local sport was the wholesale slaughter of passenger pigeons. These birds, so numerous that they were said to be breaking the tops of pine trees around Frostburg, were killed by the thousands when people took long poles and knocked them from their nighttime roosts. At times hundreds of people turned out for circular hunts in the "romantic region," which is current-day LaVale.[10]

Most marriage ceremonies were held on the farm and after a "day-long frolick" at the bride's home, the younger guests retired the following day to the home of the groom for a reception. The newlyweds and all the company rode on horseback at full gallop, yelling at the top of their voices. Near the journey's end, those with the fastest horses left the group and made a "run for the bottle." This was a bottle filled with whiskey, sitting on the gatepost or held in the hand of the groom's father. The first rider to reach the bottle took it back to the crowd and treated them, gallantly offering it first to the bride and groom.[11]

Camp meetings offered another opportunity for community—drawing from both town and farm. The "old camp ground" at the head of the Narrows, about a mile and a half from Cumberland, saw frequent use as did one east of town near Flintstone. Preachers, "travelling and local," were asked to come and congregations were "especially invited to attend with their tents." Methodism was very strong in the county; its ministers, according to one contemporary observer, were much opposed to fiddling and dancing, with some "going so far as to assert that the violin was an invention of the devil, invented by satan expressly to destroy souls."[12]

Sudden death was no stranger to Allegany County's villages and farms. Nearly every issue of the weekly newspapers reported farming or hunting fatalities, backyard mining or timbering accidents, infant mortality, death at childbirth, or suicides by drowning, hanging, or shooting. And communicable diseases like measles, smallpox, and scarlet fever were frequently noted. Consumption, typhus, and a variety of intestinal troubles also took a toll. That a family would unexpectedly lose some members was accepted stoically as the normal course of life. A pioneer farmer recalled that after a death, the family customarily stopped the clocks and turned all mirrors and pictures to the wall. The body was dressed in a white shroud by neighbors and laid out on a special "cooling board." Coffins were constructed by cabinetmakers or by the farmer himself from solid cherry or walnut. A bill from 1827 for one "Thomas Stallings, deceased," reveals that a store in Flintstone charged $11.28 for a coffin, ten yards of crepe, eight yards of cambric for a shroud, one pair of stockings, one ball of cotton for a pillow, and fifty springs and screws.[13]

The same country or general store which provided a coffin for Mr. Stallings boasted rows of hogsheads and barrels containing Potomac River herring, flour, and molasses. On the shelves were snuffboxes, clay pipes, needles and pins (purchased by the ounce), and cure-all remedies of laudanum and castor oil. Dry goods like men's shoes at $1.75 a pair or "fine" hats at $4.50 were also available. Other items included coffee at twenty cents a pound, bacon at six cents a pound, maple sugar at seven cents a pound, and chickens at a dozen for one dollar. For more selection in services and shopping, however, one needed to travel to Cumberland. Although the county seat would not pass one thousand in population until 1830, it had long offered a variety of professions and trades. By 1800 doctors, lawyers, midwives, and "professors" had settled in Cumberland. Signs advertising the shop of a hatter, tailor, boot and shoemaker, stocking weaver, milliner, or maker of buckskin breeches and gloves could be seen all along Mechanic Street. A real estate dealer was already in town, soon to be joined by others. Before long, the newspapers carried real estate ads along with lists of delinquent taxpayers. A newcomer could often pay the back taxes and find himself the proud owner of a farm with a name such as "Sinkhole Bottom," "The Third Attempt," "Taylor's Neglect," "George's Adventure," or "The New Addition." Cumberland also boasted the services of nail makers, glaziers, joiners, and cabinetmakers. The farmer came to town to sell or trade his wheat, rye, oats, green and dried apples, feathers, beeswax, honey, venison, hay, or even coal and timber. He might return home with the latest model spinning wheel, an apple-butter kettle from the coppersmith, bridle bits or stirrup irons from the blacksmith, or some "Extract of Tomato" pills to "cleanse and purify his system" from the new apothecary.[14]

The real stimulus to population growth and increased commerce and industry in the county during the first quarter of the nineteenth century was the construction of the National or Cumberland Road. By 1802, heavy settlement in Ohio had created a new state and Congress, fearful of potential disunion between the sections, took a large step in bonding the East to the West. In the enabling legislation to give Ohio statehood Congress decreed that 2 percent of the net revenues derived from the sale of public lands in the new state must be used for constructing roads to connect or "cement" Ohio to the older states. Word of a proposed new artery thrilled people in western Maryland, Pennsylvania, Virginia, and Ohio—and all wondered just where the road would run. Philadelphia, Baltimore, Washington, and Richmond all lobbied to be the origin of the road. In late 1805, Senator Uriah Tracy of Connecticut, reporting for a special committee, made this recommendation:

> The committee have thought it expedient to recommend the laying out and making a road from Cumberland on the northerly bank of the Potomac and within the state of Maryland, to the river Ohio at the most convenient place between a point on the easterly bank of said river opposite to Steubenville and the mouth of Grace [sic] Creek which empties into said river Ohio, a little below Wheeling in Virginia.

This was the most practical and least expensive route—the one laid out by Nemacolin and Gist, used by Braddock, and in 1805, still in use as a narrow, unreliable, deeply rutted track. Not only the shortest route between the mountains, the proposal provided a logical connection between older roads from Baltimore and Washington and fresh trails in ever-growing southern Ohio.

Tracy's report paved the way for an act to regulate the surveying and construction of a road from Cumberland to Ohio. After passing the Senate the bill ran into difficulty in the House before being finally passed on March 24, 1806, by a sixty-six to fifty count. Pennsylvania voted thirteen to four against the measure because the road missed Philadelphia and passed through only a small part of the state. Virginia, fearful that the route would siphon off population from the South, tallied a sixteen to two vote against the measure. But passage assured that Cumberland, not Richmond, was to be the gateway to the West.

President Thomas Jefferson signed into law on March 29, 1806, the legislation creating the Cumberland Road, the only road construction bill ever named after a town. That same year, three newly appointed road commissioners hired a professional surveyor to map the saw-toothed country between Cumberland and the Ohio River. After more political infighting between Maryland, Pennsylvania, and Virginia, a final plan was set. The route would follow the old Indian trail to Uniontown and Washington, Pennsylvania, where it would twist back west to Wheeling. Not until 1809 were funds available for road work. The commissioners had secured $12,000 from the sale of Ohio lands. This sum would complete two miles of road at the projected construction cost of $6,000 per mile. A contract to build the first ten-mile section from Cumberland was not let until May 1811.[15]

Once begun, even with a two-year lapse during the War of 1812, the work moved along rapidly. But conquering each of the thirty-three miles and thirty-four rods of the National Road between Cumberland and the state's western border demanded considerable ingenuity and persistence. The countryside was beautiful but demanding. David Shriver, later to found a prominent Cumberland banking family, was appointed superintendent of road construction. Though energetic and competent, he had his problems. Spring comes late in Allegany County, flooding swept away road markers, workers complained of low wages, and town merchants had no cash to honor government drafts. Shriver's gang of axmen, chain carriers, and polemen battled daily with stubborn scrub growth and towering oaks. Contracts called for a strip sixty-six feet wide to be cleared of all growth and ditched on either side. After grubbing, the roadbed was leveled with pick and shovels to thirty feet in width. Hills were leveled, surplus rock removed, and hollows, valleys, and abutments of bridges and culverts filled. Surveyors insisted that section contractors, usually farmers along the route, be precise in measuring angles and degrees. But because they were farmers and not engineers, regradings were frequent. The law required that twenty feet of the road's surface be covered with stones ranging from twelve inches in depth to eighteen inches. Over all was spread stone, broken small enough to pass through a three-inch ring. Groups of men sat with their legs spread out, hammering rock to specified size. While some workers cut, grubbed, ditched, and hammered, others hauled rock for bridges from local quarries. A visitor from New York marveled at the stone bridges, calling them "monuments of taste and power that will speak well for the country when the

Working on the bed of the National Road, 1815. Courtesy Public Roads Administration

brick towns they bind together shall have crumbled in the dust."

In December 1813, Superintendent Shriver reported the first ten miles finished and in use by travelers with a second stretch of eleven miles nearly completed. It had not been easy. Shriver complained that contractors shortchanged their workers in wages and that in retaliation the laborers dallied and often deliberately marred the road's surface by felling trees on it or locking the brakes on their wagons. Two years after it first opened, $1,800 had been expended to repair the initial section. For a while the substitution of slave for free labor was contemplated. But with increased wages more laborers, mostly Irish, moved into the county. Construction camps made up of weather-stained canvas tents and crude shacks lined the road from Cumberland west. An area resident of long standing decried the change in life style and the massive inflation that the new route created. A Cumberland lot with a comfortable log house of one room which sold for around one hundred dollars before the road was priced at over one thousand dollars by 1811. Rising costs forced Congress to increase the annual appropriation and in 1816, nearly $94,000 was spent. The pike was completed from Cumberland to Uniontown at a cost of $9,475 per mile. By the time the 130 miles to Wheeling was finished in 1818, the cost per mile neared $13,000.[16]

Now that the route was completed to the Ohio port, it needed continued maintenance. Upwards of a thousand freight wagons had made the trip in 1818 with loads averaging two tons, and each year brought increased traffic. The road, considered to be the best constructed highway in America, was subject to normal depreciation and also man's depravity. In the early 1820s, a stage owner noted that "on the Eastern side of the Great Savage Mountain, there cannot be found a handful of dirt on the road for some distance, it being washed out by the filling up of culverts or drains, carrying with it all the small stone on the surface. . . ." Superintendent Shriver reported to Congress on the vandalism. He told of bridge walls pried off, milestones smashed, wagoners locking their brakes and gashing the road, and people hauling away gravel for their own use. Farmers living along the right-of-way were the worst culprits. They encroached on the pike by planting gardens and shrubs or even building fences or houses upon its limits. Shriver ended his statement with this notation: "The abuses above mentioned are a growing evil, they are increasing daily."

To service the growing flow of traffic on the road, engineers believed that a new macadam surface was necessary. By the mid-1820s, the old face was entirely broken up and the original stones removed. The bed was raked nearly flat, and crushed limestone, granite, or flint was laid to a depth of three inches. Then travel was permitted for a while before another three inches were deposited. In some sections the process was repeated a third time. Although the new covering was superior to the original one, the continuous cutting of heavy wheels soon proved that there was just no way to lay down a permanent hard surface. So, because appropriations from Congress for repairs remained tied up in the constitutional and political struggles over internal improvements, the road crumbled.[17]

In 1832, Congress again appropriated funds for repairs. The people of Cumberland, overjoyed at the news, celebrated by staging a torchlight parade. Two years later, army engineers recommended that the original road across Wills Mountain (out Greene Street and up present-day Braddock Road) be changed to follow Wills Creek or the Narrows and then up the valley of Braddocks Run (through what is now LaVale). Constructed under the direction of Lieutenant John Pickell, this "new and improved link" added less than a mile to the length of the road while the slighter incline allowed wagons to pull double the weight they could handle on the old route—a real boon to the fledgling coal industry. The area marked the opening of the new link on November 11, 1834, with festivities; a newspaper reported the "grand and truly patriotic style" in which citizens from Cumberland and Frostburg and those living "on the line of the road" marched with Union flags flying, "accompanied by a full band of music." Now that all repairs and changes were completed, the United States government, which had constitutional qualms

Traffic on the National Road—congestion at bridge over Wills Creek. Courtesy Public Roads Administration

Tollhouse on the National Road—LaVale.

about erecting tollgates to collect maintenance funds, officially turned the road over to the state governments. In 1835, tollgates went up on the National Road.[18]

The turnpike brought what one historian has called the "magic of emigration" to the county. From the east came travelers on the "Bank Road," which was the "old Hancock Road" with a new surface financed by Baltimore banks. So smooth was this road that a mail coach could travel the twelve miles from Cumberland to Flintstone in one hour and twenty minutes. Up from the Shenandoah Valley moved more wagons. Day and night ponderous Conestogas, full of settlers, passed through Cumberland's public square and headed west. And from east and west came wagons piled high with goods. Tons of coal, heaps of shingles, hogsheads of nails, hinges, and bolts, and casks of salted cod filled warehouses in the county seat. Lines of canvas-covered vehicles moved across the road and frequently backed up traffic at bridges. Nevertheless, a veteran wagoner, by averaging his usual eighteen miles a day, could travel the 266 miles from Wheeling to Baltimore in fifteen days.[19]

Through the National Road at Cumberland moved countless numbers of animals on their way east. There were blooded horses from Texas, domestic turkeys from Pennsylvania, cattle from Illinois, mules and merino sheep from Ohio, and thousands of aromatic swine from Indiana and Ohio. One woman of "delicate sensibilities" revolted at the sight of so many pigs. She exclaimed: "We met the unclean beasts—by the hundreds, grunting along under the wheels of our carriage, and in the true spirit of monopolizing stupidity, endeavoring to keep the whole of the road to themselves." Not until 1839, did an increasingly sophisticated Cumberland outlaw pigs from the main thoroughfares in town. Human droves were a common sight. Negro slaves, arranged in couples and fastened to a long thick rope or cable, were driven over the road like mules. A traveler from Ohio has left us a poignant account of one of these drives.

> In the winter of 1828-29, I put up for a night at Frost Town, on the national road. Soon after there came a slaver with a drove of slaves. I then left the room and shortly afterwards heard a scream,

and when the landlady inquired the cause, the slaver cooly told her not to trouble herself, he was only chastising one of his women. . . . It appeared that three days previously her child had died on the road and been thrown into a crevice in the mountain, and the mother weeping for her child was chastised by her master, and told by him, she "should have something to cry for."[20]

Stagecoaches were the pride of the road. The earliest, called "turtle-hacks" because of their shape, were introduced around 1815. Very uncomfortable, they gave way to the Troy and Concord coaches in the 1820s. Strong and durable with upholstered interiors and three crosswise seats, these new coaches accommodated nine passengers inside and two upstairs with the driver. A Cumberland man, Thomas Shriver, invented the elliptical spring which improved the quality of the ride. Shriver also owned a large coach manufacturing establishment. One of the earliest stage owners in Cumberland, Lucius B. Stockton, at first used custom-built stages from Uniontown but also experimented with a heavier coach made by Abraham Russell of Allegany County. The most popular coach was one of the Concord type built locally by Stockton's workmen and weighing from 1,400 to 2,250 pounds. All the stages carried colorful titles—named after counties, states, cities, politicians, or whatever fancied the owner. "Ivanhoe," "Beauty," "Industry," "Allegany," and "Jackson" all plied the road to Wheeling.

James Reeside was another prominent "land admiral." After selling his tavern in Cumberland in 1820, he turned to the stage business. The initial thrice-weekly run between Baltimore and Wheeling took seventy-two hours via Cumberland. By 1836, he had adopted daily service and shortly thereafter he inaugurated twice-daily service. Not content, Reeside added another triweekly line and named his empire the Good Intent Lines. When he expanded a third time, his rival Stockton contemptuously called Reeside's line the "June Bug" because it would be defunct before the coming of the summer insects. With completion of the Baltimore and Ohio Railroad to Cumberland in late 1842, stage travel from the county seat west increased dramatically, giving rise to more stagecoach lines. Now a traveler could choose between

THE MARYLAND ADVOCATE.

Vol. 1. Cumberland, (Md.) Monday, September 13, 1824. No. 47.

PRINTED AND PUBLISHED BY
John M. Buchanan,
Opposite the BANK, South Mechanic Street, Cumberland, (Md.)

Terms of Subscription.
The 'MARYLAND ADVOCATE,' *is published every* MONDAY, *at* TWO DOLLARS *per annum, if paid any time within six months*—TWO DOLLARS & TWENTY-FIVE CENTS, *if not paid until the end of the year, and* TWO DOLLARS *and* FIFTY CENTS *will invariably be exacted, if it is not paid within eighteen months after the time of subscribing. No subscription taken for a shorter time than* SIX MONTHS, *and no paper discontinued* UNTIL ALL ARREARAGES ARE PAID OFF.

Terms of Advertising.
Advertisements not exceeding one SQUARE, *will be conspicuously inserted three times for* ONE DOLLAR, *and twenty-five cents for every additional insertion—longer ones in proportion.*

CANDIDATES
For Electors of President and Vice President, for the district composed of Frederick, Washington and Allegany counties:

For HENRY CLAY,
Gen. SAMUEL RINGGOLD, of Washington county, and WILLIAM ZOLLICOFFER, of Frederick county.

For Gen. ANDREW JACKSON,
THOMAS POST, Esq. late Sheriff of Washington county, and Doct. WILLIAM TYLER, of Frederick county.

For JOHN QUINCY ADAMS,
Col. DAVID SCHNEBLY, of Washington county—JOSHUA COCKEY, Esq. of Frederick county.

For WM. H. CRAWFORD,
BENJAMIN TOMLINSON, of Allegany county, and Doct. JOHN M. SMITH, of Frederick county.

CANDIDATES FOR CONGRESS,
For the 4th Congressional District of Maryland.
Col. THOMAS C. WORTHINGTON,
UPTON BRUCE, Esq.
JOHN LEE, Esq.

CANDIDATES FOR THE
SHERIFFALTY:

To the Free and Independent Voters of Allegany county.
Gentlemen—I again offer myself to your consideration as a candidate for the office of SHERIFF of Allegany county, at the next election. Should I be so fortunate as to meet with the support of a majority of the Voters of this county, I pledge myself to attend faithfully and diligently to the duties of said office.
I am, gentlemen,
Your ob't. servant,
WILLIAM M'MAHON.
Cumberland, Oct. 8.

To the Voters of ALLEGANY COUNTY:
Gentlemen—Permit me again to declare myself as a candidate for the office of
SHERIFF,
at the next Election. If it shall please you to elect me, I pledge myself to perform the duties attached to the office with humanity and fidelity, to the best of my abilities.
THOMAS THISTLE.
Oct. 7.

To the free and independent Voters of Allegany County.
GENTLEMEN—
I respectfully offer myself to your consideration as a candidate for the office of
SHERIFF
at the ensuing Election; and should I be so fortunate as to meet with a majority of your votes, I pledge myself to attend faithfully and diligently to the duties of said office with impartiality, humanity, fidelity and to the best of my skill and abilities.
I am, gentlemen,
Your most obt. servt.
JOSEPH CARTER.
Feb. 1824. tf.

This is to give Notice,
THAT the Subscriber, of Allegany county, hath obtained from the Orphans' Court of Allegany county, in Maryland, *LETTERS OF ADMINISTRATION* on the Personal Estate of James M. Cresap, late of Allegany county, deceased. All persons having claims against the said deceased are hereby warned to exhibit the same, with the vouchers thereof, to the subscriber, on or before the *Tenth day of FEBRUARY next*: they may otherwise by law be excluded from all benefit of the said estate.
Given under my hand, this 10th day of August, 1824.
LENOX MARTIN,
Acting Administrator.
N. B.—All persons indebted to the said Estate are hereby requested to make immediate payment.

NOTICE.
I hereby forewarn all persons from shooting on my mill dam, or any of my inclosed fields, on any pretence whatever, as I find that my family as well as property of different kinds are endangered by such evil practice.—Any person or persons acting contrary to this notice, shall be strictly dealt with according to law in the case, without respect to persons.
JAMES SCOTT.
Cumberland, Aug. 23, 1824.

STRAY COW.
Came to my place, at the mouth of Savage River, in Allegany county, Md. a *RED COW*, with a star in her forehead, the two hind feet white and white on her belly—the left ear has a crop and a slit, and the right ear has a crop and underbit—she has a calf, and appears to be about ten years old. The owner is requested to come, prove property, pay charges, and take the cow away. The cow and calf were appraised at $12.
JOHN TEMPLEMAN.
Aug. 4, 1824.

J. G. HOFFMAN,
Coppersmith & Tin-plate Worker,
South Mechanic street, next door to the Printing Office, Cumberland, Md.
MOST respectfully informs his friends and the public generally, that he continues to manufacture
EVERY DESCRIPTION OF
COPPER & TIN WARE
at the shortest notice and on terms suitable to the present times. He returns his grateful acknowledgments to those who have heretofore favored him with their custom, and assures them that nothing shall be wanting on his part to give general satisfaction to those should they continue to favor him with a call.
☞ *Old COPPER, BRASS and PEWTER, wanted.*
July 5.—40—3mo.
N. B. *AN APPRENTICE* of good moral character and study habits would be taken to learn the above business. J. G. H.

NOTICE:
Those persons who know themselves indebted to the subscriber, especially those whose accounts are of long standing, would confer a favor by making payment as soon as possible. J. G. HOFFMAN.
July 21.

POWDER
FOR SALE.
THE SUBSCRIBER HAS ON HAND, AND WILL SELL LOW FOR CASH OR APPROVED COUNTRY PRODUCE,
A QUANTITY OF
Boerstler's first quality
RIFLE POWDER,
by the keg or smaller quantity.
JOHN G. HOFFMAN,
Agent for Danl. Boerstler.
Cumberland, May 4, 1824.

CASH
WILL BE GIVEN FOR CLEAN
Linen and Cotton RAGS,
AT THIS OFFICE.

NOTICE.

AN ELECTION
WILL be held at the several Election Districts in Allegany county, on *The first Monday in October* next, for the purpose of electing a
A Representative
for the fourth Congressional District of Maryland, in the next Congress of the United States, and to elect
Four Delegates
to represent the said county in the next General Assembly of Maryland.
ALSO, to elect
A Sheriff
for said county.
AN ELECTION
Will also be held at the several Election Districts in Allegany county
On the first Monday in November next,
for the purpose of electing
Two Electors
of President and Vice President of the United States.
AND'W. BRUCE, Sh'ff.
SHERIFF'S OFFICE,
Cumberland, Aug. 2, 1824.

MILL-OWNERS
LOOK HERE
The subscriber respectfully informs owners of Mills, that he dresses, in the best manner, all sizes of
"Alleghany Burrs,"
which he will sell on moderate terms. He will furnish Mill Stones (if desired) any place along the Potomac between Cumberland and Georgetown. A few lines, from persons at a distance, forwarded to the subscriber, 9 miles North of Cumberland, or left at the Printing Office, will meet with prompt attention.
JACOB WITT.
August 30, 1824.

DOCTOR
S. P. SMITH,
Has abandoned the intention of leaving this place, as his health is restored. He will continue to attend, as usual, to calls in his profession.
CUMBERLAND,
July 19,

Doctor Hugh H. Waite,
Offers his professional services to the citizens of Allegany. He has established his office in the house formerly occupied as such by the late Doctor Head.
April 1824.

TAKE NOTICE.
The Subscriber has for Sale, for Cash or Country Produce,
Pint FLASKS, quart, half-gallon & gallon BOTTLES,
by the dozen or smaller quantity.
ALSO—6 by 8, 7 by 9, 8 by 10, 10 by 12, 11 by 15, 12 by 16 and 12 by 18
WINDOW GLASS,
by the box or less quantity.
Wm. M'Mahon.
Cumberland, July 12.

FOR SALE,
A Negro Woman and her two Children.
For particulars enquire of the *Printer*.
August 2, 1824.

Just received, and for sale at this office, price 25 cents, the
REMARKS
OF
JOHN M'MAHON,
In the House of Delegates of Maryland, on the Bill to confirm an act, entitled an act to extend to all the citizens of Maryland the same civil rights and religious privileges that are enjoyed under the constitution of the U. States.

NOTICE TO TRAVELLERS

THE U. S. MAIL COACH,
From Baltimore to Wheeling, by the great National Turnpike Road,
LEAVES the Office next door to Barnum's Indian Queen Hotel, on
Sundays, Tuesdays and Thursdays, at 4 o'clock A. M.
Connectig with the great Western Mail from Washington city at Fredericktown, and arrives at Wheeling in three and a quarter days. Returning leaves Wheeling every
Tuesday, Thursday and Saturday
and arrives in Baltimore and Washington City in three & a quarter days.
THE ACCOMMODATION LINE
Leaves the same Office on Mondays, Wednesdays, Fridays and Saturdays,
And arrives at Wheeling in four days. Returning from Wheeling arrives in Baltimore in four days. By this line the routes are performed altogether in day light.
The Proprietors have neither spared pains or expense in rendering this line equal in point of comfort to any in the United States.
REESIDE, MOORE, STOCKTON, & Co.
Proprietors.
July, 1824.—40tf.
N. B. All bagage, packages and parcels at the risk of the owners

CELEBRATED
FAMILY MEDICINES.
LEE's long and highly approved FAMILY MEDICINES,
Continue to be carefully prepared and sold WHOLESALE and RETAIL, at the proprietor's Dispensary, Number 68, Hanover street, Baltimore: sold also, by his appointment, by
J. M. BUCHANAN,
CUMBERLAND, Md.
Who has just received a fresh supply from Baltimore.
☞ Please to observe *what ever* and *where ever you buy, none can be Lee's Genuine Family Medicines*, without the signature of the proprietor,
NOAH RIDGELY,
Late Michael Lee & Co.
VIZ:
Lee's excellent Anti Billious PILLS—
They are excellently adapted to carry off superfluous bile, and prevent its morbid secretions—to restore and amend the appetite—produce a free perspiration, & thereby prevent colds, which are often of fatal consequence.
Please to ask for "*Lee's Anti-Billious Pills.*"
DEAR SIR—Having made use of the various Pills in my family, offered to the public for the last twenty-five years, and having found your celebrated Anti-Billious Pills the most efficacious in cleansing the stomach and bowels, removing head aches, sick stomach; and having used them for several years past, can have no hesitation in stating, that I believe them (as represented) a most valuable Family Medicine.
JACOB SMALL,
Conway-st. Baltimore.
Aug. 9, 1822.
To Mr. NOAH RIDGELY.
Lee's Worm Destroying LOZENGES—
A most powerful medicine—removes and destroys all kinds of worms.
Lee's Elixer—
An invaluable medicine; it never fails to cure the most violent colds, and affords instant & great relief, in all obstinate coughs—it also relieves young children from cholics, &c.
Lee's Nervous Cordial—
An excellent medicine for all nervous affections, weakness, pains in the loins, back, &c.
Lee's Essence of Mustard—
No medicine ever excelled this in curing rheumatism, sprains, bruises, frosted feet, &c.
Lee's Ague & Fever Drops—
A never failing cure. Thousands can testify of their being cured by those Drops after the bark and every other medicine has proved ineffectual; and not one in a hundred has had occasion to take more than one, and numbers not half a bottle.
Lee's Sovereign Ointment—
Warranted to cure the Itch, by only one application.
Lee's Persian Lotion—
An excellent medicine for curing tetters, ring worms, prickle heat, softens the skin and improves the complexion.
Lee's Indian Vegetable SPECIFIC—
An effectual cure for the Venereal and Gonorrhea.
Lee's Tooth ache Drops—
Which gives immediate relief in the most severe instances.
Lee's Tooth Powder—
Which cleanses & beautifies the teeth.
Lee's Eye Water—
A sovereign remedy for all diseases of the eyes, whether the effect of natural weakness or of accident.
Lee's Anodyne Elixer—
For the cure of every kind of headaches.
Lee's Corn Plaister—
An infallible remedy for speedily removing Corns, root and branch, without giving pain.
Lee's Lip Salve—
Is recommended (particularly to the ladies) as an elegant and pleasant preparation for chopped and sore lips, and every blemish and inconvenience occasioned by colds, fevers, &c. speedily restoring a beautiful rosy color and delicate softness to the lips.
Numerous cases of cures could be annexed of the happy and good effects that have followed the use of the above
Justly Celebrated FAMILY MEDICINES,
but the publisher has not room for them in this paper. A number of persons have called on the proprietor and have given it as their confident opinion that their health has been entirely restored from the most alarming diseases, and in many cases their days have been greatly prolonged by timely use of these most excellent medicines.
Country dealers in medicine are invited to call, as they will be treated on the most liberal terms. Persons wishing to sell them on commission, can obtain them in those places where no agents exist, by giving approved references—letters post paid.
July, 1824.

Courtesy Library of Congress

the National Road Stage Company, Good Intent Stage Company, Landlord's Line, and Pioneer Line. The squeeze of competition caused rates to be cut, and although the ride might still be bumpy, the four-dollar ticket between Uniontown and Cumberland was halved. Hundreds of stagecoaches, some handsome, others dilapidated, plied the road. Highland Hall, a Frostburg inn which accommodated 300 guests, served thirty to forty stages daily. When the editor of the Cumberland *Civilian* examined the books of two stage lines in 1849, he found "to his astonishment" that during the first twenty days of March, in "unusually bad weather," 2,586 passengers had been transported across the mountains. Other lines ran twice-daily coaches to Flintstone and a daily route to Petersburg, Virginia, and after 1850, to Bedford, Pennsylvania, on a road of four-inch-thick oak planks.[21]

Travel on the Cumberland Road could always be difficult, but winter passage through the mountains was especially hazardous. And winter often came early. On the night of October 3, 1836, a foot of snow fell. The wagoners took one look at the weather and decided to hold over for another day at the Sand Springs tavern at the foot of Big Savage Mountain, one mile west of Frostburg. It was no problem ascending Big Savage but descent played havoc with travel schedules. A big snow could stretch the journey between Grantsville and Frostburg into a three-day trip. A cautious wagoner would tie a large tree to the back axle in order to slow his ride down an icy slope. Even more perilous was a winter journey by stage. A coach literally danced on the "polished" road, swaying from side to side as it careened down the mountains. Seasoned travelers held on for dear life, but most newcomers to the area, including President-elect Zachary Taylor in 1849, paid little attention to personal safety as they enjoyed the winter scenery. Upon arriving in the Narrows, Taylor ordered his coach stopped, disembarked, and stared in awe at the magnificent sight.

Stage accidents were usually minor and after righting the coach and dusting off the passengers the driver would be on his way. But the upsetting of a stage four miles east of Cumberland took a life in 1825, and five years later the Episcopal

Bishop of Ohio, Philander Chase, dislocated an arm and broke three ribs when a coach leaving Cumberland ran off the road and overturned. Much less frequent but more often discussed were stagecoach robberies. The most legendary one in this area occurred in August 1834 when two highwaymen attempted to rob an "express mail" coach seven miles west of Frostburg in the heavy pine forest known as the "Shades of Death." Driver Samuel Luman ignored the robbers' pistols and with his whip chased the bandits away. When passengers gave the taciturn Luman a meager reward a Cumberland paper posed this question: "Query. Wonder if the safety of the mail and lives of the passengers were valued at only five dollars?"[22]

Among the hundreds of thousands of ordinary citizens traveling through Allegany County were a sprinkling of dignitaries. Congressmen from western states on their way to Washington seemed commonplace and rarely achieved mention in the newspapers. But large crowds applauded Presidents James Monroe, John Quincy Adams, Andrew Jackson, William Henry Harrison, James K. Polk, and Zachary Taylor. And when oddities like the midget Tom Thumb, the defeated war chief Black Hawk, the elderly hero of the American Revolution General Lafayette, the villain of the Alamo Santa Anna, or the eccentric editor of the New York *Herald* Horace Greeley, complete with oversized top hat and scraggly whiskers, appeared, they attracted spellbound audiences. Other political favorites to travel the pike were the dark-skinned Senator Thomas Corwin of Ohio, once mistaken by a Flintstone tavern keeper for Henry Clay's slave; the boisterous Jacksonian from Missouri, Senator Thomas Hart Benton; the outrageous folk hero Davy Crockett; the colorful Sam Houston; and the austere Southerner, John C. Calhoun. In early 1849, both presidential nominees of the previous November's election, Zachary Taylor and Lewis Cass, appeared in Cumberland. Cass had outdrawn Taylor in county votes but a large crowd gathered on a cold February evening to listen to President-elect Taylor's platitudinous speech. A more popular attraction with the people than either politician that year was

"Old Whitey," Taylor's famous horse from the days of the Mexican War.

For most of the first half of the century one of the area's most popular political figures, and a frequent overnight guest, was Henry Clay of Kentucky. Clay was so identified with his "American System," or program of expanding internal improvements, that the National Road was called by many the "Clay Road." When Clay as congressman, or senator, or secretary of state, or presidential candidate, or just plain private citizen passed along the road the cheering never died. How he survived the rigors of such trips, and they were frequent, is a matter for amazement. Each town and village tried to outdo the last stop in the welcome shown him. For example, when Clay arrived in Cumberland on March 25, 1829, a large delegation of townspeople escorted him the last six miles. From his hotel he greeted citizens from late morning until four in the afternoon. Then, as the editor of the Cumberland *Civilian,* which was highly favorable to Clay, reported, "a large assemblage of the town and county sat down to a most splendid entertainment." There were four toasts with brandy, a speech by Clay on the glories of internal improvements, then seven more formal toasts, thirty more recorded toasts, and "a number of toasts not recorded." The next day Clay, accompanied by a delegation, arrived in Frostburg in time for both lunch and a miniature repetition of much that had happened the previous day.[23]

Not all local citizens who ventured out to look at Clay were his partisans. Some were just curious. Indeed, during the presidential campaign of 1824, a majority in the county gave their votes to the Democratic nominee Andrew Jackson, who defeated three other candidates, including the popular Clay. In our day of sterile, look-alike campaigners and overwhelming political indifference on the part of the electorate, it is difficult to imagine both the importance of, and the fervor created by, political issues and politicians in antebellum America. Allegany County was no exception. Hardly would one election end before citizens laid plans to do better at the next one. Newspapers tacked under their mastheads the name of "their" man for the presidency as early as three years before the event. After an election, if the newspaper's candidate had lost, it often took a month before the final results were printed in a small box inside the paper with no headline. Also, in order to know what politicians had already visited or would pass through the county, one had to read the newspapers of both parties. Andrew Jackson might have been in Cumberland, but one would never know it by reading the *National-Republican* or Whig newspaper. And the Democratic paper often turned the same trick if a leading Whig, even Henry Clay, journeyed down the National Road.

When John Buchanan bought the *Alleganian,* a four-page paper of four short columns per sheet, unevenly printed on a small old wooden press, in 1823, he purchased new type and issued a larger paper called the *Maryland Advocate.* Only twenty years of age, Buchanan was determined to work for the election of Henry Clay to the presidency. With John Quincy Adams, a supporter of internal improvements, elected in 1824 and Clay appointed secretary of state, the *Maryland Advocate* parroted the Adams administration tune. But a drop in circulation from 400 to 300 readers and the problem of collecting from subscribers, some of whom were three years in arrears, forced Buchanan, eager to sell an interest in the paper for $2,000, to look outside the county for financial reinforcement. Evidently turned down by a wealthy Adams supporter in Baltimore, the editor began to herald the merits of Andrew Jackson in late 1827, after taking a mysterious stage ride with a Jackson crony, Senator John Eaton of Tennessee. One has only to compare issues of the *Maryland Advocate* in 1827 and 1828 to see the disconcerting change. Buchanan, writing about Andrew Jackson on April 28, 1827, says: "Never no never will we consent to place him at the helm of government." The same editor on February 23, 1828, writes: "We are convinced of his peculiar fitness at this time to preside at the head of government." In order to combat the *Maryland Advocate*'s espousal of General Jackson, Samuel Charles moved from Hagerstown to Cumberland and published, with financial backing, the *Allegany Journal* in late 1827. By February he owned the paper outright and renamed it *The Civilian.* This paper, which showed its

The Baltimore Pike leading into Cumberland in the 1850s.

support of non-military candidates in the selection of its name, survived the pre-Civil War period, and when the elder Charles gave up the helm after seventeen years, his son George and Archibald Cary ably carried on.[24]

Internal improvements remained the compelling issue in the county in the 1820s. Of special interest were a continued appropriation for the National Road and a new fund to help send both the Baltimore and Ohio Railroad and the Chesapeake and Ohio Canal to Cumberland. As Samuel Charles wrote in his first editorial, "No section of the country is, perhaps, more interested than this, in sustaining the existing Administration. If we are to be benefited by a liberal system of internal improvements, by roads, by canals, then we should sustain it. . . ." Charles was eager to attack the Jacksonians but politically astute enough not to offend the swing voters. He decried the belief that the Jacksonians had "all poor people move at their beck and nod" when it was clear to him that those "worthy people" could think for themselves. In retrospect it is hard to understand why more people in Allegany County did not support Adams and Clay, the ticket dedicated to internal improvements, over Jackson, a candidate lukewarm over such matters and running strictly as the hero of the Battle of New Orleans in the War of 1812. Local citizens copied fellow countrymen everywhere in showing a morbid enthusiasm for printed accounts of Jackson's alleged butchering of troops, hanging of civilians, and past adultery with his wife Rachel. Many homes in the area displayed the famous "coffin" handbills, which depicted the coffins of eighteen men whom Jackson had ordered executed and showed the general thrusting his sword into a defenseless man. *The Civilian* likened Jackson to George III and claimed that he would take nothing into the presidency but a club and rifle. The *Maryland Advocate* struck back by printing the well-circulated falsehood that Adams, while American minister to Russia, had procured young girls for the Czar. Charles called Buchanan's editorials "vulgar," "opprobrious," and "foul." So slanderous did Buchanan become that a Cumberland clergyman successfully sued him and collected $250.

Despite rallies for Adams in Frostburg, Flintstone,

Westernport, Cumberland, and Oldtown and the formation of "Administration Committees of Vigilance" in each of the nine voting districts, Andrew Jackson outpolled John Quincy Adams 856 to 741 in the county and carried with him all four Democratic candidates into the state legislature. The total number of voters had increased nearly threefold over 1824, reflecting both a heightened political awareness and a growth in the number of citizens eligible to vote.[25]

Daniel Blocher, who was trained as a printer in the *Maryland Advocate*'s office, bought an interest in the paper in 1830 and became its editor in 1832. He carried on a lively and often intemperate battle with the *Civilian.* Editor Charles had this to say about Blocher's paper: "In looking over the last *Advocate,* to find one sensible article, paragraph or sentence, or one deserving the least notice proved fruitless." Shortly after Blocher was elected to the legislature in the fall of 1837, he silenced the *Advocate*'s press. A new journal, the *Alleganian,* picked up the Democratic banner in 1838 and waged heated campaigns against the *Civilian* for the next forty years.[26]

The very fact that Allegany County had two partisan newspapers in 1830 illustrates its development from a rough frontier area to an increasingly civilized region which recognized its place in the nation. The building of the National Road had brought about these changes. It had made the county a vital link between the East and the new lands in the West.

CHAPTER IV NOTES

1. The census of 1800 lists only three slaves in the entire Georges Creek valley. Maryland Genealogical Society, *Allegany County, Maryland, 1800 Census;* F. Paul Harris, "Historical Sketch," 1932; James W. Thomas and T. J. C. Williams, *History of Allegany County, Maryland,* I (Philadelphia: L. R. Titsworth and Co., 1923), p. 150 (hereafter cited as Thomas and Williams, *Allegany County,* I); and Ele Bowen, *Rambles in the Path of the Steam Horse* (Philadelphia: William Bromwell and William Smith, 1855), pp. 253-54.

2. Will Lowdermilk, *History of Cumberland* (Washington: James Anglin, 1878), pp. 277, 286-88, 291-92 (hereafter cited as Lowdermilk, *Cumberland*); John Scharf, *History of Western Maryland,* II (Phila-

delphia: L. H. Everts, 1882), p. 1390 (hereafter cited as Scharf, *Western Maryland*, II); and Thomas and Williams, *Allegany County*, I, p. 106.

3. Every previously published account dealing with the history of the county lists the area's first newspaper as the *Allegany Freeman*. Clarence Brigham, *History and Bibliography of American Newspapers, 1690-1820* (Worcester: American Antiquarian Society, 1947), pp. 253-54; *Allegany Freeman*, June 29, 1816; *Allegany Federalist*, July 6, 1816; *Maryland Advocate*, Sept. 17 and Dec. 8, 1823; and Thomas and Williams, *Allegany County*, I, p. 143.

4. James L. Donaldson, *Speech in the House of Delegates of Maryland, on the Subject of the Allegany Election* (Baltimore: E. French and Co., 1814), pp. 1, 18; and Dieter Cunz, *The Maryland Germans* (Princeton: Princeton University Press, 1948), p. 192.

5. Lowdermilk, *Cumberland*, pp. 295-97; Thomas and Williams, *Allegany County*, I, p. 380; and Hilleary F. Willison, "History of the Pioneer Settlers of Flintstone, District #3, and Their Descendants" (unpublished typescript, 1910), p. 4 (hereafter cited as Willison, "Pioneer Settlers of Flintstone").

6. Lowdermilk, *Cumberland*, pp. 295, 301; and Thomas and Williams, *Allegany County*, I, p. 143.

7. Reprint from Baltimore *American* in *Maryland Advocate*, March 3, 1835; *Compendium of the Enumeration of the Inhabitants and Statistics of the United States from the Returns of the Sixth Census* (Washington: Department of State, 1841); and *Maryland Advocate*, July 27, 1828, and Feb. 6, 1830.

8. Willison, "Pioneer Settlers of Flintstone," p. 14.

9. Ibid., pp. 14-19; and Scharf, *Western Maryland*, II, pp. 1388-89.

10. Frederick Gutheim, *The Potomac* (Rinehart and Co.: New York, 1949), pp. 244-48 (hereafter cited as Gutheim, *The Potomac*); *Maryland Advocate*, Oct. 12, 1831, and Oct. 4, 1834; and the *Civilian*, Dec. 18, 1829. The passenger pigeon became extinct early in the twentieth century.

11. Willison, "Pioneer Settlers of Flintstone," p. 15.

12. Ibid., pp. 7, 16; and the *Civilian*, July 29 and Aug. 14, 1829, and Feb. 28, 1840.

13. Thomas D. Clark, *Frontier America* (Charles Scribner's Sons: New York, 1959), p. 220 (hereafter cited as Clark, *Frontier America*); Willison, "Pioneer Settlers of Flintstone," p. 10; and *Union*, Jan. 31, 1862.

14. Willison, "Pioneer Settlers of Flintstone," p. 24; Gutheim, *The Potomac*, pp. 187-89; and *Phoenix Civilian*, May 4, 1839. The earliest surviving newspapers in the county carry advertisements for these professions and trades. See *Allegany Freeman*, Jan. 29, 1816, or *Allegany Federalist*, July 6, 1816.

15. Philip Jordan, *The National Road* (Bobbs-Merrill: Indianapolis, 1948), pp. 72-74, 76-77 (hereafter cited as Jordan, *National Road*); and Thomas and Williams, *Allegany County*, I, pp. 181-83.

16. Jordan, *National Road*, pp. 83-84, 104-5; Scharf, *Western Maryland*, II, p. 1392; Clark, *Frontier America*, pp. 343-44; and quoted in *Two Hundred Years* (Washington, D.C.: U.S. News and World Report Books, 1973), I, p. 199. In 1825, construction on the National Road pushed westward from Wheeling. The route moved through Ohio and Indiana and finally reached Vandalia, Ill., in 1836, where it terminated.

17. Jordan, *National Road*, pp. 99-101.

18. Scharf, *Western Maryland*, II, p. 1388; *Phoenix Civilian*, June 24 and Nov. 18, 1834, and Jan. 26, 1836; and *Maryland Advocate*, Nov. 18, 1834.

19. The *Civilian*, May 5, 1878; Willison, "Pioneer Settlers of Flintstone," pp. 3-4; and Jordan, *National Road*, pp. 104, 217-18, 225.

20. Jordan, *National Road*, p. 212; *Phoenix Civilian*, Aug. 31, 1839; Thomas Searight, *The Old Pike* (Uniontown: The Author, 1894), p. 109 (hereafter cited as Searight, *The Old Pike*); and *American Anti-Slavery Almanac for 1840* (New York and Boston: American Anti-Slavery Society).

21. Scharf, *Western Maryland*, II, pp. 1335-37; Jordan, *National Road*, pp. 179-82; Thomas J. Stanton, *A Century of Growth or the History of the Church in Western Maryland* (Baltimore: John Murphy Co., 1900), I, p. 119; and the *Civilian*, March 23, 1849, and May 24, 1850.

22. Searight, *The Old Pike*, pp. 175-77, 206; Scharf, *Western Maryland*, II, pp. 1336-38; Lowdermilk, *Cumberland*, p. 321; *Maryland Advocate*, Aug. 12, 1834; and *Phoenix Civilian*, Aug. 12, 1834, and March 27, 1846.

23. Willison, "Pioneer Settlers of Flintstone," p. 3; Jordan, *National Road*, pp. 212-13; Thomas and Williams, *Allegany County*, I, p. 1454; *Maryland Advocate*, May 23, 1825, and June 26, 1830; the *Civilian*, March 27, 1829, Jan. 21, 1837, and Feb. 23 and July 6, 1849; and *Alleganian*, April 3, 1846, and June 2, 1849.

24. *Maryland Advocate*, May 31 and Nov. 15, 1824; the *Civilian*, April 10 and 17 and May 13, 1828, and Aug. 19, 1829; Thomas and Williams, *Allegany County*, I, p. 372; and Scharf, *Western Maryland*, II, p. 1455.

25. The nine voting districts in 1828 were Glades, Selby's Port, Little Crossings, Westernport (then spelled Western Port), Frostburg, Cumberland, Oldtown, 15 Mile Creek, and Flintstone. The *Civilian*, Feb. 14 and 28, July 17 and 24, Oct. 9, and Nov. 13, 20, and 28, 1828, Jan. 30, 1829, and June 3, 1834; *Maryland Advocate*, Nov. 15, 1824, and Oct. 30, 1830; Thomas and Williams, *Allegany County*, I, p. 252; and Scharf, *Western Maryland*, II, p. 1453.

26. The Times and Alleganian Company, publisher of the Cumberland *News* and *Evening Times*, evolved from the *Alleganian*. *Maryland Advocate*, Oct. 30, 1830; the *Civilian*, Jan. 30, 1829; *Phoenix Civilian*, June 3 and 18, 1834, Jan. 26 and Sept. 17, 1836, and Sept. 2 and 23, 1837; and Scharf, *Western Maryland*, II, p. 1453.

V

THE TRANSPORTATION AND MINERAL FRONTIER, 1829-1860

The small, bald, sour-looking man thrust his spade at the ground. The blade struck a root. Unperturbed, he tried once again with the same result. Now John Quincy Adams, sixth president of the United States, laid down his shovel, and to the delight of the cheering crowd, stripped off his coat. He then took up his spade and drove it home. Thus a few miles from the White House on a warm and sunny Fourth of July, 1828, the Chesapeake and Ohio Canal was officially inaugurated. Forty miles away in Baltimore the venerable Charles Carroll, sole surviving signer of the Declaration of Independence, formally opened the construction of the Baltimore and Ohio Railroad. Once again an effort would be made to use the Potomac Valley to link Allegany County and the West with the tidewater.[1]

Since the eighteenth century men had recognized the upper valley of the Potomac River as a source of raw materials and a potential future market for eastern goods. Stimulated by the growing fur trade and western settlement, many people urged that the Potomac River be developed into a usable artery of transportation. The distance from Georgetown to Cumberland was 184.5 miles and from Georgetown to Pittsburgh via Wills Creek 341 miles, thus making this route the shortest path between tidewater in the East and the head of navigation on the western waters of the Ohio River. Through the efforts of several entrepreneurs, including George Washington, the Potomac Navigation Company was chartered by Maryland and Virginia in 1785 with orders to deepen the river and cut canals around the falls. By 1789, three bypass canals were completed, permitting occasional vessels to make the trip from Cumberland to within a few miles of Georgetown. But slack-water or year-round navigation on the shallow Potomac was not feasible. Shipping by water remained limited to short periods in spring and fall when seasonal rains raised the river's level and enabled barges to be floated downstream.[2]

Prior to the completion of the Baltimore and Ohio Railroad to Cumberland in 1842, literally all shipping from the county was done in flatboats eighty feet long, thirteen feet wide, and three feet deep. Farmers and miners spent the long winter months constructing barges along Wills Creek, using the abundant white pine found west of Cumberland. During the spring freshets the boats, each one manned by four oarsmen and usually traveling in fleets of from twenty to forty crafts, carried coal, flour, and butter to the Harpers Ferry and Georgetown markets. During the War of 1812 Notley Barnard of Westernport filled a government contract by manufacturing walnut gunstocks, shipping them by water to the federal arsenal at Harpers Ferry. After the war the demand for Allegany County coal grew yearly. A bushel of coal valued at seven cents in Cumberland brought thirty cents at Williamsport and as much as sixty cents in Georgetown. By 1833, over 300,000 bushels of coal were shipped annually. Because demand outstripped supply, most of the coal was sold by the time the barges reached Harpers Ferry.[3]

The three-day trip downstream to Georgetown entailed little physical effort besides steering clear of rocks and whirlpools. To help pass the time oarsmen consumed considerable quantities of whiskey. So common was the practice that when one merchant sent three boats downstream in June 1834, "without a drop of spiritous whiskey on board," a newspaper praised the owner, called his example "a worthy one," and hoped that it would be emulated. It was not. On reaching their destination the barges generally were broken up and sold for firewood or building materials. A few broad-backed souls whose vessels had keels poled upstream for ten days in order to bring a load of salt or dried cod or shad back to the county.[4]

In November 1823, the first Chesapeake and Ohio Convention met amidst predictions of great success for the almost-completed Erie Canal in New York and a general optimism that the federal government would and should support a program of aid to public works. This meeting of dignitaries from Pennsylvania, Maryland, Virginia, and the District of Columbia generated enough enthusiasm to secure an appropriation from Congress for a detailed survey of the proposed canal route. This year-round artificial waterway would connect Georgetown with Wheeling, (West) Virginia, and the Ohio River. Its proponents argued that the canal would increase commerce and expand the markets for Maryland minerals and farm products. John C. Calhoun, the secretary of war, journeyed to the county in September 1824 to "officially" inspect the "summit level" and determine the practicality of the route surveyed by the United States Board of Engineers. In May 1828, Congress appropriated $1,000,000 of the projected $4,500,000 construction cost of building the canal as far as Cumberland. News of this bill was greeted by wild revelry in the county; a rather windy resolution declared the funding to be "the most propitious event . . . since the days of the Revolution." Five weeks later, President Adams turned the first spade of dirt in what would become a twenty-two-year construction nightmare before the waterway finally reached Cumberland.[5]

Work began immediately on the eastern division of the canal. The generous dimensions—sixty feet wide at the water's surface, six feet deep and forty-eight feet wide at the bottom—indicated that the directors of the C&O visualized the use of steamboats on its waters, factories along its banks, and centuries of unlimited service. In Cumberland, land prices shot upward as local residents speculated on warehouses, dock space, and lots along the proposed route of the waterway. People eagerly followed the progress of the great ditch as it snaked westward in fits and starts. Nearly every issue of the *Civilian*, the *Maryland Advocate*, and its successor, the *Alleganian*, carried canal news and a large crowd turned out to meet the president of the C&O Company when he visited the area in 1833. In the next year work began on

Scene on the canal.

the western end of the waterway when a crew started quarrying stone eleven miles from Cumberland. Nevertheless, many citizens began to fear that the canal might never reach the county seat.[6]

From its inception the project had encountered difficulties. A seemingly endless dispute with the Baltimore and Ohio Railroad over right-of-way hindered construction in the Potomac Valley and general inflation sent the cost of materials and labor upwards, with the price of lime alone jumping 300 percent. Although harsh winter weather and spring flooding also retarded progress, the main problem was the labor supply. Because contractors found themselves short-handed during harvest season, they demanded that the canal board encourage the migration of workers from within the states and across the Atlantic. Many new recruits were unhappy with their working conditions, shelter, and pay. Some just abandoned their shovels and departed while others took out their frustrations by fighting among themselves. In January 1834, a "war among the workers" sent two volunteer companies marching from Cumberland to Williamsport.[7]

By autumn 1834, the financial resources of the C&O were exhausted. State governments, the Congress, and private investors were all reluctant to contribute further. Over $4,000,000 had been expended to construct 108 miles of waterway and many hesitated to even guess what it would cost to push through the remaining seventy-five miles of rugged terrain to Cumberland. But the people of Allegany County refused to let the project die. Conventions of civic leaders passed resolutions in February and October 1834 urging state governments in Pennsylvania, Maryland, and Virginia and the United States Congress to fund canal construction. Legislators were assured that once the waterway reached Cumberland, "bituminous coal of the very best quality" and supply could be shipped east. Sixteen men from the area, including both Whigs and Jacksonians, answered a call to attend a large canal meeting in Baltimore in December 1834. This work reaped dividends. In March 1835, the Maryland legislature approved a loan of two million dollars to bring the canal to Cumberland. Scarcely had the votes been counted before another orgy of speculation in coal-rich lands began. Obviously many in the area believed the toast, number forty-two of the forty-three drunk at the county celebration: "Cumberland, the future compeer of Baltimore in the extent of population and trade."[8]

The only part accurate in the toast was the word "future." Fifteen more years passed before the canal was completed. In January 1836, to the consternation of the long-suffering local citizenry, shortage of funds again curtailed work. A Washington journal, *Niles' Register,* reported "considerable panic" in Cumberland. Business was "dull," the principal streets empty, the merchant "idle," and the speculator "cut to the quick." This financial trouble deepened in 1837, when a general economic decline settled over the nation, making it even more difficult for the C&O to secure capital. Still, citizens in the area, especially the mine owners, remained optimistic. The railroad was making progress toward Cumberland, and by 1839, canal digging was again under way at Little Orleans and along Wills Creek. There was even talk of creating an inland harbor at the county seat, with a basin large enough to accommodate 1,000 boats.[9]

The project seemed at times to be beset by trials. Floods in 1836, 1840, 1843, 1845, 1846, and 1847 washed out embankments. Therefore, the company needed not only a constant infusion of funds for new building but also appropriations to repair damage from floods and to maintain completed work. Moreover a scarcity of hard rock stymied construction in Allegany County. And, finally, revived labor strife hindered work in the late 1830s. On New Year's Day 1838, a group of Irish workers who were employed in building the tunnel at Paw Paw stormed into Oldtown, destroying property and threatening death to any who opposed them. The rioters, upset by large pay cuts and the wholesale hiring of Germans and Americans to displace them, were finally restrained by the "Continental Guards" and other armed men from Cumberland. Many of the Irish were dismissed and blacklisted. Then, in August 1839, violence erupted near Little Orleans, a small community at the mouth of Fifteen

Mile Creek. Militia from Allegany and Washington counties marched to the scene, seized weapons, tore down shanties, and arrested rioters. At a trial held in Cumberland fourteen Irish laborers were convicted of "assault with intent to kill" and given sentences ranging from one to eighteen years. When the Democratic governor of the state pardoned these men, local voters, already forced to absorb over $3,000 in court costs, reacted by voting Whig in 1840.[10]

By 1843, thirty-two of the fifty miles of canal in Allegany County were complete, but many again despaired that the remainder would be dug. The C&O was nearly two million dollars in debt and no one showed much interest in providing relief. The Baltimore and Ohio Railroad had reached Cumberland and its supporters advocated that it act as a "feeder" between the coal mines and the completed stretch of canal. Therefore, the B&O argued, there was no need to finish the canal. Nevertheless, strenuous effort by the C&O's board of directors convinced the state legislature to waive its lien on the receipts of the canal in favor of a bond issue sufficient to finish construction to Cumberland. The telling argument was that as long as the canal remained incomplete, the state's lien on net revenues was worthless because there would never be sufficient revenues until Cumberland was reached. Consequently, now that money was available, work on the C&O resumed in 1847, with "all classes of laborers" being hired and provided with "efficient" police protection. The eastern section of the canal, from Georgetown to Cumberland, was finished at last in the autumn of 1850; the section from Cumberland to Wheeling was never built. Total cost of the 184.5-mile ditch was $11,071,176 or $59,618 for each mile dug.[11]

The formal opening ceremony on October 10, 1850, featured countless politicians, dignitaries, and "other prominent gentlemen." To enliven the proceedings brass bands, including one from Baltimore (which came on the train), played, the Eckhart artillery drilled, cannons fired, and participants consumed "a copious supply of the finest and choicest wines." But for many the celebration came too late. The principal speaker put it bluntly but fairly:

> Many of us were young when this great work was commenced, and have lived to see its completion, only because Providence has prolonged our lives until our heads are gray. . . . Thousands have been ruined by their connection with the work, and few in the region have had cause to bless it.

Measured by the optimistic forecast made twenty-two years earlier, the canal was a failure. No packet service or "two-storied canal boats" ever materialized. Its competitor, the B&O, had been serving the area for eight years and had pushed on toward Wheeling and the Ohio Valley. The limited success due the C&O rested in hauling bulky and imperishable commodities like coal, iron, flour, and limestone products for the next three-quarters of a century.[12]

Although the Baltimore and Ohio Railroad won the race to Allegany County and would effectively outstrip its rival, the Chesapeake and Ohio Canal Company, economically, the victory did not come easily. In 1827, Baltimore was dependent on slow and expensive freight wagons to haul her commerce to the West. The city feared the competition of the completed Erie Canal and New York City to the north and the recently chartered Chesapeake and Ohio Canal and Washington City to the south. Out of a series of meetings held by influential merchants and bankers came the daring proposal to build a railroad over the mountains in order to open the port of Baltimore to the West. John V. L. McMahon, formerly of Cumberland and a past representative to the Maryland Assembly from Allegany County, drafted a charter for the Baltimore and Ohio Railroad. The state granted approval in February 1827 for the company to build a double track to the Ohio River, a route which would presumably pass through Cumberland. The first stock issue received heavy support despite the fact that no one had the slightest idea how to go about constructing America's first railroad. A survey was commissioned, however, and Charles Carroll was persuaded to lay the cornerstone.[13]

A letter sent from Annapolis to Cumberland and subsequently printed in the *Maryland Advocate* reveals how excited many were about the B&O:

> The Railroad is the *rage of the day*. . . . I was told today that a

> car, with *sails,* travelled in the road at the rate of *twenty miles an hour.* We live a century too soon.

Horses, not sails, were first considered to be the best potential means of rail locomotion. But a successful test in August 1830 of Peter Cooper's steam engine Tom Thumb settled the issue and convinced the B&O to retire the horse.[14]

The railroad's difficulties were both financial and political. The line was chronically short of funds, but unlike the canal, the B&O did generate a modest revenue as it opened each new link. Yet its early critics, usually backers of the C&O, believed that a railroad was more expensive to build and operate than a canal. And even some of the B&O's supporters in the county wondered if trains could compete successfully with canals. Tracks had passed Frederick by 1831, but the B&O found itself blocked at Point of Rocks on the Potomac because of litigation by the Chesapeake and Ohio Canal Company. A compromise in 1833, which included the payment of $266,000 to the C&O, allowed the railroad to push on. British capital recruited by Louis McLane, president of the B&O, in exchange for an agreement to buy rails made in England, kept the railroad afloat in the late 1830s.[15]

From Harpers Ferry the line crossed into Virginia and followed the twisting Potomac until it re-entered Maryland six miles below Cumberland. The city was ready, in the words of Samuel Charles, editor of the *Civilian,* "to become the most important inland town in the whole union." From June 1842 on, every issue of the *Civilian* carried at least one and usually several articles about the railroad's progress between Hancock and Cumberland. By late September construction had moved twenty-one miles west of Hancock, with nearly 1,500 laborers toiling around the clock to push the work forward at the rate of a mile a day. Residents of the county were anxious and curious. A reporter from the Wheeling *Times* interviewed people in Cumberland, noting that many refused to believe in the existence of an "Iron Horse" "capable of bringing at his heels 10 or 20 cars each loaded with 50 people and their baggage."[16]

On November 1, 1842, a large crowd gathered to watch a

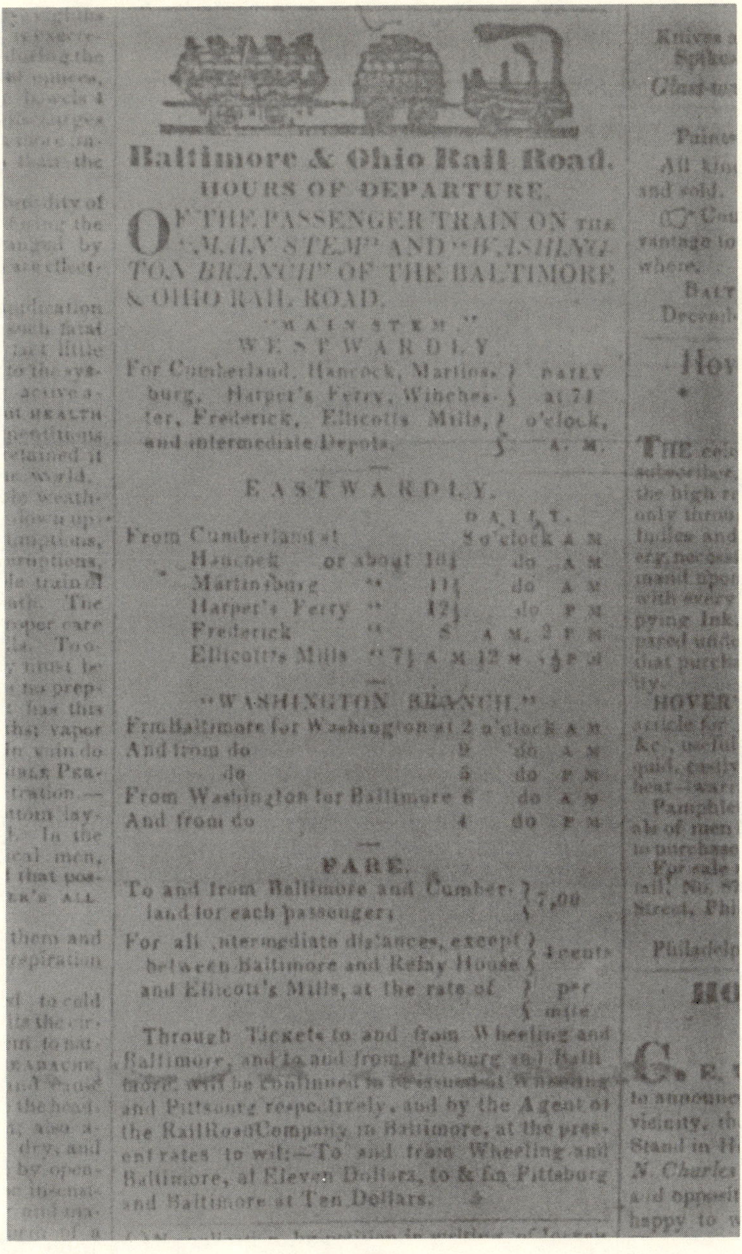

Baltimore & Ohio Rail Road.

HOURS OF DEPARTURE

OF THE PASSENGER TRAIN ON THE "*MAIN STEM*" AND "*WASHINGTON BRANCH*" OF THE BALTIMORE & OHIO RAIL ROAD.

"MAIN STEM."

WESTWARDLY.

For Cumberland, Hancock, Martinsburg, Harper's Ferry, Winchester, Frederick, Ellicotts Mills, and intermediate Depots, DAILY at 7½ o'clock, A. M.

EASTWARDLY.

		DAILY.	
From Cumberland at		8 o'clock	A M
Hancock	or about	10¼ do	A M
Martinsburg	"	11½ do	A M
Harper's Ferry	"	12½ do	P M
Frederick	"	8 A M, 2	P M
Ellicott's Mills	"	7½ A M 12 M 5½	P M

"WASHINGTON BRANCH."

Fm Baltimore for Washington at	2	o'clock	A M
And from do	9	do	A M
do	5	do	P M
From Washington for Baltimore	6	do	A M
And from do	4	do	P M

FARE.

To and from Baltimore and Cumberland for each passenger, 7,00

For all intermediate distances, except between Baltimore and Relay House and Ellicott's Mills, at the rate of 4 cents per mile.

Through Tickets to and from Wheeling and Baltimore, and to and from Pittsburg and Baltimore, will be continued to be issued at Wheeling and Pittsburg respectively, and by the Agent of the RailRoad Company in Baltimore, at the present rates to wit:—To and from Wheeling and Baltimore, at Eleven Dollars, to & fm Pittsburg and Baltimore at Ten Dollars.

B&O timetable, 1847.

test, or pilot, locomotive come into the city. As the train approached it struck a slight grade, emitting volumes of black smoke and sparks from its stack. Its appearance struck terror among the spectators, with those nearest the tracks running for their lives. On this note the B&O came to Cumberland. Four days later the *Civilian* greeted the official "first" train with the headline "Here at Last." After years of waiting the county was eager to embark on a new era, "a golden age." As the farthest point west yet penetrated by rail, Cumberland now became a great exchange or transshipment center and the "Queen City" of the Alleghenies. For nearly a decade the city would be the most important center between the Atlantic Ocean and the Ohio River.[17]

The coming of the B&O to Cumberland in 1842 and the C&O eight years later enabled the coal industry in Allegany County to increase production. Long before these two arteries of transportation existed, however, people in the county had engaged in mining. The presence of coal was recorded in 1751, when a "Frye and Jefferson" map printed the words "Coal Mine" near Georges Creek. Early discoveries of the mineral were accidental, as one Virginia traveler noted in 1789, when he wrote of the "inexhaustible beds of coal, some of which the river laid bare," near the mouth of the Savage River. In 1810, violent spring flooding of Georges Creek stripped the earth from a "mountain of coal" near present-day Lonaconing. Some of this coal was taken to Westernport and sent down the Potomac to Georgetown.[18]

There was little that was systematic in early mining—people just removed the surface coal with their farm implements. The small population in the area used relatively little of the output for fuel and coal-burning industries were few in number. In 1816, Roger and Thomas Perry burned coal from Frostburg at their glassworks in Cumberland, but the fire gave the glass a greenish hue and the Perrys turned back to wood. Construction of the National Road through the lands of George Eckhart in 1815 uncovered new deposits, with additional discoveries being made in what became Frostburg and Pompey's Smash (Vale Summit). The first recorded

The town of Cumberland in 1855.

fatality occurred in May 1824, "in one of the coal pits near Frostburg."[19]

The coal region in Allegany County consisted of an area five miles wide between Dans Mountain on the east and Savage Mountain on the west and twenty-five miles long from the Pennsylvania border to Westernport. As the region developed, Frostburg on the National Road became its center and it included the villages of Mount Savage and Barrelville to the northeast, Eckhart Mines a few miles east, and to the southwest in the Georges Creek valley the communities of Borden Shaft, Midlothian, Carlos, Klondike, Lord, Vale Summit, Ocean, Midland, Lonaconing, Pekin, Moscow, Barton, and Westernport.

In 1828, inspired by the increased shipping of coal down the Potomac and taking to heart the toast by Richard Beall at a dinner in Cumberland—"to the coal miners of Allegany, with the aid of the Canal, richer than the gold mines of Peru"—the Maryland Mining Company was incorporated by the state legislature. A prototype for future incorporations, the company was authorized to purchase up to 5,000 acres of land and to build a railroad from its mines to Cumberland or some point on the C&O. A land boom was on; rocky acreage which previously sold for a few cents and a jug of whiskey now brought upwards of three hundred dollars an acre. Between 1828 and 1850, the legislature incorporated thirty coal and iron companies, all of which hoped to dig the famous fourteen-foot-thick "Big Vein." Enthusiasm knew no limits. A construction engineer for the C&O believed the mineral so plentiful that the canal "would pass through coal banks where coal could be thrown from the mines into a boat with a shovel."[20]

Many of the initial investors in the mining region, especially in the Lonaconing and Mount Savage areas, believed that iron, not coal, would be their chief source of profit. Some of these early companies carried the word "iron" in their official titles. A syndicate of Baltimore and English investors chartered the George's Creek Coal and Iron Company in 1837, and two years later in their annual report noted that in Lonaconing, or the "Lonaconing Residency," a

View from Eckhart Mines, 1854. From Harvey, *Best Dressed Miners*

"flourishing village" of 700, one could find "neither drunkard nor beggar." And why not? This new town, planted amidst unbroken forest "in a strange and thinly inhabited district" and named for the Indian "Lonacona," chief of a tribe long since departed, was a company town. Founded and directed by outside capital, the village offered a severely restricted manner of life to its people who, if they objected, had only one recourse—to leave.[21]

The company retained absolute mastery over its Lonaconing holdings until the 1850s. Its charter gave the superintendent almost feudal rights of rule; his power even extended to the ballot. On election day, 1839, hands were told for whom to vote. Life followed a pattern and all workers obeyed the "Rules of the Lonaconing Residency." Employees worked every day of the year except Sundays and Christmas. Labor from sunrise to sunset stopped and started at the sound of the "great bell of the company." It was illegal for a man to hunt, drink "distilled spiritous liquor," gamble or quarrel, leave the community without permission, own firearms, miss work except for grave reasons, make purchases outside the company store, patronize any but the company physician, or keep a dog without securing special permission. And woe visited those who fell behind on their rent or kept a messy pigsty. The superintendent directed all these rules and others. He lived in his residency or "Grande Maison" (Grand Mansion). A worker who dared trespass on his grounds or enter to talk with him faced immediate discharge and expulsion from the community.[22]

At peak production in mid-1839, laborers composed of thirty-eight furnace hands and 140 miners (including nine boys between the ages of ten and sixteen) made up the major portion of the 220 persons employed at the Lonaconing ironworks. These men and their families brought Lonaconing's population to 700, and made it in 1839, briefly, the second largest town in the county. Company houses built by "mountaineers," the native residents of the area, flanked the main street. Nestled in their midst was the company store, which dispensed everything from soap and saltfish, brooms and tinware, to chocolate and lemons, umbrellas and fiddles.[23]

From its founding the company emphasized the importance of completing an iron furnace, believing that iron would be not only more profitable but also easier to ship than coal. When it began work on the furnace the company assumed that the C&O would reach Cumberland by early 1840. But in June 1839, the canal was still fifty miles from that city, financially drained, and going nowhere. The iron furnace was producing thirteen tons of high-grade pig iron daily which could not be sent eastward except by paying excessive wagon rates. So the smelting operation shut down until, as a caretaker superintendent wrote in September 1840, "our Legislators . . . give us a Canal." Business did resume in 1853, but in coal mining, not iron smelting.[24]

A larger, and for a time more successful, venture in iron manufacturing occurred in the company town of Mount Savage. Originally a mountain hamlet known successively as Luthworth, Arnold's Settlement, Savage Mount, and Jennings Post Office, the village was transformed in the early 1840s into a place of "smoky furnaces and forges and vast heaps of cinders" which loomed up out of the surrounding forest "like some magic place in a faraway place." The metamorphosis began in 1837 when English investors constructed the Mount Savage Iron Works. The initial rolling mill was followed by two blast furnaces in 1840. By 1842, the Maryland and New York Iron and Coal Company had built "a village consisting of 22 dwelling houses, a schoolhouse [and] a store, together with vast buildings for the manufacture of iron." The first rails manufactured in America were rolled in Mount Savage in 1844, an achievement awarded a silver medal by the Franklin Institute of Philadelphia. As business increased, 500 men mined the coal, iron, and fireclay from the surrounding mountains, worked at the mill, and tended the furnaces. The town numbered nearly 3,000 people—all of whom lived in several hundred company houses "built principally of stone and situated in parallel rows on hillsides." Each house had a small yard enclosed by a thick stone wall which gave the village "a peculiarly picturesque effect."[25]

Mount Savage experienced two decades of economic boom and bust. In 1845, it was the second largest population center

Mount Savage Iron Works, 1854. From Harvey, *Best Dressed Miners*

in the county and called by a Cumberland newspaper "one of the greatest (if not *the* greatest) Iron Manufacturing Establishment in America." Business dropped off in 1846, however, and when all work ceased in the next year, the county sheriff offered the property for sale. It was purchased by the Mount Savage Company in 1848, and prosperity returned to the area as the new owners increased production of bar iron, becoming the principal supplier of iron rails for the B&O. The town was again alive. An "excellent library" was heavily patronized and political discussion was heated as men debated whether or not the protective tariff would protect their jobs. Nevertheless, as one visitor in 1852 noted: "If iron goes down, the company and all Mount Savage go down too—the works are stopped and the village depopulated." Mining iron in the region was expensive because the ore lay in several separate deposits and was not of the best quality. With a reduced tariff in the 1850s, the Mount Savage Company found itself undersold by European manufacturers. After suffering erratic, declining output and periodic labor disputes for several years, the iron refining business shut down permanently in 1868. The production of fireclay, begun in 1839, continued, as it has until the present day.[26]

While iron mining in the county declined, coal production in the Georges Creek basin climbed dramatically as transportation facilities improved. Frostburg, sitting 2,200 feet up in the mountains, grew from a "small and straggling" village into a center of economic activity by the outbreak of the Civil War. Although the town took its name from an early resident, Meshach Frost, many then believed—and there are many today who believe—that the designation aptly described the mountain climate where "winter," as one early tourist wrote, "comes early and lingers late." Frost settled in 1812 on land formerly owned by Robert Clarke and his heirs. Meshach and his wife Catherine built a home on the spot where Saint Michael's Catholic Church now stands and began to house and feed laborers working on the National Road. Once the pike was completed, Frost's Highland Hall became a regular stopover where horses were changed and mail and freight relayed. By 1817, town lots were laid out and the

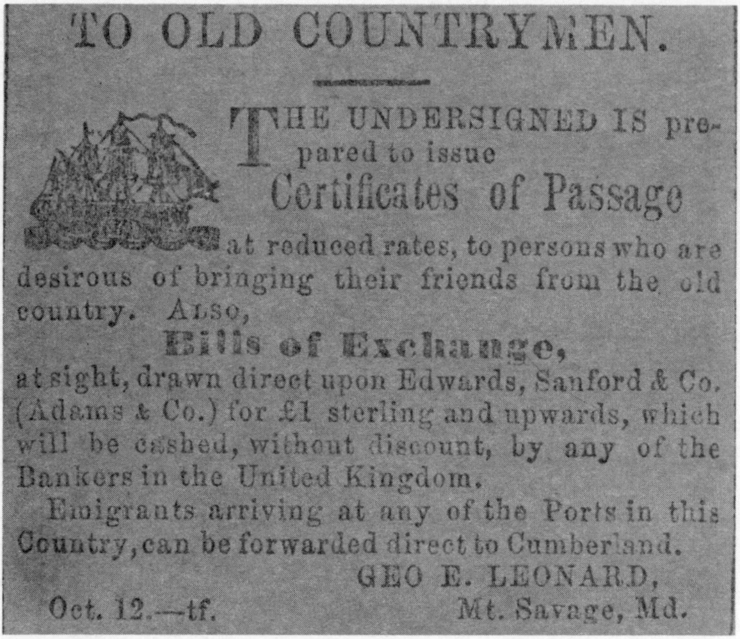

Advertisement from the Cumberland *Civilian,* June 24, 1856.
Courtesy Maryland Historical Society

settlement called Mount Pleasant. For reasons unknown, the town's name changed to Frost Town when the first post office opened in 1820, and within a few years the place became Frostburg.[27]

Although large enough to host a circus in 1833 and to sponsor its own militia unit, "The Frostburg Grey's," in 1838, the village's population trailed that of Cumberland, Lonaconing, and Mount Savage until the late 1840s. Then the reputation of its healthful location, the increase in mining, and the expanding rail transportation helped spur Frostburg's growth. In 1858, the town was prosperous enough to support a newspaper, *The Gazette and Miner's Record,* ambitiously described in its masthead to be "Devoted to the Mining, Manufacturing, and Agricultural Interests, Arts, Sciences, Literature and General News." It was the first county newspaper to be published outside of Cumberland. The *Frostburg True Union* absorbed the *Gazette* in 1862. After 1865, Frostburg's population took another jump and some of its residents believed that their town would soon displace Cumberland as the county's business center.[28]

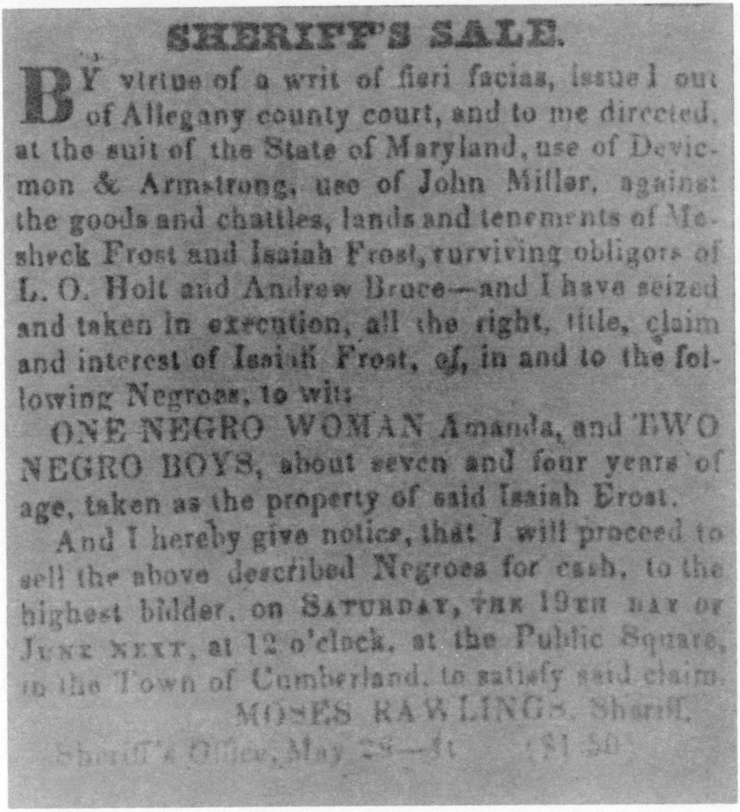

SHERIFF'S SALE.

BY virtue of a writ of fieri facias, issued out of Allegany county court, and to me directed, at the suit of the State of Maryland, use of Devicmon & Armstrong, use of John Miller, against the goods and chattles, lands and tenements of Mesheck Frost and Isaiah Frost, surviving obligors of L. O. Holt and Andrew Bruce—and I have seized and taken in execution, all the right, title, claim and interest of Isaiah Frost, of, in and to the following Negroes, to wit:

ONE NEGRO WOMAN Amanda, and TWO NEGRO BOYS, about seven and four years of age, taken as the property of said Isaiah Frost.

And I hereby give notice, that I will proceed to sell the above described Negroes for cash, to the highest bidder, on SATURDAY, THE 19TH DAY OF JUNE NEXT, at 12 o'clock, at the Public Square, in the Town of Cumberland, to satisfy said claim.

MOSES RAWLINGS, Sheriff.

Sheriff's Office, May [illegible]—4t ($1 50)

Selling slaves to settle an estate. Advertisement in Cumberland *Alleganian*, May 29, 1847.

A visitor to Frostburg in 1860 noted that from the town one looked upon several of the region's twenty-five mining villages. A mile and a half east on the National Road was Eckhart Mines, a town developed by the Maryland Mining Company. When that company was sold in 1852, the town contained "about 100 buildings of wood, brick and stone . . . among them . . . 70 Dwellings . . . all new and in the best repair," which housed a population of "7 or 800 souls." Nearby Pompey's Smash, laid out in 1851, was unique in that it was owned by Welsh, Scottish, and Irish miners "who bought the lots and built the town." An early historian of coal mining and once a resident of the Georges Creek area, Andrew Roy, related how the town received its name: "Some of the coal was hauled in wagons and sold to the neighboring blacksmiths by a negro [*sic*] slave named Pompey, who on one occasion had the misfortune to smash his wagon on the spot where the village was afterwards laid out; and it was named Pompey's Smash. Years afterwards the miners became ashamed of the name and changed it to Vale Summit."[29]

Between 1825 and the Civil War many villages in the valley, including those of Borden Shaft, Detmold, Franklin, Jackson, Midland (initially called Koontz), Barton, Pekin, and Moscow, developed around mines bearing those names. The latter three were once part of the 1,200-acre estate of the Reverend William Shaw, a Methodist minister who settled on the site of Barton in 1794. His son, William Shaw, Jr., laid out the town in 1853, naming it for his father's hometown, Barton-on-Humber, England. Miners and tradesmen filled the town and a Catholic priest from Frostburg remarked that "no matter where the devil was during the week he was sure to turn up in Barton on Sunday." Indeed, the town in 1860 was a spot where "work was plentiful, wages high and whiskey twenty-five cents a gallon."[30]

At the south end of the Georges Creek valley, and more remote from the largest mines in the region, lay Westernport, the most western navigable port on the North Branch of the Potomac. Originally called Hardscrabble, the village acquired a post office in 1802 and incorporated in 1859. Before the coming of the railroad the community contained barely thirty homes and Piedmont, directly across the river in Virginia (now West Virginia), was an open field. But once the B&O arrived in Piedmont in 1851, and the Cumberland and Pennsylvania moved down the valley later in the decade to Westernport to link itself to the larger railroad, the town's unique location stimulated population growth.[31]

The people who filled these valley towns came from a variety of places. Some were miners from Pennsylvania who left the anthracite coalfields to cross into Maryland for the higher pay in the bituminous coal region. Others were Irish workers who abandoned construction jobs on the C&O and the B&O to seek more permanent employment in the expanding mining industry. An ever-increasing number of trained colliers emigrated from the mining districts of South Wales, England, and Scotland in the 1840s, and by mid-century, growing numbers of Germans settled in Lonaconing, Frostburg, and Eckhart Mines. Once secure in their jobs, many of the immigrants responded to newspaper advertisements placed by local agents who offered to make all arrangements to bring relatives left behind in the old country directly to western Maryland. Although the greatest influx of population was to come in the first decades after the Civil War, census figures for the years 1840-1860 reveal a steady increase in the number of miners in Allegany County. As a group these men, who have been intensively studied in Katherine Harvey's superb book *The Best Dressed Miners,* were stable, economically better off than their counterparts in other states, and altogether worthy citizens.[32]

A stimulus for the expanding coal production and the accompanying increase in immigration was the building of short-line or branch railroads in the county. The idea had been discussed for years. In 1831, Meshach Frost had hosted a meeting of "the proprietors of coal mines and . . . all Senators and Delegates" of the county and "any other persons interested in procuring a charter for a RAILROAD from the mines to Cumberland." Five years later the *Phoenix Civilian* noted that the Maryland legislature was considering three railroad bills for Allegany County worth "twenty millions of dollars." And in 1838, the state did agree to allow the Maryland and New York Iron Company to construct a railroad nine miles from the Narrows up Jennings Run to Mount Savage. The road, after numerous financial tribulations, officially opened on the first of April, 1845. In May of the same year, the Maryland Mining Company began work on a line 11.25 miles in length which ran through the Narrows and up "Braddock's Valley" to Eckhart. It required a full year of construction for the railroad to literally tear its way through the "steep and rocky and rugged sides of the mountains."[33]

The Cumberland-Mount Savage Railroad extended its tracks to the foot of Frostburg in 1851, and after digging a tunnel under that town, the road, now owned by the Cumberland and Pennsylvania Railroad Company, continued the line 9.8 miles to Lonaconing in 1857. There it connected with the tracks of the George's Creek Coal and Iron Company, which in 1852 had opened the 9.2-mile line between Piedmont and Lonaconing. In 1864, the Cumberland and Pennsylvania Railroad, owned by the Consolidation Coal Company, gained control of the entire road between Piedmont and Cumberland via Mount Savage. Now the valley really was "one continuous street and town." Twice-daily passenger service allowed residents to travel from village to village or even to go as far as Cumberland for a shopping excursion.[34]

The growing prosperity found in the Georges Creek area also was evident in the county seat. Cumberland's population shot upward, doubling between 1830 and 1840 and then doubling again by 1850. With slightly over 6,000 inhabitants Cumberland had become the state's second most populous city. In 1841, the *Civilian* boasted that Cumberland was "destined . . . to become the most important inland town in the whole Union." The paper's editor described new construction: "Washington Street has been opened, graded and almost built up with very fine buildings. . . . Hotels have been improved, extensive Breweries, an immense tannery, Cement Mill, Castor Mill [erected]." The *Alleganian* reported the town in 1845 to be increasingly "crowded," with unlimited business opportunities available. The next year, the *Alleganian*'s competitor, the *Civilian,* toyed with the idea of expanding into a biweekly. A monthly publication "for farmers and mechanics of Allegany County," *The Plough, The Loom and The Anvil,* made its debut in 1848. The litany of praise and prophecy heard at the beginning of the decade was repeated in 1849, when the famed journalist Horace Greeley, editor of the New York *Tribune,* visited the city and then told his eastern readers that "Cumberland is destined to become one of the largest inland towns of America, a rival of Pittsburg and Lowell [Massachusetts]."[35]

Cumberland's economic boom continued into the 1850s as the town profited from the enormous transfer business that developed because of the common meeting in the city of the National Road, the Baltimore and Ohio Railroad, and the Chesapeake and Ohio Canal. As the western terminal of the canal, the county seat was a layover point for boatmen and a natural trading place for the hundreds of people engaged in navigation. Both the owners of storage buildings and transfer wharves and the men who hauled the freight, the teamsters, did a brisk business. Items from the county which were carried down the canal in its first year of operation included flour, wheat, corn, oats, lumber, lime and cement, coal, limestone, manure, bricks, mill offal, nails, tobacco, whiskey, beer, ale and cider, fruit, hay and straw, pig and scrap iron, rough stone, flax, hemp, bacon, butter, furniture, livestock, rails, bark, and "sundries." Old industries expanded and new ones sprung up. Beall's Foundry kept twenty men busy constructing hopper cars for the mines; Butter's Steam Cabinet and Chair Factory produced sofas, mattresses, and coffins; and the Cumberland Cotton Factory employed fifty people, most of them women, to manufacture cloth, twine, and candlewicks. A third newspaper, the *Unionist* (soon called the *Telegraph*), began printing in January 1851, and a fourth, the *Democrat,* commenced in October 1856.[36]

When a national depression hit in early 1857, Cumberland seemed to be unaffected. The editor of the *Civilian* in March 1857 asked: "Where is the town or city within a circuit of 200 miles in better condition?" In September 1857, however, the same editor wrote of "a deplorable sight," miners, mechanics, and clerks, "a good number . . . idle who want to work, and whose daily labor is their sole dependence." Then in October, the Cumberland Coal and Iron Company defaulted on its loans and its main creditor, the Mineral Bank of Cumberland, failed. Economic despair deepened in the next year when the Cumberland City Bank closed its doors and the city failed to convince the U.S. Congress to locate a national foundry in Allegany County. People asked, "Is Cumberland a finished town?" Many leaders in the region found western Maryland too dependent on the East and they urged that local factories convert the area's raw materials into finished goods. An editorial printed in April 1860 sounded a refrain familiar to citizens of Allegany County in the 1970s:

> Year after year we are compelled to witness the removal of our citizens in search of more prosperous localities. . . . A loss of part of our industrious population is a loss of wealth.[37]

Although Allegany County did recover from the depression of the late 1850s, it is interesting that Cumberland, with the canal, the railroad, and the National Road all meeting in the city, never achieved the prominence many had hoped and predicted for her.

CHAPTER V NOTES

1. Walter S. Sanderlin, *The Great National Project, A History of the Chesapeake and Ohio Canal* (Baltimore: Johns Hopkins Press, 1946), p. 60 (hereafter cited as Sanderlin, *Great National Project*); and Edward Hungerford, *The Story of the Baltimore and Ohio Railroad, 1827-1927* (New York: G. P. Putnam's Sons, 1928), I, p. 39 (hereafter cited as Hungerford, *Story of Baltimore and Ohio Railroad*).

2. Sanderlin, *Great National Project*, pp. 18, 31.

3. The *Civilian*, April 17, 1828; *Phoenix Civilian*, Aug. 6, 1833; Nellie H. McCoy, "History of Westernport," typescript, n.d. A dam built across the Potomac at Cumberland in 1845 ended flatboating. Jacob Brown, *Miscellaneous Writings* (Cumberland: Miller, 1896), p. 32.

4. *Maryland Advocate*, Jan. 21, 1834; Sanderlin, *Great National Project*, pp. 40-41; and John T. Scharf, *History of Western Maryland* (Philadelphia: L. H. Everts, 1882), II, p. 1435 (hereafter cited as Scharf, *Western Maryland*).

5. Sanderlin, *Great National Project*, pp. 52-56; *Maryland Advocate*, Sept. 18 and Oct. 4, 1824; and the *Civilian*, May 29, 1828.

6. Sanderlin, *Great National Project*, pp. 61-65; and *Phoenix Civilian*, June 25 and Aug. 27, 1833, and May 6, 1834.

7. Sanderlin, *Great National Project*, pp. 69-71, 79; and *Phoenix Civilian*, Jan. 28, 1834.

8. Delegates from Ohio, still hopeful that the canal would be pushed

as far as the Ohio River, attended the Baltimore Conference. *Phoenix Civilian,* Feb. 4 and Oct. 21, 1834, and March 24 and May 12, 1835; J. William Hunt, "Across the Desk," in the Cumberland *Sunday Times,* Oct. 10 and 17, 1954 (hereafter cited as Hunt); and *Maryland Advocate,* March 24 and 31, and April 7, 1835.

9. *Niles' Register,* Feb. 20, 1836, quoted in Sanderlin, *Great National Project,* p. 108; the *Civilian,* Jan. 31, 1840; and *Alleganian,* August 1839, quoted in Hunt, Feb. 2, 1952.

10. Sanderlin, *Great National Project,* pp. 123-24, 141, 192; the *Civilian,* Feb. 20, 1828, and Feb. 17, 1840; *Phoenix Civilian,* Nov. 3, 1838, and Sept. 21, Oct. 26, and Nov. 2, 1839. Initially called Orleans by an early settler for his former home, the town became known as Little Orleans by the time it acquired a post office in 1838. *Phoenix Civilian,* Nov. 13, 1838.

11. Sanderlin, *Great National Project,* pp. 139, 147, 153, 167; the *Civilian,* Feb. 7, 14, and 21, 1840, May 11 and 18, 1849, and May 10 and Oct. 11, 1850; and James W. Thomas and T. J. C. Williams, *History of Allegany County Maryland* (Philadelphia: L. R. Titsworth and Co., 1923), I, pp. 230-31 (hereafter cited as Thomas and Williams, *Allegany County*). The projected connection of the eastern and western waters via the Potomac and Youghiogheny or Monongahela was never achieved, but the proposed continuation of the canal to the Ohio River was discussed for years.

12. The *Civilian,* Oct. 11, 1850; Richard Walsh and William Fox, editors, *Maryland, A History, 1632-1974* (Baltimore: Maryland Historical Society, 1974), p. 197; and Frederick Gutheim, *The Potomac* (New York: Rinehart & Co., 1949), pp. 263-66.

13. John V. L. McMahon, in 1824, while a state representative from the county, collaborated with a fellow delegate to press passage of a bill giving Jews the right to vote. He left the county in 1826. *Maryland Advocate,* May 20, 1826. Ten short train ways were built prior to 1827, all rickety, wooden affairs. Hungerford, *Story of Baltimore and Ohio Railroad,* I, p. 39; Thomas and Williams, *Allegany County,* I, p. 266; and Scharf, *Western Maryland,* II, pp. 1339-40.

14. *Maryland Advocate,* Feb. 6, 1830; and Hungerford, *Story of Baltimore and Ohio Railroad,* I, p. 101.

15. The *Civilian,* Feb. 5, 1830, and April 20, 1839; *Maryland Advocate,* March 6, 1830; and Thomas and Williams, *Allegany County,* I, p. 268.

16. The *Civilian,* Jan. 2, 1841; Hungerford, *Story of Baltimore and Ohio Railroad,* I, p. 199; and Wheeling *Times,* Oct. 3, 1842, quoted in Hunt, June 18, 1961.

17. *Special 1908 Edition of Daily News;* and the *Civilian,* Nov. 5, 1842. Cumberland retained the title "Mountain City" until after the Civil War, when it became known as the "Queen City."

18. Katherine Harvey, *The Best Dressed Miners* (Ithaca: Cornell Uni-

versity Press, 1969), p. 4 (hereafter cited as Harvey, *Best Dressed Miners*); and Scharf, *Western Maryland*, II, pp. 1477-1500.

19. Harvey, *Best Dressed Miners*, p. 5; Will Lowdermilk, *History of Cumberland* (Washington: James Anglin, 1878), p. 303 (hereafter cited as Lowdermilk, *Cumberland*); Scharf, *Western Maryland*, II, p. 1500; and *Maryland Advocate*, May 31, 1824.

20. F. Paul Harris, "Historical Sketch of Barton," 1932; the *Civilian*, June 5, 1828; and Cumberland *Miner's Journal*, Feb. 4, 1853, quoted in Harvey, *Best Dressed Miners*, pp. 7-9. Despite the incorporations and the investment activity by easterners, by 1850, only four companies were actively engaged in mining. Some of these, in turn, failed or were absorbed by the Consolidation Coal Company, established in 1864. Scharf, *Western Maryland*, II, pp. 225-26.

21. *Report of the George's Creek Coal and Iron Company* (Baltimore, 1839), pp. 6, 13; Scharf, *Western Maryland*, II, p. 1499; and William M. Richards, "An Experiment in Industrial Feudalism at Lonaconing, Maryland, 1837-1860" (M.A. thesis, University of Maryland, 1950), pp. i-ii (hereafter cited as Richards, "An Experiment in Industrial Feudalism"). Translated into English, Lonacona means "where many waters meet."

22. The "Rules of the Lonaconing Residency" are listed in Harvey, *Best Dressed Miners*, Appendix B, pp. 377-79; see also page 130; and Richards, "An Experiment in Industrial Feudalism," p. 14.

23. Katherine Harvey, "Building a Frontier Ironworks: Problems of Transport and Supply, 1837-1840," *Maryland Historical Magazine*, LXX (Summer, 1975):159-60 (hereafter cited as Harvey, "Building a Frontier Ironworks").

24. Ibid., p. 165; and the *Civilian*, Jan. 10, 1840. Lonaconing would revive dramatically by the 1860s, when it would become, after Frostburg, the second community of the Georges Creek valley.

25. Thomas and Williams, *Allegany County*, I, pp. 489-91; quote from "a traveller" in Hunt, Nov. 16, 1948; quoted from Baltimore *Sun*, Nov. 24, 1842, in Harvey, *Best Dressed Miners*, p. 76; *Special 1908 Edition of Daily News;* and Ele Bowen, *Rambles in the Path of the Steam Horse* (Philadelphia: William Bromwell and William Smith, 1855), pp. 254-55 (hereafter cited as Bowen, *Rambles in Path of Steam Horse*).

26. *Alleganian*, May 10, 1845, and May 13, 1848; *Civilian* and *Journal*, June 3, 1856; Bowen, *Rambles in Path of Steam Horse*, pp. 254-55; *Civilian and Telegraph*, June 9, 1859; and Scharf, *Western Maryland*, II, p. 1496.

27. New York *Evening Post*, Oct. 22, 1860. At his death in 1794, Robert Clarke owned much of the land in and around the town of Frostburg. Frostburg *Mining Journal*, Feb. 13, 1915, quoted in Thomas and Williams, *Allegany County*, II, pp. 517, 522. According to land records, Patrick Murdock also owned several hundred acres around

Frostburg. Scharf, *Western Maryland,* II, p. 1478; *Maryland Advocate,* Nov. 10, 1823; and C. P. Cranfield to Ulysses Hanna, July 24, 1912, quoted in *Historical-Biographical Sketch of Frostburg, Maryland* (Frostburg: Mining Journal Publishing Company, 1912).

28. Scharf, *Western Maryland,* II, pp. 1389, 1478; the *Civilian,* June 30, 1838; Harvey, "Building a Frontier Ironworks," p. 161; Frostburg *Gazette and Mining Record,* Dec. 18, 1858; and Frostburg *True Union,* March 11, 1862. The *True Union* moved to Cumberland in 1862 and became the *Union. Union,* Oct. 7, 1865.

29. New York *Evening Post,* Oct. 22, 1860. The Maryland Mining Company took over the property of George Eckhart, whose heirs had no proof of ownership and received nothing for their coal-rich lands. Richard Lowitt, ed., "Frostburg 1882: German Strikers vs. German Strikebreakers," in Society for the History of the Germans in Maryland, *Twenty-eighth Report* (Baltimore, 1953), p. 73. Harvey, *Best Dressed Miners,* pp. 76, 80; Scharf, *Western Maryland,* II, p. 1444; and Andrew Roy, *History of Coal Mining in the United States* (Columbus: J. L. Trauger Printing Co., 1905), p. 48.

30. *Civilian* and *Journal,* May 27, 1856; Harvey, *Best Dressed Miners,* pp. 77, 80; Scharf, *Western Maryland,* II, pp. 1444, 1466, 1510; and Thomas J. Stanton, *A Century of Growth or the History of the Church in Western Maryland* (Baltimore: John Murphy Co., 1900), I, p. 204 (hereafter cited as Stanton, *A Century of Growth*).

31. Scharf, *Western Maryland,* II, p. 1463; and Frances D. Greaves, "Westernport Information" (typescript, 1975).

32. The 1840 census lists nearly 16,000 inhabitants in the county, of which only 140 described themselves to be engaged in "mining." A decade later the three major districts of Westernport, Lonaconing, and Frostburg reported 370 persons employed in this industry, and this number almost tripled in the decade 1850-1860. Harvey, *Best Dressed Miners,* pp. 17-20, 25-26; the *Civilian,* July 7, 1857; and Stanton, *A Century of Growth,* I, p. 206.

33. *Maryland Advocate,* Nov. 9, 1831; *Phoenix Civilian,* Feb. 23, 1836; the *Civilian,* Oct. 26, 1849; and Cumberland and Pennsylvania Railroad Company, "Ninety-two Years of Transportation Progress" (1937), p. 11 (hereafter cited as C&P Railroad, "Ninety-two Years of Transportation Progress").

34. The *Civilian,* July 21, 1857; *Civilian and Telegraph,* March 24, 1859, and March 25, 1864; C&P Railroad, "Ninety-two Years of Transportation Progress," pp. 11-12; and Scharf, *Western Maryland,* II, p. 1439. The C&P acquired the Eckhart-Cumberland line in 1870.

35. Cumberland's population was 1,162 in 1830 and 6,067 in 1850. The *Civilian,* Jan. 9, 1841, and Nov. 17, 1848; and *Alleganian,* Nov. 29, 1841, April 10, 1846, and June 2, 1849.

36. Hunt, March 1, 1953, and Aug. 5, 1962; the *Civilian,* Oct. 7, 1856, and Sept. 21, 1858; and Lowdermilk, *Cumberland,* p. 371.

37. The *Civilian,* March 17, Aug. 11 and 18, Sept. 22, and Oct. 6, 1857, and April 6 and 27 and Nov. 30, 1858; *Civilian and Telegraph,* Dec. 1 and 8, 1859, and April 5, 1860. The desire to manufacture finished goods in the county was nothing new. In February and March 1835, a large meeting of "the mechanics of Allegany County" urged the creation of new local industries. *Phoenix Civilian,* Feb. 24 and March 17, 1835.

VI

SOCIETY AND POLITICS, 1829-1860

The man preaching on the street corner was naked. The "prophet" Harris had again returned to Cumberland from his home in Virginia to warn the people to repent, or pay the consequences for their wickedness. Harris's first appearance at the corner of Mechanic and Bedford streets came in April 1828. People paid little attention to the itinerant preacher predicting Cumberland's imminent doom until he disrobed during one of his exhortations and proceeded to walk down Mechanic Street. When he was arrested, he elected to return home rather than be locked up. A year later, he appeared stark naked at a Sunday worship service. Racing to the pulpit, Harris turned, and in the same state of undress, delivered a sermon before being hustled off to jail for a brief incarceration. For the next three years he returned to Cumberland annually in April, when he would preach, naked, and would then be arrested and forced to leave town. The climax came in April 1833. When Harris suddenly materialized in the nude on Mechanic Street, he was apprehended and sentenced to be lashed on his bare back. A large crowd witnessed the punishment, which he accepted without complaint. He told observers that it was his duty to suffer, even from those he was trying to warn of impending tragedy. Impressed by his stoicism, the people of Cumberland agreed to give Harris the opportunity to disrobe and complete his walk in the hope that he might then consider his mission accomplished. With all the citizens forewarned and inside their homes, Harris strolled in splendid isolation, shouting at the top of his lungs that fire and brimstone would soon devastate the wicked city. After his walk he donned his clothing and quieted down. But when within a week the unclothed prophet again turned up on the streets, public patience had run out and Harris was escorted to relatives in Leesburg, Virginia, where he was permanently detained.

No one paid much heed to Harris's grim prophecy until most of Cumberland went up in smoke on Sunday morning, April 14, 1833. The fire started in a cabinet shop on the corner of Mechanic and Bedford streets, ironically, just the spot where Harris had done most of his preaching. Aided by a fierce wind, the flames moved 500 yards through the heart of town, destroying everything in their path. Over seventy-five houses and shops and both newspaper offices lay in ruins. The Hagerstown press reported that "nothing now remains but parts of walls and chimneys, where once the principal part of town stood."[1]

Cumberland's 1,200 citizens immediately moved to rebuild their town. Aided by subscription drives in neighboring Pennsylvania and Virginia and in Washington City, workers provided relief for those hardest hit by the disaster. President Andrew Jackson sent fifty dollars and the prominent stage line owner, James Reeside, pledged half the proceeds from the sale of his property west of Wills Creek. Contributions totaled over twenty thousand dollars in addition to the large quantities of food and clothing. Within six weeks, Samuel Charles had the *Civilian* back in print complete with a new title, the *Phoenix Civilian,* and a large replica of the legendary bird on the paper's masthead. Prominent Democrats in Baltimore, including John W. Garrett, sent money to Daniel Blocher so that he could resurrect the *Maryland Advocate.*[2]

As great a tragedy as the fire was, some benefit resulted from it. Many unsafe and unsightly buildings and "infinite amounts" of rubbish were reduced to ashes. Cumberland's two temperance societies found satisfaction in noting that every tavern in town had burned down. But new taverns quickly sprang up; other "more substantial, more durable, and more elegant" buildings were erected as well. The November 19 issue of the *Phoenix Civilian* reported the progress made on the construction of eight large two-story brick buildings. Many frame and log houses had already been completed. By 1834, Cumberland not only had recovered from the fire but had acquired professionalism in addition. In that year, the city boasted its first "real" dentist. His advertisement soon appeared:

> I. Collins, Dental Surgeon. Natural and artificial TEETH mounted and set in the most approved manner. Also, teeth partially decayed, cleaned and repaired. As to competency, Mr. C. feels no disposition to enlarge. An enlightened public must and will judge for themselves.

And the county seat acquired more polish when the town council banned "the outrage" of skinny-dipping in Wills Creek and the Potomac.[3]

The county was visited by many natural disasters during the antebellum period. A Cumberland newspaper reported an earthquake on March 7, 1828, whose tremors were "sensibly felt by many of our citizens." When locusts scourged the area in 1834, the editor of the Democratic newspaper wryly suggested that the Jacksonians would no doubt be blamed for the arrival of the insects. Much more serious—and frequent—was flooding. The coming of spring with its combination of rain and melting snow caused Cumberland annually to prepare for the worst. Especially devastating were the floods of 1816, 1828, 1836, 1840, 1846, 1847, 1853, and 1860, when the overflow from Wills Creek submerged large areas of town. A letter written after the flood of 1836, arguing that the only "proper and safe" site for the town was west of the creek, is typical of the protracted public discussion over how to save the county seat from repeated flooding.[4]

Most fearsome of all the disasters was cholera. Early in the spring of 1832, county citizens heard that cases of Asiatic cholera had appeared on the east coast. After midsummer deaths were reported in Frederick and Hagerstown, Cumberland held a public meeting and raised funds to prepare a hospital. Fortunately, although the facility was readied for the siege, it was not needed. Some people believed that Pittsburgh had escaped cholera because dense clouds of polluted air protected that city. Cumberland had no such defense, but miraculously was spared the disease in 1832. With the arrival of summer 1833 came rumors of "several cases" of cholera in Cumberland and "verified reports" of deaths from the disease all over the United States, including canal workers around

Williamsport. The first official fatality in the county was the "sudden" death of Samuel Smith in early August. Temperance advocates could take comfort in reading that the victim was intemperate, and hastened his trip to the grave by consuming a half-gallon of apple brandy every day for the previous three weeks. Actually, out of a fear of the disease and ignorance over how to treat it, let alone prevent it, many usually sober citizens sought solace in the bottle. Others believed that teetotalers were immune to cholera. But once a Baptist or Methodist minister or an officer of the local chapter of the Sons of Temperance succumbed, however, the argument for abstinence lost its punch. In 1849, the destroyer reappeared. President Zachary Taylor appointed a day of humiliation and prayer. Dr. C. H. Ohr, physician for the Cumberland Board of Health, warned the county that cholera "is slowly narrowing the circle around us" and that "no effort be spared" to mitigate the attack. Residents were ordered to clean up their premises, pour lime in damp cellars, and refrain from their usual habit of throwing refuse and offal into the street. Whether through clean habits or good luck, Allegany County once again escaped the brunt of the disease. But good fortune ended in 1853, when, with Cumberland covered with mud and filth left by spring flooding, conditions were ideal for cholera. In August, the first death occurred and the town emptied into the surrounding countryside overnight. A citizenry which thrived on detailed newspaper accounts of natural disasters and crowded to witness public executions had no stomach for the observation of a fatal case of cholera. It was most unnerving to see one's neighbor be hardy at breakfast, lose control of his bowels and vomit excessively by noon, turn "mottled" and "cadaverous" in appearance by midafternoon, suffer violent spasms at dinner time, and be in the grave by sundown. Within two weeks, fifty-five people were dead. Not until the first frost did the disease disappear.[5]

Local citizens were helpless in the face of cholera and other natural disasters, but there were areas of their lives amenable to change. Education had long been considered essential to support a democracy, and it was particularly important in frontier communities, where people were eager to acquire polish and sophistication. As early as 1795, the general assembly had granted permission to various groups in Allegany County to establish academies for educational purposes. The state chartered Allegany County School, popularly known in Cumberland as Allegany County Academy, in 1798, providing an annual appropriation of $300. In 1811, the sum rose to $500, and in 1831, a final increase brought the amount to $800 per annum, where it remained until 1916. Although this payment was never enough to do more than provide a few scholarships and secure general building maintenance, people raised quite a fuss when it was temporarily discontinued during the Civil War. The curriculum at the academy took one beyond beginning work in reading, writing, and arithmetic into instruction in geometry, composition, grammar, and the "dead languages" of Latin, Greek, and Hebrew. Although competing private schools such as the Frostburg and Flintstone seminaries opened their doors (1825), operated for a few years, and then vanished forever, Allegany County Academy survived. The state apparently voted funds in the 1820s for academies in Westernport and Frostburg, but neither school materialized. When in 1826, Thomas Jefferson McKaig became principal of Allegany Academy, the institution flourished, with an average enrollment of 150 pupils. After McKaig's resignation in 1834, however, attendance dropped to thirty-three students by 1836 and thereafter remained erratic. Nevertheless, by 1849, the school had outgrown its original building. Funds raised by private subscription allowed the academy to move into a magnificent brick structure, complete with massive Doric columns, on Washington Street opposite the courthouse. The building now houses the main branch of the Allegany County Library.[6]

In 1826, the general assembly agreed upon an elaborate system of public primary education for Maryland. County and district boards were to be established and detailed provisions made to support and operate the schools. The system was optional, requiring voter approval. Although it was accepted by thirteen of the state's nineteen counties, the people of Allegany County, fearful of increasing their taxes, rejected the proposal by a vote of 1,031 to 249. Local residents preferred to draw on the meager "free school" fund provided by the state and used by the county commissioners to send indigent children to private primary schools. The commissioners rejected a bill to establish a county system of public schools in 1837, but accepted a similar act of the general assembly two years later. By the new law, commissioners appointed trustees for each school district and the trustees in turn assumed responsibility for providing physical facilities, the apportionment of the meager state funds, and the levying of a school property tax. The plan was used only in those election districts in the county which voted its acceptance.

Schools blossomed all over the area. Those that remained open for six months were designated "full," or "whole," institutions and those operating for a shorter period were called "half" schools. In 1836, sixty-four "whole" schools and one "half" school received funding; by 1859, the numbers had increased to 112 "whole" schools, which received thirty dollars per year from the county, and twenty-two "half" schools. But the establishment of a semiuniform system brought no utopia in education. Too many local children were still denied a chance to obtain even rudimentary schooling. Boys apprenticed to learn the blacksmith, wheelwright, cooper, or brewing profession worked all day. In 1850, a Cumberland newspaper suggested that a night school for apprentices be established. Education would be served and young men would be prevented from spending their evenings "visiting worse places by far!" At best, regular daytime education was academically half-rate. Schools met in one room of the teacher's home. Only the basics—reading, writing, and simple arithmetic—were attempted. The instructor organized the work so that the writing lesson came after lunch, when the family table had been cleared. Normally each child paid fifty cents a term, a sum which doubled by the 1850s. The teachers, elected by popular vote of the people in their district, were a poor lot. For example, one sent a pupil to the local post office with this note: "Please give this boy my male."

A state report concerning education in Allegany County issued in December 1865 made several critical comments. Many of the district's trustees were "illiterate," schoolhouses were "very inferior," teachers were "often ignorant," and the entire system was one "of very bad habits for the children." The account noted that "the general intelligence of the people of the county is at an extremely low ebb." Many could neither read nor write. Surprisingly, as a group, the miners of the Georges Creek region registered a higher rate of literacy than laborers in town, or area farmers.[7]

Whatever their educational deficiencies, county citizens were literate enough to support a growing number of newspapers and interested enough to take enthusiastic part in political campaigns. The excitement generated by national and local elections in the 1820s spilled over into the next decades. The newspapers, the pro-Whig *Civilian* and the Jacksonian organs, the *Maryland Advocate*, and after 1838, the *Alleganian*, continued their attacks on each other. No twentieth century niceties were employed. Whigs or "wiggies" were described in print as elitist "Bigbugs," "Nabobs," "Enemies of the Poor," or "Humbugs." The Jacksonian Democrats were called "Jackanapes," "Jackdams," or "Buffoons." When the Jacksonians claimed that the *Civilian* did not prepare its own editorials, Samuel Charles refuted the accusation, declaring the *Alleganian*'s editorials to be so bad that it was obvious the editor had written them.[8]

Elections in this period were extremely close and campaigns vitriolic. In 1832, the Jacksonians controlled six of ten county commissioners' seats and President Jackson increased his winning majority of 1828 from 115 to 191 votes. Violence occasionally surfaced. During the county election of 1834, the editor of the *Maryland Advocate* was assaulted and an attempt made to destroy the paper's type. In 1836, a year after Cumberland mechanics had endeavored to organize a union, both newspapers sought to win the votes of the laboring class. The Jacksonian, Martin Van Buren, won the presidency but his opponent, William Henry Harrison, carried the county by 221 votes.[9]

The most famous and colorful campaign in the area during the antebellum period came during the presidential election of 1840. At the national level, Whigs hoped to place William Henry Harrison in the White House, and the people of Allegany County did their part. "Young Men's Harrison Meetings" met in every hamlet, while most Van Buren activity was limited to Cumberland. When "Granny" Harrison was sneeringly labeled the hard cider and log cabin candidate, the Whigs eagerly embraced those symbols. A county man who had fought under Harrison during the War of 1812 could not venture out of doors without being "continually cheered and feted with cider." To show their support of "old Tippecanoe" Harrison, Allegany County Whigs, led by Thomas Shriver, constructed a huge ball twelve feet in diameter. Built on a wooden frame and covered with red, white, and blue cloth, the ball had a bar through the center which extended two feet on either side. Ropes were attached to the bar to help keep it in motion and to brake it when traveling downhill. The ball represented, in the eyes of its creators, a political revolution in motion that was to roll on until the Democrats were defeated. Various political slogans graced the oval's surface: "Old Allegany; with heart and soul this ball we roll"; "Farewell dear Van, You're not our man, to guide the ship we'll try old Tip"; "Firm as Allegany's hills, pure as are her mountain rills, we proudly come our motto be, Harrison and liberty." Cumberland Whigs propelled the ball to the Baltimore convention where it was loaned to the New York delegation, who rolled it from Baltimore to Philadelphia to New York City and on to Boston. Newspapers everywhere carried stories of the giant ball from Allegany County.[10]

The climax of the local campaign occurred during the three-day "Grand Harrison Rally" in Cumberland in September 1840. Although travel was still limited to horseback, buggy, wagon, or foot, over 5,000 people poured into Allegany County for the festivities. Those who arrived on September 21 found Cumberland decked out with liberty poles, wreaths, flags, streamers, bunting, and political mottoes. On

Old Allegany you see here,
Who bids you all "be of good cheer."

"The gathering BALL is rolling still,
Sull gathering as it rolls."

With Heart and Soul
This BALL we roll.

May times improve
As on we move.

Farewell, dear Van,
You're not our man.

To guide the ship,
We'll try Old TIP.

Old Allegany!

CONVENTION Sept. 22, 1840.

CUMBERLAND, MARYLAND.

With promises we've long been fed,
But do not like the treat.
We'd rather have a little bread,
And something else to eat.

Firm as Allegany's hills,
Pure as are her mountain rills,
We proudly come—our motto be,
HARRISON AND LIBERTY.

FIRE IN THE MOUNTAINS!

GRAND

Harrison Rally,

IN OLD ALLEGANY!

Come to the rescue!

The friends of HARRISON AND REFORM, in Old Allegany, will hold their GRAND RALLY, in Cumberland, on TUESDAY the 22d day of SEPTEMBER next. The citizens of our own and the adjoining States are cordially invited to come up with us, to the rescue, on this occasion. We expect to give the *GREAT BALL* one mighty turn more on the 22d; nor will it give our friends a greater pleasure to assist us, than it will the Mountain Boys to receive their patriotic aid. We promise a warm Allegany reception—substantial Log Cabin fare, and a rich treat from some of the most distinguished champions of our cause. The Maryland Electors, and many of our ablest friends from Virginia, Pennsylvania and Maryland, will be present with us.

We would invite our friends from Union-town, Somerset, Bedford, Romney, Hagerstown, Frederick, Baltimore, &c. to bring with them their respective Banners.

Our brethren of the Van Buren party, we most respectfully and cordially invite to be present with us on the occasion, that they may hear and judge for themselves, of the many reasons which will be urged, why there is an ABSOLUTE NECESSITY for a CHANGE in the Administration of our Government at this crisis. We hope to satisfy them (if they will favor us with their presence,) that according to the principles with which the old Jackson party, of which they were members, started out—that RETRENCHMENT AND REFORM are DEMANDED at the hands of every patriotic citizen.

The undersigned Committee of Arrangements are now engaged in preparing a FESTIVAL and a LIBERTY POLE for the occasion, as well as every accommodation to make our visiters comfortable. And once and again, in the name of OUR COUNTRY, we bid you all a hearty Allegany welcome!

Thomas Shriver	Samuel Eckles	Alpheus H. Gross
Samuel Athy	William Saylor	J. M. McCleary
Daniel Wineow	Abraham Russell	Thomas Reid
William Lynn	Wm. R. M'Culley	Harrison D. Black
Thomas Rizer	Matthias Rizer	Henry Hudson
H. G. Grieves	Jonathan Butler	Henry B. Osborn
John Gephart	Aza Twigg	Wm. Cappeller
Jas H. Hoblitzell	Gustavus Beall	Fred'k Shipley
H. B. Pigman	Jacob Rizer	Robt. V. Craggs
Thomas A. Healy	John M. Maguire	Wm. L. Lamar
Michael Wilson	Patrick Crowley	Daniel Folck
Geo. W. Haller	Daniel Cresap	R. Worthington
U.R. Lowdermilk	Benjamin Davis	Isaac Rice
R. V Hook	Alexander King	Jesse Hinkle
John Pickell	George C. Perry	Joseph Shriver
Joseph Shumate	J. W. Magruder	Samuel P. Smith
J. J. Johnson	Samuel Charles	Joseph Schuck
George Mattingly	Jacob Bargdoll	Geo. Stubblefield

Committee of Arrangements.

Cumberland, August 26, 1840.

The call which brought five thousand people to Cumberland. Courtesy Maryland Historical Society

Tuesday morning, September 22, a salute was fired at sunrise to awaken the huge throng. After three hours of organizing, a procession of over 3,000 men, led by a forty-piece brass band from Wheeling, began to parade. Delegations from every county election district, including 250 miners from Frostburg and a bagpiper, participated. Representatives from Oldtown dragged a "genuine" log cabin. The Uniontown band led over 500 Pennsylvanians, with separate bodies of marchers coming from Bedford, Somerset, and Fayette counties. Support arrived from Hampshire County, Virginia, and from Hancock, Hagerstown, and Boonsboro in Maryland. Highlighting the parade was the "Great Ball," a new sphere of over twenty feet in diameter which required "60 stout athletic men" to maneuver it. A slogan on the ball's surface rang true: "Ye Allegany boys, come help us roll this Ball, It's grown so very large, we'll need you one and all." The parade proceeded to the "agreeable shade of Mr. Black's grove," one mile out the Oldtown road. There, 500 ladies dressed in white supplied the weary marchers with refreshments. After four hours of orations, the convention adjourned, to reconvene for more talks by candlelight at the "Great Pole" in Cumberland. "Because the spirit had not yet abated," the celebration continued a third day. Hundreds lingered to hear yet more rhetoric and consume yet more spirits before making the trek home.

Despite the success of the Whig rally, the actual vote was close, with Harrison squeezing out a 178 ballot majority in Allegany County. Whigs proclaimed that the margin had been reduced by the "100 spurious illegal votes" from Irish railroad workers. No matter, after twelve years of national victories by the Jacksonians, the Whigs had a winner in William Henry Harrison. The president-elect passed through the county on his way to Washington. A young boy observed a man of gray complexion and hair, appearing feeble in movement, descend from a stagecoach in fierce February weather. The youth wondered about the senselessness of forcing such an old man to travel in winter. Six weeks later, that man, William Henry Harrison, became the first president to die in office.[11]

Much of the intensity and frivolity of 1840 carried on into

the campaigns of 1844 and 1848. The Democrats courted the mechanics' vote, promising them "two dollars a day and roasted beef." Party faithful paraded along county roads carrying a stuffed ox-hide with a "Good Democrat" astride it, carving knife in his hand. The *Civilian* asked the voters to free Allegany County from Democratic tyranny while the *Alleganian* urged its readers "to get the Democracy moving." To promote the national candidacy of Henry Clay, the Whigs arranged a political rally in Cumberland in the summer of 1844. Hundreds of people, many accompanied by live raccoons, flocked to the county seat. An "immaculately" dressed politician, in the midst of a speech, stepped too close to a raccoon, the symbol of his party. As one amused observer reported: "The coon misbehaved in a manner that soiled the finest hat and suit at the rally." The politician in question subsequently switched to the Democratic Party. The Democratic nominee, James K. Polk, squeaked by in the county with a majority of only sixty-seven votes. As president, Polk was repeatedly scourged by local Whigs for his expansionistic politics and heavy-handed conduct of the Mexican War. The *Civilian* charged that the Mexican War was "conceived as much against the Whig Party as against Mexico."[12]

In 1848, nativism, the hatred of immigrants, became a local issue in the Zachary Taylor-Lewis Cass contest for the presidency. Rumors spread among the area's German-Americans that the Whig Taylor was not only bitterly opposed to foreigners but committed to a law requiring a twenty-one year residency for citizenship. The tactic succeeded, with Cass rolling up a large majority in Cumberland which enabled him to overcome a deficit outside the county seat. The congressional race also inspired local interest. The Whig nominee, Thomas Jefferson McKaig of Cumberland, debated his Democratic opponent, William T. Hamilton, over the paramount issue of the day: the tariff. Coal and iron workers turned out to hear the two men argue the merits of free trade versus the protective tariff before large audiences in Frostburg, Mount Savage, Lonaconing, and Eckhart. A fear of economic uncertainty and the belief that a tariff did save or protect jobs helped give McKaig a majority in the mining region. But the charge that McKaig was an aristocrat hurt his overall performance at the polls. Although he carried his county by thirty-eight votes, he narrowly lost neighboring Washington County and missed a seat in the United States Congress by fifty-nine votes. Not satisfied with the victory, the *Alleganian* complained that "a large number of workers" had been deterred from voting, or "induced to vote the wrong ticket," by the fear of being discharged from their jobs.[13]

Their interest in local as well as national elections demonstrated that the area's voters felt an investment in their community, even though many of them were new to the region. Allegany County continued to grow as mining, manufacturing, and expanded commerce attracted permanent residents. But, by mid-century, it began to draw tourists as well. A visitor to Frostburg in 1825 had written the *National Intelligencer* upon his return to the nation's capital, praising Allegany County as "an incomparable region of health and recreation" and wondering why more of official Washington City did not leave the intense summer heat and humidity to rest in the mountains. After the railroad reached Cumberland in 1842, vacationing in the county became infinitely more practical and the numbers of those seeking recreation increased. The valley between the Narrows and the ascent up Red Mountain, with its shade groves, was popularly called the "romantic region." Temperance societies and church revivals claimed camps along this stretch of the National Road. More popular in the eye of the pure tourist of the 1840s was rambling Highland Hall in the village of Frostburg. Some considered it to be the finest vacation hotel between Baltimore and Wheeling. A regular summer visitor recorded this impression: "The site was eligible, the building commodious and elegant, the view from its observatory unsurpassed in any mountain scene this side of Switzerland." Many of the leading families of Baltimore and Washington stayed at the hotel every summer. However, when the Cumberland to Wheeling section of the Baltimore and Ohio Railroad was completed, the stage lines dried up and Highland Hall lost all its winter trade. In 1853, the Catholic Church purchased Highland Hall and remodeled it, and the structure became Saint Michael's Church.[14]

One of Allegany County's most famous tourists during this period was Lord Napier, the British ambassador to Washington during the presidency of James Buchanan. Lord and Lady Napier, their four sons, and a small army of servants under the direction of a distinguished looking English butler, summered in the "Hamill Mansion" in Frostburg. The natural beauty which enchanted the English diplomat caused others to ask why there were so few pictures of the area's splendid scenery. In 1858, the Baltimore and Ohio moved to remedy this omission by sponsoring a special six-car train from Baltimore to Oakland in order to promote western Maryland. Fifty artists made the journey and numerous stops were scheduled to allow for sketching and daguerreotypes.[15]

For decades a popular resort in the county was at Flintstone, or Mountain Vale, as the town was called until the 1830s. Although the cold, warm, and mineral springs there never achieved the fame of Berkeley Springs, Virginia, in the eighteenth century or Bedford Springs, Pennsylvania, in the nineteenth century, they served hundreds of visitors in the antebellum period. Since the turn of the century, families had traveled to the springs, building cabins and pitching tents for a summer sojourn. There among "sublime scenery," one could partake of the waters famous for curing rheumatism and cutaneous diseases and restoring "vigor, elasticity and clearness." By the 1830s, two brick hotels accommodated guests, and in the 1840s, Colonel John Piper operated a popular summer hotel which bore his name. A carriage from Piper's ran daily in the summer to Cumberland to pick up guests arriving on the Baltimore and Ohio Railroad. Guests at Piper's could restore their "weary and overtaxed systems" by indulging in "wholesome air, wholesome food and pure wholesome water." Ten springs served the visitor, including a pungent sulphur stream and a mineral spring of "agreeable taste." The warm springs, one mile above the hotel, remained a constant sixty-eight degrees while an adjacent cold spring registered fifty-three degrees. Flooding in the late 1850s filled the springs with mud and gravel, washed away the bathhouses, and ended the resort era in Flintstone.[16]

A common form of recreation for county citizens was participation in any number of parades and banquets between George Washington's birthday on February 22 and political celebrations in November. Any excuse appeared to be reason enough for festivities, even if it had to be the forty-second anniversary of the Battle of North Point in the War of 1812. These gatherings helped bring the people of various communities and farms together. For example, in April 1840 Frostburg sent her smartly dressed militia, "the Greys," and many private citizens down the mountain to join with the "Cumberland Guards and United Riflemen" and the "Allegany Cavalry" in a parade through the county seat to honor the arrival of spring. On Saint Patrick's Day, 1846, a procession of 600 people marched in Mount Savage, led by the local Catholic priest and a band from Cumberland.[17]

Throughout the Mexican War the county celebrated word of every military victory. After Vera Cruz fell in spring, 1847, the *Alleganian* described events in Cumberland as "the handsomest affair of the kind ever witnessed in the mountain city." With the entire town illuminated, "Captain King's new cavalry company paraded." Military pageants became commonplace by the 1850s. The "Eckhart Artillery," the "Blues" and "German Yeagers" from Frostburg, and the "Guards" and "Continentals" of Cumberland eagerly exhibited their finery and drill work to large crowds of spectators. Often the day ended with fireworks exhibitions staged by a professional "pyrotechnist" brought in from Baltimore.[18]

The county reserved its greatest effort, suitably, for the birthday of the United States. Cannon salutes rang from the mountaintops, drill teams performed, brass bands provided music, and huge crowds gathered in Cumberland to hear a politician deliver "an appropriate address," before all sat down to a full-scale banquet noted for its endless toasts. In 1834, the county's Fourth of July commemoration was held in Frostburg. An observer counted sixty toasts before the festivities were closed on this note: "To the citizens of Frostburg, considerably *elevated* above the people of Cumberland." A newspaper editor, in reviewing past celebrations, pointed out that a common thread in each was "mirth, wit and champagne." He also recalled that "as the sparkling catawba went down, patriotism rose up, and there were usually six speeches being delivered at once." The county recorded two notable exceptions to a noisy Fourth of July. In 1842 and 1848, "dry" observances were held in Cumberland. Protestant and Catholic churches in the area sent delegations to unite in parade with temperance societies. A special attraction in 1842 was the appearance of 200 laborers for the C&O Canal who had "taken the pledge" in Ireland before emigrating to the United States. The Sons of Temperance organized the festivities in 1848. The ceremony began at nine in the morning when local delegations of the sons marched through Cumberland to the east of town for a day of prayers, readings, and speeches, broken up "at proper intervals with odes and songs." But perhaps the Fourth longest remembered was in 1857, when nothing happened. In late June, posters circulated around the county to announce that a Professor Culex, in order to celebrate the Fourth of July, "would perform the wonderful feat of WALKING ON WATER!" All were invited to gather in Cumberland at the canal docks to watch the professor cross the Potomac. Long before the appointed time hundreds of people of all ages and both sexes poured into town to secure a good seat on the riverbank. The Cumberland newspapers estimated that 3,000 were present "to witness the *wonderful event.*" Ten o'clock passed and eleven drew near and still no Professor Culex. As people became impatient, "it was whispered around that *culex* was the Latin word for *mosquito.*" At this point the truth "flashed upon their minds" that they had been bitten by a prankster.[19]

Cumberland was the social hub of the county. There, the possibilities for amusement depended somewhat on one's social class. Mechanics generally favored gambling games and foamy pints of the locally produced "common" beer, while the more affluent citizens attended a seemingly endless round of dinners and dances. So hectic was this schedule in the 1830s that one outsider, exhausted by his recent visit, wrote his sister: "I believe you think of nothing else in Cumberland but parties and frolicking. When do you find time for housekeeping and making butter?" This same lady also busied herself raising funds for the county's first public library, which in 1838, having acquired three hundred books and the name "Mechanics Circulating Library," made novels, biographies, and histories available to the public at a "very moderate" rental.[20]

Some people were attracted by a macabre form of entertainment. A "sensational" murder trial would draw sizeable audiences to the courthouse and huge throngs for the subsequent execution. In October 1829, between four and five thousand people witnessed the hanging of a confessed wife-slayer, George Swearingen, the former sheriff of neighboring Washington County. Six companies of infantry, a horse troop from Bedford, Pennsylvania, five ministers, and the sheriff of Allegany County escorted the prisoner from the jail to the west bank of Wills Creek near the town limit. At the scaffold nearly two hours of hymn singing and "appropriate prayer" elapsed before "the last moment arrived." The interest surrounding Swearingen's execution remained unsurpassed until January 1856 when a German immigrant, Frederick Miller, was hanged for the premeditated murder of two friends. Despite bitter cold and deep snow "thousands upon thousands" of persons gathered in Cumberland "to witness the horrible sight."[21]

Fortunately, there was a variety of entertainment choices. The circus was one of the region's most popular attractions. People flocked to see the many caravans of "strange and wonderful" animals and skilled performers who traveled the National Road in highly decorated wagons. If a circus was not in town, the county seat offered other diversions. By the late 1840s, a visitor to the "Mountain City," as Cumberland's citizens called their town, could patronize the "modern" ice-cream parlor on Baltimore Street or go upstairs above the newspaper office to sit for a "perfect picture" in the new daguerreotype studio. After partaking of a substantial meal, complete with "French" wines, at Barnum's Hotel, one could sit back in the dining room and listen to "Kneass' Celebrated Opera Troupe" present a "grand concert" or smile while "a band of darkies from Baltimore presented nigger minstrels in a scientific manner."[22]

The pinnacle of antebellum cultural progress came on July 10, 1847, with the gala opening in Cumberland of Belvidere Hall, the first real theater in the county. The inaugural performance by the Virginia Serenaders was followed by a season of dramatic offerings, including the *Golden Farmer,* presented by the famed Joseph Jefferson and his company. Among the galaxy of acts to play the Belvidere, family singers were the favorite. For twenty-five cents one could watch such groups as "The Alleganians" or "The Butlers." Clad in long-tailed, bright blue or red waistcoats, and fawn-colored trousers, these performers sang rollicking sentimental American tunes and tragic songs, and acted out impromptu musical sketches characterizing national problems. "Father Kemp's Old Folk's Troupe," dressed in powdered wigs and flowered silk of the colonial era, visited annually. This group often slipped prohibition songs into their repertoire. Most popular of all were the burnt-cork and chalk-mouthed comedians who wisecracked and danced to the brassy music of the minstrel shows. All classes mingled freely in Belvidere Hall as mechanics and bankers, farmers and railroad workers attended the theater. But on occasion a newspaper editor would protest the rowdiness of some in the crowd or complain that the incessant spitting and ever-present smell of raw onions and whiskey tended to upset those in the audience with delicate sensibilities.[23]

Although the language barrier presented a problem for some recent immigrants to the county, many were eager to take in American theater at the Belvidere. By the 1840s, the numbers of new arrivals, most of whom were Irish and Germans, increased daily. Tax rolls added the names of newcomers like John Woltz, Frederick Schmidt, and Rudolph Fogolpole from Germany, and James Kelley and Phillip Clarke from Ireland. These men went to the courthouse to make application for citizenship and then returned three years later to declare an oath to support the Constitution of the United States and "absolutely and entirely renounce and abjure all allegiance and fidelity to every foreign prince, potentate or state sovereignty whatsoever." The census of 1850 designated 5,017 of the county's 22,045 residents as having been born outside the United States.[24]

Many of the foreign-born citizens who settled in the area by mid-century did so by accident. They had landed in Baltimore, the major port farthest inland, and then traveled the pike or railroad to Allegany County. Some who originally intended to push farther west were enticed by the job opportunities available in the region's factories, mines, and shops. To a growing number this certain employment held more allure than an uncertain future beyond the mountains.[25]

The local leaders of the Democratic Party courted the immigrant vote. At election time, their newspaper, the *Alleganian,* printed notices of party rallies and the text of political speeches in both English and German. But not everyone in the county welcomed the newcomers with open arms. The specter of nativism, unfortunately, was evident in western Maryland. Some native Americans resented the recent Irish and German residents because of the clannishness and Catholicism of both groups, the presumed intemperance of the Irish, and the suspected radicalism of the Germans. Many Whigs in the area, called "Whig-Natives" by the *Alleganian,* favored legislation in 1845 requiring naturalized citizens to bring certificates of naturalization to the polls. Believing this stipulation to be a slur, Democrats successfully engineered the repeal of this state law in 1846.[26]

As the numbers of outsiders mounted, signs of tension appeared, especially in Cumberland. Whenever a threat of cholera surfaced, some were quick to blame "the filth . . . in the dwellings of the Emegrants [sic] lately located here" for causing the epidemic. In June 1847, the vestry of Christ's Church (now Saint Paul's English Lutheran), a church founded by Germans in 1794, gave notice to the German-speaking members of the congregation that after October 1, 1848, they could no longer use the church to hold services in an alien tongue. Even the kindest historian of the church admits that "some scars and hurt feelings" resulted. The Whig newspaper, the *Civilian,* warned its readers to be vigilant at election time and to reject any attempts by non-naturalized "loco-foco" Irishmen or Germans to cast a ballot. Often, when a case of drunk and disorderly conduct was discussed in the press, the *Civilian* took pains to label the culprit as Irish or "most likely" from the "shores of Erin." Political meetings of "Sag Nicht" Germans and boisterous Irishmen were always reported to be held in grogshops.[27]

Nativism had been a latent force in Maryland for years before it boiled over and became a power to be channeled into political action. In 1854, some residents of Allegany County became enamored of a new and secret organization, the American Party. A member of this party, when asked about his status, would point to his eyes, then his nose, and then his head to illustrate "Eyes nose nothing," or would whisper, "I know nothing." Thus the members of this organization earned the sobriquet "Know-Nothings." These people were expressing conservative sentiments at a time of rapid social and economic change and ever-increasing sectional animosity. They decried both the influx of foreigners and the supposed abandonment of the purer and simpler standards of America's founders. Some "Know-Nothings," such as the editor of the *Civilian,* even went so far as to criticize men who wore their hair long. Their cry of "Americans shall rule America" was heeded in Cumberland in 1854, when local nativists succeeded in electing a ticket drawn from former Democrats and Whigs. The next autumn, Henry W. Hoffman of Cumberland, the American Party's candidate for Congress, attacked those who misrepresented his party, insisting that "Americans" only wished to protect their country from "illegitimate foreign influences." He did not oppose all outsiders but urged that some controls be enacted on unlimited immigration. Although Hoffman lost Allegany County by thirty-eight votes, he won handily in Washington and Frederick counties and went off to the nation's capital for two years. In 1856, Maryland "Know-Nothings" gave Millard Fillmore his only electoral votes in the presidential race but in the county they lost to the Democrat James Buchanan by a margin of 2,248 to 1,938. Editor George Charles of the *Civilian* blamed the defeat on illegal voting tactics by the Democrats: "boozers, youngsters or illiterate emigrants." He accused them of counterfeiting ballots, using naturalization papers of persons long dead, and generally practicing "mean, low and disgusting tricks." Two years later the *Civilian* charged the Democrats with voting "the sick, the lame, the halt, the blind, the illegal."[28]

Another volatile issue which affected the county during the antebellum era was the question of slavery. The area contained only 792 slaves in 1850, the smallest number of any county in the state. Thus relatively few citizens in the region actively participated in the "peculiar institution." There were some local slave owners, such as Dr. David Lynn, who appeared in court to record a purchase and swear that "one negro girl named Susan Ann, aged about 15 years . . . is a slave for life." A George Blocher visited the same courtroom to pay a five-dollar fee and then swear to "release from slavery, liberate, manumit and set free my negro man Lewis Graham aged 29." But most people in the county remained indifferent to the activities of men like Dr. Lynn or Mr. Blocher. Many regarded slavery as a harmless institution or necessary evil. The opinion generally held was that slaves in the county were well treated and very seldom sold unless, as one chronicler noted, "they became vicious or got to stealing." Yet a study of the Cumberland newspapers reveals frequent sheriff's notices of slaves for sale. One of the largest transactions occurred in Westernport in 1834, when the heirs of John Morrison sold eighteen chattels, including children aged three, two, one, and eight months. The price of slaves increased, with "a colored man 21 years of age" selling for $1,175 in August 1859.[29]

Western Maryland was not completely isolated from agitation by abolitionists. Antislavery advocates frequently passed through the area. Occasionally passions over the slave question would flare up and fights break out among stage or train passengers. But travelers with abolitionist predilections, like a group of Quakers who stopped in Cumberland to visit the free Negro population, were given "a *general* hint to make their stay in town as short as possible." They left the next day.[30]

Because of the county's proximity to the free states, it was a common route for fugitive slaves on their way to freedom. The Cumberland newspapers carried advertisements for runaway chattels and frequent reports of "fugitive darkies" who were lodged in the county jail. Legend tells us that the underground railroad did exist in Allegany County. The "Frostburg Sesquicentennial Souvenir Book," published in 1962, lists three known stations in that city. But few white people in the area involved themselves in "the liberty line." Slaves who escaped from bondage were primarily dependent upon their own resources.[31]

For decades it had been considered "good" politics in the region to stigmatize the black man as "the curse of America" and label one's campaign opponent as soft on slavery. Any association with antislavery was pure political death. In the election of 1856, the Republican candidate for president, John C. Fremont, who ran on a platform to halt the further expansion of slavery, won a total of three votes in Allegany County out of 4,189 ballots cast. That same year the local population applauded Preston Brooks for his vicious physical attack on United States Senator Charles Sumner, a "rank, fanatical abolitionist." The *Civilian* declared that "a few more of the same feather as Mr. Sumner ought to get it next, and perhaps they will." Congressman Henry W. Hoffman lost his bid for reelection because he supported the House of Representatives' censure of Brooks.[32]

Maryland, as a border state, became entrapped on the interlocking issues of slavery and sectionalism as the nation moved toward separation and war. The "Know-Nothing" Party, which saw itself as a "Union" party in 1856, vanished from the national picture shortly thereafter, although it remained active in the state and county until 1860. Local leaders worked to form a "united conservative" movement to combat both abolitionism and secession. Their efforts must have met with some success, for in 1859, a "Union" party elected two delegates to the legislature, a sheriff, and two commissioners. People in the area continued to support the Union, denounce extremism, and pray for peace. Local military companies like the "Cumberland Continentals" still marched through the streets "with drums beating and colors flying," but the editor of the *Civilian and Telegraph* echoed the thoughts of many when he wrote of the soldiers: "Long may they live to enjoy the blessings of health and prosperity . . . and never be forced to face the raking fire of an advancing foe."[33]

In the presidential election of 1860, Abraham Lincoln, the Republican nominee, was the only one of the four candidates who lacked newspaper support in the county. The *Civilian and Telegraph* endorsed John Bell of the Constitutional-Union Party, the Democratic *Alleganian* approved the regular Democrat Stephen A. Douglas, and a new publication, the *Bulletin,* rallied behind John C. Breckinridge, the candidate of the Southern Democrats. Bell won the county with 1,521 votes, Douglas was second with 1,202, Breckinridge third with 980, and the national winner, Lincoln, a poor fourth with only 522 votes. The Democratic *Alleganian* deplored the election results but saw no excuse for separation between the North and South.[34]

There was considerable excitement in Allegany County during the secessionist winter of 1860-1861. On January 17, 1861, representatives of all political parties met in Cumberland to listen to strong "Union" speeches. The group adopted resolutions which called for preserving the nation, acknowledging South Carolina's grievances to be just but her secession not "proper or constitutional," and safeguarding the institution of slavery. In the next month, over five hundred "friends of the Union" paraded by torchlight through the streets of Cumberland. Oratory and parades, however, could not stem the coming of "the brothers' war." War was inevitable and the divisions which had hidden beneath the surface would soon be open.[35]

CHAPTER VI NOTES

1. Will Lowdermilk, *History of Cumberland* (Washington: James Anglin, 1878), pp. 315-25 (hereafter cited as Lowdermilk, *Cumberland*); and J. William Hunt, "Across the Desk," in the Cumberland *Sunday Times,* April 13, 1952 (hereafter cited as Hunt).

2. Lowdermilk, *Cumberland,* pp. 325-29; and John Scharf, *History*

of Western Maryland (Philadelphia: L. H. Everts, 1882), pp. 1381, 1453 (hereafter cited as Scharf, *Western Maryland*).

3. Scharf, *Western Maryland*, pp. 1385, 1451; *Phoenix Civilian*, Nov. 4 and 19, 1833; *Maryland Advocate*, Dec. 17, 1833. One year after the great blaze, many citizens tied black ribbons on their doorknobs to commemorate the destruction of their town. *Phoenix Civilian*, April 14 and Sept. 2, 1834.

4. The *Civilian*, March 13 and April 28, 1828, July 7, 1835, and Feb. 17, 1840; *Maryland Advocate*, May 27, 1834; *Alleganian*, July 3, 1846, and Oct. 9, 1847; *Civilian and Telegraph*, April 12, 1860; and letter of A. A. Browne to Anna Lyons, July 1836, quoted in Hunt, July 28, 1946.

5. *Phoenix Civilian*, July 9, 16, and 30, 1832, and July 9 and 23 and Aug. 6, 1833; *Maryland Advocate*, July 29, 1834; James W. Thomas and T. J. C. Williams, *History of Allegany County Maryland* (Philadelphia: L. R. Titsworth and Co., 1923), I, pp. 245-46 (hereafter cited as Thomas and Williams, *Allegany County*); and Hunt, June 5, 1955.

6. Citizens of Frostburg wanted their own academy. In 1848, the assembly chartered a Frostburg Academy and in 1850, legislation was introduced to divide the annual appropriation evenly between Cumberland and Frostburg. *Alleganian*, Feb. 15 and 22, 1848, and Jan. 19 and 26, 1850. Competition from the free county school system forced Allegany County Academy to close its doors forever in 1929.

7. *Maryland Advocate*, Oct. 3, 1825; the *Civilian*, March 8, 1850; Scharf, *Western Maryland*, pp. 414-15; Gertrude Williams, "History of Education in Allegany County, Maryland, 1798-1900" (M.A. thesis, University of Maryland, 1936), pp. 24, 30, 39-41, 51-57, 67-68, 177; and Katherine Harvey, *The Best Dressed Miners* (Ithaca: Cornell University Press, 1969), p. 29.

8. *Phoenix Civilian*, Sept. 2, 1837; and the *Civilian*, Aug. 8, 1840.

9. After the election of 1832, the *Civilian* turned its columns upside down as a gesture of mourning. The *Civilian*, Oct. 9 and Nov. 20, 1832; *Maryland Advocate*, Sept. 27, 1834; and *Phoenix Civilian*, Oct. 14, 1834, Feb. 25, 1835, and Aug. 13 and 27 and Nov. 12, 1836.

10. *Phoenix Civilian*, March 14 and 21, April 18, and May 2, 1840; and Jacob Brown, *Miscellaneous Writings* (Cumberland: Miller, 1896), p. 62 (hereafter cited as Brown, *Miscellaneous Writings*).

11. The *Civilian*, Sept. 26, Oct. 10 and 17, and Nov. 17, 1840; and Brown, *Miscellaneous Writings*, p. 126.

12. The *Civilian*, July 9, 1842, and Jan. 26, 1843; *Alleganian*, May 22 and Aug. 16 and 23, 1845, May 15 and June 5, 1846; and Brown, *Miscellaneous Writings*, pp. 62-63.

13. Allegany County shared a congressional seat with Washington and Frederick counties, and the nominees from both parties usually were selected from the more populous region to the east. The *Civilian*,

Nov. 17, 1848; *Alleganian,* Nov. 18, 1848; and Thomas and Williams, *Allegany County,* pp. 256-57.

14. *National Intelligencer,* Sept. 25, 1825; *Civilian and Telegraph,* Nov. 13, 1859; *Union,* Sept. 23, 1865; and Scharf, *Western Maryland,* p. 1436.

15. The *Civilian,* Oct. 1, 1850; Thomas H. Taylor to Frostburg Sesquicentennial Committee, May 9, 1962, in *Frostburg Sesquicentennial Souvenir Book* (Frostburg, Md.: The Frostburg Sesquicentennial Committee, 1962); *Alleganian,* June 27, 1857; *Frostburg Gazette,* Dec. 18, 1858; and Hunt, Nov. 11, 1945.

16. Hilleary F. Willison, "History of the Pioneer Settlers of Flintstone, District #3, and Their Descendants" (unpublished typescript, 1910), pp. 11-12, 26 (hereafter cited as Willison, "Pioneer Settlers of Flintstone"); Ele Bowen, *Rambles in the Path of the Steam Horse* (Philadelphia: William Bromwell and William Smith, 1855), pp. 239-42; *Phoenix Civilian,* Aug. 14, 1833; the *Civilian,* Aug. 5, 1856; and Hunt, Feb. 13, 1952.

17. *Civilian and Journal,* July 8, 1856; and the *Civilian,* Feb. 28, 1840, and March 27, 1846.

18. *Alleganian,* April 17, 1847; and the *Civilian,* Dec. 8, 1848, and Aug. 5 and Sept. 12, 1856.

19. *Civilian and Journal,* July 8, 1856; the *Civilian,* July 18, 1828, and July 7, 1857; *Phoenix Civilian,* July 8, 1834; *Alleganian,* July 8, 1848; and Hunt, July 2, 1961.

20. A. A. Browne to Anna Lyons, June 5, 1835, quoted in Hunt, June 28, 1946; *Maryland Advocate,* Dec. 17, 1833; and *Phoenix Civilian,* Aug. 25 and Sept. 29, 1838.

21. The *Civilian,* Oct. 2, 1829; and Lowdermilk, *Cumberland,* p. 383.

22. Philip Jordan, *The National Road* (Indianapolis: Bobbs-Merrill, 1948), pp. 333-34 (hereafter cited as Jordan, *National Road*); *Phoenix Civilian,* Oct. 29, 1833; *Alleganian,* Oct. 18, 1845, and Aug. 19 and Nov. 25, 1848; and the *Civilian,* Nov. 17, 1848.

23. Jordan, *National Road,* pp. 336-37, 341; the *Civilian,* Nov. 17, 1848, and Aug. 25 and Sept. 1, 1857; Lowdermilk, *Cumberland,* p. 60; *Alleganian,* Aug. 16, 1845; and Richard C. Wade, *The Urban Frontier* (Chicago: University of Chicago Press, 1972), p. 259.

24. Allegany County, Alien Docket, U.R. No. 2, pp. 7, 14, 15, 72; United States Census, 1850, Allegany County.

25. Dieter Cunz, *The Maryland Germans* (Princeton: Princeton University Press, 1948), pp. 384-85.

26. Cumberland *Alleganian,* Sept. 20, 1845, Feb. 20, 1846, and Sept. 23 and Oct. 28, 1848. When the Mexican War began in 1846, German-Americans in Cumberland demonstrated their "Americanism" by organizing a German company. Cumberland *Alleganian,* May 15, 1846.

27. *Maryland Advocate*, July 29, 1834; Hixon T. Bowersox, *History of St. Paul's English Lutheran Church* (Cumberland: Monarch Printing Co., 1944), p. 104; the *Civilian*, Nov. 10, 1848, and Oct. 21, 1856. Allusions to unseemly behavior by the Irish are scattered throughout many issues of the *Civilian*. In another church split, the German Catholics separated from Irish-controlled Saint Patrick's parish. On July 4, 1848, the cornerstone for Saints Peter and Paul's was laid.

28. Richard Walsh and William Fox, editors, *Maryland, A History, 1632-1974* (Baltimore: Maryland Historical Society, 1974), pp. 304, 305, 311, 314-17; the *Civilian*, May 13 and Nov. 4, 11 and 25, 1856, and May 18, 1859; and Lowdermilk, *Cumberland*, p. 383.

29. United States Census, 1850; Allegany County Land Records, Book 4, dated April 4, 1849, pp. 884-85; dated May 2, 1848, pp. 224-25; Willison, "Pioneer Settlers of Flintstone," p. 25; *Maryland Advocate*, Sept. 16, 1834; and *Civilian and Telegraph*, Aug. 4, 1859.

30. Jordan, *National Road*, p. 210; and *Alleganian*, Sept. 27, 1845.

31. *Frostburg Sesquicentennial Souvenir Book*, no page number; Larry Gara, *The Liberty Line* (Lexington: University of Kentucky Press, 1967), p. 18; the *Civilian*, Aug. 3, 1856, and Sept. 1, 1857.

32. *Phoenix Civilian*, Sept. 3, 1836; the *Civilian*, May 27 and Nov. 11, 1856; and *Civilian and Telegraph*, Sept. 29, 1859.

33. *Civilian and Telegraph*, March 31, April 14 and 21, and Nov. 10, 1859.

34. The *Civilian and Telegraph* did endorse Lincoln as a second choice. *Civilian and Telegraph*, Aug. 2, 1860. Lincoln's vote in the county represented nearly one-fourth of his state total. It came primarily from the pro-tariff mining districts. *Civilian and Telegraph*, Nov. 15, 1860; and Democratic *Alleganian*, Nov. 10, 1860.

35. Lowdermilk, *Cumberland*, pp. 389-91.

VII

A COUNTY AT WAR, 1861-1865

Cumberland's storefronts were barricaded, her children had been sent to relatives and friends in the countryside, the local militia unit, the Continentals, was uniformed and primed for action at the city's edge, and the bank was surrounded by a hastily organized "Home Guard" of assorted muskets and pitchforks. Less than two weeks after the firing by Confederate forces on Fort Sumter in mid-April 1861, the subsequent call by Lincoln for 75,000 troops to quell an insurrection, and the assault on Union soldiers by a Baltimore mob, the war had come to Allegany County. Information had reached Cumberland that "a large band of lawless persons from some direction" was preparing to march on the city and plunder its riches. Although none of the mysterious outlaws showed up that day, the area remained rife with dissent between Unionists and secessionists.[1]

In the months between the separation of South Carolina from the Union in December 1860 and the first bloodshed in April 1861, citizens of the county debated what Maryland's role should be if war was declared between the North and the South. Public meetings and demonstrations, including torchlight parades, were held throughout the county to debate the question. Men billing themselves as "Friends of the Union" commiserated with the South's complaint of the North's hostility to the South, but strongly condemned those who would dissolve "this glorious Union." Other groups of "Conditional Unionists" asked that Maryland remain neutral in any war and thus not compromise her honor by either aiding or subduing the seceding states.[2]

During this period, two remarkable men appeared in the

county to plead for their section. Congressman Roger Pryor came from Virginia to Cumberland to "fire the Southern heart," while Francis Thomas, ex-governor of Maryland, emerged from his hermit's retreat in the glades to visit towns and villages to speak for the Union. These men only exacerbated the tension. The Reverend A. T. Weddell of Cumberland has left a poignant observation on the effects of this uncertainty on the region. Public discussion now affected private relationships. Old friends became alienated, visits and receptions were canceled, and the sermons and prayers of ministers were scrutinized for evidence of political sympathies. Miners in Vale Summit stood guard to prevent the removal of a "Union flag," and fistfights became commonplace in the brickyards of Mount Savage, where secessionist feeling was strong among the Irish laborers.[3]

The United States government perceived the county to be Unionist though "heavily sprinkled with mischievous secessionists." Young men flocked to join both armies, with the majority serving under the Stars and Stripes. Two days after Lincoln's first call for troops, Lonaconing had formed its own company, begun regular drills, and telegraphed the Secretary of War in Washington for marching orders. Throughout the war, Allegany County stood highest of all Maryland counties in exceeding her draft quota to the Union. When a draft was ordered in October 1862 with a quota of 872 men, it was revealed that 1,463 men had already volunteered. Before the war's end, seventy-nine local men were commissioned officers by action in Washington. One enlistee, Ransom Powell, left the mines in Eckhart and joined up at age thirteen. By early 1865, the county was paying $200 to add to the state's $300 bounty for enlistees or drafted men. Cumberland still consistently filled her quota, but drafts were required in Mount Savage, Westernport, and the mining hamlets around Frostburg.[4]

Because of Maryland's uncertain status as a border slave state, many citizens in the mining regions joined Pennsylvania units. Andrew Roy, a Union volunteer himself, recalled that the Tenth Pennsylvania Volunteers was raised from "stalwart republican" miners from the Vale Summit-Frostburg region.

Other citizens enlisted in the Second and Third Maryland Regiment Volunteer Infantry, Potomac Home Brigade. Of the ten companies of the Second Regiment which were organized between August and October 1861, nine came from Allegany County. Companies E, H, and K were from Cumberland; A was recruited at Lonaconing, B at Oldtown, C at Frostburg, D at Piedmont-Westernport, G at Mount Savage, and I from the rest of Allegany County. Five of the ten companies enrolled in the Third Regiment between October 1861 and April 1862 were composed of area enlistees. The Second Regiment saw service under Generals Benjamin Kelley and Frederick Lander in the Army of West Virginia. It participated in skirmishes against Stonewall Jackson when the Confederates threatened Hancock in January 1862. After a year on the West Virginia frontier, the Second spent 1864 on duty in the Valley of Virginia under General David Hunter. By war's end, the Second Regiment had participated in twenty-three skirmishes and battles. The Third Regiment served on the upper Potomac, fell captive at the siege of Harpers Ferry in September 1862, was paroled and exchanged, and then placed on railroad guard duty until July 1864, when it fought at the Battle of Monocacy. The Third followed General Hunter in the valley against Jubal Early, and finished the war under the command of General Philip Sheridan.[5]

There were no locally organized Confederate military units to match the many legally sponsored companies and brigades formed in the county to fight for the United States. So hundreds of Southern sympathizers from the county joined Confederate regiments organized elsewhere in Maryland, or crossed the Potomac into Virginia and enlisted under the Stars and Bars. Local people served in cavalry and guerrilla units, with many following the heralded Harry Gilmor, Turner Ashby, or the McNeills. Throughout the war, Cumberland newspapers sporadically carried notices of Confederate enlistees who had been killed or wounded, captured, or "returned home." And whenever a Confederate raiding party appeared in the vicinity, the next issues of the newspapers would note that several youngsters were missing from their homes and were presumed to have joined the rebels.[6]

After the initial war scare, the county settled into an uneasy period. In all communities a sense of insecurity and mistrust prevailed, and fresh rumors surfaced daily, the most startling story being that staunchly Unionist Bedford and Somerset counties, across the Mason-Dixon line, were suspicious of their neighbors to the south. The mayor of Cumberland squelched this rumor by issuing a proclamation "to the citizens of Pennsylvania" assuring them that "a peaceful relation still exists between Pennsylvania and Maryland." Both county newspapers, the *Civilian and Telegraph* and the *Alleganian,* urged moderation on the populace, the former admonishing its readers to respect the persons and property "of the most obnoxious" from "assault and injury." But the same paper printed a warning to "our secessionist friends" that lawless activity could not be tolerated. Town dwellers were urged to plant gardens, and farmers to sow "with a liberal hand every foot they can possibly tend." And subscribers were told that the first treatment for a gunshot wound is "a little stimulant and plenty of cold water dressings," advised what to put in a soldier's kit, and warned about how much to pay for a good sword.[7]

The mayor's race in Cumberland in May 1861 focused on the war. The "True Blue Unionist" candidate, Colonel C. M. Thurston, defeated the incumbent, Jacob Humbird, a man "generally recognized as a secessionist." Oratory was fierce, and a huge American flag was strung across Baltimore Street, where it remained for months. Mass meetings continued to be held almost nightly, but those of Southern sympathizers usually ended in confusion because of an inability to resolve the question of leaving the Union.[8]

A slumping economy was everywhere in evidence. Traffic on the canal and the railroad was periodically halted. Most commerce, including the mail, fell back on the long-neglected wagon road from Cumberland to Baltimore. Local industries were shuttered for lack of business, and unemployment increased when the railroad workshops were silenced and the mining output trickled to a halt.[9]

Confederate forces had seized Harpers Ferry, Martinsburg, Winchester, and Romney, and Union troops controlled Grafton when Cumberland became an occupied city. On a foggy Monday morning, the tenth of June, the city awoke to find its main thoroughfare clogged with "hoosiers in big gray breeches." These were colorfully dressed Union soldiers commanded by Colonel Lew Wallace (the postwar author of *Ben Hur*). The Eleventh Indiana Regiment, uniformed in Zouave costumes of contrasting reds, blues, and grays, soon attracted "the entire tenantry of the town" to watch it perform its habitual double-time march to an encampment near Rose Hill Cemetery.[10]

To ease the anxiety of the county residents, Wallace's force worked to build up the confidence of the people. Discourse was encouraged between civilians and soldiers, and frequent military concerts and marches entertained the public. But military occupation was now a fact of life. As one man noted: "Soldiers meet you at every step." The political climate changed. An attempt was made to ban secessionist sentiment, and a roundup and arrest of suspected Southern sympathizers began which would stretch over four years. A "hurrah for Jeff Davis" could bring the provost marshal from Cumberland to any area of the county, and common newspaper headlines were "Arrested upon the Charge of Treason," "More Arrests," or "Another Arrest." Most of those seized were marched to Cumberland, made to swear an oath of support for the government of the United States, and then released. Some, including such notables as State Representative Josiah H. Gordon and State Senator Thomas Jefferson McKaig, were imprisoned. McKaig served time in federal prisons in Baltimore and Columbus, Ohio.[11]

Cumberland was a strategic point all through the Civil War, but most critically so in the early months of the conflict. Its location on the Potomac, the importance of the Baltimore and Ohio Railroad and the Chesapeake and Ohio Canal, its turnpike connections with the South Branch Valley and into the north by Bedford or Uniontown routes, and its gateway position to the West, all combined to make it a highly desirable location to the Federal government. In four years, no major battle would be fought in the county, but the all-important struggle to maintain the railroad from Wheeling to Washington centered on the Mountain City. From Wallace's arrival in Cumberland in June 1861 until the mustering out and transporting home of thousands of troops in the summer of 1865, the Baltimore and Ohio figured in Lincoln's grand strategy. During the course of the war, Generals Wallace, Robert F. Shenck, Benjamin F. Kelley, George C. Crook, and Franz Sigel served in Cumberland, and all were frustrated with their inability to keep the Baltimore and Ohio open. Long and difficult to hold, this lifeline of Union supply offered an easy target for Southern guerrillas.

On his way to western Maryland, Wallace had learned that a force of Confederates stationed in Romney, only twenty-eight miles from Cumberland, was able to move at will against the railroad. With 500 men, he took the train to Piedmont and then marched all night to Romney. The town was cleared of rebels with a minimum of difficulty and the June 11, 1861, "raid on Romney" hailed as a great achievement in those very early days of the war. A week later the Confederates burned the railroad bridge at New Creek (Keyser), and early on the morning of June 19 messages reached Cumberland that 5,000 men were marching against the city. The news spread like wildfire, and "excitement and consternation were almost without limits"; bells were ringing everywhere, and the streets filled with people. One message after another arrived saying that the enemy was nearer. Soon martial music was heard on Baltimore Street. "Defense was the word." The Continentals and Home Guard were under arms and the Zouaves marched just beyond town on the Bedford Road to take up positions. Messengers were sent in all directions to alert the people and ask for help. The "true men of Frostburg," responding to a telegram, raised 100 men within twenty minutes, and brass band blaring, they marched down the mountain to aid their neighbors. Other troops arrived from Grantsville, and from Centerville, Wellersburg, and Bedford, Pennsylvania. But no Confederates came to town. By late evening, calm prevailed, but not before agitators had forced the Redemptorist Brothers at Saints Peter and Paul to open their monastery for a fruitless search for a cache of Confederate weapons.[12]

Wallace, unable to secure definite information about enemy activities and to forestall any attack on Cumberland, decided to move a scouting party into the Confederate-held area of neighboring Hampshire County, Virginia. (West Virginia had not yet broken away from Virginia.) Eleven miles east of Cumberland, along and near the railroad, the Zouaves scattered the rebel force after a "bloody and desperate" fight. Back in Cumberland, the Union troops received their first pay when Joseph Shriver, president of the First National Bank, loaned Colonel Wallace $10,000 for salaries.[13]

The pressure in Cumberland only increased when the Indiana Zouaves received marching orders on July 7, struck their tents, and headed east. Their vacant camp was filled by two Pennsylvania regiments, and from that date until April 1865, Union troops continuously filtered in and out of Cumberland. Evidences of tension in the county were newspaper reports that seminarians from Saints Peter and Paul had been mistaken for a Confederate scouting party and fired upon, sniper fire had been directed at travelers on the canal, the Confederates had arrested a Unionist farmer in Oldtown, and "secessionist vandals" had sabotaged canal culverts and destroyed railroad bridges and culverts between Piedmont and Lonaconing. The culmination came with a riot in downtown Cumberland in August. A huge crowd gathered on Baltimore Street to hear Francis Thomas, then serving in the National Congress, cheer on the Union cause. His speech was interrupted first by jeers from Confederate sympathizers and then by a gigantic free-for-all. After disposing of the hecklers, the "True Blue Unionists" descended upon the office of the *Alleganian,* a newspaper that had repeatedly urged moderation toward the South. The mob smashed the newspaper's furnishings and type, and hurled its press from a second-story window. Its competitor, the staunchly Unionist *Civilian and Telegraph,* primly noted in its next issue that the *Alleganian* was out of business. (Nearly three years later, in May 1864, the *Civilian and Telegraph* would announce the resuscitation of the *Alleganian* and call it "much improved" after its "long rest.") Three days after the destruction of the newspaper, the Baltimore *Sun* reported news of an impending attack on Cumberland and the concomitant roundup and deportation of "prominent secessionists" because "their presence could no longer be tolerated."[14]

Periodically throughout the war, county citizens would be exiled from their homes. The usual reason for banishment was the suspicion that persons with relatives in the Confederate Army could serve as a source of information to them from within the Union lines around Cumberland. Such suspicion was not always unfounded; an underground mail service operated continually in Cumberland during the war, the favorite "post office" being a store on Baltimore Street. The diary of Priscilla McKaig, wife of a prominent Cumberland educator and attorney, William Wallace McKaig, details the events surrounding the commandeering of her husband's office and the seizure of the family residence for use as a Union headquarters. The mother of two sons in the Confederate Army, Mrs. McKaig was ordered into exile by General David Hunter, who commanded the Federal Department of West Virginia under whose jurisdiction Allegany County fell. On July 11, 1864, her house was surrounded by military guard, and its inhabitants given twenty-four hours to depart. She wrote on July 12: "Slept none last night and feel miserable this morning. Can't get word to or from William. . . . My husband away, my clothes wet in the washtubs and my youngest son in a distant school."

Accompanied by her sister-in-law (also an accused Southern sympathizer) and four children, Mrs. McKaig was taken under military escort to Romney, where she began three months of wandering in the South Branch Valley. By September the weary traveler had exhausted most of her financial resources; while banished, she had received from a dealer in exchange only $600 in United States greenbacks for $3,000 in Confederate money. With cooler weather approaching, Mrs. McKaig wrote to General Kelley in Cumberland for a permit to have winter clothes sent from the city, and she asked that her exile end. On October 10, she received the long-hoped-for news that her sentence was suspended, and three days later her party returned to Cumberland. She recorded the event: "Mary Patterson met us below town and said Union personnel still occupied our home. We drove up Union Street through the alley by our house. There I met again with my dear husband, so filled with emotion that he could hardly speak."[15]

As an anchor to the Baltimore and Ohio Railroad, Cumberland held a vital role in protecting the line. Early in the war, the county seat became the headquarters for both the District of Cumberland and the Railroad Department of the Department of West Virginia. As such, it became the nerve center for all railroad defensive operations between Harpers Ferry and Parkersburg. Knowing the value of the Baltimore and Ohio and its threat to the Southern cause if it were successfully used to transport troops from the Ohio Valley east to Washington, Confederate raiders continually besieged the railroad, derailed its trains, destroyed boxcars, and dismembered its telegraph lines. From June 14, 1861, until the end of March 1862, no through trains moved between Baltimore and Wheeling and at irregular intervals until April 1865 there were serious interruptions to traffic. For example, the wooden bridge at North Branch, only a few miles east of Cumberland, was burned on May 28, 1861. On June 18, 1863, its replacement, an iron span, was destroyed, and in February 1864, Confederate raiders burned twelve trestle logs and again made the bridge impassable. Five months later, Union guards from a nearby blockhouse repulsed an enemy attack.[16]

As the Union Army grew in size, better protection was given the railroad, particularly in the Cumberland area. The District of Cumberland, an organization recommended by Secretary of War Edwin Stanton, was set up in March 1862 with three regiments of infantry and one cavalry troop, a total of 2,900 men. Also operating in the area during the spring of 1862 was the Second Regiment, Potomac Home Guard. Sensitive to criticism by the Cumberland press, these local recruits protected the South Branch bridge below Oldtown. The railroad's most superb feat in transporting troops came in September 1863 when 20,000 troops were moved in eleven days from the east to reinforce the demoralized army of General W. S. Rosecrans after the loss at Chickamauga in Tennessee. For three days there was an almost constant succession of troop trains moving through Cumberland—a sight which left the local population somewhat dazed.[17]

The proximity of Confederate forces in Romney always unnerved the Union command in Cumberland. General Kelley surprised a rebel force in October 1861 and marched 400 prisoners back to Cumberland. By winter, 1862, southern forces under Stonewall Jackson had retaken Romney and planned to destroy bridges all the way into Cumberland. Severe weather canceled this strategy, but Allegany County remained jittery. In March 1862, the Union command telegraphed Washington that Cumberland was bracing for an attack by the cavalry of Turner Ashby and the infantry of Jackson. None came. Again in September panic swept over the area when Lee's troops crossed into Maryland on the way to fight McClellan's army at Antietam. At the suggestion of Governor Bradford, a city brigade for "home defence" organized in Cumberland. But once immediate danger passed, the unit disbanded.[18]

In mid-June, 1863, the Union braced for a major onslaught by Robert E. Lee's Army of Northern Virginia. President Lincoln issued a proclamation asking for new enlistments and he indicated that the Confederates hoped "to make inroads into Maryland, West Virginia, Pennsylvania and Ohio." Unknown to the citizens of Allegany County, General G. K. Warren, chief engineer of the defending Army of the Potomac, considered Green Spring, a spot fifteen miles southeast of Cumberland, to be a probable point of Lee's crossing of the Potomac. If this location were used, Cumberland would be an early objective of the invading army.

On June 15, the Union Army evacuated the Cumberland area and concentrated all forces in the county across the Potomac at New Creek to counter Lee. The Confederates, fresh from a victory at Winchester, did march into Maryland and Pennsylvania on the way to Gettysburg, but they crossed the Potomac at Williamsport. Left unprotected, Cumberland gave way to hysteria. The Baltimore and Ohio Railroad removed its rolling stock and light machinery from the city, and merchants sent wagonloads of goods north to Bedford. The excitement continued all day; signs of the invading army were expected hourly, but that day no Confederates appeared.

The next day groups of strangers were spotted on Williams Road as they approached Cumberland. A few shells fired into the city preceded the arrival of two "graybacks" with a flag of truce. The invaders, knowing the city was vacant of soldiers, met with the acting mayor, V. A. Buckley, and a deputation of citizens. A note, signed by Colonel John D. Imboden, was handed to Buckley. A surrender "as an act of humanity" was demanded and received, and no blood was shed. About 350 of Imboden's cavalry, several of whom were from the county, moved into Cumberland where they tore down telegraph lines, dismantled some railroad tracks, and requisitioned the few horses still in town. The invaders were primarily interested in purchasing hats, boots, shoes, clothing, and food, for which they paid in Confederate scrip. Aware that a large Union force was at New Creek, the Confederates stayed only a few hours before leaving. Shortly after the "capture of Cumberland" had ended, a detachment from New Creek stormed back into town and caught some of Imboden's men who had tarried to visit with friends and relatives. No one had been harmed in Cumberland but a farmer near Murley's Branch was killed when he fired upon the fleeing Confederates. The city remained tense as rebel scouts were spotted a few miles from Cumberland. And for a few weeks a pass was required from the provost marshal before one could leave Cumberland. Soon, however, the excitement abated. Citizens resumed normal routines while they read fictitious, or greatly exaggerated, versions of the raid reprinted in the local papers. The Richmond *Enquirer* told of "millions of dollars worth of damage done at Cumberland" and Baltimore and Pittsburgh papers dolefully announced a great disaster in Cumberland.[19]

Bands of Confederate raiders continued to penetrate the county at will and strike the railroad and the canal. Among the many citizens who deplored the Union's inability to protect transportation lines was A. C. Greene, a director of the Chesapeake and Ohio Canal and also a superintendent of the Borden Mining Company. Greene believed that the only sure protection for the canal was for heavy rains to keep the Potomac "unfordable" by Confederates. Only then could the coal companies do any business.[20]

During early spring, 1864, renewed threats of invasion rocked Cumberland. On one occasion General Kelley called in reinforcements from Pennsylvania, and on another he marched his army a mile east of the city to a hill overlooking the town, to form a battle line. In March, Major General Franz Sigel, assigned command of the Department of West Virginia, chose Cumberland as his base of operations. Sigel promised "to defend the city" and he had a fort built on the hill near Williams Road. Six weeks later Sigel departed, and General Kelley returned to his old post. A newspaper editor complained that Kelley's force was too small to "amount to much either of offence or defence."[21]

Although Allegany County was spared the horror of any major engagements during the war, the Battle of Folck's Mill, fought on August 1 and 2, 1864, is important for what did not happen to Cumberland and the Georges Creek mines. On July 31, the city was again panic-stricken when word arrived that Confederate troops under General John McCausland, fresh from the previous days' raiding and burning of Chambersburg, Pennsylvania, had reached Hancock and were determined to march on Cumberland. Their objective was to interrupt traffic on the Baltimore and Ohio, sabotage coal mines, and destroy tipples. Rumor (later proved unfounded) placed other rebel forces advancing on the city by way of Bedford. Wild excitement prevailed, and at a mass meeting over two hundred citizens volunteered to assist the undermanned garrison commanded by General Kelley.

Defenders dug trenches on Fort Hill and three miles from town along the Baltimore Pike overlooking Naves Crossroads. Troops were concentrated on the heights west of Folck's Mill, and other hilltops were covered with hundreds of spectators anxious to view the expected conflict. Initial scouting reports told of a line of Confederates over one mile long.

Trees were felled across the road to slow their advance. Even so, shortly after noon on August 1, advance units of McCausland's force of 3,000 reached positions west of Martins Mountain and occupied the eastern heights overlooking the grist and sawmills of Folck's farm. By late afternoon, additional Confederate units had arrived and drawn fire from Kelley's men. Surprised, the rebels took shelter behind the mills, under the Evitts Creek bridge, and behind several farms. Others took up positions in the surrounding woods, with shells from their artillery occasionally reaching Cumberland.

Apparently stalemated, McCausland and his subordinate, General Bradley Johnson, were uncertain in their estimation of the strength of the Union defenders and fearful that a retreat route across the Potomac might be sealed. Major Harry Gilmor was ordered to find a back road to the river by which the Confederates could march to the South Branch Valley and safety. In the predawn hours of the second, Gilmor reached Oldtown. At daylight Johnson's brigade joined Gilmor's small force in attacking Union infantry guarding the bridge. Joined by McCausland and the main Confederate force, the southerners fought a bitter skirmish before crossing the Potomac. After overwhelming a Union force at Green Spring and destroying some Baltimore and Ohio track, they hastened to Moorefield. Although the Battle of Folck's Mill and its aftermath produced few casualties on either side, it was important in that it saved the county from invaders who were bent on devastating the area's mines and transportation arteries.[22]

Actual military threats against Cumberland and the coal region were minor in comparison with those experienced in other areas. For example, neighboring Romney changed hands fifty-six times during the war. Yet, the War Between the States did alter much of the routine in county life. The conflict brought with it a heavy demand for coal. But the destruction of Baltimore and Ohio and Chesapeake and Ohio beds by Confederates and periodic flooding caused transportation disruptions resulting in unemployment. Adding to this problem, in 1861, the Federal government hindered canal shipments by seizing boats "on the supposition they would be useful to the military." As the war dragged on, however, the Union Navy drew heavily on "Cumberland coal," and every effort was made to keep transportation arteries open. During flush times, fifteen to twenty loaded boats departed daily from Cumberland.[23]

Any prolonged shutdown on either the canal or the railroad created a vacuum in Allegany County. Dependent once again on the "old two-horse stage system," citizens complained that merchandise from Baltimore took a month, and even letters and newspapers a week, in transit. Indeed, George T. Knorr, editor of a new weekly paper, the *Union,* lamented in the fall of 1862 that "Baltimore, for the time being, might as well be on the other side of the ocean." Inevitably, in the absence of hard news, rumors filled the gap. Periodically the Cumberland papers would announce that Jefferson Davis was "going blind" or was "fatally ill."[24]

In the early days of the war some wounded and sick federal soldiers were brought to the county to recuperate. Billeted in Cumberland's halls, churches, and warehouses, and attended by local physicians, their numbers had grown to 500 in December 1861. By spring, 1862, over 1,200 disabled soldiers overburdened the existing facilities. Cumberland women sponsored "sanitary fairs" to raise hospital funds, and they often offered home cooking to convalescing soldiers, but little was done to upgrade accommodations. An inspector for the surgeon general's office reported filthy bed sacks, unemptied bedpans, a scarcity of medical supplies, and unlimited confusion. Additional hospital space became a high priority, and a larger facility was secured eight miles west and 1,000 feet above Cumberland in Clarysville. This property, the estate of the late Gerard Clary, included seventeen buildings and a large amount of land to house new structures. Yet, overflow from Clarysville still filled fifteen scattered locations in Cumberland, and another hospital in Mount Savage also housed "a large number of troops." Bread was baked at Cumberland and sent along the National Road to Clarysville. Regardless of the nature of injury, all patients received the same diet. With the railroads frequently disabled, local citizens volunteered their carriages and farm wagons to transport convalescents.[25]

Being a garrison town provided both advantages and disadvantages for Cumberland. Military protection was nearby, but many people, including politicians and newspaper editors, were unhappy with some of the soldiers, especially those General Kelley placed in authority. Laments were heard about the "curses and horrible oaths" of military men "on our streets." Other citizens shuddered at what was to become the county's greatest wartime entertainment—military executions. These grim events, described in graphic detail in the press, drew crowds of several thousand spectators. "Burlesque Dress Parades" in which the strutting soldiers wore all manner of costumes—chimney sweep, beggar, Indian, "portly" gentleman, or scarecrow—were frequently staged to entertain the townspeople. For some, the war brought romance. Dashing cavalry officers, dressed in dark blue with contrasting bright yellow braid, picnicked on mountain slopes with pretty young ladies. Even the overbearing General Kelley fell prey to cupid. Shortly after the war ended, he married Cumberland's most eligible beauty.[26]

Juvenile delinquency was on the rise in wartime Cumberland. The editor of the *Union* thundered against "rowdyism" and fussed that "gangs of half-grown boys are permitted to annoy the peaceful inhabitants, *ad libitum*." The most frequent complaints dealt with minor theft (including the new sign over the *Union* newspaper office), false alarms for the fire companies, and disrupting performances at the local opera house. One of the more devilish pranks occurred six weeks after Imboden's raid, when the nervous town was awakened by mysterious cannon fire at half past one in the morning. The birth of a "Sunday School Association" to reform the "three-fourths of the youth in our community not in attendance at any Sabbath School" evidently produced few results. But who could blame youth when many of their elders frequented an ever-increasing number of taverns, gambling dens, and houses of ill-repute? Periodically, the community launched crusades against these evils, but the odds against abolishing sin were long. Occasionally a victory

Baltimore Street, looking west from Centre Street, in Cumberland, 1864. Courtesy Herman and Stacia Miller Collection

was recorded. During the summer of 1863, residents of Decatur Street vexed "by night and by day by continuous disturbances at a house of bad repute" took the law into their own hands and pulled the house down. The temperance movement in the county literally disappeared during the war. In September 1864, the first meeting "in years" was held in

Cumberland and a new chapter of the Sons of Temperance, "an institution which this community particularly stands in need of," was formed.[27]

A commonplace sight to anyone in Cumberland were the train cars of rebel prisoners passing through town on their way to camps in Ohio and Illinois. A unique opportunity to see soldiers in gray was to attend one of the banquets or dances sponsored in Cumberland by Phi Kappa Sigma Fraternity. Because so many of Kelley's officers were members of that fraternity, they formed an alumni chapter and sponsored parties to unite fraternity brothers (temporarily) in both the Confederate and the Union armies. An invitation to soldier members, Northern and Southern, dated June 5, 1863, reads as follows:

> You are respectfully invited
> to attend an evening party to be
> held at the St. Nicholas Hotel,
> Cumberland, Md., on the 9th of
> June, 1863, given by and in
> honor of the Phi Kappa Sigma
> Fraternity of Cumberland.

The archives of the national fraternity record many similar social events held during the war years by the Cumberland alumni chapter.[28]

Although proportionally few in number, slaves remained chattels in Allegany County until slavery was officially abolished in 1865. In December 1862, two months after the Emancipation Proclamation freed slaves in the Confederacy, two slaves were sold in Cumberland. And in November 1863, an "aged free colored man," James Harris, was sentenced to six years and six months by a local judge for aiding his own children in their escape from bondage. In January 1864, the *Civilian and Telegraph* reported all five county delegates to be "square on the mark" when they voted with the majority in the Maryland House of Delegates to call a constitutional convention to abolish slavery in the state. These same delegates reflected the wishes of their county when they announced that they favored "immediate unconditional emancipation without state compensation." But they had no de-

Union encampment during the Civil War on Camp Hill, Cumberland, now the site of Allegany High School. Courtesy Herman and Stacia Miller Collection

sire for Negro equality "at the ballot-box, in the jury-box, on the witness stand or elsewhere." When freedom did come, the farms of the county were emptied of slaves as most of the blacks cleared out "bag and baggage" and headed for Cumberland, Bedford, and other towns "carrying their goods upon their backs." At his Borden's Mine farm, William Ward, one of the area's largest slaveholders, gave each of his twenty-nine emancipated chattels a new suit and entertained them at a dinner to commemorate their new status.[29]

One of the most colorful events of the entire Civil War transpired in Cumberland less than two months before the struggle ended. Although militarily insignificant, the dead-of-night kidnapping of Generals George Crook and Benjamin Kelley from their hotel beds stands as one of the most audacious acts of the war.

By early spring, 1865, it was obvious to most Southerners that their cause was doomed. Yet guerrilla fighters in the South Branch Valley along the upper Potomac River still operated at will against the Union. One of the most persistent and vexatious bands had been McNeill's Partisan Rangers. Never more than seventy or eighty men strong, this group, first under the leadership of John Hanson McNeill and then that of his son Jesse, had harassed a 100-mile stretch of the Baltimore and Ohio Railroad for four long years. And on numerous occasions their forays had taken them into Allegany County.

The young and inexperienced Jesse McNeill, in command since his father's death in 1864, was bent on capturing General Kelley. Earlier in the war, Kelley had arrested Jesse's mother and sister and incarcerated them in an Ohio prison camp. It was this private war between Major General Kelley and McNeill's Rangers that served as a catalyst for the Cumberland raid. The chance to capture Crook was an added incentive. Aided by the advice of a number of Cumberland men in his band, McNeill had learned the location of picket posts, where the generals headquartered, and how many troops were garrisoned in town. Thus on the morning of February 20, 1865, he led sixty-four men from Moorefield on an eighty-mile dash to Cumberland where they hoped to

Clarysville U.S.A. General Hospital, 1864.

snatch Kelley and Crook from the midst of 8,000 Union soldiers.

Five miles from Cumberland the band stopped at the S. D. Brady farmhouse for consultation and to fill their canteens with apple brandy. Assignments were given out and groups of men delegated to seize Kelley and Crook, to raid the stables, and to destroy the telegraph office. Three miles from town on the New Creek Road (now U.S. 220), Federal pickets were surprised and the password, "Bull's Gap," extracted when the rangers suggested hanging a Union soldier. Another mile up the road the inner picket post of five men was secured and the way into town clear. At three o'clock in the morning on February 21, McNeill's men entered the west side of town and proceeded along Greene Street, passed Emmanuel Episcopal Church and crossed the chain bridge over Wills Creek. Whenever asked, they identified themselves as "scouts from New Creek." At Kelley's hotel sentinels were disarmed, and the general pulled out of his bed at gunpoint, ordered to dress, and taken outside. A similar scene was repeated at Crook's hotel.

The entire kidnapping lasted barely ten minutes. After a stop to obtain additional horses the raiders rode down Canal Street and onto the canal towpath. The group was five miles from town before a cannon boomed in Cumberland and told them the dash for safety had begun. They crossed the Potomac at Wiley Ford and raced to Romney. Overconfident, a few of McNeill's men tarried there and skirmished with an advance guard of pursuers. Not until late afternoon and only seven miles from Moorefield did the rangers finally stop to rest. The next morning, Crook and Kelley were dispatched to Richmond via Harrisonburg and Staunton. On February 25, they were turned over to authorities in the Confederate capital. The Cumberland *Civilian and Telegraph* on March 23 noted that the generals, who had been paroled on March 20, were back in town "and seem nothing the worse for their brief visit to Richmond."[30]

Cumberland awoke to the thunder of artillery on Monday, April 10, 1865. By day's end, two hundred rounds of cannon fire had sent the glad news of Lee's surrender over the mountains and through the valleys of Allegany County. The war was over. Continual rain postponed various civic celebrations and scarcely had citizens illuminated their houses and decorated them with red, white, and blue streamers before they heard the "sad news" of President Lincoln's assassination. A woman, writing seventy years later, recalled that as a young girl she had watched her grief-stricken mother carefully put away the "gaudy decorations" and buy yards of black goods to mark her family's mourning for the martyred president. Church bells in the county tolled hourly and businesses suspended activity for a week.[31]

Any lessening of bitterness between Unionists and Southern sympathizers in the county had been washed away by Lincoln's death. One newspaper demanded that "jollification over the assassination" be stopped. Soldiers from Clarysville assaulted a group of "Copperheads" at Eckhart Mines who were drinking and shooting guns in celebration. The *Civilian and Telegraph* printed that "hanging would not have been more than they deserved." All over the area meetings were held to discuss how Confederates who were returning home should be greeted. One man echoed the thoughts of many: "The feeling against those who went from us and joined the rebels is intense." Some communities gave the "graceless and shameless wretches" thirty hours to leave. Still the numbers of rebels streaming in to give themselves up became commonplace. George Harrison, elected mayor of Cumberland in May 1865, preached leniency to the people, asking them to accept those Confederates who are "fully repented." But others fermented over the "blackhearted rebels and traitors" and in November the editor of the *Union* was still writing that those who had chosen "Jeff Davis and Disunion" should "be willing to lie on the bed of their own making." When Will Lowdermilk purchased the *Civilian and Telegraph* in July 1865, that paper began to modify its formerly strident position toward ex-Confederates. Gradually the intensity of division lessened and most of those who had gone south returned home. But it was several years before the soldiers of both sides became friends again and neighbors renewed relationships.[32]

A mustering-out center was established in a grove on the National Road, three miles west of Cumberland. An elaborate camp was constructed with bridges, arches, and temporary buildings. Here thousands of soldiers were processed and discharged between May and September 1865. Many thousands more from the Midwest passed through Cumberland riding the Baltimore and Ohio home.[33]

Economic progress in the years following the war would signal the beginning of a great boom period. Yet business and industry stagnated in Allegany County during early summer, 1865, while the economy converted from war to peace production. The price of coal fell and work was temporarily suspended in the Georges Creek region. The Mount Savage Iron Works laid off hundreds and when wages were reduced in the Baltimore and Ohio machine shop in Cumberland, many men quit and signed with a Baltimore company to go abroad to work in the machine shops of the Russian government.

Despite an uncertain economy, the county was relaxing after four years of war. A host of entertainers descended upon the area. The Thoyer and Hayes United States Circus with "Mammoth Menagerie and Egyptian Caravan" called itself the "most colossal exhibition of the nineteenth century." Belvidere Hall in Cumberland featured local and national talent. The "Mountain Minstrels of Frostburg" and "Mr. Kemmer's Singing Class of Juveniles" vied for billing with "Ellenger and Foote's Grand Combination"—three midgets, including Commodore Foote, who claimed to be the smallest man in the world and played classical music. Spirits were high. The Fourth of July celebration in Frostburg "exceeded all expectations," and in Cumberland the sparks from an "unlimited supply" of Roman candles "in the hands of careless boys" played havoc with the finery of the town's citizens. The entire county had gone berserk over baseball—and the game was played until December. Three weeks before Christmas, the last game of the season in Cumberland commenced on a Tuesday in fifty-five degree weather. The following Friday, much of the town turned out to ice-skate on Wills Creek in ten degree climate.[34]

By early fall, 1865, the county appeared on the road to economic recovery. Coal production increased and newspapers reported the canal to be doing the best business in its history. A building boom hit, leading a resident of Frostburg to complain that all the area's "magnificent" pine forests were rapidly disappearing into the saws of the town's three lumber mills. And in Westernport, a company "encouraged by the prospects of a good supply" began to drill for oil. No oil was found, but better days had arrived for many in the county.[35]

CHAPTER VII NOTES

1. *Civilian and Telegraph*, April 25, 1861.

2. Ibid., Jan. 17 and Feb. 21, 1861; Will Lowdermilk, *History of Cumberland* (Washington: James Anglin, 1878), pp. 390-94 (hereafter cited as Lowdermilk, *Cumberland*); and J. William Hunt, "Across the Desk," in the Cumberland *Sunday Times*, Dec. 16, 1954 (hereafter cited as Hunt).

3. *Union*, May 16, 1863; Lowdermilk, *Cumberland*, p. 395; and Andrew Roy, *Recollections of a Prisoner of War* (Columbus: J. L. Trauger Printing Co., 1909), pp. 149, 156 (hereafter cited as Roy, *Recollections*).

4. Lew Wallace, *An Autobiography* (New York: Harper Brothers), p. 277 (hereafter cited as Wallace, *Autobiography*); John Scharf, *History of Western Maryland* (Philadelphia: L. H. Everts, 1882), II, p. 1503 (hereafter cited as Scharf, *Western Maryland*); Hunt, July 15, 1956, and March 10, 1963; Andrew Roy, *History of Coal Mining in the United States* (Columbus: J. L. Trauger Printing Co., 1905), p. 52; *Union*, Oct. 18, 1965; and *Civilian and Telegraph*, June 23, 1864, and Feb. 16, 1865.

5. Roy, *Recollections*, p. 149; Hunt, March 3, 1963; and Harold Manakee, *Maryland in the Civil War* (Baltimore: Maryland Historical Society, 1961), pp. 121-22.

6. Hunt, March 10, 1963. See Lowdermilk, *Cumberland*, for a partial listing of area citizens who joined the Confederate Army.

7. *Civilian and Telegraph*, April 25 and May 9, 16, and 23, 1861.

8. Ibid., May 16, 1861; and Hunt, Feb. 12, 1961.

9. *Civilian and Telegraph*, June 20, 1861.

10. Ibid., May 9 and 16 and June 13, 1861; Lowdermilk, *Cumberland*, pp. 396-97; and Wallace, *Autobiography*, p. 283. Wallace's encampment is now the site of Allegany High School.

11. *Civilian and Telegraph*, June 13, Aug. 29, Sept. 5, and Oct. 20,

1861, and July 28, 1864; *Union,* Feb. 17 and May 2 and 16, 1863; and Scharf, *Western Maryland,* II, p. 1399.

12. Wallace, *Autobiography,* p. 283; *Civilian and Telegraph,* June 20 and 27, 1861; and Hunt, Dec. 12, 1960.

13. The engagements near Frankfort (now Fort Ashby) are known as the Battles of Pattersons Creek. The encounter while Union troops were on their way back to Cumberland is known as the Battle of Kellys Island. Wallace, *Autobiography,* p. 294; *Civilian and Telegraph,* July 4, 1861; and Hunt, Feb. 1, 1953, and Feb. 12, 1961.

14. *Civilian and Telegraph,* July 4, 11, and 18, and Aug. 9, 1861, and May 19, 1864; Hunt, July 7, 1956; and Baltimore *Sun,* Aug. 30, 1861.

15. Diary of Priscilla McKaig, quoted in Hunt, Nov. 24 and Dec. 1 and 8, 1963.

16. *Civilian and Telegraph,* Sept. 26, 1861; and Hunt, Nov. 23, 1953.

17. *Union,* Sept. 27, 1861, and Oct. 4, 1862; and Hunt, Sept. 18, 1960, and April 4, 1968.

18. *Union,* Sept. 28 and Nov. 1, 1862; Hunt, Jan. 6, 1957, and April 7, 1968; and Edward Hungerford, *Baltimore and Ohio Railroad, 1827-1927,* Vol. 2 (New York: G. P. Putnam, 1928), pp. 48-58.

19. *Union,* June 20 and 27 and July 4 and 11, 1863.

20. Katherine Harvey, *The Best Dressed Miners* (Ithaca: Cornell University Press, 1969), pp. 155-56 (hereafter cited as Harvey, *Best Dressed Miners*).

21. *Civilian and Telegraph,* Feb. 5, March 17 and 24, and May 17, 1864; and Hunt, April 21, 1957.

22. Lowdermilk, *Cumberland,* pp. 415-16; Hunt, Feb. 17, 1963, and June 7, 1964; and Harry Gilmor, *Four Years in the Saddle* (New York: Harper Brothers, 1866), pp. 213-25.

23. Hu Maxwell and H. L. Swisher, *History of Hampshire County* (Morgantown: A. B. Boughner, 1897), p. 549; Harvey, *Best Dressed Miners,* pp. 150-51, 158; *Union,* June 23 and Aug. 29, 1863; *Civilian and Telegraph,* Sept. 18, 1862; and Hunt, Aug. 4, 1957.

24. *Union,* April 11 and Oct. 12 and 25, 1862; and *Civilian and Telegraph,* Sept. 12, 1861.

25. Hunt, Oct. 4, 1964, and Jan. 6, 1957; *Civilian and Telegraph,* Jan. 14 and Feb. 18, 1864; U.S. Sanitary Commission, *Report, 1862* (Washington: Government Printing Office, 1862), p. 11; and U.S. Sanitary Commission, *Report, 1864* (Washington: Government Printing Office, 1864), pp. 190-91.

26. *Civilian and Telegraph,* Feb. 18, July 14, and Oct. 6, 1864; and *Union,* Oct. 18, 1862, and Jan. 3 and Aug. 15 and 22, 1863.

27. *Union,* Sept. 20, 1862; and Jan. 3, April 18, May 30, July 25, Aug. 29, and Sept. 5, 1863; and *Civilian and Telegraph,* Sept. 1, 1864.

28. *Union,* June 6, 1863; and Hunt, May 18, 1952.

29. The 1863 tax assessment listed slaves worth $124,775. *Civilian and Telegraph,* Jan. 21, March 31, and April 7, 1864; *Union,* Dec. 20, 1862, and Nov. 14, 1863; Hilleary F. Willison, "History of the Pioneer Settlers of Flintstone, District #3, and Their Descendants" (unpublished typescript, 1910); and Scharf, *Western Maryland,* p. 1475.

30. Mark Joseph Stegmaier, "The Kidnapping of Generals Crook and Kelley by the McNeill Rangers," *West Virginia History,* Vol. XXIX, Number 1 (October 1967): 13-42; *Civilian and Telegraph,* Nov. 3 and Dec. 1, 1864, and March 23, 1865.

31. *Civilian and Telegraph,* April 13 and 20, 1865; and Hunt, Oct. 25, 1953.

32. *Civilian and Telegraph,* April 20 and 27, May 4 and 11, June 8 and 29, and July 6, 1865; *Union,* Oct. 28 and Nov. 11, 1865; and Lowdermilk, *Cumberland,* p. 423.

33. Lowdermilk, *Cumberland,* p. 423; *Civilian and Telegraph,* July 27 and Sept. 16, 1865.

34. *Civilian and Telegraph,* April 27 and July 6, 1865; and *Union,* Sept. 3 and Dec. 9, 1865.

35. Harvey, *Best Dressed Miners,* p. 162; *Civilian and Telegraph,* May 4, July 13, and Aug. 10, 1865; and *Union,* Sept. 23 and Oct. 21, 1865.

PART III

The Whirligig of Change, 1865-1920

By

John B. Wiseman

VIII

A HALF-CENTURY OF ECONOMIC GROWTH, 1865-1920

The half-century following the Civil War was a period of significant economic growth for Allegany County. Accelerated exploitation of the region's natural resources, developing manufacturing diversification, expanded railroad operations, and a steady rise in farming all bolstered the economy. As industry and trade grew, so did the county's population. In the 1860s, the number of people in the area jumped from 28,348 to 38,536, with the number of coal miners doubling. The separation of the far western part of the county to form Garrett County in 1872 caused only a slight reduction in Allegany's population by 1880 because the railroads employed more and more people and attracted many new residents. Industrial expansion in the 1890s helped produce a 30 percent increase during that troubled decade, from 41,571 to 53,694 people. By 1900, Allegany County contained 250 manufacturing concerns and ranked third in the state in population. Over the next two decades the county continued to develop, both in numbers and in wealth. In 1915, its total bank resources ranked third in the state, and by 1920, its population had risen to 69,938. Cumberland's rapid growth from 1890 to 1920 was the main source of that increase. During that period it swelled from 12,729 to 29,837, an increment due largely to the expansion of railroad activity and the development of new industry such as the production of tinplate. Its manufacturing diversity won the city, the second largest in the state by 1880, the reputation as the "Pittsburgh of Maryland" in the 1890s. Rich in natural resources, favored with extensive transportation facilities and possessed of an expanding, industrious, and homogeneous people, the county rarely doubted its capacity for economic progress.[1]

The visible signs of prosperity were not so apparent at the close of the Civil War. In October 1865, the Cumberland *Union* reported that the county roads scarcely deserved the name. Nowhere was there "an unbroken mile of good road in Allegany." Neglect had also allowed the National Turnpike, once the symbol of the area's importance, to deteriorate beyond easy repair. It remained in "miserable condition" four years later and in 1871, the stage line that operated between Grantsville and Smithfield closed down. Other county roads had failed to improve during the interim. In 1873, an irate resident of Pompey's Smash (now Vale Summit), a mining community of 500, complained that the settlement lacked a road "fit" for a wagon to drive on and that the route to Clarysville was "impassable." He also asserted that the county taxes collected in Pompey's Smash justified building an artery to Frostburg. Twenty years later, a state-supported assessment of local economic conditions indicated that its roads were still inadequate. Fortunately, Allegany's industry had the benefit of a more advanced mode of transportation in the Chesapeake and Ohio Canal and an expanding railroad system.[2]

The foundation for the county's elaborate transportation network was established before the war. Railroads had become an important contributor to the development of the region's coal and iron industry since the Baltimore and Ohio Railroad first came to the area in 1842. While the Baltimore and Ohio Railroad bypassed the immediate coal and iron fields as it veered southwest from Cumberland through Rawlings and Piedmont on its route to Wheeling, the Cumberland and Pennsylvania Railroad ran the breadth of the mineral territory. A short service railroad built by the George's Creek Coal and Iron Company before the war to haul minerals out of the mining region, the Cumberland and Pennsylvania ran one railroad from Piedmont to Frostburg, Mount Savage, and Cumberland and another one from the Eckhart coal mines to Cumberland. In the Georges Creek area it established branch lines directly to the mines and it connected with the Baltimore and Ohio and the Chesapeake and Ohio Canal in Cumberland. It was through these channels that the county's natural reserves reached Baltimore, Washington, Alexandria, and from there the Atlantic seaboard. The Cumberland and Pennsylvania linked with the Pennsylvania Railroad in Corriganville and with the Baltimore and Ohio at Piedmont.[3]

The railroad's significance in the county's postwar economy increased as did its relationship with the region's coal industry. In 1872, the Baltimore and Ohio completed the Pittsburgh and Connellsville line, thus providing it with an entry into the steel city. Only the most stubborn opponents of technological progress would quarrel with the Cumberland *Daily News* observation in 1871 that "the iron horse has conquered and steam reigns triumphant." The editor succinctly sized up both the importance of the railroad and the degree to which the fate of modern transportation and coal were intertwined. The Baltimore and Ohio, one of the nation's largest railroads, also recognized the significance of this relationship. In 1876, through stock ownership and interlocking directorships in the Consolidation Coal Company, it began to assume a monopoly of the Maryland coal industry. A few years later Consolidation's main competitors in the Maryland mining region, the American and Maryland coal companies, began to build their own railroad to transport coal from their mines. This new road, the George's Creek and Cumberland, soon became involved in a bitter struggle with the C&P, owned by Consolidation, over the local transportation trade. The C&P tried to stop construction on the George's Creek by erecting a brick station which would obstruct its competitor's tracks. The station, however, was demolished and the new line was completed in 1881. The George's Creek line started in Lonaconing, picked up coal on spur lines to mines, crossed over Midland on a wooden trestle, and then cut northeast to Clarysville and Cumberland where it connected with the Baltimore and Ohio and the Chesapeake and Ohio Canal. After the courts upheld the new railroad's right to use the Cumberland and Pennsylvania's bridge across Wills Creek, more peaceful competition ensued. The chief traffic of the local railroads was coal. In 1873, the

Cumberland and Pennsylvania moved over two million tons out of Allegany County. The George's Creek road transported over 200,000 tons of coal during its first year in 1881. By 1890, its shipments had increased to 905,731 tons.[4]

The amount of coal shipped over the Chesapeake and Ohio Canal also rose sharply as mine production accelerated in the postwar decade. The early 1870s were the canal's most prosperous years. Its rates were lower than those of the railroads until 1873, before the latter's development was complete. Despite the annual winter closing of the waterway from mid-December to mid-March, canal shipments increased to 904,898 tons in 1875. In an effort to avert a decline resulting from competition with the faster railroads, the Chesapeake Company tried steamboats in the summer of 1873. The new boats reduced the log time from Cumberland to Georgetown from six to two days, but they were never widely used because the churning propellers, operating at high speed, damaged the banks. After steamboats were abandoned, the company experimented with tractors, but tests proved that the old mule teams were cheaper and more efficient. A more successful effort to reduce expenses was the establishment of a telephone system at forty-three stations in 1879, which kept the company informed on the flow of trade. But beginning in the early 1880s, except for a sharp rise in 1883 and again in 1893, shipping on the canal declined. A massive flood in 1889 nearly destroyed it altogether. Repairs required two years to complete, and the waterway never regained its economic importance after 1893. Steam truly reigned "triumphant."[5]

The emerging importance of steam power placed Allegany County, with its abundant high-quality coal reserves, in an enviable position in the second half of the nineteenth century. Maryland's only coal lay in five basins: the Georges Creek, the upper Potomac, the Castleman, and the lower and upper Youghiogheny. The main deposits rested in the Georges Creek basin, an area extending twenty-five miles in length from Mount Savage to Westernport, and five miles in width between Savage and Dans mountains. Veins of fourteen, six and four feet lay in horizontal positions. During the nineteenth century most of the coal was taken from the "Big Vein," or what was known as the Pittsburgh seam, situated relatively high in the hills. Thus, the coal could be easily reached through tunnels dug into the side of a mountain rather than by deep perpendicular shafts with their costly hoisting operations. The "Big Vein," a semibituminous coal, was extraordinarily suited for smithing and steam purposes. It contained enough bitumen to make it readily inflammable and enough carbon to maintain a uniform heat for a long period of time. Consequently, Georges Creek coal was used extensively as fuel for locomotives, steamboats, and New England factories. Its market expanded in the last quarter of the nineteenth century. The British government supplied its naval stations in the West Indies with Maryland coal in 1873, the Klondike goldfields used it for blacksmithing in 1898, and the American battleships that destroyed the Spanish fleet in the Philippines that same year operated on Georges Creek coal. By 1893, nearly sixty-eight million tons had been shipped out of the region. Although Maryland's status as a bituminous coal producer dropped from fifth in the nation in 1880 to eleventh in 1900, all of the state's coal was extracted from the far western counties. In 1901, a state record-breaking four and a half million tons were mined.[6]

Allegany County's mining operations exhibited certain distinguishing characteristics, some of which were revealed to mining company engineers by a United States government topographical map of the Georges Creek basin, the first of its kind. The region's contour, a broad syncline, enabled miners not only to follow the seam outcrop patterns, but also to expand from the surface slope into the confining hills along the underground slope of the coal. With little alteration, the "drift" method allowed coal cars to exit from the shaft by simple gravity. Drifting also permitted natural water accumulation to follow a gravity outlet with virtually no pumping necessary. Moreover, the use of fire at some distance into a drift tunnel in order to draw air for the miners, a practice in widespread use by the late 1880s, may have been first used in the Georges Creek area. Some of these fires are still burning. The diffusion of the coal into blocks, or "slips," which ran on angles in different directions, rendered the use of explosives impracticable. Therefore, the method of mining throughout the nineteenth century was sheer manual labor with pick, shovel, wedge, and sledge. Pick mining was less hazardous than blasting. It also produced a more marketable coal, for explosives crumbled the product. More often than not headings ran through the mountains, providing a transit way for women at Hoffman Hollow who wanted to shop at the Eckhart store. Miners worked in rooms off the headings, usually in pairs. They built passages from one room to another to get coal out and to improve ventilation.[7]

The plentiful mineral deposits and the low cost of mining invited corporate investment in western Maryland. At the end of 1866, there were already twenty-three companies in operation, but a series of mergers quickly resulted in the domination of the coal business by two companies. Consolidation Coal, the emerging corporate giant of the region, marketed five million dollars in capital stock in 1864. By 1871, through purchase of smaller companies and control of local railroads, Consolidation monopolized the wealth of the coal industry. It owned about 8,000 of the 15,000 acres of coal land in the county and controlled the C&P Railroad, the mining region's only direct link with the eastern delivery system. One of its mines, Ocean Mine Number 2, took out a record 1,300 tons one day and 600,000 tons in six years. At one point it contained 214 rooms. The other major merger, which brought together the Central Coal Company and the Maryland Coal Company, comprised the largest operation in the county in 1868. Responding to local fears of alien corporate power, Consolidation moved its headquarters from New York City to Baltimore in 1877. By 1880, most of the corporations had moved their administrative operations to Baltimore and Cumberland. Company presidents maintained close liaison with locally based superintendents and personally visited mines when labor dissatisfaction erupted.[8]

While most of the profits derived from Allegany County's natural wealth flowed outside the area, local miners were a relatively prosperous group throughout much of the late nineteenth century. Easy access to high-quality veins of coal, nearby markets, and inexpensive transportation allowed mining companies to be more generous with their workers than some of their competitors in other fields were. Miners received their highest wages, one dollar a ton, during the last year of the Civil War, when the demand for coal was great and the supply of workers was low. That was an unusually high rate considering the fact that a pair of miners would normally fill five two-ton cars daily by 1869. From May 1866 to January 1877, the wage rate in the Georges Creek region was sixty-five cents a ton. It dropped to forty cents three times over the next fifteen years, periodically rising before another decline. The average days worked also varied from year to year, depending on the length of the winter layoff due to the canal closing, fluctuations in the demand for coal, and occasional strikes. The number of working days ranged from 210 in 1878 to 254 several times over the next twenty-five years. Yet despite these erratic conditions, Maryland coal miners fared comparatively well. Twenty percent of them owned their own homes in 1870. In 1884, a year when miners averaged $445 in annual income, one-third of their group boasted home ownership. Workers who rented company houses in the 1880s paid $3.50 to $7 a month. On the average, about 12 percent of their earnings went for rent, a figure which dropped to 9½ percent in 1901. Two-story frame double houses which accommodated two families were typical in the Frostburg region, but structures varied throughout the coal area from solid frame and stone houses to "mere shells." In one town, there were tenement dwellings which were said to house from three hundred to six hundred people. Housing never became an issue, however, in the labor struggles of the post-Civil War period. Georges Creek miners were generally free of the high prices that normally went with company stores. The state legislature prohibited these stores in 1868 and tightened the prohibition in 1898. Georges Creek family incomes were supplemented by half-turns, a practice where a boy, working with an adult, received half as much as a man. The highest employment of boys came in 1880, following a severe depression, when 512 mine workers, or 13.9 percent, were boys under sixteen years of age. Finally, most mining families reduced food costs by home gardening. As a result, the Maryland miner lived comparatively well. Although one descendant of an Eckhart miner claims that poverty was characteristic of the coal village in the late nineteenth century, most outside observers who investigated the standard of living in the coal region were favorably impressed.[9]

However crucial coal was to the economy of the Georges Creek area and the county, other extractive industries were also important. Coal miners constituted less than 10 percent of Allegany County's population throughout this period. Even in the mining region, coal was not always king. The once-prosperous Mount Savage iron industry closed down in 1866, but iron ore works lingered on in Frostburg into the 1880s. In November 1871, the Bowery Furnace worked 140 tons of iron in one week, a record production. By 1880, however, the Bowery mine was nearly depleted. Nevertheless, the Thomas H. Paul and Sons Iron Works Company, engaged in the building of small locomotives, employed sixty people in 1881, and a smaller company employed ten men. The fireclay industry in the mining region was more enduring than iron. Mount Savage's Union Mining Company extracted large quantities of fireclay and firebrick as well as coal from its 600 acres of mineral land. During the late nineteenth century its plant was the largest manufacturer of firebrick in the country. It still operates, although on a much smaller scale. In the 1890s, this company, along with the Standard Savage Firebrick Works in Ellerslie, employed several hundred men. Frostburg had at least three brick refractories in the postwar period, using fireclay from Big Savage Mountain and processing it in the valley below. The Savage Mountain Firebrick Works in Frostburg manufactured about one and a quarter million firebricks annually in the early 1870s, shipping most of its product to Pittsburgh and Wheeling.[10]

Mount Savage was also the center of a major railroad industry in the late nineteenth century. The C&P Railroad established its construction operations in Mount Savage before the war. Between 1855 and 1917 the Cumberland and Pennsylvania shops built twenty-eight engines, and in a twenty-year period beginning in 1868, rebuilt twenty-two engines. In addition, the Mt. Savage Locomotive Works, established in the early 1880s, built engines for various companies as far away as New Mexico. The number of men working in these shops ranged from 250 to 600 during peak periods. Eighteen train operating crews also worked out of Mount Savage, moving in convoy fashion throughout the western part of the county in the 1880s and 1890s. These men commanded the highest wages in the area in 1880. Engineers received $3.50 a day, conductors $2.50, firemen $2.10, and brakemen $1.95 and $1.65. Blacksmiths and boilermakers in the shops earned $2.10 a day at the turn of the century. In 1891, the C&P also built two passenger depots in the mining region, one in Mount Savage and the other in Frostburg.[11]

The transportation industry was instrumental in the economy of other towns. Ellerslie's life revolved around the railroad. Established on the eve of the Civil War, it became an important rail center in the last half of the nineteenth century. The Pittsburgh and Connellsville line ran through the town as did the extension of the Western Maryland after the turn of the century. Westernport was another town nourished by the railroad. The C&P had shops there and the West Virginia Central, built in the late 1880s to haul coal and lumber out of the neighboring state, traversed the growing town on the edge of the mining region. Many Westernport residents also worked in the thriving Baltimore and Ohio shops across the river in Piedmont.[12]

Cumberland's location on the railroads and canal assured its growth. Eager to help stimulate industrial development, the city gave the Baltimore and Ohio thirty acres of land in 1867 to build a rolling mill plant with the understanding that the land would revert to the city if the mill ceased operation. Between seven hundred and a thousand men were employed in constructing the mill, which was completed in 1870. In 1873, it employed 750 men, who turned out 2,500 tons of steel rails every month for the company roads. These workers received the highest wages ever offered in Cumberland, ranging from three to ten dollars a day. The rolling mill plant also prompted the development of related business concerns. A merchant bar mill, in association with the steel rail plant, produced a variety of iron products and employed 300 people. Boatbuilding was also a major industry in Cumberland in 1873. Ninety-one canal boats were built that year, ensuring one hundred jobs. Workers on the canal and at the wharves must have been numerous, for 554 boats moved on the waterway during the peak year of 1873, when company profits exceeded half a million dollars. The canal was completely overhauled to accommodate the larger new boats, and the wharves were expanded in anticipation of continued prosperity.[13]

Older industries, largely based on the region's natural resources, provided Cumberland with a diversified economic base. Two foundries produced agricultural implements, gristmills, stoves, engines, and car wheels, and the city boasted three carriage factories. Brick manufacturing, employing about seventy people, and quarrying, another extractive industry, were lively businesses. Tanneries, a long-established operation in the county, continued to thrive, especially during busy seasons. Forty-five men worked in a Cumberland branch, which was one of seven tanneries within forty-three miles of the city, all under the direction of one big regional company. During the months of April and May as many as 2,000 people in the tri-state area were employed as bark peelers or teamsters, or in other jobs related to the tanning industry. The lumber business flourished in the early 1870s. Coal mines required great quantities of mine props, pit ties, and mine rails, railroads needed crossties, the canal boom increased boat construction, and other wood-using industries drew heavily on the county's timber reserves. Sawmills and lumber-oriented concerns provided work for hundreds of men. There was a growing demand for building materials to build houses for the new residents coming in to work in the rolling mill. One Cumberland lumber manufacturing company kept two sawmills in constant operation and produced two million feet of lumber in 1873. A furniture company employed eighty-three men. In Frostburg the A. J. Willison Steam Planing Mill and Sash Factory was an immense business.[14]

The county's timber resources, mostly dense pine and hemlock forests, contributed to the area's economic development. White pine was the most valuable and easily exploited, encouraging small logging operations in different parts of the region. In the eastern section several companies took timber off Green Ridge and transported it by portable railroad lines which they moved every few months. But most of the logging concerns worked in the western part of the county, especially in the southwestern corner. Logging companies near Westernport could use the Savage River to move timber to the Potomac, which was dammed for sawmills after the war. The Davis Sawmill, operating where Westvaco's lower paper mill now stands, produced crossties for the Baltimore and Ohio.[15]

Another old industry, agriculture, continued to play an important role in the economy. Wheat, oats, potatoes, and corn were the main crops and most farming was done in the valleys and on low adjacent hills. According to the 1878-79 county directory, there were 133 farmers in Flintstone and 38 in Oldtown, two distinctively rural communities. But agriculture was a countywide occupation. One hundred and fifteen Cumberlanders listed themselves as farmers; forty-eight did so in Frostburg, and eighteen in Mount Savage. Present-day Cresaptown was largely an agricultural community as was today's LaVale, known in the mid-nineteenth century as Percy, after a farm in that region. While the Mount Savage and Frostburg area contained a few large, prosperous farms, notably the Porter and Arnold estates, smaller holdings were characteristic of the mining territory. Lonaconing had thirty-one full-time farmers in 1878 and Barton had sixty-one. How many Georges Creek farmers were miners who saved enough money to buy land is impossible to tell, but agricultural habits were persistent. As late as the early twentieth century most Frostburg families had a cow which grazed on the edge of town. Homes without gardens in the mining region were rare. During extended strikes and the worst years of the depression in the 1870s these gardens became a means of survival.[16]

The postwar prosperity came to an end in the mid-1870s

The West Virginia Pulp and Paper Company mill at Luke in the 1890s.
Courtesy Westvaco Corporation

when a national depression finally engulfed western Maryland. Coal shipments, so vital to the economy of the region, declined one-third in 1876. Wage cuts in some of the mines prompted a strike in April of that year and most miners experienced erratic employment throughout 1876. In Cumberland the rolling mill closed down entirely then. Its workers, who had previously enjoyed high wages, roamed the area looking for dollar-a-day "pick and shovel" jobs. Nearly every day in 1877 the Cumberland and Pennsylvania carried people away from the Georges Creek region in search of employment. Businesses built on credit were unable to meet their debt obligations and consequently went bankrupt. As industries collapsed, unemployment soared. Families who failed in their house payments lost their entire investment. Matters became so desperate during the height of the local depression in the winter of 1877-78 that local charities opened public soup kitchens to feed hungry people with no means of support. Finally, in the spring of 1878, the economy began to recover, but it took several years for families to make up severe losses; many in Cumberland were never able to regain their previous economic stability. This insecurity derived partly from the uncertain status of the rolling mill and related industries. The mill resumed full production in 1879. However, after 1883, the Baltimore and Ohio began to buy its rails from other manufacturers. In 1888, the plant closed. It remained idle until 1890, when a Johnstown, Pennsylvania, iron company leased it for a few years while it was rebuilding its own plant following a fire. By the time the rolling mill became idle again in 1893, it had long before lost its position as the city's major industry.[17]

Despite the decline of the rolling mill operation, Cumberland entered a new period of economic growth. Glassmaking began its most productive years in the 1880s, with the establishment of what would become two major firms, the Warren Glass Works Company, located in south Cumberland, and the Cumberland Glass Works, situated at the west end of North Mechanic Street. Using cheap fuel provided by local coal and native pure silica sandstone, both companies employed about twenty-five workers in 1885. As new plants and more so-

The National Glass Company plant at the end of North Mechanic Street in Cumberland. The Wellington Glass Company acquired it in 1909. Fire leveled the works in 1920. Courtesy William P. Price Collection

phisticated production developed over the next thirty-five years, so did the number of those employed in glassmaking increase. The Warren Glass Works became the Queen City Glass Company in 1890. Its plant soon covered seven acres, employed between 150 and 225 men, and shipped its products throughout the country. By 1910, the glass industry was the sixth largest employer in the county. Effectively represented by the American Flint Glassworkers Union, glassmakers were the highest paid workers in the area, earning from $2.60 to $4 a day in 1911. Few employees remained at one plant throughout their careers because of the high incidence of fires, but they rarely had difficulty finding jobs.[18]

Breweries and liquor distilleries also expanded in the 1880s and 1890s. The renewed influx of beer-drinking miners from the British Isles after the Civil War and the continued flow of Germans into the county prompted the growth of the brewing industry. Germans monopolized the business and Cumberland contained the biggest and most specialized plants. Paul H. Ritter produced a lager beer, called Bavarian, in a brewery on Paca Street and installed the first ice machine in western Maryland in a new plant built in 1889. While Ritter's brewery was the largest one at that time, there were twelve other brewers and bottlers operating in the city in 1888. However, the industry was a countywide one and included at least one businesswoman, by the name of Beck, whose Cumberland establishment lasted from 1858 to 1911. Mount Savage, Frostburg, Lonaconing, and Westernport had breweries prior to the expansion of the Cumberland industry in the late nineteenth century. The area's largest and most important brewery, the German Brewing Company, was established in 1901. Its plant on Wills Creek in west Cumberland featured modern equipment and covered an area 250x250 feet. The brewery, which had a capacity of 75,000 barrels, provided jobs for seventy-five to one hundred people. Later known as the Queen City Brewery, it acquired a regional reputation for its product. A local distillery, during its brief career, surpassed German's beer renown. The Braddock Pure Rye and Whiskey Distillery had a broken history. Built in 1856 immediately west of the Narrows, it ceased operations during the

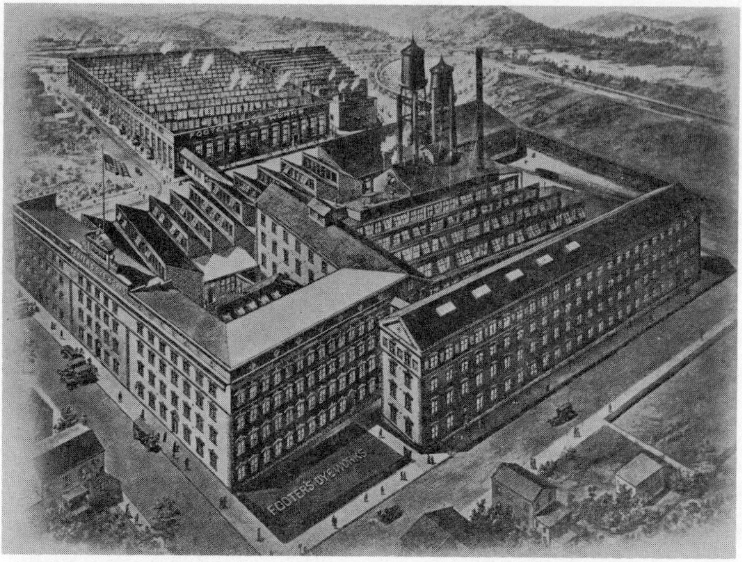

The enormous, world-famous Footer's Dye Works in Cumberland, a major area employer until the Great Depression. Courtesy William P. Price Collection

war and was converted into a chemical works in 1877. In 1883, James Clark bought the property, reconverted it into a distillery, and produced two barrels a day the first year. By 1896, the Baltimore *American* touted it as one of the most modern plants of its kind in the country. The Frostburg *Mining Journal,* emphasizing the medicinal value of the product, attributed this quality to its special sources, Braddock stream and the spring issuing from the limestone cliffs of Knobley Mountain. In 1903, there were 15,000 barrels of bonded whiskey aging in the distillery and the company had sales headquarters in Virginia and West Virginia.[19]

Another local industry, the Footer's Dye and Cleaning Works, also catered to an extensive market. The story of its owner, Thomas Footer, is a classic Horatio Alger tale. Orphaned as a child in England, he worked in a textile mill during the day and attended school at night. Arriving in this country at the age of twenty-three with his wife and two young children, he labored for nearly a decade in textile mills in Philadelphia, Oswego Falls, and Harpers Ferry. In the late 1870s, he came to Cumberland, where he established a cleaning and dyeing works in a one-room basement on South Centre Street. After careful expansion, the Footer plant covered a half block from Liberty to Mechanic streets in the 1890s. In 1904, Footer acquired new property on South Mechanic and Howard streets where he soon erected a number of four-story buildings. By the end of that decade the Footer Works was the largest and most complete business of its kind in the country. Nearly 500 people worked for the company, including 200 women and girls. Everything from the heaviest fabrics to lace curtains from the White House went through the plant, described by one contemporary as "spotless as a lady's parlor." There were separate buildings for cleaning specialty items such as hats, gloves, and feathers. During the early twentieth century, branch establishments opened in McKeesport, Baltimore, and twenty other cities in the East. Whether or not Footer delivery trucks "were seen on the streets of America everywhere," as one county historian has claimed, the Cumberland plant processed fabrics from cities throughout the eastern section of the country. The care which the employees took with each item and the size of the business later made the company vulnerable to competition from the less expensive quick-order cleaning enterprises that emerged after World War I.[20]

Cumberland's economy was further stimulated by expansion of the Baltimore and Ohio Railroad operations and development of the tinplate industry. Despite fears of the working class that a new business would result in rent increases, residents voted two to one for the city to extend an interest-free loan of $150,000 and a tax exemption to the railroad so that it might purchase ninety acres of land for construction of a terminus of three divisions of its roads and move the repair shops of Martinsburg, Keyser, and Piedmont to south Cumberland. Observers correctly predicted that the railroad center would more than double the city's 1,043 skilled mechanics and laborers before it was finished. The complex, which included an immense roundhouse and a yard to accommodate 3,000 cars, took four years to complete. By 1906, it employed over 2,000 people. During the 1890s, the tinplate industry also developed, creating jobs for many Cumberland residents. A new company engaged in the manufacturing of thin steel sheets, mixed with tin, opened in June 1892 with a working force of 100. Within a year 400 more were employed in the production of tinplate, iron, and steel. The availability of superior steam-producing coal at the low rate of $1.15 a ton, equally inexpensive coke and iron ore from a dozen Pennsylvania fields, and the area's transportation facilities made Cumberland an attractive place to produce goods for a growing national economy. Congress sweetened the opportunity with the passage in 1890 of the McKinley Tariff Act, which protected American iron, steel, and tin products against European competition. The manager of the new company, euphoric over the tariff, proclaimed that it "has given us the whole of this country as a market." A decade later, a Philadelphia-based concern, the N&G Taylor Company, took over the Maryland Sheet and Steel Company in south Cumberland and moved its headquarters to Maryland. By 1910, the tinplate industry, with a work force of 476, was the fourth largest employer in the county. A smaller establishment, the Potomac Paper Company, hired over 100 people in the 1890s.[21]

Cumberland's physical development gradually reflected its burgeoning economic activity. After a decade of relatively few changes in the general appearance of the city in the 1880s and only moderate increase in population, a dramatic spurt in real estate expansion, urban modernization, and number of inhabitants took place. Both the south and the north ends of the city experienced significant housing construction in the early 1890s; one pasture area, known as the Stone Battery section, was transformed into a community of "comfortable dwellings" under the direction of active realtors. Transportation innovations accompanied the housing boom, providing Cumberland the conveniences of a modern city. Ignoring derision of the idea of paying a nickel to ride a trolley when walking was free, the Cumberland Electric Railway completed its trolley line from the center of the city to Narrows Park in late June 1891. Over the next decade, it extended tracks to south Cumberland and linked up with electric railways in the Georges Creek region to form an efficient and inexpensive interurban system. On the eve of a national depression in 1893, Cumberland had fifteen miles of paved streets and an extensive gas and electrical system. Neither the national economic decline nor disastrous downtown fires long impeded the city's growth. It weathered both crises and emerged from them confident of continued development. New buildings quickly rose on Baltimore and Mechanic streets. The second floor of an enlarged county courthouse, destroyed early in 1893 by fire, was completed by the end of the year.[22]

Cumberland's diversified economy lured new workers and their families. The city experienced a ten-year population percentage gain in the 1890s exceeded only by that in the second decade of the twentieth century, climbing from 12,729 to 17,128. The increase in the following decade, 4,711, was the result of fresh economic stimulants. In 1906, the long-awaited entrance of the Western Maryland Railway into the county seat and its absorption of the West Virginia Central extended the area's shipping facilities. The city was served by five railroads, including a terminal of three divisions of the B&O. Altogether, the railroad industry furnished employment to over 2,000 people in Cumberland. The city also contained twenty-nine factories, mills, and foundries, two business colleges, and nine banks, all of which survived the national financial panic of 1907. The business recession of that year ultimately drove 300 families elsewhere in search of work, but the decline was short-lived. The tinplate mills, running at full blast in 1909, reported record high employment. Cumberland even had two telephone companies competing for customers. Its final modernistic touch was the introduction in 1900 of a horseless delivery truck by the city's branch of Swift and Company meat-packers, a company that came to Cumberland in 1895.[23]

The economic outlook outside the county seat was also bright. In the southwestern corner of the area a Scottish immigrant family, the Lukes, took over the Davis Sawmill in 1889, and expanded its operations. Exploiting a good local supply of mountain water, white spruce, and inexpensive coal, the family-owned corporation, which became known as West Virginia Pulp and Paper Company, also had immediate access to the West Virginia Central. By 1894, the Luke plant consisted of nine buildings and produced 40,000 pounds of paper daily. It employed 200 men in the pulp factory and 75 men, women, and children in the paper department. Over the next two decades the employment figure steadily increased until it reached 1,000. The Luke-Piedmont community added two foundries in the 1890s and the Davis Coal and Coke Company, which owned 50,000 acres of coal land in the Georges Creek region and West Virginia, had its headquarters in Luke. Luke also claimed one of the nation's three steam car manufacturing firms in 1900. Known as the Maryland Automobile Manufacturing Company, it produced the Maryland Steamer for a national market for one year before its collapse.[24]

An established industry, farming, maintained its level of importance during the first two decades of the twentieth century. In 1910, there were 894 farms in the area covering 163,287 acres of land. The number of agricultural units increased to 999 in 1920 while the amount of acreage under production declined to 152,974. Nevertheless, 54 percent of the county's land area was farmed, the average unit was 153 acres, and the value of agricultural property was $7,395,000. As if determined to show the rest of the state that they could farm as well as they could mine and manufacture, agricultural groups explored ways of increasing production. The Flintstone School devoted so much time to improving farming techniques that it won a reputation as the western branch of the University of Maryland Agricultural School. In 1915, the Allegany and Garrett County Agricultural Society, holding its fifth annual festival in Lonaconing in October, discussed ways of making the two western counties the leading agricultural producers in the state. Even Consolidation Coal involved itself in scientific farm demonstrations, producing nearly thirty-six bushels of wheat per acre on a ninety-acre plot between Frostburg and Eckhart in 1915. World War I, with the accompanying federal assistance to agriculture, accelerated experimentation and production. Allegany was one of the first dozen counties in the country to take advantage of the provisions of the 1914 Smith-Lever Act. The law established the Extension Service of the Department of Agriculture, which included a county agent and a home demonstration system. Dairying also increased during this period. The Queen City Dairy, a cooperative plant owned by local producers, had a $200,000 annual business by the early 1920s. Besides the orchard of fruit trees present on most farms, there were also a number of sizeable commercial fruit growers in the county.[25]

The coal mining industry increased its output sharply in the first decade of the twentieth century, maintaining a high level of production until World War I. Between 1900 and 1910, twenty-six new companies entered the region, making a total of forty companies operating seventy-one mines. This did not include family diggings from small banks for home consumption or local trade. In the 1890s, these operations numbered fifty. While the bulk of coal mining in western Maryland continued to take place in Allegany County, Garrett contained the vast majority of the family efforts. Coal production peaked at five million tons in 1907 for a total value of $6,623,697. Over the next eleven years output leveled off, averaging from four to four and a half million tons, and rising to four and three-quarter million tons in 1917 before the wartime shortage of men caused production to decline. The number of miners employed in western Maryland increased from 2,700 in 1873 to a record high of 6,436 in 1906. In 1910, approximately 4,000 miners were employed in Allegany County alone. While production increased in the late nineteenth and the early twentieth centuries, wages declined. The average annual income for miners in 1870 was $542.59, as compared with $489.97 in 1906, a year in which the average miner worked a respectable 250 days. The banner year for wages was 1891, when the average miner earned $635 and worked 254 days. Allegany's miners continued to fare better than many of their counterparts elsewhere, but they hardly shared equitably in the profits that they produced for the major companies. In 1909, Con-

Typical of large mines in the Georges Creek area was Koontz Mine near Lonaconing at the turn of the century. Courtesy Westvaco Corporation

The interior of a Georges Creek coal mine. This is Koontz Mine near Lonaconing.
Courtesy Westvaco Corporation

Photo of a typical Georges Creek miner
after leaving the mines.

solidation, through absorption of coal companies in West Virginia and Pennsylvania, became the largest coal mining company in the country. Its cash dividends that year were $1,009,882.50; its stock dividends were $6,150,000. The total amount of coal mined in western Maryland through 1920 was about 190 million tons, which sold for an average price of over a dollar a ton. As the major companies were externally controlled corporations, most of the profits flowed outside the region.[26]

The search for increased profits sometimes produced imaginative efforts. Such was the case with the digging of a drainage tunnel through Hoffman slope which Philip Jenkins, his three sons, and a group of laborers constructed for Consolidation between 1903 and 1906. This engineering feat, which occurred without fanfare, benefited all parties involved in the industry. A structural lag in the strata beneath the Hoffman mines had frequently resulted in water accumulating to a depth of one and a half feet in some of the active shafts. Production loss and complaints from mine inspectors prompted the company to correct the condition. Originally designed to drain one of Consolidation's big mines, the drainage tunnel diverted water through bored conduits four to six feet in circumference over a total distance of nearly one mile. The water discharged into Braddock Run at Clarysville. Later, the feeder was expanded in order to drain other nearby mines.[27]

The area's economic growth was reflected in its population centers, which provided more visible signs of change and development. Early in the twentieth century, companies in Frostburg and Westernport built streetcar lines which were soon connected and merged with the Cumberland street railway in 1905 to form twenty-eight miles of track operated by the Cumberland and Westernport Electric Railway Company. Bold planners envisioned a subsequent connection to Salisbury, Pennsylvania, which would join the region with a trolley line then running to Meyersdale and ultimately to Pittsburgh. This regional interurban system never materialized, but innovations in transportation continued in Cumberland, signs of its development. In October 1913, an automobile

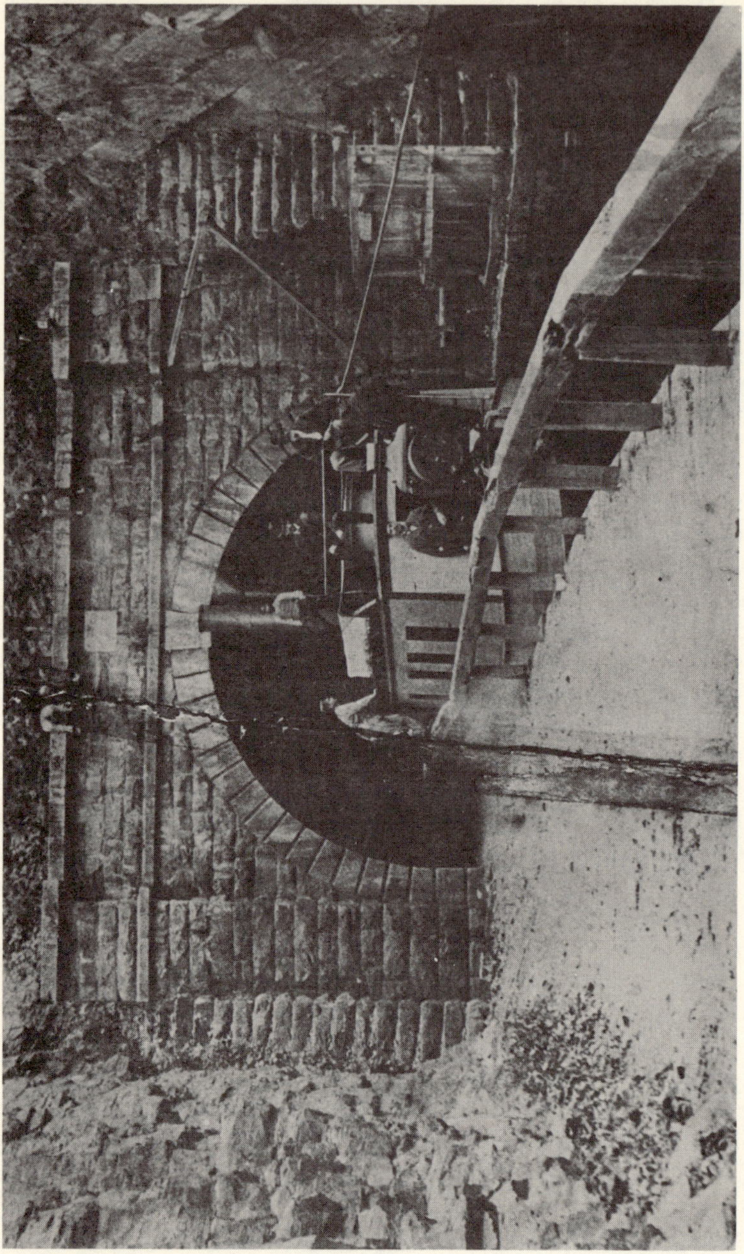

The C&O Canal at the east portal of Paw Paw tunnel. Randolph Spriggs, the superintendent of the canal, in derby hat, is sitting on top of boat. Courtesy William P. Price Collection

The Chesapeake and Ohio Canal Company boatyard on Wineow Street in Cumberland. Coal from the Georges Creek region was transferred from trains to canal boats here for the trip east. Courtesy Growden Collection, Allegany County Historical Society

The first interurban car from Cumberland arrives in Frostburg. Courtesy Growden Collection, Allegany County Historical Society

The George's Creek and Cumberland Railroad maintained a large roundhouse for its locomotives at the end of North Mechanic Street in Cumberland. Courtesy William P. Price Collection

omnibus running from city hall to the property of the Dingle Company in the area now known by that name carried passengers for a nickel to visit housing sites. The community already contained four houses and several others were in the planning stage. In the meantime, LaVale was undergoing organized settlement. D. P. Miller bought a half-mile strip along the old National Road in 1909 for the purpose of real estate development. He named his property LaVale in honor of his birthplace on a farm in western Pennsylvania. What was then a cluster of farms and a recreation area for local people was quickly transformed into a residential section. By 1920, LaVale had 1,288 residents.[28]

Cumberland also underwent significant expansion during the second decade of the twentieth century. Its population growth, from 21,839 to 29,837, actually exceeded the county's increase, from 62,411 to 69,938. The absorption of outlying areas near industrial tracts and new housing projects accounted for most of Cumberland's rise in population. In 1913, the Cumberland Heights Improvement Company developed the eastern part of the city between Williams Street and Oldtown Road. The Campobello, or Camp Hill, area near Allegany High School was also built up that year. An even larger addition to the city took place in 1914, when an extensive settlement below the B&O shops was annexed. Popularly known as Egypt because of its lack of lighting, the area had been divided into more than 700 lots by the Humbird family in the late 1890s to house workers from the railroad shops. Tinplate mill and box factory workers also lived there, making it a sizeable community extending from the railroad headquarters to the Chesapeake and Ohio Canal. After its incorporation into the city, it became known as Humbird Division.[29]

Industrial developments stimulated by World War I aided in Cumberland's growth. In 1916, the Cumberland Development Company, composed of prominent businessmen, negotiated a contract with Kelly-Springfield Tire Company in which the local group pledged $750,000 to help establish a plant in the Queen City. The following year 200 men began preparations for building a massive structure. Their number grew until construction was completed in late 1920. Wartime demand for industrial goods also spurred production in an established business. A United States government order for steel processed parts for aircraft engines prompted the N&G Taylor Tin Plate Company to increase its work force to nearly one thousand between 1917 and 1920. Most of the city's other major industries also maintained a high level of employment. The end of the war stopped construction of the half-completed Cumberland plant of the American Cellulose and Chemical Manufacturing Company, Ltd., now known as the Celanese Corporation. However, the shift in production plans from war-oriented materials to more stable fibers and yarns made it a more secure business when it opened in the 1920s.[30]

The introduction of new industries to Cumberland came at an opportune time, for the economic future elsewhere in the county was ominous. Depletion of the valuable Pittsburgh coal vein and growing competition from other coalfields and from other sources of power meant that mining would soon cease to be the bulwark of the area's economy. Coal production in the smaller seams would continue, but 1920 was the last prosperous year for the coal industry. Systematic exploitation of the region's forests had also exhausted much of the marketable timber. More than sixteen million board feet were cut in the area's mills in 1909, and the paper industry was the county's third largest employer in 1910. But by 1912, farm clearing had reduced the wooded tracts to less than two-thirds of the total region. More important, 99 percent of the virgin forest was gone. Excessive logging operations, followed by fires and the absence of reforestation, had virtually removed white pine and yellow poplar in some places. Consequently, the county's mines, railroads, telephone and telegraph companies, and sawmills would increasingly look outside the region for their timber needs. West Virginia Pulp and Paper Company expanded on the strength of lumber hauled in from West Virginia on the Western Maryland Railway. A silk mill in Lonaconing provided some diversification in the mining region, but Frostburg, the area's major urban center, failed to expand its economic base beyond the brick industry, sawmills, a brewery, an electrical company, and a silk and stocking factory. None of these industries added significantly to either the city's or the county's economy. Frostburg's dream that its location on a railroad trunk line would attract large manufacturing operations came to naught.[31]

Another inauspicious sign for the area was the closing of the canal in 1924. Just as the deterioration of the National Pike in the previous century symbolized the end of an era, so did the gradual demise of the canal. Railroads had long since made the slow-moving boats an obsolete method of transporting goods, but canal shipping lingered on into the twentieth century. After 1909, when shipments dropped to less than 200,000 tons, consignments steadily declined to 64,477 tons in 1920. The company operated at a severe loss until the 1924 flood finally ended the canal's commercial career. Railroads were now the undisputed king of transportation, but half-empty coal hoppers would not make it a very prosperous reign. Allegany County needed a transfusion of new industry if it hoped to engage in another half-century of growth.[32]

CHAPTER VIII NOTES

1. Katherine A. Harvey, *The Best Dressed Miners: Life and Labor in the Maryland Coal Region, 1835-1910* (Ithaca: Cornell University Press, 1969), pp. 19-20 (hereafter cited as Harvey, *Best Dressed Miners*); W. L. Fairbanks, *A Statistical Analysis of the Population of Maryland* (Baltimore: Maryland Development Bureau, 1931); *Seventeenth Annual Report of the Maryland Bureau of Industrial Statistics* (Baltimore: Kohn and Pollack, Inc., 1908), p. 55 (hereafter cited as *Seventeenth Annual Rep. Md. Bur. Indus. Stat.*); W. L. Fairbanks, *The Manufacturing Industry of Maryland* (Baltimore: Maryland Development Bureau, 1932), p. 174; Henry A. Grine, *Preliminary Economic Studies of the Western Allegany County Area* (Annapolis: Maryland State Planning Commission, 1941), p. 9 (hereafter cited as Grine, *Preliminary Economic Studies*); *Fourteenth Census of the U.S., 1920 Bulletin, Population: Maryland* (Washington, D.C.: Department of Commerce, 1921), pp. 2, 5 (hereafter cited as *Fourteenth U.S. Census, 1920 Bulletin, Maryland*); and the Johns Hopkins University Faculty, *Maryland: Its Resources, Industries and Institutions* (Baltimore: The Johns Hopkins University Press, 1893), pp. 22-23 (hereafter cited as the Johns Hopkins Faculty, *Maryland: Its Resources*).

2. Cumberland *Union*, Oct. 28 and 31, 1865; Cumberland *Civilian and Telegraph*, April 15, 1869; Frostburg *Mining Journal*, March 29,

1873; and *Fifth Annual Report of the Maryland Bureau of Industrial Statistics* (Baltimore: King Brothers, 1897), p. 205.

3. Harvey, *Best Dressed Miners,* p. 12; and John T. Scharf, *History of Western Maryland* (Philadelphia: L. H. Everts, 1882), II, pp. 1429-30 (hereafter cited as Scharf, *Western Maryland,* II).

4. Cumberland *Daily News,* May 11, 1871; Harvey, *Best Dressed Miners,* p. 12; Scharf, *Western Maryland,* II, p. 1430; *Fourth Biennial Report of the Maryland Bureau of Industrial Statistics* (Annapolis: C. H. Baughman and Company, 1892), chart insert, n.p. (hereafter cited as *Fourth Biennial Rep. Md. Bur. Indus. Stat.*); and Cumberland *Sunday Times,* Bicentennial Edition, June 8, 1975.

5. Angela Carraway, "The Chesapeake and Ohio Canal in the Early 1870's" (Frostburg State College: unpublished paper, 1975), pp. 2-6; J. William Hunt, "Across the Desk," in the Cumberland *Sunday Times,* April 13, 1947, and Feb. 19, 1950 (hereafter cited as Hunt); and *First Annual Report of the Maryland Bureau of Industrial Statistics* (Baltimore: William J. C. Dulany Company, 1893), p. 216 (hereafter cited as *First Annual Rep. Md. Bur. Indus. Stat.*).

6. *Seventeenth Annual Rep. Md. Bur. Indus. Stat.*, pp. 48-50; *First Annual Rep. Md. Bur. Indus. Stat.*, pp. 213-15; and Harvey, *Best Dressed Miners,* pp. 9, 13-15.

7. Letter from Don W. Duckson, Jr., to John B. Wiseman, Feb. 20, 1976; *First Annual Rep. Md. Bur. Indus. Stat.*, pp. 217-18; and Harvey, *Best Dressed Miners,* pp. 35-36.

8. Cumberland *Civilian and Telegraph,* Nov. 11, 1866; Harvey, *Best Dressed Miners,* pp. 9-10, 165-66, 186; and Frostburg *Mining Journal,* Nov. 9, 1872.

9. James B. Crooks, review of Harvey, *Best Dressed Miners,* in *The Maryland Historical Magazine,* Spring, 1971: 82-83; *Fourth Biennial Rep. Md. Bur. Indus. Stat.*, p. 226; and Harvey, *Best Dressed Miners,* pp. 62-66, 72, 80-81, 83-84, 90-92, 95.

10. Harvey, *Best Dressed Miners,* p. 53; Hunt, Nov. 6, 1949; Frostburg *Mining Journal,* Nov. 25, 1871, and June 4 and Aug. 6, 1881; U.S. Census Office, *Tenth Census of the U.S.: 1880 (Report on the Mining Industries in the U.S.)* (Washington, D.C.: Census Office, 1886), pp. 259-60; *St. Patrick's Church, Mt. Savage, Maryland: Special Centennial Issue, 1873-1973* (Mt. Savage, Md.: St. Patrick's Centennial Committee, 1973), no page number (hereafter cited as *St. Patrick's Centennial Issue*); and the Johns Hopkins Faculty, *Maryland: Its Resources,* p. 23.

11. *St. Patrick's Centennial Issue,* n.p.; and Tim Aaron, "A History of the Cumberland and Pennsylvania Railroad" (Frostburg State College: unpublished paper, 1975), pp. 14-15.

12. Mrs. Frances D. Greaves's notes on local newspapers (hereafter cited as Greaves notes); and *Special 1894 Edition of the Piedmont Herald.*

13. *Special 1908 Edition of The Daily News;* Cumberland *Daily News,* June 5, 1873; and Hunt, Jan. 22 and Feb. 19, 1950.

14. Cumberland *Daily News,* June 5, 1873; and F. W. Besley, *The Forests of Allegany County* (Baltimore: State Board of Forestry, 1912), p. 5 (hereafter cited as Besley, *Forests of Allegany County*).

15. Besley, *Forests of Allegany County,* p. 8; and *Town of Luke, Maryland: Fiftieth Anniversary of Incorporation, 1922 through 1972* (Luke, Md.: privately published, 1972), pp. 7-8 (hereafter cited as *Luke Fiftieth Anniversary Issue*).

16. *Boyds Cumberland City and Allegany County Directory, 1877-78* (Cumberland, Md.: Alleganian and Times Publishing Company, 1878), pp. 132-56; Harvey, *Best Dressed Miners,* pp. 28, 94-95; and Ward Orem interview with James Elias, April 1975 (Frostburg State College History Department).

17. Harvey, *Best Dressed Miners,* pp. 186-92; *Special 1908 Edition of The Daily News;* and James W. Thomas and T. J. C. Williams, *History of Allegany County, Maryland,* Vol. I (Philadelphia: L. R. Titsworth and Co., 1923), pp. 122-23 (hereafter cited as Thomas and Williams, *Allegany County*).

18. James W. Bishop, *The Glass Industry of Allegany County, Maryland* (Cumberland, Md.: Commercial Press Printing Company, 1968), pp. 7-15, 18-20; *Eighteenth Annual Report of the Maryland Bureau of Industrial Statistics* (Baltimore: George W. King Printing Company, 1910), p. 57 (hereafter cited as *Eighteenth Annual Rep. Md. Bur. Indus. Stat.*); and Cumberland *Evening Times,* April 8, 1911.

19. William J. Kelley, *Brewing in Maryland from Colonial Times to the Present* (Baltimore: John D. Lucas Printing Company, 1965), pp. 630-32, 662-64; *The Heritage Review,* July 1974; *The Courier Cumberland City Directory, 1888,* n.p.; *Special 1908 Edition of The Daily News; Special 1896 Illustrated Edition of the Baltimore American,* p. 219; Frostburg *Mining Journal,* Jan. 4, 1896; and Cumberland *Daily News,* May 19, 1903.

20. Thomas and Williams, *Allegany County,* Vol. I, pp. 549-51; B. F. Johnson, *Men of Mark in Maryland,* Vol. III (Baltimore: B. F. Johnson, Inc., 1911), pp. 188-89; *Special 1908 Edition of The Daily News;* and Cumberland *Daily News,* Aug. 15, 1904.

21. Cumberland *Civilian,* June 8 and 22 and Aug. 22, 1890, March 25 and June 10, 1892; *Special 1908 Edition of The Daily News;* the Johns Hopkins Faculty, *Maryland: Its Resources,* p. 23; letter from Leslie L. Helmer to James W. Bishop, November 1975; and *Eighteenth Annual Rep. Md. Bur. Indus. Stat.,* p. 57.

22. *Special 1908 Edition of The Daily News;* Cumberland *Civilian,* Jan. 5, 1894; and the Johns Hopkins Faculty, *Maryland, Its Resources,* p. 23.

23. *Fourteenth U.S. Census, 1920 Bulletin, Maryland,* p. 2; Cumberland *Evening Times,* Oct. 24, 1908, and Sept. 17, 1909; and Cumberland *Daily News,* April 7, 1900, and March 6, 1905.

24. *Luke Fiftieth Anniversary Issue*, pp. 9-16; and Piedmont *Herald*, April 20, 1894.

25. *Twentieth Annual Report of the Maryland Bureau of Industrial Statistics* (Baltimore: King Brothers, 1912), p. 21; Thomas and Williams, *Allegany County*, pp. 407-8; *The Advocate* (Lonaconing), Sept. 9, 1915; and Hunt, Oct. 26, 1947.

26. Harvey, *Best Dressed Miners*, pp. 10, 53, 62-63, 172, 360, 367; *Seventeenth Annual Rep. Md. Bur. Indus. Stat.*, pp. 50-51; and *Eighteenth Annual Rep. Md. Bur. Indus. Stat.*, p. 57.

27. Letter from Don W. Duckson, Jr., to John B. Wiseman, Feb. 20, 1976; and Ian McHaig and Nicholas Muhlenberg, *George's Creek* (Philadelphia: University of Pennsylvania Department of Landscape, Architecture and Regional Planning, 1966), p. 112 (hereafter cited as McHaig and Muhlenberg, *George's Creek*).

28. *Historical-Biographical Sketch of Frostburg, Maryland and Its Citizens* (Frostburg: Mining Journal Publishing Company, 1912), p. 9 (hereafter cited as *Historical Sketch of Frostburg*); Cumberland *Daily News*, Sept. 17, 1913; *A Brochure About LaVale, Maryland* (no date), p. 5; and U.S. Census Office, *Fourteenth Census of the U.S.* (Washington, D.C.: Census Office, 1921), p. 228 (hereafter cited as *Fourteenth Census of U.S.*).

29. U.S. Census Office, *Thirteenth Census of the U.S.* (Washington, D.C.: Census Office, 1912), p. 221; *Fourteenth Census of the U.S.*, pp. 228-29; and Cumberland *Daily News*, April 4 and Sept. 9, 1913, April 2, 1914, and April 22, 1897.

30. Hunt, Nov. 12, 1967, and May 3, 1953; Cumberland *Daily News*, Aug. 21, 1917; and letter from Leslie L. Helmer to James W. Bishop, November 1975.

31. McHaig and Muhlenberg, *George's Creek*, p. 17; W. L. Fairbanks and W. S. Hamill, *The Coal Mining Industry in Maryland* (Baltimore: Maryland Development Bureau of the Baltimore Association of Commerce, 1932), pp. 26-27, 68; Harvey, *Best Dressed Miners*, p. 367; Besley, *Forests of Allegany County*, pp. 6-7; *Historical Sketch of Frostburg*, p. 10; and *Nineteenth Annual Report of the Maryland Bureau of Industrial Statistics* (Baltimore: Kohn and Pollack, Inc., 1911), p. 56.

32. Hunt, Feb. 5, 1950.

IX

SOMETHING FOR EVERYONE: POPULAR ENTERTAINMENT AND CULTURAL DEVELOPMENTS, 1865-1920

Opportunities for entertainment and cultural enrichment kept pace with the expanding economy after the Civil War. Indeed, there was a significant correlation between the two phenomena. The railroads that transported coal and firebrick out of the region brought in entertainers and lecturers to perform in the area's opera houses and outdoor groves. Open-air activity remained popular. Throngs of people gathered outside for parades, patriotic rallies, picnics, or simply walks in the woods. In the words of one novelist writing about America at the turn of the century, "There seemed to be no entertainment that did not involve great swarms of people. Trains and steamers and trolleys moved them from one place to another. That was the style, that was the way people lived." Such was the case with Allegany County. An interurban electric streetcar system closely linked the towns in the western part of the county together early in the twentieth century, making a variety of stage fare available to more people and enhancing social interaction among the region's different ethnic groups. Modern technology also produced silent movies, adding a new source of diversion. During the period between 1865 and 1920 the state mandated a complete public educational system, including a teachers' training school in Frostburg in 1898. Traditional institutions, moreover, continued to function as significant social centers. A great variety of churches served cultural as well as spiritual needs. Almost alongside the churches were saloons, which abounded at this time.[1]

While society in this region was certainly not idyllic, it was a remarkably cohesive and rich one culturally. Most Alleganians had ties with the British Isles and Germany and shared a common heritage and set of beliefs. Even minorities, such as blacks, subscribed to most of the dominant cultural ideals and practices. Their social life revolved around churches and fraternal orders and many of their organized activities followed the prevailing ones of the day. Of course, not everyone shared the same levels of enjoyment and enrichment. Negroes faced the humiliation and inequality of opportunity that went with Jim Crow. Children whose family income required them to work in the mines or on the farms were unable to take full advantage of the new schools. Moreover, frequent fires and other adversities, often compounded by negligible public services, made for a harsh environment. But everyone participated, in varying degrees, in a plentiful social and cultural life. There was something for everyone to enjoy and a wide array of entertainment for those who could afford it or had access to it.

In the immediate post-Civil War period many people took advantage of the diversified stage entertainment that the railroads brought here. One dramatic troupe made its premiere performance in Cumberland's Belvidere Hall in 1865 before it went on to Ford's Theater in Washington. A New York orchestra played in the hall in 1870, and a variety show, a musical festival, and a magician were among its main attractions in 1871. Much of the entertainment was tailored for families and so were the prices. A family of six could see the magician for only a dollar. With a motto of morality and sobriety, a European variety show, featuring twenty performers, came to Cumberland for a two-day visit in June of that year. Responding to the growing demand for amusement, Cumberland included a large theater in its new city hall.[2]

Touted as one of the most modern theaters between Baltimore and Pittsburgh, the Academy of Music opened on March 7, 1876, with a dramatic company headed by John T. Ford, one of the leading stage promoters of the time. The star of the company delivered an opening address before the group performed *The Big Bonanza, The Two Orphans,* and

The Academy of Music in Cumberland was one of the cultural and entertainment centers of Allegany County until destroyed by fire in 1910. Courtesy Growden Collection, Allegany County Historical Society

Jane Eyre on consecutive evenings. *The Two Orphans,* a tear-jerker about a blind girl and her sister, was the most popular play of the era. Equipped with the most modern stage trappings, a large orchestra pit, and a seating capacity of twelve hundred, the academy was well suited for the melodramas of the time, which depended heavily on stage effects to portray train wrecks, steamboat explosions, forest fires, earthquakes, and other natural disasters. Important contemporary morals were also celebrated in the theater. The rewards of honesty, industry, and chastity, and the perils of drunkenness, gambling, and infidelity, depicted by countless Horatio Alger novels, found their way to the stage. For those who wanted assurances that these verities paid off there were lectures on Lincoln and other inspiring figures. In 1882, Frederick Douglass, one of the great self-made men of the nineteenth century, spoke to an audience in Frostburg.[3]

The Georges Creek region had an active theater life of its own. Before the advent of opera houses in that area, theatrical troupes performed in local halls. Frostburg had several halls large enough to attract performing companies prior to the erection of its two theaters in 1876. The first one, built by the Independent Order of Odd Fellows as part of a large four-story structure, was dedicated in February 1876. It contained a large stage and an orchestra pit, and seated 750 people. A few months later, Paul's Hall, which later became known as Moat's Opera House, opened as a full-fledged theater. Dramatic troupes performed in both houses, scheduling both one-night stands and longer runs with different plays, concluding with a rerun of the most popular attraction. While the Cumberland and Pennsylvania Railroad made it possible for many of the people in the region to patronize the Frostburg theaters, it also brought touring companies right to their own communities. After a week's stay in Frostburg, a theatrical troupe moved on to Lonaconing in May 1872. *East Lynne,* the region's most popular play, drew an audience of 900 in Piedmont in 1874. When Westernport's opera house burned down in 1876, residents in that area were without a regular theater until the burgeoning railroad town of Piedmont built a new opera house in 1885. In the interim, the-

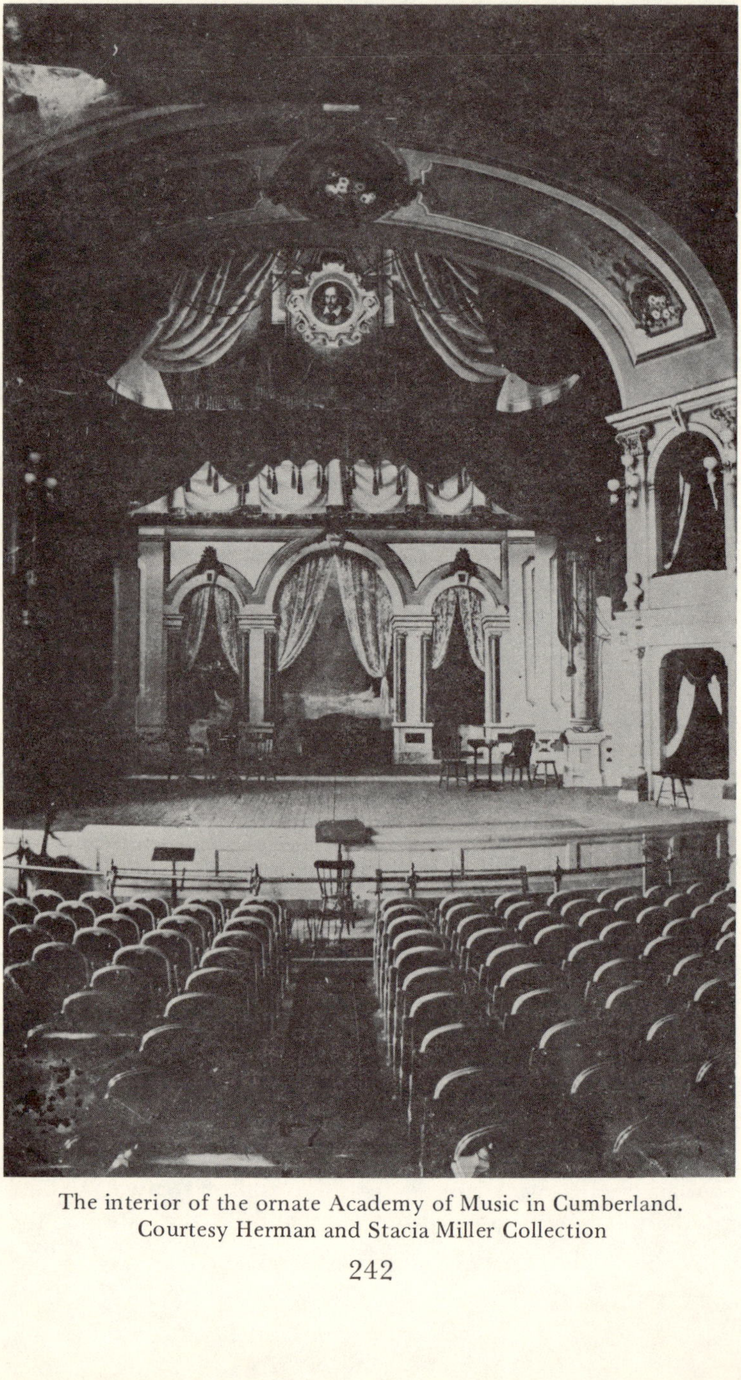

The interior of the ornate Academy of Music in Cumberland.
Courtesy Herman and Stacia Miller Collection

atrical companies staged productions in local halls or people took the train to see stage performances elsewhere in the county.[4]

These opera houses provided audiences a wide variety of fare. During the heavy theater season in the fall and winter, the Academy of Music sometimes ran a new show every three or four days. In addition to serious drama, famous minstrel and vaudeville companies, the most popular form of stage entertainment from the 1880s until World War I, kept theatergoers coming back for more. When familiar light operas such as the *Pirates of Penzance* came to Cumberland, the academy advertised reserved seats for twenty-five cents extra. In the 1890s, the visit of the Boston Grand Opera Company, offering such selections as *Faust* and *Il Trovatore,* was regarded as the highlight of the theater season. Choruses, humorists, and Civil War dramas, including the perennial classic, *Uncle Tom's Cabin,* rounded out the road shows that came to Allegany County during the late nineteenth century. In the absence of traveling companies, local musical organizations filled in as the theaters furnished a place for home talent to perform.[5]

The summer months brought the circus to the bigger towns. One circus featuring fifty acts and three clowns stopped in Grantsville, Frostburg, and Cumberland in July 1867. By the 1870s, the people could count on at least two tent shows each summer, preceded by a parade of animals. Three played in Frostburg within a three-week period in 1872, and at least that number, including one from Japan, came to Cumberland in 1899. The annual visit of the Carl Hagenbeck-Wallace Circus brought 400 performers and tango horses from London to the county seat in 1915. A variety of Wild West shows, including Buffalo Bill's extravaganza, also entertained in the area. More specialized animal shows exhibited such rarities as Philippine water buffalo after the Spanish-American War brought those islands to the nation's attention.[6]

People took to the outdoors for a variety of activities before the radio and television lured them indoors. Weekend family and organizational picnics in the numerous parks which dotted the county were popular pastimes. Some people preferred simply walking in the woods, collecting flowers and herbs. Those who left home without something to eat sometimes found refreshments along the way. One Frostburg woman who grew up on a farm outside town still remembers helping her mother feed as many as fifty strollers on Sunday afternoons. Fishing in Georges Creek became a casualty of acid iron waste from the mines, which by 1907, if not sooner, had destroyed all forms of life in the stream by the time it reached Westernport. But the area's many streams and rivers still provided plenty of good angling. They also furnished holes for swimming. Children in Westernport and Luke had the extra benefit of the log booms near the paper mill to swim in, and those in Cumberland had the canal. In outlying regions boys stripped bare; in heavily used waters like the canal, cooperative boat captains warned them of approaching mixed company. As rowing and canoeing became more popular after the turn of the century, bathing suits were required in the Potomac River. The Cumberland *Daily News* reported over one hundred boats on the river nearly every afternoon in July 1908, and warned the nude bathers that the sheriff would clear them out. Winter failed to deter outdoor activity significantly. Skating, "coasting," and sleigh riding often involved groups of people, sometimes to the point of endangering public safety. When coasting got out of hand on one occasion in Cumberland, the police stopped it. There were also periodic sleighing accidents, such as the one in which a couple were thrown from their sleigh when a freight train frightened their horse. More often than not, however, sleighing parties concluded happily in someone's country home.[7]

The warmer seasons allowed for a greater diversity of outdoor entertainment. Both fairs and horse races were held at the fairgrounds in south Cumberland. Jousting enjoyed a brief popularity in the 1870s. Cumberland Negroes sponsored a tournament two miles east of Cumberland at Thurston Grove in August 1871 to an "unusually large" group of people. A band, drum corps, and numerous string instruments made it a festive occasion, capped by the crowning of a queen. The black population of Frostburg staged a tournament at the end of Broadway in August 1875, and at least three others were held in the county in the summer of 1876. On William Shaw's property near Barton spectators could watch the twenty-five knights entered in a private tournament from a 100-foot-long grandstand built for the event. Baseball was a more enduring sport. Most of the communities had regular teams and the rivalry between them was sometimes intense. Frostburg applied the name "canal rats" to the Cumberland players, who reciprocated by referring to their Frostburg opponents as the "slag diggers." The games were characterized by high emotion and by the practice of ejecting the umpires rather than the players from the contest. Throughout this period baseball became a standard part of holiday festivities.[8]

National holidays and local celebrations sometimes involved whole communities and were marked by parades, athletic contests, music, and speeches by local notables. Ordinarily no holiday excelled the Fourth of July for sheer entertainment value. In 1876, the celebration of the national centennial made the day even more festive despite the severe depression that gripped the county. Frostburg began its celebration on New Year's Eve 1875, when several hundred men led by the public school principal marched to the mayor's house at midnight, fired a volley of rifles, and then rang church bells. On the Fourth of July the town woke up to the same bells and cannon blasts between five and six in the morning. This was followed by a parade a few hours later which included all the cornet bands of the area. In the afternoon, 3,000 people attended a picnic and heard speeches, choir music, and a reading of the Declaration of Independence.[9]

The county's centennial in 1889 featured a special celebration in Cumberland. The George's Creek Railroad ran excursion trains between Lonaconing and Cumberland with reduced fares; the Cumberland and Pennsylvania did the same for citizens of the Westernport area; and the two railroads which reached outside the county, the Baltimore and Ohio and the Pittsburgh and Connellsville, offered special services

Cumberland fire engines on parade at the turn of the century.

for people coming to the area from Baltimore and Pittsburgh. The most spectacular day of the half-week festivity began with a military parade headed by President Benjamin Harrison, followed by a balloon ascension which concluded with a parachute jump from 5,000 feet by a Professor Hunt. Other activities of the day included baseball and football games, lawn tennis, an evening bicycle parade, and an entourage of illuminated canoes on the Potomac River. Whenever a town birthday arrived, such as Frostburg's centennial in late August 1912, a familiar pattern of parades and games took place. Lonaconing celebrated even without a birthday; pride in its physical development sufficed. In September 1907, its "face washed, its hair combed and its best frock gotten out of the deep drawer from beneath the sweet lavender," the town staged a homecoming week. There were games and parades during the day, movies and concerts at night. Earlier in the year, as was the periodic custom in the mining region, Lonaconing devoted a day to dancing, singing, and banqueting in honor of the Scottish poet Robert Burns's birthday. The party ended with a public reading of his poetry.[10]

The Burns celebrations were evidence of the continuing cultural importance of northwestern Europe in Allegany County. Although by 1900 the foreign-born population had declined to about 4 percent, in 1870 roughly one-fifth of the county's 38,536 people had been born outside the United States. In 1880, Allegany County had five times as many foreign-born residents as any other county in the state except Baltimore and Baltimore City, totaling nearly 7,000. Virtually all of them came from the British Isles and Germany, a homogeneous group of people who had much in common with each other and with those already here. Immigration from the mining countries of England, Scotland, and Wales increased threefold in the 1860s as coal production accelerated. In the three major mining areas of Frostburg, Lonaconing, and Westernport, 1,970 people listed themselves as miners and foreign-born in the 1870 census. The Irish-born population grew more slowly, but the thriving railroad centers of Cumberland and Mount Savage and increased employment on the canal continued to attract laborers from that country. First-generation Irish numbered 1,847 in 1870. Immigration from Germany decreased in the 1860s, but Allegany County residents born in that western European country, 2,312, still numbered more than any one of the groups from the British Isles. Germans tended to gravitate toward farming, manufacturing, and business activities, with few of them becoming miners.[11]

Despite the general coherence of nationalities and cultures, certain ethnic and religious boundaries did exist. In Cumberland the German Catholics attended Saints Peter and Paul's Parish while the Irish predominated at Saint Patrick's. Midland was almost entirely Irish and Catholic, but in Lonaconing, where the Scotch prevailed, Catholics had difficulties finding jobs. Moreover, after strikebreakers from southeastern Europe arrived in the coal region beginning in the early 1880s and a number of Spanish people came to Luke to work in the paper company at the turn of the century, the area's cultural homogeneity was eroded. However, in spite of the strained relations that existed at times among residents of different heritages, congeniality generally prevailed. Women traded recipes across the fence, a sharing which resulted in the Welsh trying matzo ball soup, the Scotch eating Irish stew, and the few Jewish families learning to like finnan haddie.[12]

The various groups preserved their religious heritages, and sometimes their identities, in the county's many churches. The 1870 federal census listed seventy-four churches in the westernmost part of the state. Nearly half of them were Methodist. Frostburg's 3,500 people supported eleven churches in 1872, and added two more over the next five years. In 1877, Methodist, Baptist, and Lutheran congregations were the most numerous. Episcopalians and Congregationalists, however, also had their churches, and Roman Catholics worshipped at Saint Michael's. Since churches, like other institutions, practiced racial segregation, Frostburg's black population met in its own two places of worship. Outside Cumberland and Frostburg, Westernport was the only town with a black congregation. Lonaconing, with its large Scotch population, was proud of its Presbyterian church.

Cumberland possessed the only Jewish synagogue in 1877, but the Frostburg Jewish community soon acquired its own. In Mount Savage, Irish Catholics predominated at Saint Patrick's and apparently prospered, for they built a new parish church in 1873. Lonaconing, Barton, and Westernport also had Catholic churches, and Midland built a new one in 1891. Some smaller villages like Oldtown contained only one church, a Methodist Episcopalian. Whatever the denomination, religion seemed to flourish. The 1870 census listed 70 percent of the county's population as members of religious groups. While the Frostburg *Mining Journal* bewailed in 1872 that 1,000 out of 3,500 people in Lonaconing failed to attend Sunday services and that the Baptist church had "gone to pieces," this center of so-called apathy boasted seven churches in 1878 and impressed one outside observer as a "hive" of Sabbath religious activity. Barton, with a population of about 1,100, had five churches, and Eckhart's 822 people supported three. Cumberland's range of seventeen churches satisfied nearly every conventional religious need. The black community had three churches, each one with a regular pastor.[13]

Whatever their denominational differences, the people in the county perceived themselves as bound together by commonly shared values generally referred to now as the Puritan ethic. They frequently described themselves as "sober," "honest," "moral," and "industrious," and they put a high premium on education and religious instruction. Visitors to the area generally agreed with this assessment, and if the numbers of churches, home owners, and banks are any indication of the commitment to Puritan values, their perception was not far off the mark. Churches assumed the responsibility of instilling right behavior in their congregations. It was not uncommon for several hundred people to listen to two-hour Bible lectures, and the Cumberland clergy introduced "open air" park preaching on Sunday afternoons in 1872 to provide religious instruction to strollers seeking "fresh air and rural scenery." Fearful that the growing number of taverns was undermining the town's moral welfare, Frostburg churches sponsored meetings of temperance groups. The results were sometimes impressive. Fifty people took the no-drinking pledge following a temperance lecture at Saint Michael's in May 1872. A year later, the Frostburg Temperance Society attracted 175 people to one of its meetings. Convinced that unmarried young men flocked to saloons for lack of something better to do, the *Mining Journal* proposed that the "best remedy" for the "evil practice was marriage."[14]

Judging by the number of saloons in the county, temperance groups must have fought an uphill battle. Contemporary estimates of the number of "drinking resorts" in Frostburg in the summer of 1872 vary from thirty-two to thirty-eight. Whatever the exact number, it is clear that prohibition was not in fashion. Cumberland contained thirty-nine drinking establishments in 1888. The saloon traffic was especially heavy on weekends, and sometimes the camaraderie got out of hand. A report of a Saturday night in Frostburg in 1879 told of seven or eight different fights. One man had his finger broken and "his ear badly bitten," many others were injured and laid up for several days, and a "number" of arrests were made. Saloons located on the canal stops also drew rowdy crowds on weekends. Shantytown in Cumberland was notorious for its brawls, and Oldtown, which attracted drinkers from Green Spring, West Virginia, after the Mountain State went dry in 1883, experienced some tumultuous Saturday nights. While drinking was common, however, drunkenness was not. The German and Irish people were accustomed to drinking beer, and British miners had a tradition of washing down coal dust with a glass of ale. As for the inordinate number of saloons, estimated by contemporary observers at different times in the late nineteenth and early twentieth centuries to number five in Oldtown, forty in Lonaconing, and twenty-six in Midland, the most convincing explanation is that many of them were family saloons established to supplement other sources of income. In many cases they became the sole means of support. Men who were too old to work or who were disabled opened up their homes as drinking spots. Area breweries provided inexpensive beer and the Braddock Distillery sold rye whiskey for $1.25 a gallon. Consequently, the employed patronized the unemployed. How could temperance advocates castigate such self-help operations?[15]

Hard work, thrift, and self-reliance sometimes led to even more successful careers. By 1900, as a result of state laws against company stores, former miners or miners' sons operated general stores, specialty shops, restaurants, and hotels. Several former miners organized banks, and mining families produced a small professional class, most notably lawyers. One of them, David J. Lewis, represented the classic Horatio Alger rise from youthful employment in the mines to self-taught lawyer, and eventually, United States congressman. John J. Price, a miner for thirty-seven years, ultimately became a prosperous grocer and substantial property owner, serving four terms as mayor of Frostburg and three terms as county commissioner. In Cumberland there were the examples of Thomas Footer, who founded the Footer's Dye Works, and George Wellington, who rose from business clerk to head both a bank and the Cumberland Electric Railway Company and to serve in the United States Senate. While such triumphant ascents from obscurity to prominence served as models for what was possible for some, others simply went from half turns to full turns in the mines or moved from farm to factory. Blacks, who were accustomed to hard work, rarely saw their labor yield much change in their status. One Negro, who had served as a scout and guide for Union forces during the Civil War, and who achieved some renown in Cumberland as a phenomenal weight lifter, worked long hours selling newspapers. Sixty-four years after coming to the Queen City, he died at the age of 103 with the distinction of being the nation's "oldest active newsboy."[16]

There were also limits to the cooperative impulse. A food and dry goods cooperative in Lonaconing, beginning with 130 stockholders in 1874, sold staple supplies at reduced prices for forty-seven years. But county residents never derived benefits that might have passed to them through cooperative acquisition of the fabulous wealth in natural resources that lay literally at their feet. Enterprising efforts such as family "diggings" in coal which lay on their own land barely affected the flow of coal profits from Frostburg to

New York. Consequently, most people failed to realize the social welfare gains that might have accompanied public control of natural resources. Cumberland had no general hospital until 1892 and the coal region went without one until 1912. When a smallpox epidemic struck Cumberland during the winter of 1876-77, city authorities moved the sick to an almshouse farm conveniently located near a cemetery.[17]

Outside of education, public services were limited to absolutely essential matters. County tax levies produced $131,000 in revenue in 1881. School appropriations constituted nearly one-fourth of this money. Over $15,000 went to pay juries and court witnesses, while courthouse and jail expenses, sheriff fees, and other law-related items took another $20,000. The county spent only $5,900 on almshouses that year, $3,500 on pensions, and $1,900 on orphans court fees. Appropriations to corporations matched those made to "sundry charities," $3,500. Municipal services were equally minimal. Cumberland established a waterworks system in 1871, but until 1910 it obtained its water from the Potomac River, a common receptable of human waste. The city waited until 1888, when pollution threatened to make city water a health menace, before it built a sewage line. Primitive sanitary conditions prevailed throughout most of the county, resulting in occasional epidemics. Typhoid fever swept through Lonaconing in 1877 and through Mount Savage in 1904. Until Cumberland turned to Evitts Creek for its water supply in 1910, the Potomac water produced hundreds of cases of typhoid fever every summer. Of the mining towns in 1885, only Frostburg had good water supplied by the Savage River through a reservoir on Mount Savage. Public health officials described Lonaconing's water as a constant menace to its residents. Local streams throughout the Georges Creek region were polluted with refuse from slaughterhouses, stables, and family privies. Hogs, cattle, and horses roamed county streets throughout the nineteenth century, leaving piles of waste.[18]

The absence of municipal fire departments sometimes proved costly. Frostburg experienced two major fires in 1874, when the north side of town burned in February and the south side in September. The second blaze caused damages amounting to $150,000 before the Cumberland Fire Department, carried by train, arrived to assist local volunteers. The young men of Frostburg organized a fire company four years later. Lonaconing suffered even more extensive losses in a fire that started in a horse stable on September 7, 1881. Fifty-three buildings went up in smoke in three hours. Overcome by panic, men broke open whiskey barrels and lay intoxicated in the street while the Westernport Fire Department put out the blaze. Few businesses survived the fire and many families were left homeless. In the long run, however, the Lonaconing fire was a blessing. Before the calamity the main street was a six-inch slough of mud for half the year, the long steps of houses ran to the streets, and there were no sidewalks. A year later the town organized a volunteer fire department, and a new sense of public-spiritedness, rekindled by a devastating flood in 1884, would lead to Lonaconing's incorporation in 1890, paved streets, and modern architectural touches. Cumberland escaped major conflagrations for sixty years following the great fire of 1833. Then it experienced two disasters within a three-month period in 1893. The first one destroyed the courthouse on January 5. Exactly three months later, half of Baltimore Street lay in ashes. Referred to for years as the "Baltimore Street Fire," it took six hours for the city volunteer fire companies and organized help from Frostburg, Piedmont, Bedford, and Martinsburg to control the blaze. High winds and a second fire which broke out on Wineow Street complicated matters and temporarily conjured up fears of total destruction before the rescue effort averted the holocaust. Midland suffered a big fire in February 1905, losing its opera house and very nearly the train trestle which crossed over the town, and four years later, Lonaconing experienced another blaze. A different kind of disaster, a cyclone, devastated much of Frostburg in 1891.[19]

The natural adversities of the times and the absence of modern services failed to impede the growth of the larger towns and cities. More than one-fifth of the county's population, 8,056 out of 38,536, lived in Cumberland in 1870. The establishment of Garrett County in 1872 stunted Allegany's population growth during that decade, but it made the county more compact and increased Cumberland's share of its people. Allegany's population declined to 38,012 in 1880, while the number of people living in the county seat grew to 10,693, as railroad workers gravitated to the jobs created by the movement of the B&O Railroad headquarters to Cumberland. The B&O's construction in 1872 of a magnificent hotel, featuring marble fireplaces, exquisite chandeliers, and a plush dining room, as part of its enormous new station, made Cumberland's importance apparent to both local citizens and travelers. Trains stopped there to allow passengers dining or overnight accommodations in what became known as the Queen City Hotel. Taking note of its growing significance, Cumberland called itself the Queen City. With its transportation connections and its diversified economic base, Cumberland was destined to grow. By 1880, it was the second largest city in the state, and its population increased from 12,729 in 1890 to 17,128 in 1900, while the county's population rose to 53,694. The fire of 1893 brought new buildings and enterprises to Baltimore Street and the city claimed four national banks, several savings banks, an electric railway system, electric lighting, one of the state's finest theaters, and a wide array of churches, schools, newspapers, and businesses that met virtually every need of the times.[20]

Frostburg, which took over Cumberland's title as the Mountain City in the 1870s, also experienced rapid development in the last three decades of the nineteenth century. Incorporated in 1870, it was the most important town in the coal region with a population of 3,400 in 1873, and it served several thousand more. Although it lacked Cumberland's potential for varied economic growth, Frostburg possessed a thriving business section which included twenty-seven grocery and provision stores, thirteen general merchandise stores, and a number of specialty shops in the 1880s. Its newspaper, the *Mining Journal,* was a jealous guardian of local interests which would soon include successful agitation for a state normal school in Frostburg. Flanked by mountains, blessed with cool summer evenings and pure air, it had become a summer resort area of some renown. It boasted two hotels in 1871, added at least one more over the next decade

The magnificent Queen City Station and Hotel provided Baltimore and Ohio Railroad patrons with good food and pleasant accommodations before the advent of dining and sleeping cars. Courtesy Herman and Stacia Miller Collection

Mount Savage was a major railroad shop town and industrial center in the nineteenth century. Courtesy William P. Price Collection

and a half, and in 1897, the Gladstone Hotel, a $100,000 structure, opened for business. Several boardinghouses, including the old Frost mansion, also accommodated distinguished visitors such as Lord Lyons, the British minister in Washington, who summered in the Mountain City in 1876. Always pleased to remind Cumberland that size wasn't everything, Frostburg boosters invited the "sweltering denizens" of the rival city to "cool off" in their town during summer heat waves. By 1900, Frostburg's population had increased to 5,274. The city contained a gas and electric plant, clean water, modern stores, two opera houses, three banks, a large number of churches, and people with considerable confidence in its future.[21]

Contrary to the general pattern of growth, Mount Savage declined in importance in the late nineteenth century. Its early promise as a major industrial town was never fulfilled because the nearby iron ore deposits were low-grade, its fireclay resources were limited, and the town lay outside the main coal region. When the C&P Railroad made Mount Savage the site for its car-building and repair shops in the 1860s, the town became an active railroad center, but its social significance was largely self-contained and hampered by its ephemeral economic status. During the 1890s, Franklin D. Roosevelt sometimes spent part of his summers at the grand Bruce estate, the home of his mining official uncle, Warren Delano. Mount Savage had other distinguished estates set off from the center of town, indicating a more clearly defined hierarchical social structure than existed elsewhere in the mining region. Perhaps the pattern of absentee ownership which the Delano family investment signified was a reason for the town's decline. Once the natural resources were gone, whether they were iron ore, coal, or fireclay, so were the town's wealth and promise. In any case, the rhythm of life in Mount Savage, as in most railroad towns, was governed by train schedules. People woke up, ate, and socialized by the engine whistle or the movement of cars. Moreover, the train runs to Frostburg and Cumberland were so convenient that the residents of Mount Savage often went elsewhere for their theater entertainment. The railroads encouraged this practice by offering to wire ahead for reserved seats.[22]

Lonaconing, Westernport, and Barton were the other towns with a population of more than 1,000 in 1880. Lonaconing was the largest, with 2,808 inhabitants, and the most prominent. Its opera house, large general merchandise store, saloons, hotels, banks, and two newspapers served a satellite of small villages that grew up around mine sites. Barton, with a population of 1,112 in 1880, was an independently active community although its residents probably gravitated to Lonaconing for theatrical entertainment. It contained two general stores, two hotels, a number of saloons, a restaurant, and a circulating library, and it boasted a town orchestra. Westernport was the only town outside of Frostburg and Cumberland to witness a steady increase in population, from 1,468 in 1880 to nearly 4,000 in 1920. The growth of the Luke paper mill and expanding railroad operations in that area accounted for Westernport's gain. Incorporated in 1859, the town had a cultural life which revolved around an opera house until its destruction by fire in 1876, a YMCA established in 1892, and a phenomenal number of fraternal organizations which mixed with people from Luke and Piedmont. As was true throughout the county, Westernport's churches also served as active social centers. While each of the towns from Mount Savage to Westernport possessed its own special forms of entertainment, the railroads, and after the turn of the century, the interurban electric railway system fused some of their cultural life.[23]

People living in the eastern part of the county lacked connecting transportation facilities, but they shared a rural, predominantly agricultural experience that was more representative of the region's population contour than life in the western towns. Using 2,500 as a dividing point between a rural and an urban community, 25,038 of the county's 41,571 residents lived in a rural setting in 1890. As late as 1910, rural residents still outnumbered their urban counterparts, although the margin was reduced to slightly over 1,000. The 1,016 people who lived in the area between Sideling Hill Creek and Green Ridge in 1881, the Orleans District, led a relatively contained existence, but the canal which linked Little Orleans with Georgetown and Cumberland, and later, the Western Maryland Railway provided the region with regular contact with the outside world. One Catholic and four Methodist Episcopal churches furnished centers for organized social life. Residents in the Flintstone District to the west were dispersed over a wide area. The village of Flintstone contained 315 people in 1881, while 1,200 more were scattered, living mostly on farms. This section had three churches, a fraternal lodge, and a Grange organization where farmers could socialize. South of Flintstone in the Oldtown District, 180 people lived in the main village, while another 1,400 were spread out over flat farmland. Much of Oldtown's social life centered in a new Methodist Episcopal Church, but eastern Alleganians turned outdoors for much of their entertainment. Rawlings, bound by two mountain ranges and located near the Potomac River, provided ideal fishing, hunting, swimming, and sledding for the approximately 800 people who lived in the district. Following a county pattern, those who made their homes in the country flocked to the parks, which blanketed the whole region, for dancing, band concerts, picnics, athletic contests, and revival meetings.[24]

Allegany Grove quickly became the county's foremost summer religious center following its incorporation as a revival meeting site in 1890. Originally used by a few Cumberland families for summer homes, the area was soon transformed by religious groups into a place where spiritual instruction, Christian fellowship, and summer family recreation could be combined. Located in the center of today's LaVale, immediately east of Vocke Road, it had access to water from Braddock Run and to the transportation facilities of the two local railroads, and later, the Cumberland Electric Railway Company, all of which had stations within a mile of the grove. The meeting site featured an open-sided tabernacle, ninety by seventy feet, where local preachers and visiting evangelists exhorted large crowds brought in by rail or horse-drawn carriages. There was also a smaller pavilion used for Bible study classes for the permanent summer residents who lived in the grove's cottages, which ultimately numbered

Allegany Grove as a summer resort for Cumberland residents until the early twentieth century. The large tabernacle was the location for many religious meetings and other functions until destroyed by fire. Courtesy Herman and Stacia Miller Collection

seventy-five. Sundays at the big meeting grounds were characterized by religious inspiration and social fraternity. Following the eleven o'clock service, families spread out a picnic lunch and then returned for a two o'clock service. Farm families often had to go home to perform chores in the afternoon, but some of them came back for evening vespers. Families who had cottages or tent sites on the grounds made the grove their summer home; working fathers simply commuted to their jobs by train.[25]

The grove's popularity soon stimulated more diversified attractions. Chautauqua programs brought national figures in July and August to speak on character building, patriotism, and temperance. Humorists provided light fare; and renowned opera companies and choruses, which often allowed local groups to sing with them, delighted music lovers. John Philip Sousa and Helen Keller were among those who provided inspiration consistent with the aims of the camp. As the flow of temporary visitors to the campground increased, a hotel was built to accommodate them. In 1904, it charged seven dollars a week for board; five- and six-room cottages were rented for thirty to forty dollars for the whole summer. Tickets, good for fifty lectures and concerts, sold for $2.50. By the early twentieth century the grove's reputation had extended beyond Allegany County, prompting the B&O and the West Virginia Central to run excursion trains to the center. The camp meetings ended in April 1914, when a fire destroyed the tabernacle and sixty-five of the cottages. After another fire in 1918 leveled the hotel, Allegany Grove became only a pleasant memory.[26]

Musical societies and organizations were a more enduring part of the county's cultural activities. Even the smaller towns like Barton had their orchestras, and religious choral societies flourished. They performed in local halls, the best ones being invited to Allegany Grove or to the Academy of Music. But the local band was the most popular musical organization. Both Westernport and Frostburg had two bands in the late nineteenth century and Frostburg added another early in the next century. The Arion Band, one of Frostburg's earliest, has been in continuous existence for nearly one hundred years. The Midland Independent Cornet Band played at picnics and holiday celebrations and provided background music for performances at the local opera house. These bands practiced regularly, and at least one of them, the Gilbert Cornet Band of Westernport, won a prize at the World's Fair in Chicago in 1893. While area musicians rarely achieved such national fame, band music was an integral part of organized social gatherings.[27]

A new form of outdoor entertainment emerged with advances in transportation in the late nineteenth century. The completion in the summer of 1891 of the Cumberland Electric Railway line through the Narrows into what is now the east end of LaVale made it possible for Cumberland residents to spend their idle summer hours in an amusement center. Narrows Park, built by the enterprising railway company as a lure for traffic as well as for its own intrinsic profits, contained a roller coaster, miniature railroad, dance hall, skating rink, restaurant, and picnic ground. If contemporary observers are to be believed, virtually all of Cumberland took the nickel ride on the inaugural run to the park on the Fourth of July. When Frostburg businessmen built an electric railway to Narrows Park in April 1902, and other entrepreneurs linked a Georges Creek line with Cumberland a few months later, the entire western part of Allegany County had easy access to the amusement center. The streetcar further enhanced the social ties of the people in the county, especially in the coal area. The editor of the Frostburg *Mining Journal* noted in 1912 that it made the region "practically one town."[28]

The most important social phenomenon after the Civil War was the development of public education. Although a significant number of children had received at least a smattering of formal instruction in county schools before 1865, an 1864 state law, which provided for a uniform public school system and standardized education, made it available to even more people. The challenges were great and the results were slow, sometimes painfully so for those who watched them. At the end of the first year of operation, the county superintendent was "horrified" at what he saw in the Cumberland schools.

Mature boys and girls could "scarcely read," he reported. Many were "extremely dirty" and nearly all of them were "unruly." Worse yet, attendance was "irregular" and Cumberland adults appeared to be indifferent to the higher value of education. Only twenty-two people attended a lecture in early 1866 given by the principal of Allegany County Academy, the region's only high school. Two months later, the Cumberland *Union* estimated that 4,000 out of nearly 11,000 children between the ages of five and twenty were not attending either public or private schools. The number in that age category increased to 14,000 over the next decade, but the average public school enrollment was only 6,000. A new state law, providing for decentralized educational authority, went into effect in 1869.[29]

Insufficient financial support hurt the system throughout its early years. The county tax, which supplemented meager state aid, amounted to $0.21 on each $100 of taxable property in 1872. In comparison with other sections of the state, Allegany County was generous in its public support of education. Nevertheless, the schools would have been primitive shells had it not been for land donations by some mining companies and fund-raising efforts by students and concerned citizens. As it was, nearly one-half of the county's 130 schools in 1870 were makeshift log cabin structures. Gradually, new buildings went up. Frostburg completed a $12,000 structure for 300 students in 1869, and the rest of the mining region put its energies into fund raising and building programs during this period. By 1881, every community had at least one public school. County appropriations for education that year were $35,000, or less than $6 per student. The development of Catholic schools relieved some of the drain on inadequate financial resources. As early as 1868, Saints Peter and Paul's parish reported 239 students in its school, the parochial school in Lonaconing claimed 81, and one in Barton had 52. The private nonsectarian schools continued to offer a more diversified curriculum than the public schools, including courses in German and French.[30]

Considering the limited appropriations, the state's decision to support racially segregated schools was tragic for everyone concerned. The delay in establishing primary schools for Negroes indicated that the area's black population suffered most. The 1864 law, and subsequent legislation, earmarked county taxes paid by Negroes and designated private donations, as well as special county and state grants, for the development of black schools. From the public source, the county spent only $200 in 1868, or approximately $3.30 per student on the basis of sixty black students attending school in Cumberland in 1869. Even by 1867, the county was spending $5.44 per white student. Moreover, the Negro school in Frostburg was established only after the Beall family donated land, and Lonaconing did not open a black school until 1887. Westernport had twenty-five to thirty black students receiving instruction in the African Methodist Episcopal Church in 1894 before a school was built in 1896. By 1894, there were 211 Negro students in the county, and by 1900 black illiteracy had declined to 360 from the 542 who were unable to read and write in 1870. While the attendance rate of Negro school children was higher than that of whites, a significant number of both races either were not attending classes at all or were doing so irregularly. In education, as in other areas of public or social life, the practice of racial separation took its toll. Not only did Negroes face the stigma of inferiority which white-imposed segregation carried with it, but their schools remained financially short-changed. The quarterly share of state aid for black schools in 1902 was $246.21 as compared with $5,675.50 for white schools. The diffusion of limited funds hurt Negroes more than it did whites, as did the whole system of segregation. However, the absence of interracial contact in the county schools also deprived white children of knowledge of the black experience, an understanding which would have curtailed racial ignorance, perhaps lessened racial prejudice, and most certainly enriched the lives of the dominant population.[31]

Once the initial building program for the lower schools was finished, a more rigorous and sophisticated program of instruction was developed. Terms gradually increased from three months in 1865 to nine months in 1900. Although attendance remained irregular, the number of students attending public schools increased to about 8,000 by the end of the century. By this time, more advanced institutions offered students a higher level of education. The early free public schools were limited chiefly to the first four grades. Some high school subjects were available as early as 1878 at the Maryland Avenue School in Cumberland for students who had passed sixth grade examinations, officially justifying the use of the name Allegany County High School. But until the end of the century, the Allegany County Academy, which had offered college preparatory courses since its inception in 1798, was the region's only truly advanced educational institution. Although it operated partially on state funds, it charged tuition. This expense, and the exclusion of girls until 1879, limited its availability. Upgrading of the free schools' curriculums came in the 1890s, when institutions began to give first preference to teachers with professional training. Frostburg, Lonaconing, and Westernport also opened high schools during that decade even though their curriculums and staffs may not always have merited the advanced title. The most significant progress during the last two decades of the nineteenth century was the increase in literacy. Illiteracy for people ten years of age or older had been reduced from 4,037 in 1880 to 2,792 in 1900, of whom 699 were foreign born. There was a slightly lower percentage of illiterate voters in Allegany County (1 out of 11.42) than in the city of Baltimore.[32]

The establishment of a state-supported teacher training school in Frostburg at the turn of the century climaxed a half century of educational progress. Sparked by I. Benson Oder, editor and publisher of the Frostburg *Mining Journal,* a small group of Alleganians pressed for enabling legislation and appropriations for such a school in early January 1898. A month later, Senator David E. Dick, a veteran of the labor struggles in the mining region, introduced a bill to appropriate $25,000 to create State Normal School No. 2. Local enthusiasts were divided on the question of the proposed school's location. Cumberland began with the best case. It had the advantage of size, superior transportation facilities, and a good academy which could easily expand its curriculum to include the training of teachers. Oakland also had its supporters who lobbied in Annapolis. Frostburg's principal champion was Oder. He made concern over the students' health his main argument. Oakland's glade land fostered malaria, he asserted, while human and industrial waste made the Potomac River a carrier of typhoid fever. The Cumberland group, realizing that the division over the location was hurting what chance the normal school appropriation had in the face of the legislature's relative indifference and fiscal conservatism, conceded to Frostburg in early March. Even then the appropriation remained in doubt. Finally, an official in the state comptroller's office, who had family ties in Frostburg, proposed that the state provide an initial $20,000 and $5,000 annually on the condition that the people of Frostburg buy the land for the school. The citizens of Frostburg did just that, spearheading a successful fund-raising effort and purchasing a suitable site. The first students enrolled for classes at the new State Normal School No. 2 in September 1902.[33]

The institution's impact on the county during its first decade and a half is difficult to assess. It did improve the training of some of the area's teachers. There were no students from western Maryland in the state's only other normal school in Baltimore in 1901. Of the ninety-four members of the first class at Frostburg, all but two came from Allegany County, and half of them lived in the Mountain City. In addition, 151 elementary students attended a model school, crowding into three classrooms under the supervision of three of the seven normal school teachers. All 245 students occupied the campus's one building, what is now Old Main. The curriculum until 1917 included Latin, math, history, rhetoric and literature, natural and physical sciences, drawing, music, and physical education. However, a state study of public education, published in 1916, reported that the school's equipment was "altogether inadequate" for instruction in most of the science courses, manual training, and the fine arts. Grudging state support also impeded hiring a qualified staff. Moreover, the underpaid teachers spent much of their time working with students who came with no high school background.

Admission standards were tightened in 1917. Another building was added in 1913, making it possible to separate elementary school children from the others and to provide better opportunities for observation and practice teaching. Despite the low level of public funding and the school's divided services, 156 students completed the teacher training study through the class of 1914, and 131 of them were shortly engaged in teaching.[34]

In Allegany County, interest in learning transcended the development of local educational institutions. Visitors to the mining region were often impressed with the extent and size of home libraries. Moreover, beginning in the 1870s, Frostburg residents had access to a number of circulating libraries. One of them, operating out of Hitchins Brothers Store, rented books for ten cents a book for two weeks, and the Frostburg Circulating Library charged a one-dollar membership fee in 1875. Barton also had a circulating library in 1880. There were undoubtedly others throughout the county. How many people used these libraries is impossible to estimate, but there were enough examples of successful careers built through a zeal for knowledge to indicate that the area was not backward in this respect. David J. Lewis carried books to the mines as a young boy. Later, his disciplined reading of law led to a prosperous legal practice and a prominent political career. Some people born into more comfortable circumstances attended some of the nation's leading universities. A number of Lonaconing young men studied at Princeton University, noted for its academic excellence and Presbyterian heritage. George Henderson, a mining superintendent at Eckhart Mines, also sent his son Robert to Princeton, where he graduated in 1879 as a classmate of Woodrow Wilson. After a short apprenticeship in a law office, he attended the University of Maryland Law School and later became a prominent jurist. Judge Henderson's son graduated from Princeton University and the Harvard University Law School, and one of his daughters received a degree from Bryn Mawr. Even more significant, a local woman, Emily Campbell, earned an M.D. in 1898. There were limits to the public's appetite for the printed word, however, if it involved a sizeable outlay of money.

In 1901, Cumberland residents, in a citywide referendum, soundly defeated a proposal in which Andrew Carnegie offered to donate $25,000 for a public library building if the city would provide the site and $2,500 annually for upkeep and a general fund.[35]

The large number of newspapers in Allegany County also served an educational function, for they featured excerpts from literary works as well as trenchant editorials on important social and political issues. In 1893, Cumberland alone had eight newspapers. They were the *Civilian,* the *Courier,* the *Independent,* the *Alleganian, Die Freie Presse,* and the *Sunday Times,* all weeklies; the dailies were the *Daily News* and the *Evening Times.* Some of them had long, checkered careers. The *Alleganian,* a Democratic weekly established in 1820, was absorbed by the *Daily Times* in 1876, becoming its weekly edition until 1893, when it reestablished a brief independent life. From 1869 until 1872, the *Mountain City Times,* a daily, was under the control of the *Evening Times* Company, which changed the paper's name to the *Daily Times* in 1872 and finally to the *Evening Times* in 1892. By the twentieth century the *Times* publication had the largest circulation of any daily outside Baltimore. In 1871, the *Daily News* began its long life as a Republican organ. The *Civilian,* a Republican weekly founded in 1828, was merged with the *Telegraph* in 1858, continuing to operate until the end of the century. Cumberland also had a German-language newspaper, *Die Freie Presse,* which served parts of western Maryland, Pennsylvania, and West Virginia from 1891 to 1907. The *Courier,* the *Independent,* and a Sunday paper called the *Scimitar* had shorter lives. Frostburg had two newspapers for a brief period in the early 1870s, but the *Mining Journal,* which ran from 1871 to 1919, was clearly the foremost paper in the mining region. The George's Creek *Press,* which ran periodically from 1872 until 1907, was published in Lonaconing. Throughout the late nineteenth and the early twentieth centuries, Lonaconing could claim a number of other short-lived publications. They included the *Weekly Review,* the *Star,* the *Advocate,* and the Lonaconing *Mail.* All of these papers kept county readers abreast of local, national, and international news and their editorial columns often became fierce battlegrounds for divergent political viewpoints.[36]

Residents of the county, however, were never so engrossed in reading as to allow recreational opportunities to suffer. Cumberland built a YMCA on Baltimore Street in 1893, blacks soon organized their own YMCA on Independence Street, and railroad workers formed one in south Cumberland. The Potomac Club, providing a tennis court for its 100 members, opened renovated facilities on a Ridgeley hilltop overlooking the Potomac in 1905. Canoeing was another organized activity. The Shawnee Canoe Club, established in the 1890s with headquarters in Riverside Park, had fifty members and a long waiting list in 1912. During the first decade and a half of the twentieth century, Cumberland also sponsored the Western Maryland and Allegany Mountains Tennis Tournament. A more glittering social affair during this period was the Allegany County Ball held in the Queen City Hotel on New Year's Eve. Admission was limited to the city's elite society. Countless numbers of women's clubs and fraternal organizations throughout the county involved many more people in a more informal social life. Over 800 members of the Ancient Order of Hibernians converged by train on Reynolds in the coal region for their annual reunion and picnic in 1907. In 1911, West Virginia Pulp and Paper Company opened a three-story recreation building for its male employees. The Devon Club, as it was called, contained a library, cardrooms, billiards, a bowling alley, and a motion picture theater.[37]

Silent movies introduced a new dimension of entertainment during the first decade of the twentieth century. The Savoy, opening on Baltimore Street in 1907, was Cumberland's first regular movie house. Its predecessors were makeshift nickelodeon operations in business establishments. By World War I the Queen City had seven downtown theaters and two in the south end, some of which lasted only a few years. Those that survived the competition provided the most popular movies of the day. In Frostburg, Moat's Opera House was remodeled so that it could show moving pictures in 1907, increased its seating capacity to 400, and became known as the Wonderland Theater. The highlight of the first season was the showing of *The Great Train Robbery.* The Dreamland opened as a nickelodeon in 1904 and became the Palace in 1911. Both theaters changed movies each week, showing them every day except Sunday. In 1916, the Palace bought out the old Moat theater, changed its name to the Lyric, increased its seating to 700, and brought the year's most dramatic movie, *The Birth of a Nation,* to the Mountain City. Not all movie theaters prospered; one closed in Lonaconing for lack of patrons. Moving pictures, however, were a popular form of entertainment between 1914 and 1930.[38]

Live entertainment, which was supplanted by the moving pictures elsewhere in the area, continued to flourish in Cumberland through the 1920s. Two or three different productions sometimes appeared weekly at the Academy of Music before it was destroyed by fire in 1910. After 1910, stage shows came to the Maryland Theater, which opened in 1907. This theater, with a capacity of 1,500 to 2,000 seats, mixed live productions with movies beginning in 1912. Al Jolson performed at the Maryland in 1915 and William Jennings Bryan lectured there on the virtues of prohibition in 1919. Excursion trains and special streetcars took patrons home after the performances. For people seeking additional diversion, several restaurants catered to the after-theater crowd. In Frostburg, the Lyric, true to the opera house tradition, mixed the new and the old entertainment, but with less success than its Cumberland competitors. Fewer and fewer theatrical troupes came to Frostburg, so the old opera house showed more and more films.[39]

Racial phobias continued to haunt Negroes during this period of diversified entertainment. While a few light-skinned Negroes passed as white and went where they pleased, most members of their race were admitted only to the Maryland Theater, where they sat in Jim Crow sections in the balcony. Always a small minority, the black population of the county rose from 1,436 in 1890 to 1,827 in 1920, but this represented an actual decline from 3.5 percent to 2.6 percent. Segregation forced them to turn to their own churches and fraternal orders for organized social activity. On special occasions, such as the placing of a cornerstone for a new African Methodist Episcopal Church in Cumberland in September 1892, a significant part of the white community joined in the celebration. Regular interracial social contact, however, was never established in the modern era.[40]

Other modern social phenomena signaled both the joy and the pain of the new century. A cocaine traffic in the Queen City, described by police as "very deeply rooted" in 1905, was transforming people into "physical wrecks." Technological innovations evoked more positive attention. In 1904, three men made a record-breaking twenty-two-hour trip by automobile from Baltimore to Cumberland. Four years later the county sheriff talked fearfully of speeds of twenty-five to fifty miles per hour at car races in Narrows Park. Once again, new forms of transportation would emerge to compete with older means of transit, with equally significant social implications.[41]

CHAPTER IX NOTES

1. E. L. Doctorow, *Ragtime* (New York: Random House, 1974, 1975), p. 3.

2. J. William Hunt, "Across the Desk," in the Cumberland *Sunday Times*, Oct. 27, 1963 (hereafter cited as Hunt); and Cumberland *Daily News*, June 3 and 8, July 26, and Dec. 11, 1871.

3. Hunt, Jan. 2, and July 9, 1964; Russel Nye, *The Unembarrassed Muse* (New York: The Dial Press, 1970), pp. 158-60; Cumberland *Daily Alleganian*, March 7, 1876; and Scott Reinhart, "The History of Frostburg Movie Theatres" (Frostburg State College: unpublished paper, 1972), p. 2 (hereafter cited as Reinhart, "Frostburg Theatres").

4. Mary Elizabeth H. VanNewkirk, "Frostburg After Hours, Recreation: 1871-1877," *Journal of the Alleghenies*, Vol. 9, 1973: 22-23 (hereafter cited as VanNewkirk, "Frostburg After Hours"); Nellie Dowling, "The Story of Westernport" (Westernport Public Library: unpublished paper, no date), p. 18 (hereafter cited as Dowling, "Story of Westernport"); and Frostburg *Mining Journal*, May 18, 1872.

5. Hunt, July 9, 1967; and Dowling, "Story of Westernport," p. 19. The information on Cumberland's theater life was acquired from scattered issues of the Cumberland *Civilian* in 1890.

6. Cumberland *Civilian and Telegraph*, July 25, 1867; VanNewkirk, "Frostburg After Hours," p. 23; Hunt, June 16, 1963, and July 9, 1967; and the *Advocate* (Lonaconing), Sept. 23, 1915.

7. David W. Vaughan, taped interview with Mrs. Elsie Cutter, April 1975; interview with James Klippstein and Alvin H. Ternent, Oct. 1, 1975 (hereafter cited as Klippstein-Ternent Interview); H. S. Cummings, ed., *An Investigation of the Pollution and Sanitary Conditions of the Potomac Watershed* (Washington, D.C.: Hygienic Laboratory, 1916), p. 25; H. N. Parker, ed., *The Potomac River Basin* (Washington, D.C.: U.S. Geological Survey of Water Supply and Irrigation, Paper, 1907), No. 192, p. 217; U.S., *Congressional Record,* 55th Cong., 2nd session, 1898, Senate Document 90, pp. 14-27; Dowling, "Story of Westernport," p. 17; interview with John W. Shannon, Oct. 4, 1975; Cumberland *Daily News,* July 21, 1908; and Cumberland *Civilian,* Jan. 4 and Feb. 8, 1895.

8. VanNewkirk, "Frostburg After Hours," pp. 25-26; Cumberland *Daily News,* Aug. 25, 1871; and interview with James G. Conway, Sept. 16, 1975.

9. VanNewkirk, "Frostburg After Hours," pp. 26-27.

10. Hunt, May 22, 1955, and Jan. 4, 1959; James W. Thomas and T. J. C. Williams, *History of Allegany County, Maryland* (Philadelphia: L. R. Titsworth and Co., 1923), Vol. I, p. 288 (hereafter cited as Thomas and Williams, *Allegany County*); and The George's Creek *Press* (Lonaconing), Aug. 29 and Sept. 5, 1907.

11. Katherine A. Harvey, *The Best Dressed Miners: Life and Labor in the Maryland Coal Region, 1835-1910* (Ithaca: Cornell University Press, 1969), pp. 19-26 (hereafter cited as Harvey, *Best Dressed Miners*); Dieter Cunz, *The Maryland Germans* (Princeton: Princeton University Press, 1948), pp. 384-86 (hereafter cited as Cunz, *Maryland Germans*); and U.S. Census Office, *Tenth Census of the U.S.: 1880* (Washington, D.C.: Census Office, 1883), p. 435 (hereafter cited as *Tenth Census of U.S.*).

12. Interview with James W. Bishop, Nov. 4, 1975; Harvey, *Best Dressed Miners,* pp. 116, 238; *Town of Luke, Maryland: Fiftieth Anniversary of Incorporation, 1922 through 1972* (Luke, Md.: privately published, 1972), p. 8; and Florence Yankelevitz, essay submitted for "I Remember When" Contest, 1976.

13. U.S. Census Office, *Ninth Census of the U.S.: 1870, I* (Washington, D.C.: Census Office, 1872), p. 542 (hereafter cited as *Ninth Census of U.S., I*); Frostburg *Mining Journal,* Feb. 3, March 30, July 30, and Sept. 14, 1872; *Boyds Cumberland City and Allegany County Directory, 1877-78* (Cumberland, Md.: Alleganian and Times Publishing Company, 1878), pp. xxi-xxiii; Cumberland *Civilian and Telegraph,* March 7, 1867; *St. Patrick's Church, Mt. Savage, Maryland: Special Centennial Issue, 1873-1973* (Mt. Savage, Md.: St. Patrick's Centennial Committee, 1973), no page number (hereafter cited as *St. Patrick's Centennial Issue*); Harvey, *Best Dressed Miners,* p. 84; and Thomas J. Stanton, *A Century of Growth or the History of the Church in Western Maryland* (Baltimore: John Murphy Co., 1900), I, pp. 153-67, 176-203, 206-21, 223-27.

14. Harvey, *Best Dressed Miners,* pp. 16-17, 30-31, 80-85; and Frostburg *Mining Journal,* Feb. 3, May 11, June 8, and Aug. 31, 1872, and June 28, 1873.

15. Frostburg *Mining Journal,* May 11 and July 30, 1872, Dec. 23, 1882, and Feb. 28, 1883; *The Courier Cumberland City Directory, 1888* (Cumberland, Md.: Courier Publishing Co., 1889), no page number; the *Valley Times* (Lonaconing), Nov. 22, 1879; interview with Mrs. Gladys Rice, Oct. 10, 1975; and Klippstein-Ternent Interview.

16. Harvey, *Best Dressed Miners,* pp. 85-88; B. F. Johnson, *Men of Mark in Maryland* (Baltimore: B. F. Johnson, Inc., 1912), Vol. IV, pp. 319-21 (hereafter cited as Johnson, *Men of Mark*); Cunz, *Maryland Germans,* p. 387; and Cumberland *Daily News,* Nov. 24, 1915.

17. Harvey, *Best Dressed Miners,* pp. 182-84; and *Special 1908 Edition of the Daily News.*

18. John T. Scharf, *History of Western Maryland* (Philadelphia: L. H. Everts, 1882), II, pp. 1359-60, 1376-77 (hereafter cited as Scharf, *Western Maryland*); Harvey, *Best Dressed Miners,* pp. 86-87; Hunt, Nov. 19, 1961; and *Special 1908 Edition of the Daily News.*

19. Scharf, *Western Maryland,* II, pp. 1494, 1508-9; Thomas and Williams, *Allegany County,* Vol. I, pp. 526, 535, 542-43; the George's Creek *Press,* Sept. 5, 1907; *Special 1908 Edition of the Daily News;* and Cumberland *Daily News,* Feb. 23, 1905, and March 18, 1909.

20. *Ninth Census of U.S., I,* p. 214; Henry A. Grine, *Preliminary Economic Studies of the Western Allegany County Area* (Annapolis: Maryland State Planning Commission, 1941), p. 9 (hereafter cited as Grine, *Preliminary Economic Studies*); *Fourteenth Census of the U.S., 1920 Bulletin, Population: Maryland* (Washington, D.C.: Department of Commerce, 1921), pp. 2, 5; the *Heritage Review,* February 1973; Hunt, Nov. 19, 1961; Cumberland *Civilian,* Sept. 26, 1890; and *Special 1908 Edition of the Daily News.*

21. Harvey, *Best Dressed Miners,* pp. 85, 95-97; Frostburg *Mining Journal,* Sept. 30, 1871, Aug. 24 and 31, 1872, and Nov. 11, 1876; Cumberland *Daily News,* Jan. 4, 1897; Grine, *Preliminary Economic Studies,* p. 9; and U.S. Census Office, *Twelfth Census of the U.S.: 1900, I* (Washington, D.C.: Census Office, 1902), p. 176.

22. Charles Carney, "The History of Mt. Savage" (unpublished paper prepared for the Maryland Cooperative Extension Service, 1967), pp. 7-8; and *St. Patrick's Centennial Issue,* n.p.

23. *Tenth Census of the U.S.*, p. 204; Harvey, *Best Dressed Miners,* pp. 84-85; *The Heritage Press,* August 1972; Grine, *Preliminary Economic Studies,* p. 9; Mrs. Frances D. Greaves' notes on local newspapers; Dowling, "Story of Westernport," pp. 17-18; and Piedmont *Herald,* April 20, 1894.

24. W. L. Fairbanks, *A Statistical Analysis of the Population of Maryland* (Baltimore: Maryland Development Bureau, 1931), p. 41 (hereafter cited as Fairbanks, *Statistical Analysis of Pop. of Md.*); and Scharf, *Western Maryland,* II, pp. 1457-62.

25. Dorothy Gerbing Kave, "Allegany Grove Campground," *The Heritage Press,* April 1972; Cumberland *Civilian,* July 20, 1890; Hunt, Aug. 20, 1950, and April 3, 1955; and J. Marshall Porter, essay submitted for "I Remember When" Contest, 1976 (hereafter cited as Porter, "I Remember When").

26. *The Heritage Press,* April 1972; Hunt, Aug. 20, 1950, and April 3, 1955; Porter, "I Remember When"; and interview with Miss Olive Simpson, Sept. 3, 1975.

27. *The Heritage Press,* August 1972; Hunt, Dec. 11, 1949; *Historical-Biographical Sketch of Frostburg, Maryland and Its Citizens* (Frostburg: Mining Journal Publishing Company, 1912), p. 10 (hereafter cited as *Historical Sketch of Frostburg*); the George's Creek *Press,* Aug. 29, 1907; Piedmont *Herald,* April 20, 1894; and Dowling, "Story of Westernport," p. 19.

28. *Special 1908 Edition of the Daily News;* and *Historical Sketch of Frostburg,* p. 9.

29. Harvey, *Best Dressed Miners,* pp. 108-12; Gertrude Williams, "History of Education in Allegany County, Maryland, 1798-1900" (M.A. thesis, University of Maryland, 1936), pp. 72-99 (hereafter cited as Williams, "Education in Allegany County"); and Cumberland *Union,* Nov. 25, 1865, and Jan. 13 and March 31, 1866.

30. Williams, "Education in Allegany County," pp. 113-18, 139-54; Scharf, *Western Maryland,* II, pp. 1355-60; Cumberland *Union,* Jan. 13, 1866; Harvey, *Best Dressed Miners,* pp. 110-12; and Cumberland *Civilian and Telegraph,* Feb. 19, 1868, and April 15, 1869.

31. Williams, "Education in Allegany County," pp. 155-72; Piedmont *Herald,* April 20, 1894; Cumberland *Daily News,* Dec. 15, 1894; and Cumberland *Alleganian,* Jan. 9, 1902.

32. Williams, "Education in Allegany County," pp. 32, 97-113, 121-38; Scharf, *Western Maryland,* II, p. 1358; and Frostburg *Mining Journal,* March 30, 1901.

33. Mary Elizabeth H. VanNewkirk, "The Origins of Frostburg State College" (Frostburg, unpublished paper, 1975), pp. 1-10 (hereafter cited as VanNewkirk, "Origins of Frostburg State College"); and Frostburg *Mining Journal,* Feb. 10, 11 and 12 and April 5 and 23, 1898.

34. VanNewkirk, "Origins of Frostburg State College," p. 1; Mary Elizabeth H. VanNewkirk, "The Evolution of a College," *The FSC Journal of Mathematics Education,* No. 8 (1974): 6-12; and Abraham Flexner and Frank P. Bachman, *Public Education in Maryland: A Report to the Maryland Educational Survey Commission* (New York: The General Education Board, 1916), pp. 70-71.

35. Harvey, *Best Dressed Miners,* p. 107; Frostburg *Mining Journal,* Jan. 3 and March 13, 1874, and May 8, 1875; the *Heritage Press,* August 1972; Johnson, *Men of Mark,* Vol. IV, pp. 319-20; Thomas and Williams, *Allegany County,* Vol. I, pp. 305-7, and Vol. II, pp. 771-72; and Hunt, Feb. 6, 1949.

36. Hunt, March 6, 1949, April 8, 1945, and Jan. 23, 1955; and Thomas and Williams, *Allegany County*, Vol. I, pp. 372-76.

37. Hunt, Jan. 27, 1952, and Sept. 24, 1950; Cumberland *Daily News*, March 7, 1908, Nov. 21, 1905, and May 29, 1912; interview with Herman J. Miller, Oct. 30, 1975 (hereafter cited as Miller interview); the George's Creek *Press*, Sept. 5, 1907; and Dowling, "Story of Westernport," pp. 19-20.

38. Miller Interview; Reinhart, "Frostburg Theatres," pp. 3-5; and the George's Creek *Press*, Sept. 5, 1907.

39. Hunt, Jan. 31, 1954, and May 19, 1946; Cumberland *Daily News*, Nov. 15, 1907, and Feb. 22, 1919; and Reinhart, "Frostburg Theatres," p. 7.

40. Miller Interview; Fairbanks, *Statistical Analysis of Pop. of Md.*, pp. 75, 87; and Cumberland *Daily News*, Sept. 10, 1892.

41. Cumberland *Daily News*, July 19, 1905; Aug. 15, 1904; and Aug. 10, 1908.

X

TUMULT AND CHANGE, 1865-1920

Dramatic events often produced special currents of social and political change in the years between the Civil War and the end of World War I. Popular feeling against Republican Reconstruction policies in the South helped revitalize the county's Democratic Party before the tariff issue made the GOP the dominant political force in the 1890s. Capitalizing on a statewide rebellion against Democratic bossism in 1895, a Republican gubernatorial candidate from Cumberland, Lloyd Lowndes, overthrew the organization which had ruled the state for twenty years. Five years later, a coal strike would propel a former miner and Democratic convert, David J. Lewis, into the state legislature, where he would pioneer social welfare laws. The period from 1865 to 1920 also saw labor unions gaining a foothold in the county and Alleganians fighting their first overseas wars, rallying nobly to the defense of Cuban insurgents in 1898 and western European democracies in 1917. Taking a cue from the idealism of World War I, women activists in the region intensified their struggle for their own rights.

Yet, the "good old days" were also leavened with baser passion. Lingering frontier traditions not only prompted people to pitch in and help others, but often impelled them to gain violent retribution when they felt they were wronged. Crimes of passion were frequent well into the twentieth century and the vigilante impulse was never fully curbed. A large crowd witnessed a mob-inspired racial lynching in Cumberland in 1907. Women in the county were not immune to acts of violence when the labor struggles of the era threatened their family security.

Lawlessness frequently erupted in the immediate post-Civil War era; wartime emotion and frontier traditions did not die easily. In the spring of 1869, the Cumberland *Civilian and Telegraph* reported that murder, once "a rarity," had become almost a monthly occurrence in the county. Editorializing nine months later, the paper attributed the mounting violence to the wartime repeal of a state law prohibiting possession of concealed weapons. Consequently, thousands of men and boys had become "familiarized" with murderous weapons and were using them at the "slightest provocation." Furthermore, arson and robbery grew to such proportions in Cumberland in the winter of 1870 that a vigilante committee was formed to assist the police and the sheriff's office in ridding the city of the menace. But not even the Committee of Safety was prepared to deal with the consequences of a turbulent love affair.[1]

Both passion and tradition converged in the famous murder of William W. McKaig, Jr., and subsequent trial, a case which captured the attention of Alleganians and which continues to intrigue local people today. The main actors in this tragic melodrama besides young McKaig were Myra Black, her father, H. D. Black, and her brother, H. Crawford Black. McKaig, a handsome, dashing veteran of the Confederate Army, city councilman, and heir to the McKaig Foundry, had a flourishing social life which he divided between Washington, D.C., and Cumberland. After the war he had frequently escorted the vivacious Miss Black to social functions in Cumberland. Apparently the romance continued even after his marriage to a Virginia woman. Myra possessed love letters from McKaig written after the marriage and she claimed that he was the one who was responsible for impregnating her. Meanwhile, her brother, another Confederate veteran, had returned from service in Maximilian's army in Mexico to take a job with the Franklin Coal Company in the lower end of Georges Creek. What could have passed as a loss of pride and perhaps exile for young Miss Black soon became a matter of family honor and tradition, which mandated that the closest male relative gun down the man responsible for the girl's ruination. In early June 1870, the elder Black went after

McKaig with a shotgun, but only wounded him. When young Crawford Black discovered what had happened, learned that McKaig had made insulting remarks to his sister at the Belvidere Hall, and read the tempestuous letters, he went gunning for McKaig on Baltimore Street on the morning of October 17. After killing him, Black immediately gave himself up to a deputy sheriff in the courthouse.[2]

The ensuing funeral and trial resembled a novelist's script. McKaig's funeral procession contained the largest concourse of people ever seen on such an occasion and local emotion required moving the trial to Frederick. Three judges presided over the proceedings, which took place in April 1871. The state's attorney general led the prosecution and a well-known Indiana congressman defended Black. While crowds packed into the courtroom, Myra sat in a local hotel with her baby in her arms. Her family's honor was upheld and her brother's life was saved by eleven witnesses who testified that McKaig had a pistol in his hand when young Black found him on that fateful morning in Cumberland. An acquittal verdict amidst a tumultuous courtroom ended the melodrama.[3]

The penchant for violence, frontier justice, and crimes of passion continued. When Negroes were involved, tradition invariably worked against them. A black man accused of raping an "aged" white woman near New Creek in the eastern part of the county in August 1872 stood little chance against the prevailing practice of assuming guilt on the part of Negroes charged with sexual attacks on white women. He was convicted the same day the incident occurred and executed several months later. Blacks were also vulnerable to more spontaneous violence. Ethnic slurs exchanged between an Italian immigrant and a Negro in a Cumberland saloon in January 1895 led to an abortive pistol attempt on the life of the black man. The assailant received only forty-five days in jail for assault and carrying a concealed weapon. Four years later a white man received a jury verdict of justifiable homicide for killing a black man accused of assaulting two white women. The death penalty was not reserved for Negroes, however. The last legal execution in the county during this period was that of a white man in 1890, convicted of shooting his wife on a

Cumberland street. Husbands avenging their wives' affairs with other men continued to be the most frequent crimes of passion. Two such murders took place within an eight-month period in 1903. Area Negroes were the most vulnerable to mob violence. On the evening of October 5, 1907, in Cumberland, a thousand people witnessed the lynching of an out-of-town Negro, William Burns. Burns's killing of a police officer following an attempted arrest triggered the formation of a vigilante group of about twenty masked men who received aid from thirty others in battering down the jail door. The mob dragged him feet first down the steps at Prospect Square before a number of armed men riddled his battered body with bullets. The lynching became simply a symbolic gesture of race control. Local ministers condemned the action and a judge urged a grand jury to secure indictments against the mob's ringleaders. There was no prosecution, however, and the threat of lynch mobs remained a constant reminder to Negroes who openly challenged the racial status quo.[4]

Emotion also characterized the politics of the immediate postwar era. The majority of the people in Allegany County, which at that time extended to the far western part of the state, were loyal to the Union during the Civil War. Determined to enforce the Union victory and to punish those who had actively supported the Confederacy, Cumberland's two leading newspapers emphatically supported a state law which disfranchised opponents of the Union. When five applicants from the county appealed to Governor Thomas Swann for pardon and renewal of their civil rights in 1866, the *Union* reminded its readers of the Cumberland boy lying in Rose Hill Cemetery who had died of starvation in a Confederate prison. The paper also noted the "nearly" twenty others who died in the infamous Andersonville camp as well as the Union soldiers who died on the battlefields. "They have made their bed, let them lie in it until they consent to act as men and not as traitors," editorialized the unforgiving *Union.*[5]

Most Alleganians, however, were opposed to harsh federal treatment of the defeated South and to federal guarantees of the Negro's rights. Because the voters associated these stands, as well as the issue of Union, with the Republican Party, the county's Democratic Party rapidly recovered its lost strength. The area's most prominent Democrat, William Walsh, presided over mass meetings in Cumberland in March and September of 1866. Resolutions supporting President Andrew Johnson's lenient Reconstruction policy were adopted at both meetings, the second of which was attended by 12,000 people. Even Republican newspapers were divided on the major national issues. The Cumberland *Union,* denying the Democratic claim that the Republicans were the "Negro party," accused Democrats of using the specter of racial equality as a "smokescreen" for the return of "Jeff Davis rule." While the Republican paper opposed Johnson's pardoning of former Confederates, it endorsed the president's position against federal protection of the Negro's civil rights. The Cumberland *Civilian and Telegraph* was consistently critical of Johnson's policies, although the Republican organ indicated that its support of voting rights for blacks did not mean that it favored racial equality. In 1868, the Democratic presidential candidate, Horatio Seymour, narrowly defeated the Republican war hero Ulysses S. Grant in Allegany County; the Democratic congressional candidate, Patrick Hamill, also carried the county by a small margin. Despite its efforts to avoid association with the movement for Negro equality, the Republican Party lost ground in the area. In 1869, Freedmen's Bureau officials ducked eggs and "other missiles" during a meeting in Cumberland. Allegany Negroes, nevertheless, were happy to vote for the first time in 1870. They held a celebration in Frostburg, an emerging Republican stronghold, in September 1871.[6]

Neither major party gained the upper hand in the county's politics during the two decades following the Civil War, but a few notable trends did develop. With party fortunes fluctuating sharply, the small black vote, estimated by the *Civilian* as numbering 202 in 1870, acquired unusual significance for its size. The black political presence may have produced a white backlash in 1870, as the *Civilian* claimed, for the Democratic majority in the congressional race that year increased from 300 to 800. In a county election in 1877 and a congressional race in 1878, however, the *Alleganian,* a zealous Democratic paper, tried to woo black voters away from their Republican base. Democrats were more consistent and more successful in courting the immigrant vote. The *Alleganian*, apparently confident of the Irish vote which traditionally went Democratic, reminded German immigrants in 1877 that the Democratic Party was the one that represented the interests of the wage earner and the foreign-born voter. The Democrats' identification with the Catholic immigrants, common laborers, and white supremacists explains why the party of Andrew Jackson generally won the support of Cumberland and Mount Savage, with their large working-class and Catholic populations. Not all immigrants or wage earners were Democrats, however. The towns west of Cumberland, especially Frostburg and Lonaconing, helped keep the Republican Party alive and well in Allegany County. Coal miners in the two major towns in the coal region, many of whom were also recent immigrants, often voted overwhelmingly Republican. This phenomenon may be attributed partly to cultural factors such as the preponderance of Protestants and the pockets of temperance sentiment in that region. But the main factor was the Republican Party's unequivocal support of the protective tariff on coal in contrast to the Democratic position of tariff for revenue only. As the county's economy was so heavily dependent on coal, interest in the tariff extended beyond the mining areas. A Democratic congressman who ignored the tariff issue in 1869 failed to survive a primary challenge in 1870. Commenting on a public meeting in support of a high duty early that year, the *Civilian and Telegraph* asserted that "repeal or reduction of the coal tariff would prove fatal" to the region.[7]

The separation of the western half of the county in 1872 failed to stir such cataclysmic fears among those who appeared to lose most by the division. Few eastern Alleganians took much notice of the campaign by their neighbors to establish their own governmental unit even though it would entail loss of more than half of their territory and about one-fourth, 8,267, of their population. Perhaps they sympathized with the dissidents' complaints about the neglect of roads in the outlying regions, underrepresentation in the general assembly, inequitable disbursement of tax revenues, and the hardships that citizens in the far western districts faced in getting to the courts. Outsiders who measured the separation movement in materialistic terms believed that the area petitioning for separation held little importance except for its timber. Such a move would, however, increase western Maryland's representation in the legislature. The new county leaders moved swiftly toward their goal once the campaign began in earnest in 1871. By April 1872, Governor William P. Whyte had approved an act providing for a local referendum on the issue in the fall election. In November, western Alleganians supported separation by a vote of 1,297 to 405 and selected Oakland as the county seat. Earlier in the year the movement's chief promoters won approval for naming the new county after John W. Garrett, president of the B&O Railroad. Some problems persisted, however. County commissioners who lived outside Oakland delayed appropriations for a new courthouse for several years and the final boundary was not determined until 1898. The ease with which western separatists achieved their objective, moreover, encouraged dissatisfied Georges Creek residents to try to form their own county in the middle of old Allegany. Claiming that the coal region's wealth justified such an action, they started a petition campaign in 1873. However, the area lacked sufficient population or enough support in the legislative judiciary committee for the campaign to amount to anything.[8]

While the movement to create a new county in the coal region soon collapsed, the resentment in parts of Allegany County, particularly in Frostburg, against Cumberland's domination of political offices continued. When county conventions in 1873 selected nearly half of forty-one candidates from the Queen City, and only five from Frostburg, the *Mining Journal* railed against the disparity. Congressional candidates from the area were invariably Cumberland politicians, whatever their party affiliation. A young lawyer with a family history in the state dating back to the colonial era, Lloyd Lowndes, won a Republican seat in 1872. Two years later, Cumberland's most prominent lawyer, William Walsh, defeated Lowndes in the general election. A native of Ireland and the city's leading Democratic stalwart, Walsh was renominated by his party in a convention held in the Academy of Music in 1876. Stressing the party's support for the foreign-born residents, Walsh defeated his Republican opponent, Louis E. McComas, by a handful of votes, even though he failed to carry Allegany County. Perhaps sensing the ascendancy of the protective tariff issue and the Republican Party in his district, Walsh declined to run for renomination in 1878.[9]

Depressions and strikes, which intermittently dominated the life of the county for two decades beginning in the mid-1870s, often reduced conventional politics to relative insignificance. As if sporadic employment during the severe hard times of 1875-1876 were not a sufficient burden on coal miners, the companies cut wages to correspond with those in the Clearfield, Pennsylvania, region early in 1877. Angry miners responded with a strike, but faced with the prospect of a general lockout and defection from their own ranks, they soon returned to work in March at the lower rate of pay. Subsequent canal and railroad strikes, however, forced a curtailment of mining production. In mid-June, canal boatmen struck for higher wages and blockaded the waterway. Federal troops finally opened the canal to the accompanying jeers of striking workers in a prelude to the larger conflict to come. In mid-July, 10 percent wage cuts on the B&O and other railroads triggered a national strike which swept Allegany County into a social upheaval. It began in Martinsburg, West Virginia, on July 16, when the B&O reduced wages for the second time in eight months and doubled the length of freight trains without increasing the size of crews. The strike and the ensuing intervention of federal troops quickly engulfed western Maryland. A train, operated by soldiers, which broke through barriers in Martinsburg was uncoupled by a crowd of railroad, canal, and unemployed rolling mill workers in Cumberland. In the coal region, miners joined the battle when they helped forcibly remove train operators in Keyser in the presence of federal troops. As resistance to railroad movement deepened, the conflict which it fostered became too great for local authorities to handle. A riotous crowd successfully demanded the release of two men charged with wounding a trainman, carrying the men off on their shoulders in triumph. Finally, after a week of strife, the state national guard moved trains through the area.[10]

The workers' revolt in 1877 introduced an era of unionization and labor-management conflict that the county had generally avoided since the strikes of 1854. There was a flurry of miners' organizational activity in the coalfields in 1873-1874, and immigrant miners tried to infuse their union loyalties into their neighbors' hearts, but the labor struggles of 1877 were spontaneous actions rather than union-organized endeavors. However, when coal operators reduced wages again in March 1878, the Knights of Labor, the dominant union movement of the time, finally established a foothold in the Georges Creek area. Its efforts, including sponsorship of a two-month strike in the fall of 1879, restored pre-depression wages. By 1880, about one-third of the region's coal miners had joined the Knights. Both the pay and the union gains were short-lived, however. In 1882, the companies, aided by imported strikebreakers and a new state law which allowed the use of state police to protect the new workers, defeated a six-month strike for a ten-hour day. The operators also took the opportunity to reinstitute the previous wage cut. A severely weakened Knights of Labor organization collapsed in the county two years later when companies successfully reduced wages even more. Other labor groups, however, tried to fill the vacuum. A broad, regional three-month strike organized by the National Federation of Miners, beginning in May 1886, may have ultimately pressured Allegany County coal companies to rescind the wage cuts of the previous ten years. The return of higher wages to miners in 1887 ended a decade of erratic pay and employment. Unions, however, had failed to establish a secure base in the county. Although a large number of miners and a smaller number of laborers and mechanics were sympathetic to unionization, company policy still held sway. Determined to retain their authority, moreover, mining companies would mount a more vigorous counteroffensive against unions in the last decade of the nineteenth century.[11]

A familiar pattern of depression, strikes, and strife again interrupted general prosperity and economic expansion in the 1890s. While the national depression, which began in 1893, produced less hardship in Allegany County than the economic disaster of the 1870s, it did result in some business failures, significant work layoffs, and general wage reductions. In protest against lower wages, Cumberland tinplate workers staged a three-month strike in late 1894. Earlier in the year, Coxey's Army, a group of unemployed workers en route to the nation's capital to petition for federal job programs, stopped off in the Queen City to rest and to enlarge its recruits. Ridiculed by the Cumberland *Daily News* as purposeless "mud-bespattered vagrants," the jobless army was nevertheless met by an "enormous crowd" of people who turned out to observe and visit them in Narrows Park. The main stage of the union drama, however, again took place in the coal region. Pay cuts prompted the recently organized United Mine Workers to call a national strike in early 1894 to raise wages by reducing the surplus of coal. Many Georges Creek miners, recalling that the national Knights of Labor leaders had failed to provide financial support for them in 1882, opposed a local walkout. Others left work in May to demonstrate their sympathy with the general principles of the strike. The division among Allegany miners became a bitter one, involving "the gentle sex" in not-so-gentle modes of action. Eckhart women accompanied their husbands to the mines and threatened to replace men forced out of the mines by strikers. On the other hand, their Carlos sisters stoned workers coming out of the tunnels. Frostburg miners encountered sixty women "armed with tin pans, buckets, baseball bats, and babies" as they returned home from work. The coal companies finally compelled dissidents to return to the mines through the use of strikebreakers, state police forces, court indictments of union organizers, and reports that they were prepared to construct housing projects for imported workers.[12]

A statewide political upheaval, involving Cumberland leadership, would soon eclipse labor strife and hard times as the dominating event in the county. For twenty years, a Democratic organization, headed by Arthur Pue Gorman and I. Freeman Rasin, both from Baltimore, had controlled the state government in an increasingly arrogant fashion. Bossism, Democratic rule, and eastern control of state politics all came to an abrupt end in 1895 with the election of a Republican governor, Lloyd Lowndes, from western Maryland. A descendant of a distinguished Maryland family who could trace his ancestral roots to a colonial governor, Lowndes symbolized the popular desire for a return to high-minded leadership. Born in Clarksburg, West Virginia, in 1845 and educated in Pennsylvania at Allegheny College and the University Law School, Lowndes came to Cumberland, where his father had begun a business, in 1867. Although his early years in the Queen City were largely devoted to his legal practice, he also quickly became connected with a number of banks and mining companies, and with Republican politics. In 1872, at the age of twenty-eight, Lowndes was elected to Congress. As the youngest member of Congress during his single term, he demonstrated a streak of independence when, along with five other Republican colleagues, he voted against a civil rights bill. Following a narrow defeat by another Cumberland lawyer, William Walsh, in his bid for reelection in 1874, he returned home, where he continued to mix law, business, and politics, attending national Republican nominating conventions and maintaining his ties within the state party. After rejecting gubernatorial overtures in 1891, Lowndes accepted them four years later. His timing was perfect.[13]

Rarely was a popular mood for political change, or Allegany County's opportunity for statewide leadership, so great as it was in 1895. The Republican Party turned west, not only for its gubernatorial candidate, but for its state chairman, George L. Wellington. A Cumberland native, Wellington rose from humbler origins than did Lowndes. Relying largely on his own resources since the age of eleven, he worked as a clerk in a canal store and as a bank accountant before he directed his indefatigable energy toward politics. His dedicated and effective service to the Republican Party won him selection as a delegate to the national convention in 1884, a congressional nomination in 1892, and finally, election to that position in 1894. Known for his organizational ability and tireless efforts, the party found in Wellington the right person to capitalize on the popular revulsion against insulated and strong-arm Democratic rule. Independents wanted freedom from machine politics; Republicans wanted power, as well as honest government; and Democrats were anxious to avenge Senator Gorman's support for a high tariff in 1894. All reform-minded elements believed that political progress required a purging of the Democratic establishment. As one progressive Democrat from outside the state summarized it, the only way Marylanders could "redeem" the worst "boss ridden state of the Union" was to let Republicans "beat the bosses and open the way for the Democratic party to regain control of its destinies." Sensing the widespread desire for emancipation from political bondage, Lowndes, in his opening campaign speech in Oakland, visualized himself as a "Joshua" who would "bring our people into the Promised Land of reform and good government." Pledging his administration to honesty and economy, election reforms and more equitable tax evaluation laws, Lowndes withstood a Democratic effort to identify the Republicans with the "threat of black rule" to win the governorship for the Republican Party for the first time.[14]

While Lowndes's political leadership was brief and his program was limited, his election symbolized the growth of Allegany County's influence in state and national affairs. The benefits of this rising status, however nominal insofar as concrete change in the region was concerned, lifted the spirits, if not the physical welfare, of the people of western Maryland. A "cheering throng" of "many thousands" escorted the governor-elect from his residence to the B&O station as he prepared to take office in January 1896. Referring to the "phenomenal uprising of the people" to reclaim their government in his inaugural address in Annapolis, Lowndes reiterated his campaign promises. Judging him by his own objectives, he was remarkably successful. With prodding from Lowndes, the legislature corrected electioneering abuses, removed inequities in tax assessments, created a Bureau of Immigration, established a Geological Survey Office, and practiced fiscal conservatism. Retrenchment nearly cost Allegany County a state teachers' school, but a visit by the governor to examine possible sites in Frostburg helped keep the project alive. A geological team also finally determined the official boundary line separating Allegany from Garrett County. Unfortunately for Lowndes, his independent streak alienated Republicans, including Wellington, who abandoned him in 1899. His inability to work with party leaders, coupled with Republican abuses outside his administration, and the return of Democrats to the party fold, defeated his bid for reelection. However, the momentum of 1895 carried Wellington to the United States Senate the following year, and helped elevate the political career of another Cumberlander, George A. Pearre. Pearre moved from state attorney general under Lowndes to six terms in the United States Congress, beginning in 1898. The "star of political empire" may not have left the eastern part of the state for "the rock-ribbed hills and mountains of ole Allegany" for very long, as the *Mining Journal* prophesied in 1896, but county politicians did leave their mark on the state.[15]

Events in the coalfields would soon make another political candidate as irresistible to the voters of the mining region as Lowndes was to the state electorate in 1895. The miners' strike of 1900 and subsequent conspiracy trial catapulted David J. Lewis, a self-made Cumberland lawyer and former mine worker, into the state legislature, where he effectively championed the interests of the workingman. One of the many issues that Lewis would bring to Annapolis, compulsory arbitration of strikes, grew out of the protracted labor upheaval in 1900. Soaring coal production in the late 1890s prompted miners to ask for full restoration of wages, which had been reduced in the depression earlier in the decade. Workers had accepted pay cuts with the understanding that companies would raise wages once prosperity returned. Operators rescinded part of the reduction in 1896, but they cited lower wages in competing fields as reason to oppose further increases. Angered by the owners' obduracy, activist miners requested United Mine Workers organizers to come to their

Lloyd Lowndes

David J. Lewis. Courtesy Herman and Stacia Miller Collection

J. Benson Oder, publisher and editor of the Frostburg *Mining Journal.*

aid in late 1899. They also prepared for a mass meeting to show their support for unionization as a means of redressing wage and other grievances. On March 31, 1900, 1,000 miners from the Meyersdale area and 2,500 from the Georges Creek region converged on Lonaconing to hear speeches by the nation's most prominent labor leaders, including Samuel Gompers, John Mitchell, and Eugene Debs. Area businessmen, anxious to avert a work stoppage, urged coal officials to confer with workers about wages. Company managers expressed their willingness to grant some pay increases, but refused to negotiate with union organizers. Their mounting anti-unionism, reflected in the firing of scores of miners who took a day off to attend the rally, provoked a mass walkout on April 11 in the Meyersdale and Georges Creek regions. The ensuing four-month strike took a heavy toll. Wages and trade were lost, and the coal companies secured court indictments against labor leaders for breaking up an anti-strike meeting in Lonaconing. Lewis, the defendants' counsel, lost the case, and the miners lost their battle for higher wages, but industrial wage earners would soon gain an effective champion in the state legislature.[16]

Lewis's extraordinary rise from youthful employment in the coal mines to one of Cumberland's leading lawyers prepared him for his defense of striking miners. When he came to Mount Savage in 1887 at the age of eighteen looking for work in the mines, he had already spent half his life laboring in the Pennsylvania coalfields. The young miner's lack of formal education only seemed to foster an insatiable thirst for knowledge, which he gained by struggling through primers and self-improvement literature at night after work and on lunch breaks. A speech he made on the Knights of Labor in Cumberland in 1888 won him the attention of one of the city's most prominent attorneys, who gave Lewis a set of law books which he studied over the next four years. Admitted to the Queen City bar in April 1892, Lewis, by his assiduous performance, won a partnership in 1898 with Colonel Pearre, the county's most successful politician. The junior lawyer handled the practice, which included local legal representation for the C&O Canal, while Pearre served as congressman.

But Lewis's heart lay with reform causes. His vivid memories of harsh and dangerous conditions in the mines nurtured a vision of a better life for workingmen. He intended to apply his legal training toward that end. His defense of labor organizations and his election to the state senate in 1901 provided him with the opportunities to do so.[17]

Lewis's political career, which included four years as state senator and seven intermittent terms in the United States Congress, was significant in several ways. First of all, he left the Republican Party, the base of his natural constituents, the coal miners, in 1896 to support William Jennings Bryan's Democratic crusade against economic privilege at a time of Republican ascendancy in the county. Secondly, as a progressive legislator his activities embraced a wide variety of reform efforts, ranging from the democratization of the state's political and fiscal processes to the elimination of exploitative labor practices. Not all of his endeavors were successful, but Lewis did secure local application of state laws providing for compulsory education, primary election of party candidates, and the requirement of the minimum age of fourteen for work in mines and factories. His most impressive achievements in the state legislature were a law which tightened accident safeguards in Allegany County mines and the nation's first workmen's compensation law. The latter law, which covered mine, streetcar, railroad, and construction workers, established a systematic program of compensation for financial loss sustained by injury or death on the job without regard to negligence. Elected to Congress in the Democratic upheaval in 1910, Lewis spent a long career in Washington, interrupted by election defeats, advancing similar social programs. What distinguished him from like-minded progressives were his broad, forward-looking interests. Before the country entered World War I in 1917, Lewis outlined the general concept of the League of Nations in a House speech.[18]

The county's response to idealistic foreign adventures demonstrated that its citizens were also capable of far-reaching humanitarian causes. The war to free Cuba from Spanish oppression in 1898 evoked the prompt mobilization of Allegany's state National Guard unit. Nearly two decades later another unit served in Mexico in President Woodrow Wilson's attempt to impose his brand of constitutional government upon a neighboring republic. In the case of the Mexican venture, 10,000 supporters, many of them armed with a goodwill package of fried chicken, gave the soldiers a rousing farewell at one o'clock in the morning. About two thousand welcomed them back four months later.[19]

American intervention in World War I in April 1917 struck a similar chord among the area's residents, who rallied enthusiastically behind the banner of making the world "safe for democracy." A total of 3,206 people from the county, including 99 nurses, went off to war, an extremely high percentage of the available manpower. Those who stayed at home supported the overall effort in a number of ways. They organized patriotic rallies, fund-raising concerts, Liberty Loan drives, and a whirlwind of other activities. Women, anxious to demonstrate their physical as well as their moral support, filled jobs left by departing soldiers. The president of the local Women's Preparedness Committee proudly proclaimed that the ladies were "fast taking their place in all walks of life." This included "hustling freight cars" at the Baltimore and Ohio yards and working in most of the local industries. In their more traditional sphere of activity women organized menus and gardening in such a way as to increase the flow of food overseas. Black women, organized into separate clubs, reported 111 war gardens in Cumberland in November 1917. Early the next year the County War Gardens Association announced the goal of making "every inch of available ground productive" by the end of spring. Every conceivable wartime need soon had its organized club, all of which ultimately came under the umbrella organization known as the Allegany County Chapter of the Maryland State Council of National Defense. The region had never before experienced such singleness of purpose. When news of the armistice arrived in the early morning hours of November 11, 1918, noisy demonstrations followed until midnight. For the families of the 106 natives who died in the conflict

Returning World War I veterans march in a homecoming parade in Lonaconing on September 30, 1919. Courtesy Herman and Stacia Miller Collection

their only consolation was their belief that these deaths had advanced the broad ideals of the war.[20]

Women were particularly moved by the spirit of democratic idealism. They had long worked for civic improvement. Western Maryland Hospital, built to take care of victims of railroad accidents in the early 1890s, owed its existence largely to their efforts. Their projects increased in the new century and so did their growing tendency toward organizations. Seventeen women established the Cumberland Civic Club in 1909 to work for the city's improvement. In 1913, a group of like-minded women consolidated numerous clubs into the Allegany County Federation of Women's Clubs. Anne M. Sloan from Lonaconing soon became a prominent figure in launching social welfare projects ranging from prevention of tuberculosis to world peace. Suffrage was never far removed from the minds of the activist leaders, who, taking a cue from loudly proclaimed ideals justifying American intervention in the World War, formed a local branch of the National Women's Suffrage Association in June 1917. Its members, while eschewing a militant posture, nevertheless advanced women's voting rights as a means to help infuse the political order with greater compassion and decency. In the interim, women continued their accustomed role in health care. They were active in an intensive campaign to lower infant mortality rates in the summer of 1918, and in helping to stem a major flu epidemic in the fall of that same year. Following the war, leaders in the Women's Council of National Defense decided to continue the organization to meet emergency needs. Finally, in August 1920 the long-awaited suffrage right for women arrived.[21]

The new status of women symbolized the many changes the county had undergone in the years following the Civil War. Allegany County in 1865 still showed vestiges of a frontier society, particularly in the tendency toward self-imposed justice. As the twentieth century approached, the area had begun to feel the strength of labor dissatisfaction and had produced leaders of state and national stature. The enthusiastic participation of its citizens in the World War I effort illustrated how the county had by 1920 entered the mainstream of American political and social life.

CHAPTER X NOTES

1. Cumberland *Civilian and Telegraph,* April 29, 1869, and Jan. 27, 1870; and J. William Hunt, "Across the Desk," in the Cumberland *Sunday Times,* Jan. 15, 1956 (hereafter cited as Hunt).

2. Tom Kelly, " 'Seducer' Murdered: Girl's Brother Held," *The Washingtonian Magazine,* November 1971: 81-82, 125-27 (hereafter cited as Kelly, " 'Seducer' Murdered"); and Cumberland *Mountain City Times,* June 4 and Oct. 22, 1870, and April 4, 1871.

3. Cumberland *Mountain City Times,* Oct. 22, 1870, and April 4, 1871; and Kelly, " 'Seducer' Murdered," pp. 126-27.

4. Cumberland *Daily News,* Jan. 10 and 11, 1873; and Jan. 25 and Aug. 14, 1903; Cumberland *Civilian,* Jan. 18, 1895; James W. Thomas and T. J. C. Williams, *History of Allegany County, Maryland* (Philadelphia: L. R. Titsworth and Co., 1923), Vol. I, p. 340 (hereafter cited as Thomas and Williams, *Allegany County*); Cumberland *Evening Times,* May 9, 1899; and Hunt, March 9, 1952.

5. Thomas and Williams, *Allegany County,* I, p. 259; Cumberland *Union,* Jan. 27 and Feb. 10, 1866; and Cumberland *Civilian and Telegraph,* Jan. 25, 1866.

6. Thomas and Williams, *Allegany County,* I, p. 260; Cumberland *Union,* March 3, April 7 and 14, and Sept. 17, 1866; Cumberland *Civilian,* Nov. 1 and Oct. 25, 1866, July 25, 1867, Sept. 9, 1869, and May 6 and Nov. 17, 1870; and Cumberland *Daily News,* Sept. 9, 1871.

7. Cumberland *Civilian,* Jan. 13, May 12, June 9, 23, and 30, Oct. 20, and Nov. 17, 1870, Nov. 7, 1880, and Oct. 15, 1882; Cumberland *Daily Alleganian,* Oct. 20, 1877, and Nov. 5, 1878; and John T. Scharf, *History of Western Maryland* (Philadelphia: L. H. Everts, 1882), II, pp. 1368-69 (hereafter cited as Scharf, *Western Maryland,* II).

8. Thomas and Williams, *Allegany County,* I, pp. 409-10; Thekla Fundenberg Weeks, *Oakland Centennial History, 1849-1949* (Oakland, Md.: Oakland Centennial Commission, Inc., 1949), pp. 25-27; Frostburg *Mining Journal,* Nov. 22 and 29 and Dec. 13, 21, and 27, 1873, and Feb. 28, 1874.

9. Frostburg *Mining Journal,* Sept. 13, 1873; Thomas and Williams, *Allegany County,* I, pp. 260-61, 312-13; and Cumberland *Daily Alleganian,* Nov. 3, 1876.

10. Katherine A. Harvey, *The Best Dressed Miners: Life and Labor in the Maryland Coal Region, 1835-1910* (Ithaca: Cornell University Press, 1969), pp. 186-99 (hereafter cited as Harvey, *Best Dressed Miners*); John F. Stover, *American Railroads* (Chicago: University of Chi-

cago Press, 1961), p. 119; and Jeremy Brehger, *Strike!* (Greenwich, Conn.: Fawcett Publications, 1974), pp. 20-29.

11. Frostburg *Mining Journal,* July 5 and Sept. 6, 1873; and Harvey, *Best Dressed Miners,* pp. 166-84, 203-6, 228-77.

12. Cumberland *Civilian,* Jan. 5, May 4, and June 1, 8, 25, and 29, 1894; Cumberland *Daily News,* April 12 and 16, 1894; Hunt, April 20, 1952; and Harvey, *Best Dressed Miners,* pp. 278-96.

13. Frank R. Kent, *The Story of Maryland Politics* (Baltimore: King Brothers, Inc., 1911), pp. 195-96 (hereafter cited as Kent, *Story of Maryland Politics*); Frank F. White, *The Governors of Maryland, 1777-1970* (Annapolis: The Hall of Records Commission, 1970), pp. 221-22 (hereafter cited as White, *Governors of Maryland*); Thomas and Williams, *Allegany County,* I, pp. 323-26; and *Special 1896 Illustrated Edition of The Baltimore American,* p. 211.

14. B. F. Johnson, *Men of Mark in Maryland* (Baltimore: B. F. Johnson, Inc., 1911), III, pp. 224-28; Thomas and Williams, *Allegany County,* I, p. 259; and Baltimore *Sun,* Aug. 16 and 20 and Oct. 2 and 8, 1895.

15. Cumberland *Civilian,* Jan. 10, 1896; *Proceedings of the Executive Department: State of Maryland Executive Minutes, January 8, 1896-January 6, 1904* (Annapolis: Hall of Records), pp. 2-5; White, *Governors of Maryland,* pp. 222-24; Mary Elizabeth H. VanNewkirk, "The Origins of Frostburg State College" (Frostburg: unpublished paper, 1975), p. 6; Thomas and Williams, *Allegany County,* I, pp. 320, 410; Kent, *Story of Maryland Politics,* pp. 215-16; John R. Lambert, *Arthur Pue Gorman* (Baton Rouge: Louisiana State University Press, 1953), pp. 258-59; Richard Walsh and William Lloyd Fox, editors, *Maryland: A History, 1632-1974* (Baltimore: Maryland Historical Society, 1974), pp. 609-10 (hereafter cited as Walsh and Fox, *Maryland*); Baltimore *Sun,* Aug. 26, 1899; Baltimore *American,* Nov. 8, 1899; and Frostburg *Mining Journal,* Jan. 25, 1896.

16. Harvey, *Best Dressed Miners,* pp. 297-320; Hunt, Dec. 29, 1946; and Thomas D. Masterson, "The Formation of a Progressive: Early Career of David J. Lewis of Maryland" (M.A. thesis, Georgetown University, 1969), pp. 42-45 (hereafter cited as Masterson, "Early Career of David Lewis").

17. Masterson, "Early Career of David Lewis," pp. 8-16, 29-32; B. F. Johnson, *Men of Mark in Maryland* (Baltimore: B. F. Johnson, Inc., 1912), IV, pp. 316-23; and F. Allan Weatherholt, Sr., "A Tribute to Honorable David J. Lewis" (Cumberland: unpublished paper, 1975), pp. 1-2 (hereafter cited as Weatherholt, "Tribute to David Lewis").

18. Masterson, "Early Career of David Lewis," pp. 32-36, 68-90, 103-30; Weatherholt, "Tribute to David Lewis," pp. 4-7; and Walsh and Fox, *Maryland,* pp. 645-46.

19. Thomas and Williams, *Allegany County,* I, pp. 401-4; and Cumberland *Daily News,* July 1 and Oct. 24, 1916.

20. *Maryland in the World War, 1917-1919: Military and Naval Service Records* (Baltimore: Maryland War Records Commission, 1933), Vol. I, pp. 197-99; Thomas and Williams, *Allegany County*, I, pp. 404-6; Cumberland *Evening Times*, May 18, Nov. 6, and Dec. 3, 1917; Cumberland *Daily News*, May 23 and Aug. 31, 1917; and Hunt, Aug. 19, 1945.

21. Hunt, April 4, 1946, and March 4, 1951; the *Heritage Press*, May 1972; *Allegany County Federation of Women's Clubs* (Cumberland: n.p., 1925), pp. 5-6; and Cumberland *Evening Times*, June 6, 1917, May 7 and 15 and Oct. 17, 1918, and Feb. 20, 1919.

PART IV

From Industrial Boom To an Uncertain Future Allegany County, 1920-1975

By

Harry Stegmaier, Jr.

XI

THE LAST GREAT BOOM ERA, 1920-1929

Allegany County, Maryland, in 1920, was a thriving industrial area, replete with rich natural resources and a skilled, hard-working labor force. Economic prosperity, based on the abundant coal deposits of the Georges Creek region and the many diversified small manufacturing concerns of the county, as well as on available transportation, made possible a life style unfamiliar to the present age. Cumberland had become a flourishing business, cultural, and entertainment center, the second largest city in Maryland. Other county towns also benefited from the prosperity, each with its own industries and entertainment facilities. Moreover, the unmarred natural beauty of much of the county, particularly the eastern half, provided recreational opportunities for its citizens. This easy access to recreation spots proved quite important, because in 1920 most people still took vacations close to home, not yet possessing that freedom of mobility which automobiles and paved roads would bring a little later on. What did Allegany County look like to the citizens of the early 1920s? How did they travel? Where did they do their shopping? How did they spend their free time? Let us go back over fifty years and observe the county as it was in 1920.

The urban center of the county is Cumberland, a growing industrial city and supply center for the surrounding area. The best way to see Cumberland is by trolley car. Trolley lines crisscross the city, serving the downtown, west side, south Cumberland, and Narrows Park. But before boarding a trolley, let's walk around the downtown area.

Baltimore Street appears quite different than it will to

those walking its pavements half a century later. Many of the vehicles are still drawn by horses, their hoofs clacking along on the wooden block pavement. (Baltimore Street would not receive a brick surface until 1927.) City street crews are constantly busy trying to keep the downtown streets clean. Starting at the concrete bridge over Wills Creek, let's stroll down Baltimore Street. The main street is bordered by two railroads, the Baltimore and Ohio on the east and the Western Maryland at the Wills Creek end. The latter's elevated two-story red brick passenger depot, with its wooden platform shelters and pedestrian tunnel to Tracks 2 and 3, sits right along the edge of Wills Creek. Just below the passenger depot, bordering Mechanic Street, is the railroad's freight depot, built of corrugated iron with a plank roof. Freight could be shipped to Cumberland from anywhere in the United States in the early 1920s.

Walking east on Baltimore Street toward Mechanic Street, one sees on the south side several retail stores, and on the north side the Olympia Hotel. Between Mechanic and Liberty streets are a number of retail stores, including on the north side the Gross Brothers Department Store. At the corner of Baltimore and Liberty streets stands the modern Fort Cumberland Hotel, completed in 1918. Only the Fort Cumberland is fireproof, but most of the other downtown edifices are of brick construction. Between Liberty and Centre streets, on the north side there are retail stores and another hotel, and on the south side three banks, the Second National Bank, the Liberty Trust Company, and the Third National Bank. The latter leases its rear rooms on Centre Street to the Cumberland and Westernport Electric Railway, which maintains in the building an express office and a waiting room for passengers. The intersection of Baltimore and Centre streets is protected by traffic signals, manually operated by a traffic policeman. On the northeast corner of Baltimore and Centre streets stands Saint Paul's English Lutheran Church. Farther up Baltimore Street on the north side are Rosenbaum's and the McMullen Brothers department stores. On the south side are a dance hall, the Cumberland *News* Building, the Empire and the Belvidere theaters, and the First National Bank Building at the corner of Baltimore and South George streets. Between George Street and the Baltimore and Ohio Railroad tracks stand the old Windsor Hotel, and next to the tracks, the huge Kenneweg Company grocery warehouse. Opposite the warehouse is the Plaza Hotel. The Baltimore Street railroad crossing is guarded by a watchman as are all the other Baltimore and Ohio Railroad crossings in the downtown area. Looking right from Baltimore Street we see the elegant Queen City Station with its porches and balconies girded by splendid grilled ironwork and its platform containing fountains filled with goldfish, all surrounded by well-manicured lawns colorful with flowers in spring and summer.

Having seen the main street, let's wander down some of the other streets in the downtown area. On North Mechanic Street we find the Cumberland and the Crystal laundries, as well as an automobile showroom, the Maryland Theater, the Coca-Cola Bottling Works, the Cumberland Milling Company, the Salvation Army headquarters, the Mechanic Street School for black children, and the Pennsylvania Hotel, one of the places you may go to place an illegal bet on your favorite horse. From the Market Street Bridge, one can gaze upon the high, gray wall of Saints Peter and Paul's Monastery. Within the walls, Capuchin friars toil in the vineyards and vegetable gardens that supply many of the necessities for this religious community. Between Mechanic and Centre streets, huddled around the intersection of Little Frederick and Liberty streets are the United States Post Office Building (where police headquarters is located today), Central Fire Station, police headquarters and the city jail, both in the same building, and the new city hall, on the location where the old Academy of Music once stood. On North Centre Street we may see an ice-cream factory, a tin shop, and Carroll Hall, a Catholic high school near the magnificent Saint Patrick's Church, which is set back among trees and well-kept lawns. Walking down South Mechanic Street we find the Ironing and Finishing Plant of the Crystal Laundry and the enormous, world-famous Footer's Dye Works. Off Mechanic, on Howard Street, stand the Cessna Lumber Company, the Cumberland Sash and Door Company, and the Maryland Mould Foundry

Company. South Centre Street, lined with trees, not only is a fine residential area but also has doctors' offices, Saint Stephen's Lutheran Church, and a synagogue. On Union Street are the offices of the growing Chesapeake and Potomac Telephone Company, the power plant and offices of the Edison Electric Illuminating Company, which supplies electric power to the city, and the Union Street School. J. N. M. Brandler's Coal Yard, the Baltimore and Ohio Railroad freight station, and the substantial yards of the Western Maryland Lumber Company all border North George Street. There are, of course, other buildings in the downtown area but we have described those of the greatest interest and significance. Now let's hop a trolley car on Baltimore Street, pay our five-cent fare, and head for the other business district in south Cumberland. Today, we'll ride the line that runs via Park Street and Maryland Avenue to Virginia Avenue, although we could ride the other line to south Cumberland via Wineow and Thomas streets if we wished. If so, we would roll by, among other things, the R. D. Johnson Milling Company and the Chesapeake and Ohio Canal basin, where coal from the Georges Creek region is transferred from railroad hopper cars to canal boats for the trip to Georgetown. We would also pass through a run-down section of town near the canal basin called Shanty Town, once replete with saloons and ladies of questionable reputation.

Our ride is quick, with the trolley stopping only to discharge and pick up passengers along the way, until we reach the business section at Virginia Avenue. We pass two movie theaters, including the New Theater, many retail stores and churches, a post office, and a bank before the trolley line ends at the Baltimore and Ohio Railroad tracks. Across the tracks, looking southwest, are the large brick buildings of the Maryland Glass Company and the wooden structures of the South Cumberland Planing Mill Company. In the distance, iron chimneys indicate the presence of the huge, sprawling N. & G. Taylor Company mill. Scores of buildings, some of wood, some of brick, and others of corrugated iron, house offices, a bar mill, an open hearth mill, a tin house, and a black plate mill. The site of this enormous enterprise is crisscrossed with railroad sidings. The company employs almost 900 people and even maintains its own gymnasium and baseball field complete with a grandstand. Directly across the tracks is another large concern essential to Cumberland's economy, the plant of the Baltimore and Ohio Railroad Company. Here we would find a car rebuilding shop located in the old roundhouse. Next to it, a new thirty-stall roundhouse is home to scores of steam locomotives, mountain maulers which haul freight and passengers over the heavy grades to the west. An oblong, red brick building on Offutt Street houses the locomotive repair shop where major work is done on locomotives from all over a system that stretches from Jersey City to Chicago, Saint Louis, Buffalo, and Detroit. To the east is a railroad yard of tremendous size where trains are classified. Cumberland is a key junction of the B&O system. The main line from the east splits here into routes for Pittsburgh-Chicago on one hand and for Cincinnati-Saint Louis on the other. Trains must be divided and classified here, necessitating large railroad yards.[1]

Now that we have looked at Cumberland, we should move on and see the rest of the county. The best way to do so is to board one of the daily passenger runs of the Cumberland and Pennsylvania Railroad, a subsidiary of the Consolidation Coal Company. This railroad line with its many branches serves both Mount Savage and Frostburg, traverses the towns of the Georges Creek mining area, and terminates in Piedmont, West Virginia, just across the Potomac River from Westernport, Maryland. A ride on a C&P train is one of the best ways to take a quick look at these towns and the mining industry. C&P trains leave from the Queen City Station on their 31.8-mile runs. The timetable lists twenty-one stops from Cumberland to Piedmont, but actually the train will stop at just about every road crossing or house if there is a demand. One has the choice of either a morning or an afternoon train, and the railroad also runs a late evening train on weekends to bring Georges Creek residents to Cumberland for theatrical or sporting events.[2]

The train we board at the Queen City Station is made up of cars pulled by a black steam locomotive belching soot and cinders, a nuisance to trackside residents who have just hung out the wash. The three cars, one for mail and express and the other two for passengers, are all wooden, painted vermilion red. Hardbacked, plush seats mounted on cast-iron frames welcome the passenger aboard the train. After several shrill blasts on the engine's whistle and the clanging of the bell, we're moving. Our car is filled with merchants returning on the afternoon train to the Georges Creek region after conducting business in Cumberland as well as mining company officials and other travelers. Now we're crossing Baltimore, Frederick, and Bedford streets, soon slowing for a brief stop at the Hay Street Station, which sits at the junction of the Baltimore and Ohio Railroad lines from Saint Louis and Chicago. Soon we pass the Richards and W. R. E. King coal yards, the abandoned George's Creek and Cumberland Railroad roundhouse, and the remains of the Wellington Glass Works, once a tremendous frame building which was destroyed by a spectacular fire on February 29, 1920.[3] Sheer rock walls close in, and our little train is in the Narrows. This scenic canyon supports a railroad on each side, separated by Wills Creek and the recently paved National Road. Along the road lie the tracks and catenary of the Cumberland and Westernport Electric Railway, which also serves the Georges Creek region, following the National Road through LaVale, Allegany Grove, Clarysville, and Eckhart to Frostburg. The cars of the Cumberland Electric Railway, too, use these tracks as far as Narrows Park, a popular summertime recreational area just beyond the Narrows. As our train leaves the Narrows, we notice the C&P's Eckhart branch break off, cross Wills Creek on an ancient brick masonry bridge, and head off through the open countryside to tap the rich mines at Eckhart and Hoffman.

After a quick stop at Mount Savage Junction, our train heads away from the main line of the Baltimore and Ohio's Pittsburgh Division. The staccato exhaust of the engine indicates that the train is beginning to climb. Past the limestone and rock quarries at Kreigbaum and through Barrelville we roll. Now the mines begin. To the left of the train, in quick succession, are Mount Savage George's Creek Coal Company

Mine Number One and the Cumberland and Potomac Coal Company Cassanave Mine. Soon our train is whistling and slowing for Mount Savage, one of the oldest communities in Allegany County. Its main industries are the railroad and the sizeable brickyards operated by the Union Mining Company. A town of narrow, winding, unpaved streets and frame buildings, Mount Savage is operating headquarters for the C&P Railroad. The railroad maintains a major yard and a twelve-stall roundhouse adjacent to the passenger depot, where our train pauses to unload passengers, mail, and express. Leaving town, we pass the railroad's car repair shops, machine shop, and paint shop. At one time, the C&P built locomotives on this site, not only for its own use but for sale throughout the United States. Those days, however, are long past.[4]

The engine ahead is really working now, twisting around the many curves as our train climbs through Morantown and Allegany. At the latter point, two spur lines break away, one to the left to serve Union Mine Number Two and the other to the right to Union Mine Number One. The Union Mining Company also operates a refractory here. Our train climbs steadily until we pull into Frostburg, where it pauses at the depot to unload a large pile of mail and express and also a number of passengers.

Frostburg is quite a city—a coal mining town and marketing center for the Georges Creek coal mining region. It boasts neat, well-shaded streets, many of them paved with brick or cobblestone, and handsome Victorian houses. Most of the leading citizens live on the showplace streets of the city, West Union Street and Frost Avenue. Among the city's inhabitants there are also many miners, employed by the nearby coal companies in the district. The main street is a busy commercial thoroughfare. Most of the buildings here are brick. Retail stores, restaurants, the Lyric Opera House, and several banks line the street. Two of the most impressive buildings are the four-story, brick Frostburg Opera House, where city residents can enjoy both stage plays and moving pictures, and the ornate Gladstone Hotel with its iron-railed porches. Frostburg is also a city noted for both churches and saloons. The skyline is dominated by church steeples, particularly those of

Saint Michael's Catholic Church, Saint Paul's Lutheran Church, and the First Methodist Episcopal Church. Prohibition, dictated by the Eighteenth Amendment to the United States Constitution, has had serious consequences for the saloon business. However, even though they are illegal, many of these establishments are still operating as speakeasies despite the fact that some residents view them as a "disgrace" to the town. Frostburg supports a substantial black community, a rarity in the Georges Creek area. These blacks live on Park Avenue and maintain their own church and school. Nearby is the State Normal School Number Two for the training of teachers. Founded at the turn of the century, it is still a small operation, with dormitories, classrooms, and auditoriums all housed in a few buildings on East Loo Street. Frostburg has good transportation, too; it is served by the trolley cars of the Cumberland and Westernport Electric Railway, which has just opened a new waiting room on Main Street.

Just over the hill toward Cumberland, to the east along the National Road and the interurban line, lies the little mining town of Eckhart. Dominated by Mines Four and Ten and the operations of the Cumberland Big Vein Coal Company, Eckhart also boasts a substantial C&P railroad yard and an enginehouse. However, this town of mostly frame buildings has little in the way of retail business establishments. Its proximity to Frostburg makes them unnecessary. A railroad branch line from here winds around the mountain to serve the rich mines at the village of Hoffman. Farther down the mountain is Clarysville, famous for its historic inn. Once the site of a Civil War hospital, Clarysville now is home for the car barns and power station of the Cumberland and Westernport Electric Railway.

The engine's whistle announces our departure, and the train is soon passing through the tunnel that carries the C&P Railroad under Frostburg. As our train moves out of town, it passes the Johnson and Willison lumberyards, the glowing kilns of the Savage Mountain Fire Brick Company on McCullough Street, and the plant of the Frostburg Illuminating Company, which supplies electricity to the city. Also to the left is the high red brick building of the Frostburg Brewing

Company, supposedly still producing beer despite the Eighteenth Amendment. After a stop at Grahamtown, the train pauses at Borden Shaft, site of a deep shaft mine, where the men are carried to their jobs far underground by an elevator. This is a rarity in the area, as most mines are of either the drift or the slope variety, built at an angle into the hillside. A branch breaks off to the right near here to serve the Piedmont and George's Creek Coal Company Bowery Furnace Mines One and Three, the Midlothian Coal Company Mine One, and the McNitt Coal Company Mine Number Two, all at Midlothian. Soon we are at Carlos Junction. The C&P maintains a yard and an enginehouse here. At this site locomotives are serviced that run on the Carlos branch, which wanders off to the right to serve the Sullivan Brothers mine at Carlos and the Consolidation Coal Company Mine Number Seventeen at Klondike, one of the richest mines in the entire Georges Creek region, producing 5,000 tons per day. Before entering Midland, the train passes the huge Consolidation Coal Company Number One Mine at Ocean, distinctive because of its red brick powerhouse and the electric mine engines which haul the coal from deep in the earth to the mine portal. Shortly, the train pauses at Midland, another town dominated by the coal mining industry. Other firms here are the shirt factory owned by Solomon Rosenbloom of Baltimore and a bakery. A large wooden railroad trestle of the recently abandoned George's Creek and Cumberland Railroad runs right through the center of the town.[5]

Soon our train is at Lonaconing, a major town of the region. Before reaching the depot, we pass the Klots Silk Mill, which processes silk and employs many of the women and young girls of Lonaconing. Across the railroad tracks from the silk mill is the Utility Glass Company plant, with its large chimney shaped like an inverted funnel. This company produces nonglare glass for automobile headlight lenses, as well as pressed and blown tableware and leaded and colored glass. But Lonaconing's lifeblood, like that of its neighbors, is coal. Railroad branches high on the hills on both sides of the town serve mines with such names as "Waddell" and "Sonny." Neat homes set off by iron fences dot the town. These are the residences of the many mine superintendents who live in Lonaconing. Workers' houses of frame construction line the side streets. We find the main street an active place with its large number of retail stores. Near the C&P depot is a fashionable department store, owned by the Ternents and their descendants since before the Civil War.[6]

Now we are rolling again through Detmold, Pekin, and Moscow. The mines pass by one after another—Lonaconing Big Vein Coal Company, Old Colony Coal Company Number Four, Moscow George's Creek Mining Company Mines Two and Three, and the works of the Shaw Coal Company. Soon we are in Barton, which still shows the ravages of the terrible fire of February 2, 1919. Barton was without fire protection at that time; consequently, when the fire broke out in the Junior Order of Mechanics Hall during the showing of a movie there was little anyone could do. Before it was brought under control by dynamiting buildings in its path, the fire had destroyed over twenty homes and business establishments as well as the Presbyterian Church. Shortly thereafter, the town formed Barton Hose Company Number One in order to prevent a repetition of the disaster in the future. The main street of Barton lies right beside the railroad tracks. Opposite the frame C&P depot, with its semaphore order signals, is the tipple of Lonaconing Big Vein Company's Caledonia Mine, right in the center of town.[7]

Our train moves on past more mines—Maryland Big Vein Coal Company's Barton Mine, the McDonald Mine, and Campbell Coal Company's Hampshire Mine at Reynolds, which is also the site of another power station of the paralleling interurban railway. Now come Hoffa Number Two and the Donald Mine at Lauder, the Burtner Company's Mines Six and Seven at Gannons, Washington Number Five, the Allegany Coal Company's Tacoma Mine, and Campbell Coal Company's Franklin Mine. Their number is unbelievable. One begins now to sense the critical importance of the coal industry to the entire economy of Allegany County. Coal created the towns and gives employment to the people. Without the money spent by the coal companies and their employees, the many retail outlets and service industries upon which Cumberland, Frostburg, Lonaconing, and Westernport are based would suffer. Without coal there would be no need for the railroad and its employees, nor for shop towns like Mount Savage. Coal is truly the heart of Allegany County's economy—the basis of its prosperity in the early 1920s.

We're almost at the end of our journey now as the train pauses at Franklin, where the railroad maintains an engine-house and small yard. Soon we pass the siding of the Clarion Coal Company and White's Foundry before we disembark in Westernport. The train actually continues across the wooden railroad trestle over the Potomac River into Piedmont, West Virginia, where it terminates. Westernport is another town with a flourishing commercial district. Most of its inhabitants work either in the coal mines or for the nearby Luke paper mill. Others are employed by the large locomotive repair shops of the Baltimore and Ohio Railroad in Piedmont, at the foot of the famous seventeen-mile grade that lifts the B&O's Cumberland Division over the Alleghenies.[8]

Just up the road from Westernport is Luke. Luke is a company town, dominated by the huge works of the West Virginia Pulp and Paper Company. It takes its name from the Luke family, owners of the company and the major influence here. Most of the residents are employed at the mill, and the frame, two-story dwellings, the majority of them built to the same specifications, indicate company housing. A large part of the town's social life is centered in the Devon Club, established by the company for its employees. The club building contains a library, auditorium, billiard tables, and bowling alleys. Here movies are shown, cultural programs given, and banquets held. It is quite a place, modern for its day, providing for the mill's employees recreational and educational opportunities that are lacking in many of the other towns in the county.[9]

To return to Cumberland from the tri-towns of Westernport-Piedmont-Luke, we have the choice of trains on the Cumberland and Pennsylvania, the Western Maryland, or the Baltimore and Ohio Railroad—or, if you prefer a more leisurely journey, on the C&WE interurban cars. Our choice will be a train of the B&O, which leaves from the large, red brick depot across the river in Piedmont, West Virginia. This train will carry us through the richest farmland in the county, along the Potomac River valley south of Cumberland. On our ride we pass well-maintained farms with large barns and substantial houses, such as the one at Black Oak Bottoms. As the train is a local, it makes several stops after crossing from West Virginia into Maryland just south of Keyser, including Dawson, Rawlings, Brady, and Amcelle, soon to become a huge industrial complex. At Cumberland we leave the train, our tour at an end.[10]

The eastern part of Allegany County between Cumberland and the dividing line for both West Virginia and Washington County, Maryland, is rugged territory. Just east of Cumberland, the mountains rear their heads, creating a patchwork pattern of valleys running north and south. There is no major industry in the eastern part of the county to support the small population in places such as Spring Gap, Oldtown, Town Creek, Kiefer, Little Orleans, Flintstone, and Twiggtown. Some logging, on a small scale, is done in these mountains, but the industry is only a shadow of its former greatness. The tannery at Flintstone has disappeared, a symbol of the decline of that enterprise throughout the county. Many of the people in this section are farmers, but the rocky, hilly terrain and submarginal soil make this a risky undertaking at best. In fact, many so-called farmers must take other part-time jobs, either with the railroad or with industries in Cumberland, to make ends meet. Farming in the Georges Creek area in the western part of the county is in the same shape. Many farmers in the Georges Creek region work in the mines to make a living for themselves and their families.[11]

Now that we have had a general overview of the county as it was in the 1920s, we might look more specifically at how some of its people lived. A farm family near Midlothian was fairly typical of others in the rural areas. Their frame house contained three bedrooms, a family room, a living room, and a kitchen. Indoor plumbing was something dreamed about; a trek to outdoor facilities in a snowstorm when nature called was not an experience one relished but it was a fact of life. Those same storms blew through the cracks in the upstairs, covering the beds with a fine layer of snow. The entire house was heated by a big, cast-iron stove in the kitchen; a grate in the dining room carried heat to the upstairs. Hot water came from a tank at the back of the stove. Small children always slept in the warmest room, because in the days before modern medicine and miracle antibiotics they would find it more difficult than would adults to fight off illness during cold weather. A kerosene lamp in each room except the kitchen, where there were two, provided light. Fuel for the stove came from the nearby woods or mines. Kerosene for the lamps and other necessary supplies were purchased from Willetts General Store in Midlothian.

The farm family bought only the minimum requirements, however, attempting as much self-sufficiency as possible. Meat came from hogs, butchered and smoked over green hickory wood in the smokehouse. A few cows, sheltered in a big barn, furnished milk and cream, kept cool in the summer in the springhouse, where water was obtained. The chicken house provided eggs and, occasionally, fresh meat. The family grew and canned peas, corn, carrots, beans, potatoes, tomatoes, and other vegetables. A nearby orchard supplied apples, which were prepared in countless ways. To clear the winter snow away, a horse-drawn plow was used.

There was very little time left for recreation when all the farm chores were done. If the family was fortunate, as Elsie Cutter's family near Midlothian was, then the house had a foot-pedal organ, and as the 1920s wore on, a battery-powered radio. Women did a great deal of sewing by the light of kerosene lamps. On Sundays, there was church, followed by enormous dinners for relatives and friends, sometimes numbering as many as fifty. After dinner, in spring, summer, and fall, pleasant walks in the woods helped to burn up some of the calories everyone had just consumed. Farm life in the 1920s was arduous by modern standards, but its problems were more than made up for by a family closeness now lost in the age of the automobile and the television set. People then depended on God and each other, and were aware of the beauty of nature.[12]

Farming was neither easy nor prosperous, but Allegany

County as a whole, in the decade from 1920 to 1930, was entering its last great industrial boom after two decades of declining fortunes. Between 1880 and 1920, the county's population growth had slowed, except for the city of Cumberland, which continued to move rapidly forward. This trend reversed itself in the 1920s as new businesses moved into the area. More workers were needed, and the resulting population increase gave a boost to older service industries during that period. To a large extent, the thriving economy of the 1920s would be based on these older manufacturing and service firms, as well as on the arrival of new plants such as Kelly-Springfield and Celanese Corporation.[13]

One of the striking facts about Allegany County's economy in this decade was its diversity. Not dependent only on one or two large industries, the region was extraordinarily healthy. Even the post-World War I depression of the early 1920s seems not to have struck the area so hard as it did many other sections of the United States.

During that period the people of the county worked in many different lines of manufacturing. Some of these have been mentioned previously, such as the West Virginia Pulp and Paper Company at Luke, which employed hundreds of people to turn out its many lines of paper products, and the N&G Taylor Company, where between 700 and 1,000 people worked throughout most of the decade. The latter made its own steel in open-hearth furnaces at the south Cumberland plant, rolled it into steel bars in the bar mill, and then into sheets in the hot rolling mill. These steel sheets were then dipped into molten terne metal, a mixture of 70 percent tin and 30 percent lead, to produce terneplate, used as roofing material all over the United States. Even the White House in Washington had a terneplate roof at one time. In the 1920s, the company also began manufacturing pure tinplate, steel sheets dipped in pure molten tin, for the canning industry.[14]

Many county residents were employed at the two silk throwing mills of the Klots Company, one located in Lonaconing and the other in Cumberland on Gay Street. These plants spun textiles and also did some dyeing. Berry's Throwing Works on Mechanic Street, a small enterprise, also spun textiles. Involved with textiles, but in a different fashion, was the enormous Footer's Dye Works plant in Cumberland. Footer's had become world-famous as one of the finest cleaning establishments in the United States. It had the largest rug cleaning equipment in the entire country. The White House sent not only rugs but even everyday linens to the Footer plant for cleaning. In addition to the White House, establishments all over the United States, including hotel chains, used the services provided by this company.

Allegany County also had a large tannery, the Union Tanning Company, located in long wooden buildings between Lee Street and Wills Creek in Cumberland. Even though it employed many people, the tannery's effects were not all beneficial to the area. The company polluted Wills Creek, dumping enormous amounts of waste from the tanning process into what was fast becoming an open sewer.[15]

A new factor, with all of its ramifications, that had a tremendous effect on Allegany County in the 1920s, as it did throughout the United States, was the automobile. There had been automobiles before 1920, but this form of transportation really came into its own in that decade. In 1919, there had been roughly 6,771,000 passenger cars in the United States. By 1929, this number had increased to 23,121,000, a fantastic jump. By the mid-1920s, automobile dealerships dotted the main streets of Cumberland, Frostburg, and surrounding towns. Concomitant with the growth of the automobile was the increasing number of gasoline filling stations and auto repair shops, which sprang up not only in the cities and towns of the area but in the surrounding rural countryside as well. At one time some people even felt that Cumberland would become a major automobile manufacturing center.[16]

In April of 1921, the Paragon Motor Company opened offices in the J. P. Wiesel building on Baltimore Street. Philip W. Blake, local director, announced that the company had perfected four different automobile models and would construct a plant, employing about 600 people, to make the engines near Cumberland. Many local persons invested money in the venture. The local chamber of commerce remained skeptical of the whole enterprise, and after checking on the financial status of the firm, refused to support it, stating: "The Board of Directors . . . do not agree with the proposition as a whole and, therefore, regret that they cannot see their way clear to give you anything for publication. . . ." Nevertheless, the cornerstone for the proposed plant on Mount Savage Road was laid on August 28, 1921, graced by the presence of Mayor Thomas W. Koon of Cumberland. Mr. Blake spoke at the ceremony, saying:

> We are conservatively optimistic and we feel that our twelve hundred stockholders will be augmented by many hundreds more who will all come to realize what Paragon means to them as an investment.
>
> My policy . . . is to make Paragon pay the little investor, who seldom has a chance to participate in ground floor financing, a real return on his money.

The company even produced three models of its cars, driving them around town in order to interest people in the project. Pity the poor investor who, lacking the foresight of the chamber of commerce, sank his hard-earned savings into Paragon stock. The plant on Mount Savage Road was never built. Many local residents lost large sums of money in what soon was revealed as nothing more nor less than a fraudulent stock-selling scheme.[17]

While the automobile brought new business, more substantial than the Paragon Motor Company, to the area, it also had the effect of destroying what had been the mainstay of local transportation up to that time—the horse. Horse-drawn wagons had provided most of the delivery service before 1920. They brought the ice for the icebox, the morning milk, the groceries, and countless other items of everyday life. Most retail stores provided delivery service by horse-drawn vehicle. Every town had its livery stables, with the larger towns, such as Cumberland and Frostburg, boasting a great many of these establishments. As the horse-drawn vehicle gave way throughout the county to the internal combustion engine during the 1920s, the fortunes of the feed and livery stable waned and finally died. By the end of the decade, the products of Ford and Chevrolet had replaced the horse for both personal transportation and retail delivery on the streets of Allegany County.

The brewing industry also suffered a decline, although not because its products were no longer wanted. The Eighteenth Amendment to the United States Constitution, and the accompanying Volstead Act to enforce it, compelled the three county breweries to stop producing beer. The Old German Brewing Company, renamed the Liberty Brewing Company in 1917 as a result of the anti-German hysteria which swept the country during World War I, changed its name again in 1920 to the Queeno Company. Company facilities along Wills Creek in Cumberland soon were producing a cereal beverage with less than one-half of 1 percent alcohol, labeled Queeno, described by author William J. Kelley as "disappointingly pallid and a dismal failure as a substitute for real and authentic beer." The Cumberland Brewing Company on North Centre Street also turned out a similar beverage for a time. Neither proved very popular. The much smaller plant of the Frostburg Brewing Company, with an annual capacity of only about one thousand barrels, simply shut down. Most people, however, knew that while its stocky, red-haired proprietor, Karl Schlossstein, had "officially" closed down, the brewery remained in operation clandestinely throughout the 1920s notwithstanding the Eighteenth Amendment and the Volstead Act.[18]

An important industry in Allegany County's economic structure in the 1920s was glassmaking. Blessed with natural gas piped in from West Virginia for fuel and with good glass sand from Berkeley Springs, West Virginia, fifty miles east, the glass business reached peak production about 1920, employing over one thousand people at its height. Moreover, skilled glassworkers, organized in the powerful American Flint Glassworkers Union, made excellent wages in comparison with laborers in other county firms. In a sense, glassworkers were the elite of the county labor force. Already mentioned was the Utility Glass Company in Lonaconing. Most plants, however, were located in Cumberland. The Potomac Glass Company plant, along the Western Maryland Railway tracks between Baltimore and Market streets, was one of the largest firms. It produced blown tableware, both cut and etched, of superior quality. The Maryland Glass Company, located along the B&O tracks near Virginia Avenue in south Cumberland, made glassware for nationally famous stores such as Hutzler's, Wanamaker's, and Gimbel's. Among its products was cut and polished blown flint glassware of all sorts, including sandwich trays and candlesticks. Business was so good that the company added a $20,000 brick addition to the existing plant in 1923.[19]

Unfortunately, at the beginning of the decade, on February 29, 1920, fire wiped out one of the major glass factories, owned by the Wellington Glass Company and situated at the end of North Mechanic Street near the old George's Creek and Cumberland Railroad roundhouse. In "one of the most spectacular fires in the history of the city," the conflagration, fed by thirty tons of straw used for packing and helped by a high wind, consumed the entire five-hundred-foot-long frame building. Flaming debris carried as far as Cumberland Street. The destruction of the company, only partially covered by insurance, threw over 250 employees out of work; fortunately, some found jobs with other firms. Fire seemed to be the curse of Cumberland's glass industry. Later in the decade, on April 29, 1929, a fire of "suspicious" origin ravaged the Potomac Glass Company plant, which was at that time owned by the Sloan family, with Matthew Sloan serving as president. Over 325 employees lost their jobs. Another company, the Queen City Glass Company, a small firm formed in March 1926 with a plant in the rear of 400 North Centre Street, burned less than four months after opening. Fifty people were out of work as a result of that fire on July 9, 1926.[20]

New glass operations were formed as the 1920s progressed. The Braddock Glass Company operated for a time in 1927 and 1928 in the former buildings of the James Clark Distilling Company, which had been put out of business by the Eighteenth Amendment. Another firm, the Independent Glass Company, produced glass in the same buildings in 1928 and 1929 after the Braddock Glass Company had also ceased operations. The Zihlman Glass Company, also short-lived, turned out tableware and stemware in 1927 and 1928 at a factory south of Columbia Avenue along the B&O Railroad tracks. Of these smaller businesses of the later 1920s, only the Queen Glass Company, formed in 1929, survived. It cut and engraved glass, but never produced its own raw material.[21]

By the late 1920s, the local glass industry had declined badly. Fire had destroyed two major and one minor firm. In addition, foreign competition had made it impossible for smaller companies ever to become well established. Of the larger, only the Maryland Glass Company in south Cumberland remained. Even the Utility Glass Company in Lonaconing had closed down in 1929, unable to compete with cheap foreign glass from Japan and Czechoslovakia. What had happened to this business was symptomatic, a preview of the fate that would befall many of the county's small industries in the Great Depression of the 1930s.[22]

Much of the health of Allegany County's economy in the 1920s depended on the state of the coal industry. Coal had long held this predominant position and on the surface it appeared that the 1920s would be a great decade for the business locally. On June 11, 1920, for example, a Cumberland *Evening Times* article described the shipment of area coal to eastern markets as having reached "unprecedented proportions." But beneath the outer face, all was not well. Coal production for the entire state of Maryland, most of it coming from the Georges Creek region, peaked in 1907 at 5,532,628 tons. After that the trend, looking at it over a long period of time, was steadily downward. Between 1914 and 1918, Georges Creek area totals hovered around 3.5 million tons, sank to barely over 2.1 million tons during the postwar recession of 1919, and then zoomed to about 3.01 million tons in 1920, the last time the western Maryland coalfields would generate over three million tons. In 1921, output fell drastically to a little under one and a half million tons. What was wrong with the coalfields?[23]

Many people in Allegany County have blamed labor for the economic decline of the area. Organized labor remains a convenient scapegoat, even in the 1970s. Labor, however, with its part in the great mine strike of 1922 and 1923, is only one factor in the picture. The major reasons for the decline of the area's coal business lay far beyond the boundaries of Allegany County. Historians and others who have written about the economic prosperity of the 1920s have frequently ignored the fact that the coal regions in the United States never shared in that prosperity. Overproduction of coal kept the industry depressed throughout the decade. The cause of this overproduction can be traced to World War I. Wartime demands for coal and accompanying high prices had resulted in the opening of thousands of new mines during the conflict. Between 1915 and 1919, the number of coal mines in the United States jumped from approximately 5,500 to 9,000. Once the fighting ended, however, demand for coal dropped and prices fell. Yet the new mines continued to produce, driving prices for unneeded coal further and further down. Faced with this competition, the Georges Creek region found itself in an unenviable position. Being an old field, most of the easily obtainable coal had already been mined. This left fuel that would be more expensive to mine than that produced by newer soft coal regions, especially those in Pennsylvania and West Virginia. The high quality of Georges Creek coal, particularly from the Pittsburgh seam, helped the area hold on to its markets for a time, but its future was bleak. Eventually, the Georges Creek region would lose out to the newer mining areas in the country. When that time would come, no one knew for certain.[24]

Even though organized labor did not cause the ruin of the Georges Creek coal region, it is nevertheless undeniable that the miners' strike of 1922-1923 hastened the end. It all began on April 1, 1922, when the United Mine Workers, led by crusty John L. Lewis, struck the soft coal industry after the operators and the union failed to agree on a contract. The Cumberland *Evening Times* called it the biggest coal strike in history. The western Maryland coalfields were nonunion, but miners in the Georges Creek region walked out in support of the United Mine Workers. One of the aims of the region's miners in the strike was to obtain recognition of the union by the companies. For this reason, when the nationwide strike ended on August 15, 1922, the Georges Creek miners stayed out. The United Mine Workers supported the local effort, pouring roughly three-quarters of a million dollars into the attempt to unionize the Georges Creek fields. The union even established a food commissary in Frostburg to help the miners survive. But if the union and the miners were determined to unionize, the operators, led by the Consolidation Coal Company and the George's Creek Coal Company, were just as determined to resist.[25]

Consolidation flooded the area with strikebreakers, brought in by train from Pittsburgh, Cleveland, and West Virginia. Company police and guards, armed with automatic rifles and even submachine guns, poured in to protect the mine property and the strikebreakers. Striking miners also had weapons, or soon obtained them. This explosive situation was further complicated when many of the local miners who did not agree with continuing the strike went back to work. Strikers threatened reprisals against them and their families. Violence was bound to occur, and it soon did. Company police attacked strikers, who in turn assailed "scabs" and guards. In Frostburg striking miners converged on one of the men who had returned to work. He escaped on a motorcycle amidst a hail of bullets. A company guard lobbed a hand grenade into a picket line and two of Consolidation's guards shot down a striking miner while he was walking on a public road, away from any coal company property. The Georges Creek region finally learned how the companies had controlled the West Virginia coalfields for years. Violence became so prevalent that the Allegany County grand jury, after considering numerous cases of assault and intimidation, recommended that a special constabulary be formed to preserve order. The grand jury described conditions, particularly in Frostburg and Midland, as "a disgrace to the county."[26]

In November 1923, the international executive board of the United Mine Workers called off the strike. By this time it had become obvious that the companies would not capitulate and recognize the union. Many striking miners, feeling that they had been sold out by the union, wanted to continue the strike, but it had become a lost cause. A large number of miners had lost their jobs permanently; the companies rehired carefully. Consolidation and George's Creek both declared they would operate on the open-shop principle—"Radicals and others who have been the source of trouble in the past will not be considered in the reemployment of the striking miners." The old jobs of the blacklisted miners were now held by strikebreakers who had decided to remain in the area. It was fortunate for the displaced miners, however, that new industries were opening up job opportunities in and near Cumberland. Many soon found jobs with the Kelly-Springfield Tire Company or the Celanese Corporation. But these men never forgot their union tradition. Many of them would resurface in the labor movement in Allegany County in the 1930s.[27]

The long strike, which had lasted almost twenty months, from April 1922 to November 1923, killed the United Mine Workers in the Georges Creek region. In July 1925, Consolidation Coal announced that it would operate on a nonunion basis. Other companies rushed to follow the leader. The mines were run strictly on an open-shop basis throughout the remainder of the 1920s and into the 1930s. More important, however, the strike had hastened the decline of Allegany County's coal industry. Markets that might have held up a few more years were lost as buyers turned to other sources of coal when Georges Creek supplies became unavailable. Moreover, the strike destroyed many small coal operators who were unable to survive the effects of the prolonged siege. Twenty-seven area coal companies went out of business between 1923 and 1930. By 1930, there were nearly one thousand fewer miners working in the Georges Creek region than there had been in 1921. Only a dozen companies then remained that were large enough to produce 50,000 tons annually, and only one mine employed over one hundred people. In fact, forty-one of the seventy-two firms still in operation in 1930 employed under ten persons. Competition from large companies in other areas of the United States would destroy many of these tiny operations during the Great Depression of the 1930s. Coal production rose after the strike to a high of 2,275,374 tons in 1926, but by 1930, it had fallen again to 1,528,431 tons. General conditions in the coal industry dealt the death blow to the Georges Creek fields. The miners' strike succeeded only in bringing the inevitable end a little sooner.[28]

One of the main reasons that Allegany County's economy did not suffer to any great extent in the 1920s from the decline of the Georges Creek coalfields was that two new major industries located plants in the Cumberland area during that period. Employment opportunities at Kelly-Springfield Tire Company and Celanese Corporation not only were sufficient to absorb unemployed miners, but also brought new workers to the county. It is very possible, however, that neither company might have chosen Cumberland had it not been for an extremely aggressive and active Cumberland Chamber of Commerce. The chamber, composed of many of Cumberland's business leaders, was determined to attract new industry to Allegany County. These men sacrificed their time and energy, not to mention their wealth, in a bold campaign to contact industrial concerns and convince them of the advantages the area could offer. This willingness to take the offensive produced many dividends for the county and for business and financial institutions. To support their program, the leaders of the chamber of commerce formed the Cumberland Development Company, with John Keating at the head, Charles G. Holzshu as treasurer, and energetic George G. Young as secretary. Other prominent citizens involved in the project were Hugh A. McMullen, Tasker G. Lowndes, and attorney William C. Walsh. The development company set about organizing the drive to obtain new firms, raising money to be given them as an enticement to locate plants nearby, and finding suitable industrial sites for development. Soon they had "Cumberland . . . in the throes of an economic and civic crusade," as editorial writer J. William Hunt once put it.[29]

The idea for attracting the Kelly-Springfield Tire Company to Allegany County apparently resulted from a conversation overheard by Philip W. Blake, later of Paragon Motor Company infamy, but in 1916, the energetic secretary of the Cumberland Chamber of Commerce. While aboard a train returning to Cumberland, Mr. Blake heard a group of businessmen discussing the fact that a large rubber company was searching for a plant site. With the approval of the chamber of commerce, he wrote to a number of rubber firms, inquiring whether they were looking for a new location. Only the Kelly-Springfield Tire Company answered in the affirmative. This large company wanted to build one new plant to replace their older installations at Akron and Wooster, Ohio, and at Buffalo, New York. Kelly-Springfield's reply set the wheels in motion. Negotiations to bring the plant to the county soon commenced in New York at the firm's corporate headquarters, with George G. Young of the chamber of commerce acting for Cumberland.[30]

While the talks in New York continued, the city itself took steps, backed by the chamber of commerce, to lure the plant to the area. A bond issue was planned to raise money for the venture. Local newspapers and civic groups urged its passage. When the vote finally came, only 153 of the 3,587 people who visited the polls cast a negative vote. This bond issue provided $750,000, considered an enormous amount in those days, which would be given to Kelly-Springfield as operating capital in order to build the plant and begin production. This was apparently the first time a city in the United States had ever given so large a sum to an industry to help it locate. The Baltimore and Ohio, undoubtedly mindful of the new business a firm of this size would create for the railroad, even got into the act. It promised to relocate the main-line tracks of the Cumberland division so that they would not cut directly through the proposed plant site.[31]

Largely because of the civic effort and the offer of funds, Kelly-Springfield made the decision in the fall of 1916 to locate its plant in Cumberland. Other factors, including good rail transportation, the proximity of the Georges Creek coalfields, and the abundant water supply from the Potomac River, influenced Kelly-Springfield to choose Cumberland over forty-one other cities that had tried to attract the company. Groundbreaking ceremonies took place early in 1917, soon after Kelly-Springfield's decision. Construction crews quickly erected a machine shop. Then the United States entered World War I, and work temporarily stopped on the project, not resuming until 1918. Soon the buildings of this huge new enterprise were rising, consuming ten million bricks and eighty-five hundred tons of steel. The local construction industry also reaped benefits from the new company. In addition to the plant, housing for workers and their families, who would soon be moving into the area, had to be completed. New suburbs grew. The Dingle, on the west side of Cumberland, soon reverberated with the sound of building crews putting up plush homes for management personnel. Near the plant, the Boulevard Hotel was erected. Members of the chamber of commerce financed the construction of a big, new downtown hotel, the previously mentioned Fort Cumberland, to accommodate the out-of-town businessmen who would soon be pouring into the city. All of this activity brought prosperity to the area. Retail business boomed. As a result, Cumberland did not suffer as badly as did other cities and towns in the nation from the severe recession that followed World War I.[32]

On February 3, 1920, Kelly-Springfield began manufacturing rubber at the Cumberland plant. Soon the rest of this modern industrial operation was completed. Tires began to roll off the assembly line to equip the ever-increasing number of automobiles beginning to appear on the streets of American cities and towns in the 1920s. Kelly-Springfield held an open house soon after production began. Over ten thousand people came to see the new plant and view its operations. Cumberland and Allegany County had a new industry that would be of tremendous importance to the local economy for decades to come. The devoted efforts of many individuals and the leadership of the chamber of commerce had proved what could be accomplished when enough local citizens worked together to support a project.[33]

Having acquired one new plant, the chamber of commerce did not rest on its past achievements. Soon negotiations were under way to attract another firm, a plant of the British Cellulose and Chemical Manufacturing Company. This organization was the brainchild of Dr. Camille Dreyfus, a research chemist. By 1910, he and his brother Henry had built a small plant on the banks of the Rhine to produce cellulose acetate for making, among other things, a nonflammable movie film. But the brothers' dream was to create a cellulose acetate fiber that could be used to make fabrics for clothing, a fiber with the quality of silk but without its bad features. World War I intervened, however, and eventually brought the company to the United States. The Dreyfus brothers did not like the German state and fled to Great Britain. The Allied powers discovered that nonflammable acetate dope lacquer was an excellent coating for the wings and fuselages of military aircraft. Soon Dr. Camille Dreyfus had set up the British Cellulose and Chemical Manufacturing Company, Ltd., in Great Britain to manufacture acetate dope. As relations between the United States and Germany deteriorated, the United States War Department invited Dr. Dreyfus to establish a plant in this country also to produce the dope. The company began looking for a site, the decision having been made to locate away from the seacoast at the suggestion of the war department, which was fearful of Zeppelin attacks because of the recent German raids on London. The new plant would require a location where the large volume of water necessary for the acetate production process would be available and also one near the cotton belt, as cotton linters were the primary source of basic cellulose raw material. The Cumberland Chamber of Commerce began negotiations with Dr. Dreyfus, promising funds and a site in the area. Cumberland's location suited the company's requirements. Moreover, it possessed good rail transportation and lay near a source of cheap fuel. Dr. Dreyfus soon decided to bring his enterprise to Allegany County. The Cumberland Development Company raised the money to buy three farms and parts of three others along the Potomac River near Cresaptown, deeding them to the Dreyfus firm for a plant site.[34]

Construction quickly started, but before much could be accomplished, World War I ended. The fierce wartime demand for acetate dope lacquer vanished. Work soon halted on the Cumberland plant. Moreover, the company suffered severe financial problems resulting from the economic recession in Great Britain. The collapse of the London Exchange wiped out one-third of the firm's capital. An embargo on the export of dollars created serious barriers for Americans wishing to invest in the enterprise. Funds were finally made available by using a Canadian bank as a medium. A dispute between the local construction company and the trade unions created more delays. The Cumberland Chamber of Commerce began to wonder whether the whole affair would collapse, leaving a white elephant in its wake and wiping out the local investment in the project. Dr. Dreyfus, however, gave assurances that the plant would be built. Construction started again but proceeded very slowly. While the new building went on, some small-scale production of acetate molding compounds for the plastics industry began.

The company spun its first commercial cellulose acetate yarn at its Spondon, England, plant in 1921. The yarn sold for nine dollars per pound, compared with the twenty-dollars-per-pound price for silk. There were still problems to overcome with the process, however. Uniformity in the denier and diameter of the yarn had to be obtained. Technical personnel ironed out difficulties in the revolutionary dry-spinning process. The biggest stumbling block lay in the fact that existing textile machinery was not designed to handle the new acetate yarn. Furthermore, existing dyes were of no use in dyeing it. The company, therefore, had to develop its own machinery for weaving the yarn, new dyes to color it, and a new finishing process. Technicians had to adjust looms and knitting machines to handle the yarn without breaking it. All of this work on the new process took time. Complicating matters further, a textile depression in 1923 dealt another blow to the company.

Nevertheless, the American Cellulose and Chemical Manufacturing Company, Ltd., sister company to its British counterpart, was ready to begin manufacturing cellulose acetate yarn in the United States by 1923. Major construction began at the Cumberland plant site, now named Amcelle, a contraction of the full company name. By early 1924, the spinning and textile buildings were going up. Management personnel arrived to prepare the plant for production. Nature then intervened to throw one more roadblock in the company's path. The great flood of March 1924 sent the Potomac River pouring over its banks upon the plant site, sweeping away materials and covering sensitive machinery with mud. No sooner had the mess been cleaned up than another deluge hit in May of the same year. This one, fortunately not as serious as the first, nevertheless caused additional damage to buildings and machinery. It seemed that the gods themselves had declared war on the Cumberland plant. These dual disasters convinced the company to build an extensive levee system in order to prevent a recurrence of flooding in the future. But the destruction had again thrown the firm into financial difficulties. Sometimes money was so short it seemed doubtful that the payroll could be met. Men worked around the clock, seven days a week, to put the plant into operation so that it could begin paying for itself. Hard-driving Arthur J. Fitch, plant manager, and associates like Charles Beran, the chief engineer, and Fred T. Small, a spinning expert, knew that if they did not soon begin production, the whole enterprise could conceivably collapse. The situation remained shaky through the summer and fall of 1924. Finally, the men succeeded. On Christmas day, 1924, the first cellulose acetate yarn was spun at the Amcelle plant of American Cellulose and Chemical Manufacturing Co., Ltd.[35]

Once under way, the company began to expand its operations immediately. Opposition to the new artificial yarn caused some problems. Silk manufacturers, threatened by the new competitor, spread adverse propaganda to discourage use of the new fiber. But sales resistance gradually broke down as textile experts began to see the advantages of a product with silk's good qualities that would not be at the mercy of the uncertain supply of raw materials often faced by the silk industry. Moreover, stable prices for cellulose acetate base yarn as compared with unstable prices for silk was another factor in favor of the artificial yarn. The fabric made from this new process possessed many other desirable properties such as excellent wrinkle recovery and good draping quality; it was also quick-drying. Business grew rapidly in an effort to keep up with the ever-increasing number of orders being received. The name of the company was soon changed to "Celanese Corporation of America."

Because other textile firms did not have the machinery to handle the cellulose acetate yarn, the company was forced to set up a weaving operation at the Amcelle location in 1926, as well as a dyeing and finishing plant. A revolution was taking place in the textile industry, much of it at Amcelle. A 1926 issue of the *Textile Bulletin* stated:

> The remarkable rise in the use of Celanese yarns by the mills in this country has been responsible for one of the most interesting chapters in fabric development that has been noted in the textile markets since the development of synthetic fibers.

Soon Celanese products, both those that were totally synthetic and others that were blends of synthetic and natural fibers, were being used for a variety of items, including rugs, carpets, bathing suits, and outerwear for men and women. By 1930, employees at the Amcelle plant would number in the thousands. This industry, along with Kelly-Springfield, boosted Allegany County's economy tremendously in the 1920s.[36]

The growth of these two firms was particularly significant because of the decline of the Georges Creek coalfields in the 1920s. Celanese and Kelly-Springfield would prove their economic importance to an even greater degree during the Great Depression of the 1930s.

Allegany County's excellent rail transportation in the 1920s was a factor not only in attracting industry to the area but also in providing its citizens with mobility. In that decade, before the automobile and the truck began to dominate America's transportation habits, an area's economy as well as its people literally depended upon the railroad and the streetcar. The county was fortunate then to have good rail service in all directions. The main line of the Baltimore and Ohio linked the area with Washington, Baltimore, Philadelphia, and New York to the east, and with Pittsburgh, Cleveland, Detroit, Chicago, Cincinnati, and Saint Louis to the west. On the Western Maryland Railway one line ran east to Hagerstown and Baltimore, and another ran to Connellsville, where through freight connections were available to the West; another branch ran south to tap the coal and lumber market near Elkins, West Virginia. In addition, the Pennsylvania Railroad came as far as State Line, where it connected with the Western Maryland, providing both freight and passenger service north to Bedford and Altoona, Pennsylvania. At the latter point, the branch linked with the main trunk of the vast, sprawling Pennsylvania Railroad system. As we have already seen, the short-line Cumberland and Pennsylvania Railroad supplied good service to the Georges Creek region. This area also derived benefits from the frequent passenger and fast express freight service of the Cumberland and Westernport Electric Interurban Railway. That company also provided local trolley car and commuter service within and between Frostburg and other Georges Creek towns. Within Cumberland itself, a network of streetcar lines furnished fast, frequent mass transit to all parts of the city. Local public rail transportation in the 1920s reached a zenith which would never again be equaled.

The railroad, interurban railway, and trolley car lines all employed Allegany County residents in large numbers. Local people worked on road crews and in the locomotive facilities, repair shops, and yards of the various railroads. All of these jobs helped bring prosperity to the county, and for the most part, relations between employers and workers were good. The Western Maryland Railway, however, was hit by a long strike in the early 1920s when the construction company that had taken over the railroad tried to reduce wages and abolish the seniority system. Despite arbitration, the strike continued indefinitely. Many workers eventually resumed their jobs on the company's terms. But the Western Maryland, like the coal companies, blacklisted strike leaders, a favorite corporate tactic of the 1920s. These men were forced to find other employment, some of them eventually being hired by Celanese.

Employment opportunities were not the only advantage the county derived from the railroads. Good freight service gave all the local industries an edge, and proved a strong asset when the area set out to attract new businesses. Rail service not only provided access to raw materials, but made it possible to ship the finished goods quickly and dependably to the large eastern and midwestern markets for sale.[37]

In the 1920s, however, railroads were used for more than just freight transportation. In that decade, before people had turned to the automobile, they used the train for virtually all long-distance travel and for most local travel as well. Some excellent passenger trains served Allegany County at that time. The large, ornate Queen City Station of the Baltimore and Ohio Railroad in Cumberland was a bustling place. Travelers and businessmen thronged the platforms at departure time, joined by people who simply came to watch the trains come and go. Easy access to both East and West was furnished by trains such as the New York-Cincinnati-St. Louis Limited, the New York-Chicago Limited, and the New York-Chicago Special. There were also lesser runs with such names as the Middle West Express and the Wheeling-Baltimore Express. Most of these through trains carried dining cars and provided first-class service in either parlor or sleeping cars. Dining on the railroad in that era was a gastronomic experience. Rail historian Lucius Beebe has written:

> B & O diners in the great years ran to rich and somber decor and their staffs, recruited from the best available pools of domestic help, suggested ante-bellum days on the old plantation and urged corn pone and hush puppies on patrons in defiance of modern notions of caloric intake.

Trim, polished steam locomotives handled the long trains of heavyweight cars, often having at the end an open observation car with the train's name emblazoned on a drumhead attached to the platform. On May 13, 1923, the Baltimore and Ohio inaugurated the crack Capitol Limited, all-pullman and extra-fare, between New York and Chicago. This train, one of the premiere limiteds on the North American continent, provided Allegany County travelers with a restful, fast, overnight journey to Chicago. Most businessmen rode the train in that era. In fact, in the 1920s, Cumberland had its own sleeping car from New York, the car being cut off a through train in the early hours of the morning and put on a nearby siding. The patrons, many of them Kelly-Springfield and Celanese executives, could remain in their berths until morning, their sleep undisturbed when their journey ended.[38]

Besides Baltimore and Ohio's through trains, a number of local runs originated and terminated in Cumberland, providing service to the county as well as to more distant localities. Two eastbound locals connected at Green Spring, West Virginia, with trains serving the South Branch Valley communities of Romney, Moorefield, and Petersburg, all in West Virginia. Westbound locals on the Pittsburgh Division stopped at Ellerslie. Others on the Cumberland Division served Brady Station, near Cresaptown, Rawlings, and Dawson, and provided service to McCoole and Westernport by making stops in nearby West Virginia at Keyser and Piedmont. These trains also stopped at the Amcelle plant, and for a time, employees used them to commute from Cumberland to their jobs. In fact, for several years, the trains stopped at the Beall Street crossing on the west side of Cumberland to entrain and detrain Celanese employees. As already noted, the Cumberland and Pennsylvania Railroad provided two round trips daily between Cumberland and the Georges Creek area. In addition, this railroad ran a special train known locally as the "theater train" on Saturday and Sunday evenings as well as on special occasions. This train, which made it possible for Georges Creek residents to attend movies, stage shows, and boxing matches in Cumberland, arrived at 7:50 p.m. and left at 11:00 p.m., when the events were over.

But the Queen City Station was not the only busy depot in town. The Western Maryland Railway's station, situated near Baltimore Street along Wills Creek, also witnessed a considerable amount of activity each day. A through train from Baltimore and Hagerstown to Elkins, West Virginia, stopped in Cumberland. This train served the eastern Allegany County communities of Spring Gap, Oldtown, Town Creek, Kiefer, Green Ridge, and Little Orleans, providing the only public transportation to this somewhat isolated region. West of Cumberland, it, along with another Cumberland-to-Elkins local, furnished Rawlings, Dawson, McCoole, Westernport, and Luke with twice-daily service in each direction. Another

Narrows Park, a popular amusement area near Cumberland in the 1920s. The Depression killed it in 1931. Courtesy Herman and Stacia Miller Collection

Interurban cars, such as this one of the Cumberland and Westernport Electric, shown along Route 40 in LaVale, brought people from Westernport, the Georges Creek area, and Frostburg to Cumberland and Narrows Park. Courtesy Growden Collection, Allegany County Historical Society

"daily except Sunday" Cumberland-to-Connellsville train stopped at Mount Savage and Frostburg. The twice-daily Pennsylvania Railroad trains to and from Altoona also used the Western Maryland depot. Pulled by small American and Atlantic locomotives, these trains served Hyndman, Buffalo Mills, Manns Choice, and Bedford in neighboring Bedford County, Pennsylvania.[39]

Cumberland itself had an extensive network of trolley car lines of the Cumberland Electric Railway that provided fast, dependable intra-city service. In addition to the two lines to south Cumberland described earlier in the chapter, other routes ran to the west side and Narrows Park. The Narrows Park line was simply a continuation of the route from Virginia Avenue to Baltimore Street via Thomas and Wineow streets. This line moved across Baltimore Street and up North Centre Street, past the company's carbarn and the Cumberland Brewing Company, and then on through the picturesque Narrows to Narrows Park, which boasted a merry-go-round, roller coaster, dancing pavilion, and picnic areas. Traffic was heavy on this line in the summer months, particularly on holidays. Cars, sometimes operating in pairs, on ten-minute headways, made frequent trips to the popular amusement park. In fact, the company even maintained some cars with open sides for the summertime Narrows Park traffic.[40]

Another trolley route served Cumberland's west side, a continuation of the Virginia Avenue to Baltimore Street line via Maryland Avenue. After traversing the length of Baltimore Street, it crossed the Western Maryland Railway tracks and headed out Greene Street. At Lee Street, the line split. The main route continued out Greene Street to the Dingle. It terminated at the Dingle Drugstore, where a bell on a pole outside the store warned patrons of the approaching car. The branch route broke off and ran up Lee Street, across Washington Street to Fayette Street. Here it turned west and ran for three blocks to its terminus near the cast-iron gates of serene Rose Hill Cemetery. All the trolley cars drew their power from an overhead power source. At the end of each line, the conductor had to reverse the catenary before the car could begin its return trip.[41]

The Cumberland Electric Railway was a first-class mass transit system hauling businessmen, office workers, and shoppers to all parts of the city. The system improved as the 1920s progressed. On May 7, 1922, the Cumberland Electric Railway merged with the Edison Electric Illuminating Company. The new company soon changed its name to Potomac Edison. It bought new cars as the decade wore on, and also renovated some of the older ones. An apple green and yellow color scheme, new red seats, and white ceilings marked new and renovated cars alike. In the fall of 1925, the company extended the south Cumberland line through the newly completed Virginia Avenue subway beneath the Baltimore and Ohio tracks. The railway now possessed 7.89 miles of track. Of course, accidents were not unknown. A head-on collision in the Narrows in October 1921 between a streetcar and a Cumberland and Westernport Electric interurban car caused panic.

> None of the passengers were injured, although several women in the cars fainted and pandemonium prevailed, several of the passengers being restrained with difficulty from jumping out of the cars as they rushed together.

On May 11, 1922, a Western Maryland train struck a streetcar on the Baltimore Street crossing, killing one young girl. And a motorcycle hit a streetcar broadside on March 1, 1923, at Fayette and Chase streets on the Rose Hill line. Despite these dangers, however, the Cumberland trolleys gave the city a mass transit system in the 1920s which it never again would have once automobiles became the accepted mode of transportation. By the 1950s, faced with traffic jams and a scarcity of parking, the city would wish for a decent mass transit system once more.[42]

Other towns in the western part of Allegany County also had trolley car service, although not on the extensive scale of that of Cumberland. Their service was provided by the heavy interurban cars of the Cumberland and Westernport Electric Railway. This company served the main streets of Midland, Lonaconing, Barton, and Westernport, and also furnished frequent service between these towns and other smaller Georges Creek communities. Miners often used the interurban to commute to and from work. The electric railroad was especially important in providing trolley car transportation to the city of Frostburg and frequent through service between Frostburg, Eckhart, Clarysville, LaVale, and Cumberland. In fact, the Cumberland and Westernport Electric found business so good that it added cars to its Frostburg rush-hour service in 1921. Furthermore, it leased a modern waiting room at Main and Water streets. In the summer, people from all over the Georges Creek area, as well as from Frostburg, Eckhart, and LaVale, frequently rode the interurban to Narrows Park for a day of pleasure and entertainment. Fares were only ninety cents from Westernport, and a mere thirty cents from Frostburg. Just as the Cumberland Electric Railway gave the Queen City good mass transit, the Cumberland and Westernport Electric provided excellent service to Frostburg and the Georges Creek region.[43]

Before the day of radio and television, people had to go outside the home for their diversion. In the 1920s, some form of public entertainment could be found in almost all the towns of western Allegany County. Cumberland, with its many theaters and its fairgrounds, was the amusement capital of the county. The magnificent Maryland Theater, the Liberty, the Empire, the Capitol, and the Belvidere, all in downtown Cumberland, provided entertainment in the form of movies. The New Theater in south Cumberland also showed movies, as did the Opera House and the Lyric in Frostburg, the Santoy in Lonaconing, and the Star Theater in Westernport. On a typical day in 1922, one might see Billie Burke in *The Education of Elizabeth* at the New Theater, Wallace Reid in *What's Your Hurry?* at the Santoy in Lonaconing, or Agnes Ayres in *The Lane That Had No Turning* at the Opera House in Frostburg. The importance of the movies to the public was evident when the splendid Strand Theater opened in Cumberland on September 3, 1920. Part of the Crandall chain of theaters operating mainly in the Washington, D.C., area, the Strand had an outside finish of marble-cement stucco, which gave "the exterior of the building the effect of being of beautiful scintillating marble that sparkles and glints under the blaze of floodlights with the dazzling effulgence of a Gargantuan diamond." Inside, the structure was famous for its lobby trimmed with Italian marble, its domed ceiling with bronze palace chandelier in the auditorium, its $12,000 triple-manual pipe organ, and its large stage with $15,000 worth of scenic drops.

> Long before the hour announced for the beginning of the premiere performance, crowds had gathered at the corner of Liberty and Pershing streets patiently awaiting the opening of the ticket sale. During the course of the evening, hundreds were turned away; the theater's capacity, although in the neighborhood of 2000, was totally inadequate to accommodate the clamoring throngs intent upon gaining admittance.

Big theaters such as the Strand, Maryland, and Liberty did not only exhibit motion pictures. Stage shows and other theatrical performances were also popular. Many residents of the Georges Creek area came on the theater trains of the Cumberland and Pennsylvania Railroad. Prices were cheap for such events; tickets for a performance by New York comedian Ed Wynn, at the Maryland Theater in January 1920, cost only 50¢ to $2.50, depending upon the seat location. Big bands, including Peck Mills and his orchestra and Fred Waring's Pennsylvanians, often played here in the 1920s. In addition, the theaters frequently held style shows, and for the more culturally inclined, the Concert Course series organized by newspaper editorialist William Hunt. One group of people excluded from most of this entertainment was the black population of the county, particularly in Cumberland. Blacks were prohibited by segregation laws and by the policies of the management from attending all but one of the theaters. Only the Maryland Theater admitted these citizens and there they were segregated into a special section of the balcony. In November 1927, a special theater intended for blacks was opened on North Mechanic Street. Soon it became apparent, however, that the Negro population was too small to support the new Garden Theater, built on the old location of the Howard Theater and the Dancing Academy. Before long whites were being admitted, and the idea of having a theater strictly for the black population died.[44]

Many other possibilities for the use of leisure time existed

Riverside Park, Cumberland, provided a pleasant setting for Cumberland residents to relax. Highway construction and the flood control project would destroy it. Courtesy Herman and Stacia Miller Collection

Buck Dreyer's *Potomac Queen*, a paddle-wheel excursion boat, carried picnickers and swimmers from Riverside Park in Cumberland up the Potomac River to Dreyer's Beach. It last ran in 1923. Courtesy Herman and Stacia Miller Collection

Fairgo, Allegany County's beautiful racetrack, provided enjoyment to horse fanciers from the 1920s until the last races run in September 1961. Courtesy Growden Collection, Allegany County Historical Society

in Allegany County in the 1920s. In the summer, people went to Narrows Park, or they rode the river boat "Olympic" from pleasant Riverside Park on Greene Street up the Potomac River to Dreyer's Beach, where there were picnic grounds, a lunch counter, and swimming facilities, just upriver from the site of the new Kelly-Springfield plant. Residents also danced at the rickety Roseland Dance Academy at Mechanic and Pershing streets. However, marathon dancing, a popular endurance sport of the decade, could not be held in Cumberland because of the opposition of Mayor Thomas Koon, backed by a city ordinance that forbade dancing within the city limits from midnight to 7:00 a.m. Books were available at the public library on Greene Street. Horse racing was another popular amusement. In the early 1920s races were held at the old fairgrounds off Virginia Avenue in south Cumberland. Then in 1924, stockholders of the Cumberland Fair Association bought 125 acres of land on McMullen Highway near the Amcelle plant. That site became the new fairgrounds where each year horse races were put on in conjunction with the Cumberland Fair.[45]

Of course, residents of the Georges Creek area did not have to come to Cumberland for their entertainment. In Frostburg, stock companies performed at the Opera House, and at the Junior Order of Mechanics Park, located where the College Garden Apartments now stand, there were band concerts and picnics. Lonaconing had one of the oldest organized bands in the state, and the band pavilion in Alexander Park was the stage for many of its concerts. Stock companies also played in the opera house there. Movies were particularly cheap in Lonaconing, twenty cents for adults and ten cents for children. At the Star Theater in Westernport, there were both movies and theatrical presentations, including the Buffalo Bill Show in the 1920s. All over the coal district, people went swimming in Georges Creek in the summer. Tri-Towns residents could take a dip in the millpond above the paper mill in Luke. In the fall came hayrides, and in the winter, tobogganing. One of the thrills the children of Westernport enjoyed was riding big Eastern toboggans all the way from the top of the hill down to the Cumberland and Pennsylvania

Railroad tracks. There were also bowling alleys and roller skating rinks throughout the area. Too, people simply amused themselves in that era by hiking through the woods, going on picnics, or visiting neighbors and relatives. On holidays came the big parades, with patriotic speeches and fireworks added on the Fourth of July. And whenever one of the many circuses of the decade came to town, there was a circus parade, filled with animals and performers, attracting large and enthusiastic crowds.[46]

One very important source of recreation for county citizens in the 1920s was sports. Almost every town of any size boasted its own baseball team. Intense rivalry marked the games between towns; it was almost a certainty there would be a fistfight or two to add to the excitement. Many industries also fielded baseball teams. One of the great major league pitchers of all time came from Allegany County. Robert Moses (Lefty) Grove, born in Lonaconing in 1900, won 300 games during his career on the mound with the Philadelphia Athletics and the Boston Red Sox, from 1925 to 1941. In 1923, Cumberland completed a new baseball stadium, with a capacity of 6,000 people and parking for 300 cars, on Wineow Street near the old Chesapeake and Ohio Canal wharves. The Mid-City Ball Park, modeled after the stadium in Newark, New Jersey, opened on May 4, 1923, with the Cumberland Colts defeating the Smithton, Pennsylvania, semipro team 16-7 behind the pitching of spitball artist "Count" Hilty. One of the great moments for the ball park came in 1927 when the Colts, now a professional team, won the Middle Atlantic League championship under Manager "Gus" Thompson with a lineup that included Eckhart's Johnny Byrnes at first base, Dave Black at second, Johnny Boyle at shortstop, Joe Conti at third, and "Cy" Morgan, Eddie Conley, and Frank Gleich in the outfield. The park was also used for college and semipro football and for carnivals and boxing matches. Boxing was another big local sport in that era. Matches were held, among other places, at the Liberty and Maryland theaters in Cumberland and at the Lyric Theater in Frostburg. Local names such as Gene Roman, Ray Miller, and "The Maryland Bearcat," Fay Keiser, often appeared on the card against big-name fighters from New York and other large cities. One could see most matches for as little as a dollar, or a dollar and a half for a choice ringside seat.[47]

One of the forms of pleasure prohibited, at least legally, to Allegany County residents in the 1920s was the consumption of alcoholic beverages. The Eighteenth Amendment to the Constitution and the Volstead Act, passed during the crusade atmosphere of World War I and its aftermath, banned the manufacture and sale of alcoholic beverages in the United States. This piece of legislation, dealing as it did with moral behavior, never really stood a chance. To expect people to obey the law was unrealistic; to presume it could be enforced

Illegal whiskey flourished in Allegany County in the 1920s. Shown is bootleggers' paraphernalia captured by federal agents after a raid near Westernport in that era. Courtesy Westvaco Corporation

was quixotic. With World War I over and the aggressive movement of the Wilson years disintegrating, the American people wished to return to "normalcy," as Wilson's successor, Warren G. Harding, put it. To the majority of those in the United States, a normal state of affairs included the availability of alcoholic beverages.

The Prohibition era contributed one of the more colorful chapters in Allegany County's history. Illicit liquor, manufactured in countless stills in homes, farmyard barns, and even auto repair shops, could be bought all over the county. A gallon of first-class liquor cost only about two dollars, and at those prices, county residents apparently drank it in prodigious quantities. It was fortunate for the area that most of the spirits were manufactured by local entrepreneurs. This circumstance spared the region the violence that struck other places in the nation, particularly the urban areas, when organized crime moved in to take over the illicit liquor business. Much of the potent liquid consumed in the area was simply made in small stills, which were readily available, by people at home. However, there were also big operators who made their product for sale.[48]

The king of the bootleggers in Allegany County was Harry Klosterman of LaVale. This amazing gentleman had stills scattered all over the area, including one in a house on Washington Street in Cumberland, right under the nose of the chief federal agent in the area, who lived nearby. With ample supplies on hand, speakeasies or undercover saloons soon sprang up as rapidly as flowers in spring. In Cumberland, there was one on Harrison Street near the American Legion Club and another on Cumberland Street between Baltimore and Market streets. Many restaurants sold liquor. One of the earliest raids of the era occurred at the Vimy Restaurant on North Mechanic Street. The proprietor caught his wife "lavishing her affections on a Spaniard" and "became highly peeved," as the Cumberland *Daily News* put it. Beer bottles flew, and the bleeding Spaniard summoned help from nearby police headquarters. A search of the proprietor's residence at 72 North Centre Street disclosed two stills. Liquor could also be bought by the bottle at many of the shoe repair and tailor shops in Cumberland. Federal agents made frequent raids on these establishments.[49]

Cumberland, of course, did not have a monopoly on illicit liquor. All the towns of the county had their sources of supply. One well-known family in Frostburg made moonshine which one resident who remembers the era considered "as good as bonded whiskey." In the Georges Creek region, abandoned mines proved convenient for housing stills and storing moonshine. Private homes in Lonaconing often served as speakeasies. A Westernport native recalls periodic federal raids on one particular house. The sight of revenue agents tossing a prominent Westernport bootlegger's still, mash, and other paraphernalia out the window usually attracted many onlookers.[50]

Chief nemesis of area bootleggers and speakeasy owners was federal agent William R. Harvey. This tough, dedicated civil servant was a rarity in his profession because he remained honest. He could not be bribed, and he achieved quite a local reputation for his persistence in tracking down illicit whiskey. At one point, he trailed a bootlegger through the snow for several miles, from the swamp where the man maintained a still to his home in Midlothian, where Harvey confiscated a cache of moonshine. Agent Harvey led most of the raids in the area. At times, the job became dangerous. Another federal agent, George W. Hawkins, became involved in a shoot-out on the old Daugherty farm on McMullen Highway after uncovering liquor stolen at gunpoint from the Clark Distillery warehouse in LaVale. Even courtroom hearings involving prohibition cases could be frustrating for the men. For example, a raid in January 1923 on Poole's Garage on Frederick Street in Cumberland netted three stills, six 500-gallon steel vats, 2,300 gallons of corn mash, and 295 gallons of finished liquor. Proprietor Ben Poole and his son were arrested. The hearing was held in the small civil service room on the third floor of the post office building after clerk of the Federal Court, William J. Feaga, refused to open the courtroom lest members of the unruly Law and Order League appear. Despite Feaga's stance, a crowd packed the civil service room. Ben Poole's attorney, J. Philip Roman, a man with quite a reputation both as a lawyer and as an eccentric, gave such a glowing description of his client's character that the assistant United States district attorney suggested he be referred to as "Saint Poole." City police officers who frequented the garage testified that they had never smelled moonshine. Ben Poole himself, "a citizen of righteousness and honesty," in his attorney's words, denied that he was aware of a still located in his establishment. Poole's son took the blame and pleaded guilty, and his father was set free for lack of evidence.[51] This scene was typical of the frustrations suffered by federal agents like William Harvey.

Nevertheless, Harvey had become an unbearable thorn in the side of the bootleggers. In 1926, he was made county sheriff; the bootleg powers considered this a good chance to rid themselves of his interference. Once ensconced in the office, the indomitable Sheriff Harvey proceeded to crack down on the slot machine racket in the county. Under his direction, 120 deputies took part in the largest raid ever conducted in the state of Maryland. Armed with warrants and with trucks with which to haul the confiscated equipment, the deputies seized scores of machines, filling up the entire jail cellar with the one-armed bandits. William R. Harvey later went back to the federal service, but he left behind him in Allegany County a reputation that few who had run afoul of him would forget.[52]

No discussion of Allegany County in the 1920s would be complete without mention of the Ku Klux Klan. The Klan sprang up in the early twenties in the county as it did elsewhere throughout the United States. It stood for 100 percent pure Americanism, which meant that it was anti-Semitic, anti-black, anti-Catholic, and anti-foreigner, and for the protection of the white Anglo-Saxon Protestant. The Klan's appeal is well described by author Frederick Lewis Allen in *Only Yesterday*.

> Its white robe and hood, its flaming cross, its secrecy, and the preposterous vocabulary of its ritual could be made the vehicle for all that infantile love of hocus-pocus and mummery, that lust for secret adventure, which survives in the adult whose lot is cast in drab

places. Here was a chance to dress up the village bigot and let him be a Knight of the Invisible Empire.

The Fort Cumberland Klan, Number Thirty-Seven, claimed to have 3,200 members from Allegany County at its height, with 1,800 from Cumberland alone. It was fortunate for the area that the local Klan stuck to making noise, burning crosses, and holding parades rather than whipping or murdering people as it did in other parts of the country. Its favorite tactic locally was to burn a large cross on one of the hills in the area, setting off loud firecrackers to attract attention to the escapade. Occasionally, after such antics, the Klansmen would ride around in their automobiles, dressed in their white robes and hoods so that no one could identify them. Often the Klan held big parades in downtown Cumberland which were observed by thousands of spectators, some of them undoubtedly awed by the secret legions tramping past. Many residents still remember those spectacles, which frequently ended in an initiation rite and cross-burning on one of the nearby hills or at Wolfe farm on the National Highway just east of Cumberland. The KKK died in the area as quickly as it had arisen as interest waned and political divisions tore it apart. The local group was also hurt by a mild scandal—disaster for an organization preaching high morality. When the Klan promoted a local circus, Graham E. Finch, a member, absconded with about five hundred dollars of the advertising money. Exalted Cyclops James W. Webster, admitting the scandal, shamefacedly promised all creditors that they would be paid. By the late 1920s, the Ku Klux Klan was disappearing in Allegany County, just as it was throughout most of the nation. A remnant would resurrect itself in the 1960s and 1970s, but it was a mere skeleton of an organization that once numbered thousands locally.[53]

To the businessmen, civic leaders, and citizens of its environs, Allegany County appeared to have a promising future in the late 1920s. Kelly-Springfield and Celanese, two large new industries, had brought new prosperity and employment opportunities. These two giants augmented an already diversified economic and industrial base. This variety was important in that it prevented a shock to one sector of the economy, as had occurred in coal mining, from destroying the well-being of the region as a whole. Burgeoning entertainment and sports businesses gave county citizens a wide choice when they decided how to spend their leisure time. Good transportation made such pastimes easily accessible. Cumberland in the late 1920s had become a truly metropolitan center. Frostburg was a growing city. Other towns, such as Mount Savage, Midland, Lonaconing, Barton, Westernport, and Luke, thrived on the area's prosperity. The future appeared bright in those days. Clouds were gathering, however, that would change the county as well as the rest of the nation. Events were soon to occur that would deal a devastating blow to the area's economy and industrial base, and in the process, radically alter the life of its citizens as well.

CHAPTER XI NOTES

1. This information on Cumberland, Md., was gathered from *Insurance Maps of Cumberland, Maryland* (New York: Sanborn Map Company, 1921).

2. *The Official Guide of the Railways, August, 1922* (New York: National Railway Publication Company, 1922), p. 392 (hereafter cited as *Official Guide of the Railways, August, 1922*).

3. James W. Bishop, *The Glass Industry of Allegany County, Maryland* (Cumberland, Md.: Commercial Press Printing Company, 1968), p. 40 (hereafter cited as Bishop, *Glass Industry*).

4. Tim Aaron, "A History of the Cumberland and Pennsylvania Railroad" (unpublished graduate paper, Frostburg State College, 1975), pp. 14-16.

5. *Insurance Maps of Frostburg, Maryland* (New York: Sanborn Map Company, 1910); interview with Ralph M. Race, July 30, 1975; *Historical-Biographical Sketch of Frostburg, Maryland, and Its Citizens* (Frostburg, Md.: Mining Journal Publishing Company, 1912); and Agnes M. Davis and Sally Cutter Butler, *History of Midland, Maryland* (privately published, 1975), p. 2.

6. Bishop, *Glass Industry*, pp. 46, 58; and interview with James Klippstein and Alvin H. Ternent, Oct. 1, 1975 (hereafter cited as Klippstein-Ternent Interview).

7. The *Heritage Press*, August 1972.

8. Much of the information about mines, industries, railroad operations, and railroad lines is taken from the blueprints of the Cumberland and Pennsylvania Railroad entitled *Side Track Record, 1927;* also from

interview with Mrs. Frances D. Greaves, Oct. 23, 1975 (hereafter cited as Greaves Interview).

9. *Town of Luke, Maryland: 50th Anniversary of Incorporation, 1922 through 1972* (Luke, Md.: Privately published, 1972), pp. 9, 20.

10. *Official Guide of the Railways, August, 1922,* p. 407.

11. Henry A. Grine, *Preliminary Economic Studies of the Western Allegany County Area* ("Allegany County, Maryland: Economic Conditions"; Annapolis: Maryland State Planning Commission, 1941), p. 35 (hereafter cited as Grine, *Preliminary Economic Studies*); and David W. Vaughan, taped interview with Mrs. Elsie Cutter, April 1975 (hereafter cited as Cutter Interview).

12. Cutter Interview.

13. Grine, *Preliminary Economic Studies,* pp. 2-4.

14. Letter from Leslie L. Helmer to James W. Bishop, November 1975.

15. Interview with William L. Wilson, Aug. 18, 1975 (hereafter cited as Wilson Interview).

16. Frederick Lewis Allen, *Only Yesterday* (Bantam ed.; New York: Bantam Books, 1959), p. 115 (hereafter cited as Allen, *Only Yesterday*).

17. Cumberland *Daily News,* April 15, 1921, and Aug. 29, 1921; note, James W. Bishop to author, November 1975; and F. H. Ankeney, secretary, Cumberland Chamber of Commerce, to Philip W. Blake, July 27, 1921, in Minute Books of the Cumberland Chamber of Commerce, 1921.

18. William J. Kelley, *Brewing in Maryland from Colonial Times to the Present* (Baltimore: John D. Lucas Printing Company, 1965), pp. 663-64, 681-82.

19. Bishop, *Glass Industry,* pp. 7-8, 33, 49; and Cumberland *Evening Times,* June 15, 1923.

20. Bishop, *Glass Industry,* pp. 34, 40, 62.

21. Ibid., pp. 65-66, 68-69.

22. Ibid., p. 59.

23. Grine, *Preliminary Economic Studies,* p. 11; and Cumberland *Evening Times,* June 11, 1920.

24. Katherine A. Harvey, *Best Dressed Miners: Life and Labor in the Maryland Coal Region, 1835-1910* (Ithaca: Cornell University Press, 1969), p. 367 (hereafter cited as Harvey, *Best Dressed Miners*).

25. Ibid., p. 364; and Cumberland *Evening Times,* March 31, 1922, and Nov. 22, 1923.

26. *Frostburg Sesquicentennial Souvenir Book* (Frostburg, Md.: The Frostburg Sesquicentennial Committee, 1962), no page number; Harvey, *Best Dressed Miners,* pp. 364-65; and Cumberland *Evening Times,* Oct. 10, 1923.

27. Harvey, *Best Dressed Miners,* p. 364; and Cumberland *Evening Times,* Nov. 22, 1923.

28. Harvey, *Best Dressed Miners,* p. 365, 367-68; and Grine, *Preliminary Economic Studies,* p. 11.

29. Abundant evidence of this can be seen in the Minute Books of both the Cumberland Chamber of Commerce and the Cumberland Development Company for the years from 1916 to 1923; see also J. William Hunt, "Across the Desk," in the Cumberland *Sunday Times,* Dec. 16, 1951 (hereafter cited as Hunt).

30. Cumberland *Daily News,* Oct. 27, 1931; and Hunt, Dec. 16, 1951.

31. Cumberland *Daily News,* Oct. 27, 1931.

32. *Kelly-Springfield Today* (Cumberland Edition), June 1975; Cumberland *Evening Times,* March 3, 1920; Cumberland *Daily News,* Oct. 27, 1931; *Thirty-Fifth Anniversary: Kelly-Springfield Cumberland Plant, 1920-1955* (Cumberland: Kelly-Springfield Tire Company, 1955); Wilson Interview, Aug. 18, 1975; and the Greater Cumberland Chamber of Commerce, *A Challenge for Today* (Cumberland: The Greater Cumberland Chamber of Commerce, 1975), p. 2 (hereafter cited as Cumberland Chamber of Commerce, *A Challenge*).

33. Cumberland *Evening Times,* Feb. 3, 1920; and Cumberland *Daily News,* Oct. 27, 1931.

34. Material for this section is drawn from the following sources: *Amcelle: First Link in a Global Chemical Chain* (Cumberland: Celanese Corporation of America, 1974), pp. 4-6, 22 (hereafter cited as *Amcelle*); and Harold Blancke, *Celanese Corporation of America: The Founders and the Early Years* (New York: The Newcomen Society in North America, 1952), pp. 7-10 (hereafter cited as Blancke, *Celanese Corporation*); see also Cumberland Chamber of Commerce, *A Challenge,* p. 2.

35. Blancke, *Celanese Corporation,* pp. 10-15; and interview with William E. Crooks, Nov. 5, 1975 (hereafter cited as Crooks Interview).

36. Blancke, *Celanese Corporation,* pp. 15-17; Crooks Interview; and *Amcelle,* p. 22.

37. Interview with Mrs. Frank Birmingham and Miss Mary M. Birmingham, Aug. 20, 1975 (hereafter cited as Birmingham Interview).

38. *Official Guide of the Railways, August, 1922,* pp. 398-411; Lucius Beebe and Charles Clegg, *The Trains We Rode,* Vol. I (Berkeley, California: Howell-North Books, 1965), p. 124; and Arthur D. Dubin, *Some Classic Trains* (Milwaukee: Kalmbach Publishing Company, 1964), p. 98.

39. *Official Guide of the Railways, August, 1922,* pp. 364, 392, 398-411, 420-23.

40. Birmingham Interview; and Cumberland *Daily News,* May 10, 1924.

41. Interview with Mr. and Mrs. Harry I. Stegmaier, Aug. 20, 1975 (hereafter cited as Stegmaier Interview); and Cumberland *Daily News,* Jan. 9, 1927.

42. Cumberland *Daily News,* Oct. 5, 1921, May 12, 1922, March 2,

1923, July 31, Oct. 27, and Dec. 24, 1925, April 28, 1926, and Feb. 15, 1927.

43. Cumberland *Evening Times*, Jan. 2, 1920; Cumberland *Daily News*, June 4, 1920; and Greaves Interview.

44. Cumberland *Daily News*, Jan. 20 and Sept. 3 and 4, 1920, March 6 and Sept. 14, 1925, and Nov. 1, 1927; interview with William F. Baker, Dec. 5, 1975; and interview with Herman J. Miller, Oct. 15, 1975.

45. Cumberland *Daily News*, May 7 and 8, 1923, March 3 and May 30, 1924, Aug. 4, 1926, and Oct. 27, 1931; Birmingham Interview; Fr. Blaine Burkey, *Als Ich in Cumberland War . . . : Capuchin Franciscan Memories of 100 Years in Cumberland, 1875-1975* (privately published, 1975), p. 6.

46. Interview with Ralph M. Race and Matthew Skidmore, July 30, 1975 (hereafter cited as Race-Skidmore Interview); Klippstein-Ternent Interview; and Greaves Interview.

47. Cumberland *Daily News*, June 24, 1920, May 4 and Dec. 14 and 18, 1922, April 5 and May 4, 1923, and Sept. 18, 1927.

48. Stegmaier Interview.

49. Wilson Interview; and Cumberland *Daily News*, June 2, 1920, July 18, 1923, and Nov. 17, 1925.

50. Race-Skidmore Interview; Klippstein-Ternent Interview; and Greaves Interview.

51. Race-Skidmore Interview; and Cumberland *Daily News*, Jan. 24, 25, and 30, and Oct. 31, 1923.

52. Interview with Edgar M. Lewis, Dec. 10, 1975.

53. Allen, *Only Yesterday*, pp. 46-48; Cumberland *Daily News*, May 20, 1922, May 17 and 19, and Oct. 13, 1924, and Aug. 31, 1925; Race-Skidmore Interview.

XII

HARD TIMES AND WAR, 1929-1945

The great stock market crash of October 1929 ushered in the longest depression the United States had ever encountered. The economic crisis worsened in 1931 and 1932, despite the constantly repeated promise of President Herbert Hoover that "prosperity is just around the corner." Even though President Franklin D. Roosevelt, inaugurated in 1933, provided some relief through the New Deal programs, the Depression lingered throughout the 1930s. Allegany County was no exception to the national situation, suffering high unemployment and declining industrial activity. The hard times destroyed much of the county's economic base and weakened even those industries strong enough to survive the crisis. Although few people perceived it at the time, the radical changes wrought by the 1930s would profoundly affect the area's economic future, particularly after World War II.

The Depression devastated many of the region's industries. The glass business, already in trouble in the late 1920s, was particularly hard hit. By 1936, only one small factory remained from what had once been a thriving local art. The Maryland Glass Company, hurt by a loss of sales, closed in 1935, and sold in carload lots the $96,000 worth of finished glass on hand to the Gimbel's Department Store chain. An attempt by employees to revive the company in 1936 failed completely. The Utility Glass Company in Lonaconing had collapsed in 1929. Its facilities were leased in January 1930 by Dixon and Alexander Sloan, whose Potomac Glass Company had been destroyed by the fire of April 1929. The Sloan Glass Company, as it was now called, soon began operations in Lonaconing. Its life span was short; on March 6,

1932, at around three o'clock in the morning, a mysterious explosion rocked the building with terrific force. Four volunteer fire companies battled the resulting fire for over four hours, but they were unable to prevent major damage. This disaster threw 220 people out of work and permanently ended glassmaking in Lonaconing. The peculiar circumstances surrounding this fire, a previous case of attempted arson at the plant, and the similarity of the blaze to the earlier one at the Sloan-owned Potomac Glass Company prompted a thorough investigation by the fire marshal, the office of the state's attorney, and law-enforcement authorities. Nothing, however, could be proved. Lonaconing lost a $300,000 monthly payroll in one of the Depression's worst years. The only glass company still in business by the mid-1930s was a new firm, the Cumberland Glass Company, formed in 1932. Using an old warehouse of the Clark Distilling Company in LaVale, it produced drinking glasses of all types for the hotel and restaurant business. This company survived the hard times because the repeal of Prohibition stimulated the sale of its products. It became the last remnant of a once-prosperous industry, operating in LaVale and later in Mount Savage until 1961.[1]

One of the county's most famous industries, the Footer's Dye Works, also fell victim to the times and closed permanently in July 1937. The company had been in trouble throughout the Depression, many of its problems caused by the competition of the corner dry cleaning businesses which had sprung up everywhere. Thomas B. Finan's efforts as receiver could not save the company. Eventually one of its buildings became the first A&P supermarket in the area. Today all that remains is a faded sign on the old red brick building, now occupied by the Tri-State Mine and Mill Supply Company, to remind residents of that once great enterprise.[2]

The economy dealt a severe blow to the Georges Creek coal industry, already reeling from its problems in the 1920s. Coal prices dropped sharply as demand disappeared. Moreover, its high cost made it impossible for Georges Creek coal to compete with cheaply produced Pennsylvania and West

Virginia coal. Most of the companies kept operating in 1931 and 1932, although they were selling their product for less than it cost them to mine it. Miners were employed part-time to spread out what little work remained and avoid large-scale layoffs. Men came to the mine head each day, not knowing whether there would be jobs or not. Wages were about $2.50 per day, and those lucky enough to work were happy to get even that. The coal companies, led by Consolidation, which itself went into receivership in 1932, tried to help their employees through those difficult times. Rent payments for company-owned houses were deferred, cooperative welfare projects set up, and credit arranged at local grocery stores. Nevertheless, conditions had become "deplorable" for operators and miners alike. Production fell drastically, reaching bottom in 1932, when the net tonnage mined was only 926,777 tons.[3]

The New Deal in 1933 improved the situation to some extent. Under the National Recovery Administration's bituminous coal code, prices were set and output rose to 1,257,417 net tons in 1935. But it was only a temporary recovery, followed by another precipitous decline. In 1937, only 762,053 net tons were produced, a far cry from even the two million plus tons of 1926 and 1927. The area's miners had finally unionized the local fields under provisions of the NRA's bituminous coal code. The 1934 contract negotiated between the companies and the United Mine Workers gave local miners what they had worked so long to achieve: the seven-hour day, the five-day week, check-weighmen, grievance procedures, and a wage rate of 72.2 cents per short ton. However, it was a Pyrrhic victory for the region's now-unionized miners. The Georges Creek coalfields, victims of competition and depression, would never again approach their former greatness.[4]

Even the new industries, Kelly-Springfield and Celanese, soon found themselves in trouble. Hardest hit of the two was the Kelly-Springfield Tire Company. Bad management in its New York headquarters had already put the company's future in jeopardy in the late 1920s. By 1928, Kelly-Springfield was losing close to one million dollars a year, and these losses continued during the ensuing years. With the Depression, demand for tires fell sharply. By the spring of 1935, sales were so low that every available space at the Cumberland plant was being used to store surplus tires. The economic crisis, coupled with management problems and heavy losses, finally drove the company into bankruptcy. Trustees were appointed, one of whom was Thomas B. Finan, and reorganization of the firm was begun. Kelly-Springfield, still losing approximately a million dollars a year, cut the work schedule at the local plant to three days a week. Wages were sharply reduced, and in a final effort to save money, the company moved its executive offices from New York to a site at the Cumberland plant.[5]

The man who revived Kelly-Springfield was operations expert Edmund S. Burke. Burke, who had little formal education, nonetheless made use of a brilliant mind. He immediately set out to bring competent people into the company, his goals being to establish efficient operating procedures and boost sales. Burke ran the local factory with an iron hand. He liked to say: "I don't get ulcers. I give them." This handsome, well-dressed gentleman was also a moving force in raising money for community action projects. His successful endeavors included saving both the YMCA and the Shrine Club as well as starting the local Community Chest, now called the County United Fund. Under Burke's leadership and a vigorous reorganization effort, the company's situation stabilized. Burke and the trustees negotiated the sale of Kelly-Springfield to the giant Goodyear Tire and Rubber Company. Under the new ownership, increased production orders soon had the plant again operating five days a week. Employment and wages rose. Sales began to pick up. Between August 1935 and June 1936 the company's losses dropped to $200,000, a far cry from the deficits of earlier years. By 1937, Kelly-Springfield was rapidly approaching its former state of health.[6]

While the Celanese Corporation never experienced the almost fatal difficulties of Kelly-Springfield, hard times in the 1930s nevertheless had serious effects on the Amcelle plant. A generally depressed national market for textiles forced the company to furlough employees, thereby dealing another blow to the local economy. Celanese tried to lay off as few people as possible by giving as many employees as it could two or three days' work each week. Throughout the 1930s the situation was unstable at the local factory; production would rise for a time, then fall off again. In spite of the company's efforts to spread out the work, one-quarter of the firm's 11,000 employees had been furloughed by the fall of 1937.[7]

The transportation industry, so important to the county's economy in the 1920s, also suffered with the Depression, with serious unemployment as a consequence. Railroad freight traffic fell off sharply and remained unstable throughout the decade, rising or falling with the struggling national economy. Passenger traffic declined as well. Because people had less money to spend in the 1930s, they traveled less. The Baltimore and Ohio's long-distance trains continued to serve Cumberland throughout the Depression, but many of the amenities which had marked passenger travel in earlier years disappeared. By the early forties, Cumberland had lost its set-out sleeping car service from New York. While long-distance trains held up fairly well, local rail service dropped off badly. The latter had come under increasing pressure in the late 1920s as the trains' patrons began to find the automobile more attractive. The Depression brought an end to many of the local trains which had served Allegany County residents. The Baltimore and Ohio Railroad cut off locals to Connellsville, Grafton, and Washington. The Western Maryland Railway service to Connellsville disappeared early in the 1930s. Twice-daily trains to Altoona over the Pennsylvania Railroad had been consolidated to a one-run schedule, daily-except-Sunday, in the late 1920s. By 1938, all passenger service on the Cumberland-Altoona line had been abandoned. The Cumberland and Pennsylvania Railroad trains to the Georges Creek area lasted a bit longer. In May 1929, as an economy measure, the railroad replaced the locomotive-hauled trains with a one-unit, self-propelled, gas-electric motorcar built by the Brill Company in Philadelphia. Painted vermilion red, the "June-Bug," as local residents called it,

Westernport in the early 1920s, served by the Cumberland and Westernport Electric Railway interurban cars. Courtesy Growden Collection, Allegany County Historical Society

provided local service throughout the 1930s. Declining patronage finally finished the Georges Creek run in 1942. The trains, whose passing over the rails had regulated the lives of Georges Creek residents for ninety-seven years, disappeared forever.[8]

An earlier victim of the automobile was the Cumberland and Westernport Electric Railway. In 1923, buses replaced the interurban service from Frostburg to Westernport, and in 1928, the Cumberland to Frostburg line. The rails from Frostburg to Cumberland were removed in 1929 so that Route 40 might be widened to accommodate increased traffic. The Cumberland trolley car system survived to a later date. As early as November 16, 1927, the Potomac Edison Company replaced streetcars with buses on the Rose Hill line. It was the beginning of the end. The company let tracks, equipment, and service deteriorate. Gradually, other lines were abandoned. By 1930, only the Narrows Park-Centre Street-Virginia Avenue line remained, and because of traffic congestion, service was restricted to the early morning and late evening hours. At 1:30 a.m. on May 16, 1932, the last streetcar left the turnaround at the now defunct Narrows Park, itself a victim of the Depression. Cumberland's mass transit system had lost its fight to the internal combustion engine.[9]

By the 1930s, the great nemesis of the railroads and the trolleys had appeared on the Allegany County scene. Automobiles could be seen in abundance clogging the downtown streets of Cumberland, Frostburg, and other major towns in the county. There is no question that the automobile gave people, no longer dependent on public transportation, more mobility and personal freedom. In the 1930s very few criticized the automobile, now a status symbol in American society, nor did many perceive the immense social cost of this new form of transportation. They accepted, in exchange for their new freedom, the traffic jams on narrow streets built for a horse-and-buggy era, the exhaust pollution, and the noise. Trucks had also replaced the horse-drawn delivery wagons of an earlier decade. Buses dislodged the trolleys and local trains, although they were slow and unreliable, particularly in bad weather. By the thirties, the Blue Ridge Bus Line route through Cumberland and Frostburg linked the area with Baltimore, Washington, and Hagerstown to the east, and with Pittsburgh, Cleveland, Wheeling, Clarksburg, and Uniontown to the west. The Blue and White Bus Line operated five daily trips to Altoona. Cumberland and Westernport Electric buses connected the Georges Creek region with the rest of the county. Within Cumberland itself, the buses of the Potomac Edison Company ran all over the city. In those days of cheap and abundant energy, no one really questioned the positive benefits the internal combustion engine had brought with it. The automobiles, trucks, and buses required improved roads, of course. Highway construction and improvements moved ahead in Allegany County even in the Depression years. Not only were main routes such as U.S. 40 and U.S. 220 paved and widened, but work was begun on paving state routes and improving secondary county roads. All of this activity boosted the area's economy, and consequently, proved a boon in otherwise hard times.[10]

The automobile was not the only new form of transportation on the local scene in the 1930s. Airplanes also appeared, using Cumberland's airfield at Mexico Farms. People seemed thrilled with the airplane and the idea of flying, in spite of its dangers in those early years. On April 16, 1933, the county obtained its first regular passenger air service when Johnson Air Lines began trips to Hagerstown, Baltimore, Washington, and Pittsburgh. A large and enthusiastic crowd came to see the big air show at Mexico Farms in July 1935, staged in conjunction with Cumberland's Sesquicentennial. The Goodyear blimp, stunt flying, and a bomb-dropping demonstration by five National Guard Douglas observation planes highlighted the events. A twenty-eight passenger Boeing commercial aircraft was on hand to take local people for short rides. Truly, the air age, like that of the automobile, had come to Allegany County by the mid-1930s. Cumberland began building a new municipal airport near Wiley Ford, West Virginia, in 1941, at a projected cost of $2,300,000. Because the United States government had approved the airport as a national defense project, a large part of the expense was absorbed by federal aid. WPA crews did much of the early work of clearing the land. Construction of the new facility proceeded sporadically during World War II, often stopped by a shortage of workers, who were needed by other local industries for war production. The new airport was not completely finished until after the war was over.[11]

Just as county industries suffered reverses similar to businesses nationwide during the Depression, so area banks experienced the same difficulties as banks throughout the country. By 1932, their problems, in many cases, had become insurmountable. Many financial institutions had made bad loans, often secured by depreciating real estate or securities with rapidly deteriorating values. Bank failures occurred throughout the United States in the fall of 1932 and the winter of 1933. Maryland proved no exception. In late February 1933, Maryland Governor Albert C. Ritchie proclaimed a state bank holiday, closing banks lest the panic topple the sound institutions along with the unsound. On March 4, 1933, the Maryland Emergency Banking Act went into effect, placing all financial establishments under the control of the state banking commissioner. This act, coupled with the national bank holiday proclaimed by the new Democratic president, Franklin D. Roosevelt, and new federal legislation, stabilized the situation. One of the most beneficial pieces of legislation created the Federal Deposit Insurance Corporation. This agency insured bank deposits up to $2,500 and went a long way toward preventing bank failures in the future.[12]

In spite of the state and federal legislation, however, several Allegany County banks collapsed. Most Cumberland banks survived quite well, with the exception of the Commercial Savings Bank of Cumberland, located on North Liberty Street. It was reorganized under the Maryland Emergency Banking Act and reopened for business on a restricted basis on July 20, 1933. Not so lucky were other parts of the county. The smallest bank in the county, the First National Bank of Midland, with assets of only $371,222 in 1931, fell and went into receivership. The Lonaconing Savings Bank, with assets of over one and a half million dollars in 1931, was allowed to reopen, but on a restricted basis. All attempts to save it failed. It went into receivership on December 27, 1934, and was finally liquidated. Its depositors eventually were paid at least part of their money. Frostburg was hardest hit. Two of the three banks there collapsed; only the Fidelity Savings Bank endured the storm. The First National Bank of Frostburg, with supposed assets of $1,782,019 in 1931, went into receivership. An investigation uncovered serious dishonesty. President Robert Annan and one of the bank's employees went to prison for their crimes, which included breaking into and looting customers' safe deposit boxes. Annan and his cashier had milked the bank of approximately one million dollars. Many people lost almost their entire savings in this failure; during liquidation proceedings, the First National Bank of Frostburg paid out only a fraction of the money due its depositors. The Citizens National Bank, with declared assets of $1,654,078 in 1931, also went into receivership, but returned to its customers roughly 80 to 90 percent of their savings. President Emory Hitchins went to prison as well; however, many felt that his crimes were of a technical nature involving bookkeeping procedures, and not an attempt to steal from the bank. A new bank was formed in 1934, the Frostburg National Bank, to acquire the assets and deposits of the Citizens National Bank. Operating in the old Citizens Bank building, the Frostburg National Bank became a solid financial institution in the mountain city.[13]

Industrial depression and bank failures were not enough. At times in the 1930s it seemed as though nature itself had turned against Allegany County. Because of the county's mountainous terrain, weather had always presented a hazard. In winter, severe snowstorms sometimes crippled the area, halting highway and rail transportation alike. Often during the summer months, dangerous thunderstorms, building over mountains to the west, would dump torrential rains on the area. Cumberland and Georges Creek residents feared the floods most of all. Yet even after the flood of March 1924 had struck the area, leaving Cumberland and other towns under water, causing considerable damage to Westernport and Luke, including the washing away of the Westernport-to-

Piedmont highway bridge, and destroying machinery at both the West Virginia Pulp and Paper Company and Celanese, little was done about flood control. Cumberland seemed particularly vulnerable. A later study made by the United States Army Corps of Engineers stated:

> The intense development of the narrow flood plains of Will's Creek and the North Branch of the Potomac River produce higher flood stages in this immediate section than would normally occur. The construction of the Chesapeake and Ohio Canal with its high embankments, the construction of numerous bridges of insufficient waterways, . . . the cutting off of flow through the flood plains by the building of earth embankment for approaches to the bridges, . . . and the gradual filling out into the channel of Will's Creek to provide additional building sites, have so restricted the former flood channels of these waterways that floods of any considerable size no longer have free passage and must overflow the adjoining developed actions.

In spite of the fact that Cumberland's bridges and embankments acted as a natural dam, especially on Wills Creek, the city made little effort to implement a flood control project. WPA crews did clean some of the trees and debris off the islands in the creek in the mid-1930s; however, nothing substantial was done to alleviate the problem. Cumberland invited disaster, which soon came.[14]

The flood of Saint Patrick's Day, 1936, is indelibly impressed on the memories of area residents. The winter of 1935-1936 had been extraordinarily severe, with heavy mountain snows and extremely low temperatures. In some places, the ice and snow, with an unusually heavy water content, was over forty inches deep. In mid-March 1936, a low-pressure system moving up from the Gulf of Mexico dropped heavy rains on the area. This downpour, added to the water runoff from the thawing snow, meant trouble. By midday on March 17, Cumberland had recorded two and a half inches of rain, and it was still pouring. The flood came suddenly. By midafternoon, much of downtown Cumberland lay under water. Merchants moved their goods to upper floors. People did the same with their household furnishings, and then moved upstairs themselves. On some streets, floodwaters threatened even the second stories of houses. Downtown

Wills Creek inundates the Market Street Bridge in Cumberland during the 1936 flood.
Courtesy Growden Collection, Allegany County Historical Society

Cleanup of Baltimore Street, Cumberland, after the 1936 flood.
Courtesy Growden Collection, Allegany County Historical Society

Liberty Street, Cumberland, after the 1936 flood. Courtesy
John E. Byrd Collection

workers who lived on the west side were trapped, as all bridges leading across Wills Creek except the railroad viaduct were flooded. Oil tanks broke loose in the Narrows and careened down Wills Creek, adding the threat of an explosion to the already mounting danger. The flood paralyzed Cumberland. All Western Maryland Railway service ceased. Banks, theaters, and business establishments closed for days. When the rain ended, 4.25 inches had fallen. Receding floodwaters left property damage of two million dollars and the danger of typhoid in their wake. The National Guard was brought in to keep order amidst the chaos. Georges Creek towns also suffered, but not quite as severely as Cumberland. In Westernport, for example, the water ran waist-deep on Main Street, and firemen were called upon to help people to safety. Transportation broke down. Many flooded mines in the region, which had been in a precarious financial state for some time before the tragedy of March 17, never reopened. After this disaster, the Cumberland city government finally decided that a flood control project might be appropriate. Unfortunately, it had taken a catastrophe to get some movement started.[15]

Notwithstanding the urgency of the situation, flood protection for Cumberland proved a long time in coming. On April 25, 1936, the United States Senate Commerce Committee reported a bill that included a proposed appropriation of approximately $900,000 for flood control protection for Cumberland and Ridgeley. The project envisioned the construction on both Wills Creek and the North Branch of the Potomac River of levees, retaining walls, and a new dam, and provided for channel clearing as well. This bill became the Flood Control Act of 1936. A new flood control act in 1938 supplemented the original proposal for Cumberland-Ridgeley flood protection. Authorization was only the first step. Plans had to be made, funds pinned down, and other problems of jurisdiction worked out. The Army Corps of Engineers did a study of what Cumberland-Ridgeley needed to prevent a recurrence of the 1936 debacle. Not until the fall of 1940 did their work reach the stage where some definite proposals could be made to local officials. World War II soon intervened, however, and the flood control plan was shelved for the duration of the conflict. The war also halted construction of the Savage River Dam in nearby Garrett County, another project designed to control the flow of water on the North Branch of the Potomac River and prevent flooding downstream in Luke, Westernport, and Cumberland, among other places. Allegany County would have to wait for flood protection until world problems could be resolved. Fortunately, no repetition of the 1936 disaster occurred during the intervening years.[16]

During the bleak years of the 1930s, with the Depression everywhere in evidence and natural disaster adding its toll, one bright spot appeared in the economy and in the social life of local citizens. Just before the Roosevelt administration took office, Congress voted to repeal the Eighteenth Amendment. While the states took up approval of the generally popular Twenty-first Amendment to repeal Prohibition, Congress passed a temporary measure, enthusiastically signed by President Franklin D. Roosevelt on March 22, 1933, to allow the sale of beer and wine. On April 7, 1933, Prohibition ended in the United States when beer and wine flowed freely again. Approval of the Twenty-first Amendment soon followed, permitting the sale of all alcoholic beverages. The death of Prohibition touched off widespread celebrations throughout most of the county. Bars sprang up everywhere. The sale of alcohol did more than boost depressed spirits; it resurrected the brewing industry, which had been defunct in the 1920s. The small Frostburg Brewing Company never reopened, but both the Cumberland Brewing Company and the Queeno Company started, the latter quickly resuming its old name, the German Brewing Company. Amidst great activity, Old German, Old Export, and other brews soon appeared to satisfy the thirsts of local residents.[17]

Another positive aspect of the Depression years in Allegany County came with the government work-relief projects initiated by FDR's New Deal from 1933 on. The assistance the county received under these programs helped many of its citizens survive the Depression. Moreover, some of the projects brought real material benefits to the area. Obviously, the majority of local people favored the New Deal. Normally a Republican stronghold, Allegany County voters chose the Democrat, Roosevelt, in 1932 and again in 1936. In the latter election, voters gave FDR an overwhelming 19,566 votes compared with only 11,131 for his Republican opponent, Alf Landon of Kansas. Many of Roosevelt's programs left their impact locally. The Civilian Conservation Corps, or CCC, designed to employ young men in conservation and reforestation projects, set up camps in both the eastern and the western sections of Allegany County. Many unemployed youths in Westernport and Luke went to CCC camps in Garrett County along the Savage River and at New Germany. Others lucky enough to be selected planted thousands of trees and improved roads, fire trails, and other facilities in Allegany County's forests. The Public Works Administration, or the PWA, under crusty, cantankerous Secretary of the Interior Harold Ickes, undertook a number of local projects including providing assistance in school construction and in the renovation of the old post office building for use by the city of Cumberland. The Civil Works Administration, or the CWA, a short-lived program of the early New Deal years designed to put money in people's hands quickly to increase their purchasing power, employed 744 Allegany County residents and spent almost nine thousand dollars locally during its brief existence. The Works Progress Administration, or the WPA, a massive national public works program, had the most impact of all the new federal agencies on the area. At one time, the WPA employed 3,356 county residents. In Cumberland, WPA workers cleared Wills Creek of debris, paved many streets, particularly in south Cumberland, and removed the now useless streetcar tracks from downtown streets. Other WPA projects included repairs to the library and city sewer system, construction of Constitution Park and Fort Hill High School's football stadium, improvements to parks and playgrounds, and later, work on the construction of the new municipal airport. In Frostburg, WPA workers built a wall on Main Street and paved many streets, among them Maple and Charles streets. Walls were put up and roads improved in the Georges Creek area. In Lonaconing, the WPA crews constructed retaining walls along stream beds and gave the VFW building a new stone face. The workers also paved streets in Westernport, some with cobblestones. All in all, WPA's presence proved quite beneficial to the county. Another government program, the National Youth Administration, or the NYA, employed hundreds of local young men and women on projects ranging from hospital work to landscaping public buildings.[18]

Despite their many benefits, especially the employment given to county residents, these government agencies faced much criticism. It must be pointed out, however, that most of those who were critical of the New Deal agencies were upper- or middle-class people who already had jobs. This group, some of them quite well-off and firmly established, complained about waste and corruption at the federal agencies. Many condemned those employed by the agencies as being poor workers, claiming that they spent a great deal of time leaning on their shovels. These critics failed to recognize the economic and social advantages that such government programs brought the county in years of double-digit unemployment. At times, the WPA faced not only criticism but the opposition of local government as well. Mayor Thomas W. Koon of Cumberland, leader of a highly conservative city government in the 1930s, constantly fought the WPA over wage scales and government regulations. His successors finally refused to provide any new projects, forcing the WPA to close down temporarily and dismiss workers. In another instance, the city turned down a PWA grant proposal of $113,000 for an addition to Memorial Hospital, located in south Cumberland. Fire and Police Commissioner Harry Irvine, a Republican who despised Roosevelt, claimed that the reason for the city's refusal lay in the PWA wage scales, which would force Cumberland to raise wages for poorly paid municipal workers. He went on to accuse the federal government of "strong arm methods." In view of incidents like this, it is not difficult to see why south Cumberland residents resented a city government controlled politically by the west side and north end. Nevertheless, in spite of the opposition to them, federal projects in the Depression years did alleviate some of the county's economic distress and left many material benefits in their wake.[19]

One of the most significant events in Allegany County in the 1930s, in both its immediate and its long-range effects, was the unionization of the area's labor force. To understand what happened locally, it is necessary to look at national events for a moment. Basically, the industrial worker in the United States was in an unenviable position in the early thirties. Subject to firing at the whim of management, beaten by company police if he tried to organize, and ignored by a skilled craft union like the American Federation of Labor, the industrial worker was forced to accept whatever wages, working conditions, and benefits management wished to bestow upon him. He possessed little power to change the situation. Two factors altered the national labor picture in the mid-1930s. One was the National Labor Relations Act, the other the formation of the Congress of Industrial Organizations, the CIO.

In 1933, Congress passed and President Roosevelt signed the National Industrial Recovery Act, which established the National Recovery Administration, or the NRA, designed to help check the industrial depression. Section 7A of this act gave labor the right to organize and bargain collectively with employers. Some companies simply ignored Section 7A; others circumvented it by forming company unions, which were worthless to employees because management controlled them. Moreover, enforcement of the new law remained weak. The American industrial worker, however, would be denied no longer. In February 1935, Senator Robert F. Wagner introduced a new labor bill. The Senate passed the bill in May by an overwhelming 63-12 vote, overriding in the process an antiunion amendment offered by Maryland Senator Millard Tydings. President Roosevelt now swung his support behind the Wagner bill, which the House of Representatives passed in June. The president signed it on July 5, 1935. The National Labor Relations Act, or the Wagner Act as it is sometimes called, established the National Labor Relations Board. This board was a permanent, independent agency with the power to designate the union that would represent workers in a plant or industry after it had won majority support in a secret ballot election conducted by the board. Furthermore, once the union had been chosen it would act as sole bargaining agent for the employees. The board also had the authority to prevent unfair labor practices by business, such as financing company unions, discriminating against union members, or interfering with workers, who now had the legal right to form unions. A key provision of the new law required employers to bargain with a union representing its employees. The law had been passed. Labor, however, still had to act.[20]

The biggest union federation, the AFL, had organized skilled workers, but under conservative leadership, had little interest in unionizing unskilled industrial labor. One group within the AFL, John L. Lewis's United Mine Workers, disagreed with the overriding philosophy of that organization's leadership. On November 10, 1935, three weeks after the AFL Convention in Atlantic City, at which there had been a fistfight between Lewis and William L. Hutcheson, conservative president of the Carpenters' Union, Lewis and the heads of seven other AFL unions met and formed the Committee of Industrial Organization. Ultimately ten unions, including the United Textile Workers, the United Rubber Workers, and the Amalgamated Iron and Steel Workers, combined in what now became the Congress of Industrial Organizations, or the CIO, and proceeded with a unionization plan aimed at unskilled workers. Resultant strikes, among them the famous auto industry sit-down strikes, occurred throughout the nation in 1936 and 1937 as American industrial workers unionized, often amidst fierce resistance from employers. An industrial area such as Allegany County could not expect to escape this trend. At a big labor rally on August 30, 1936, at the State Armory in Cumberland the CIO announced a unionization drive aimed at Kelly-Springfield, Celanese, and the N&G Taylor Company. Allegany County was in for an interesting time.[21]

Actually, trouble had begun even before the labor rally. On August 24, the United Rubber Workers had struck the Kelly-Springfield tire plant in an attempt to win company recognition of the union as bargaining agent for the employees. They also asked for wages comparable with those at the Akron plants of Kelly's parent, Goodyear, improved working conditions, and shorter hours. The strike had been called so hastily that many workers learned about it only when, on their way to the plant for the morning shift, they were greeted by signs on Kelly Boulevard which read "Don't be a Scab—Be a Man!" The Employees Protection Union, a typical company union, denounced the strike as depriving labor of the right to work. Nevertheless, it soon became apparent that the walkout among production workers was 75 percent effective. Pickets and the men who remained at work clashed when the latter tried to leave the plant on buses. State police dispersed the strikers with tear gas. This prompted a protest from the Allegany Trades Council to Governor Harry Nice over the use of the state police to intimidate and harass the strikers. In the face of massive resistance and violence, Kelly-Springfield shut down. The Cumberland *Evening Times,* strongly antiunion in philosophy, bemoaned the walkout, claiming that workers already had rights, mainly the right to work, and cited the prophet Jeremiah in predicting imminent disaster. It was fortunate for the community that Kelly-Springfield's farsighted leader, Edmund S. Burke, realized that unionization was inevitable. On September 1, Kelly-Springfield workers returned to work, and on September 2, Local 26 of the United Rubber Workers ratified an agreement worked out with the company. The contract provided for the return of striking workers to their jobs without action being taken against them, a survey which would be conducted to find ways to increase wages, and most important, recognition of the union as bargaining agent for the employees. In the fall of 1936, workers received a 5 percent wage increase, and in February 1937, another of approximately 6 percent. The National Labor Relations Board ordered in 1937 that the company union, sponsored and financed by Kelly-Springfield, be dissolved. The United Rubber Workers and the employees at Kelly-Springfield had won. The fight had been short, marred by only a minimum of

The enormous Celanese Corporation plant at Amcelle, shown here around 1940, employed over 13,000 during World War II. By 1975, workers numbered fewer than 1,000, indicative of Allegany County's economic problems in the 1970s. Courtesy Growden Collection, Allegany County Historical Society

violence, because of the willingness of both management and union leaders to compromise.[22]

The next CIO target was the huge Amcelle plant of the Celanese Corporation. This plant seemed particularly ripe for unionization. Many workers at the local plant had come from the Georges Creek mining region, the majority of them having union backgrounds themselves or coming from families that had been deeply involved in earlier attempts to unionize the miners. Some had been blacklisted after the 1922-1923 coal strike. These men carried their union sympathies and knowledge of organizing tactics with them when they came to Celanese. Moreover, they were among the lowest paid industrial workers in Allegany County. When the attempt to organize the plant came in the fall of 1936, they were ready. By November, negotiations had begun between the company and the United Textile Workers, represented by International Vice-President William F. Kelly. These talks proved fruitless. Amcelle works manager Charles D. Walton announced on November 11 that the company would not grant a request for a 15 percent wage increase. Moreover, on the same day Celanese ran a two-column newspaper advertisement in the Cumberland *Evening Times* defining the firm's position. In this public appeal the management announced that it would not agree to a closed union shop, would deal with employees over wages and seniority only on a departmental basis, and would not grant across-the-board pay increases under any circumstances. Company officials also threatened to close down and move the plant in an attempt to frighten employees and stir up community support for the firm's position. Celanese workers, disgruntled over low wages, discriminatory pay scales within the plant, and a lack of machinery to handle grievances, would not be intimidated.[23]

At 11:00 p.m. on November 12, the United Textile Workers struck Celanese. Over nine thousand employees walked out. The company's immediate reaction was to shut down and then attempt to bring the community to its support by newspaper advertisements and other statements. The firm declared that it would grant a $900,000 annual wage increase, but this increment amounted to only approximately half of the wage raise the union demanded. In the beginning the strike was calm, although Governor Nice did assign additional state police to the area to be on hand if trouble broke out. Mass picketing of the plant started on November 13. The strikers booed Celanese staff workers brought to the plant by train from Cumberland. Supervisory personnel began staying at the scene, eating and sleeping there for up to two weeks at a time, in order to protect valuable machinery should serious rioting take place. As was expected, the Cumberland *Evening Times* supported the company, urging strikers to reject the United Textile Workers and join instead a proposed company union, the Celanese Employees Association. Enclosing a clip-out application form, the newspaper appealed:

> Why not keep control of your own affairs by supporting a bona fide organization, free from outside influences and over which you have sole control? Why should any member of any other organization vote on continuing the strike at the Celanese?[24]

It was an explosive situation. Everyone knew that violence might result. What started it was a rumor that the company would bring in strikebreakers on Baltimore and Ohio trains. When a train attempted to discharge staff employees on the morning of November 27, a wild melee broke out. State and local police, aided by plant guards, finally quelled the riot. During the fight a plant foreman and two policemen were stabbed, and thirteen rioting strikers were clubbed. One sheriff's deputy still clearly remembers being hit on the head from behind with a baseball bat. On the morning of November 28, the scene was repeated. Police, protecting staff employees, again charged the workers; four strikers were arrested. Governor Harry Nice, in a telegram to UTW leader William Kelly, threatened "such drastic official action as neither you nor I would welcome." The governor, surrounded by state police, visited the scene to survey the situation for himself. While in the area, he felt compelled to stay overnight at the Town Hill Hotel on Route 40 rather than in Cumberland because of the bitter feelings on both sides there. An anti-union organization, the Citizens Committee of Business, Professional Men, and Property Owners, decried the situation in a full-page newspaper advertisement on November 29. Blaming outside agitators and urging labor to "hold the radical element in check," the committee begged Celanese workers to support law and order and return to work lest Cumberland become a "ghost town."[25]

The strike neared its end. The union had presented a united front to the company and proved its strength. Celanese, like Kelly-Springfield, realized that unionization had become inevitable. By December 4, employees were returning to work, and production resumed after the company agreed to recognize the union as bargaining agent and meet other union demands. Final official recognition of the United Textile Workers as sole bargaining agent for the plant's employees came after another strike in August-September 1939. Celanese workers had achieved their goal. Nevertheless, the strike left a residue of bitterness in a polarized community. The state charged twenty-one strikers with riot, rout, unlawful assembly, and inciting to riot, and another thirty-two with riot, rout, and unlawful assembly. The trial of this second group of men opened in the January 1937 term of the circuit court. All defendants, assisted by a brilliant local attorney, Eddie Ryan, pleaded not guilty. Lack of convincing evidence produced a hung jury. Faced with this verdict, the state refused to retry the case, nor did the other twenty-one strikers ever come to trial. In the long run, thousands of Celanese workers had won better wages, fringe benefits, and working conditions, but Allegany County would pay the price in increased class tension for years to come.[26]

Two of the county's largest industries, Kelly-Springfield and Celanese, had been unionized. Of course, most railroad workers had organized even before World War I, so the railroads were unaffected by the labor agitation of the 1930s. And the Georges Creek miners had unionized successfully in the early thirties with little opposition from the companies. One large industry remained unorganized, however, the N&G Taylor Company. In discussing the labor drive at this firm, we must take two factors into account. First, the N&G Taylor plant in Cumberland had become obsolete by the 1930s and was definitely a marginal operation. Moreover, newer and better products, including plastics, had begun to provide

The N&G Taylor Company in Cumberland produced terneplate and tin. A victim of obsolescence and the Depression, it died in the late 1930s. Courtesy Herman and Stacia Miller Collection

stiff—eventually overwhelming—competition for N&G Taylor Company goods. In the late 1920s, the company decided to purchase bar steel from larger and more efficient mills rather than manufacture it at the south Cumberland plant. It shut down the open hearth furnaces, blooming mill, and bar mill as a consequence, laying off hundreds of employees in the process. The Corrigan-McKinney Steel Company supplied most of the basic steel to the N&G Taylor Company and finally bought the smaller firm, although N&G Taylor continued to operate under its original name. In the thirties, the Corrigan-McKinney Steel Company merged into the Republic Steel Corporation, thereby bringing another important factor into play on the local scene. The head of Republic Steel at that time was Tom Girdler, a tycoon with a violent hatred for all labor organizations. Girdler was determined never to deal with the CIO under any circumstances. He and his comrades in several other smaller steel companies known collectively as Little Steel assembled an arsenal of guns, munitions, and tear gas worth $141,000 with which to resist their workers. Girdler once stated: "I won't have a contract, verbal or written, with an irresponsible, racketeering, violent, communistic body like the CIO. . . ." On Memorial Day, 1937, Girdler's company police, with the assistance of Chicago's finest, opened fire without provocation upon peaceful marchers at Republic's South Chicago plant. The attack may very well have been planned, as the shooting was not spontaneous. Organized volley fire mowed down over one hundred marchers, including women and children, most of them shot in the back. Ten died in what became known as the Memorial Day Massacre. When local workers tried to organize the N&G Taylor Company, they found themselves dealing with a ruthless, vengeful parent corporation.[27]

In early 1936, Republic Steel shut down the local plant. Company spies spread the word among suddenly unemployed workers that the plant would reopen if they agreed to a 10 percent wage cut. John M. Reed, the plant manager, protested these wage-cutting tactics despite his dread of Republic Steel's management. Charles A. White, a Republic vice-president and a native of neighboring Garrett County, told

Reed: "I don't give a damn about people. All I care about are profits." The approximately five hundred workers offered to take the wage reduction. Republic Steel now proceeded to bargain with the city of Cumberland for concessions as a provision for reopening the plant. On the condition that the plant operate six months a year the city willingly granted it a ten-year tax exemption. Having received what it wanted, Republic opened the local plant again on February 10, 1936. The south Cumberland industry operated throughout 1936. In early 1937, the Steel Workers Organizing Committee, having signed a contract with giant U.S. Steel without a strike, turned its attention to Republic and its allies in Little Steel. These companies resisted labor overtures, with strikes and violence as the result. Republic even developed the so-called "Mohawk Valley Formula" for breaking strikes; this formula included using court injunctions to prevent picketing, giving police extralegal powers to break strikes, labeling all union organizers as radicals and communists, and mobilizing public opinion to force workers back to their jobs. When strikes shut down Republic plants throughout the Midwest, union leaders organized a walkout at the local plant in sympathy with the others, although no specific issues were involved at the south Cumberland site. As expected, the Cumberland *Evening Times* denounced the strikers for showing their ingratitude to the company after it had agreed to resume operations at the local mill in February 1936.[28]

Following a long strike, workers voluntarily returned to their jobs. The N&G Taylor Company finally reopened in the late summer of 1937. The company worked up the raw materials already on hand and cleaned out inventories. In November 1937, the hot mills shut down for good, and after the manufactured products were sold the entire plant closed in early 1938. Republic Steel had simply decided to write off an antiquated operation, conveniently leaving the impression that labor trouble was responsible for the shutdown. Cumberland Mayor Thomas Koon, not surprisingly, blamed the CIO for the loss of this once-prosperous local industry. Allegany County lost a payroll of $50,000 per month and hundreds of workers were out of jobs. In 1938, Republic Steel removed all usable machinery and material from the local plant. Rumors spread in November 1938 that Republic might reopen locally, but they proved to be false. The old N&G Taylor Company was dead.

Labor organization and strikes at three of the big area industries stimulated general worker agitation throughout Allegany County. Many other local firms soon found that organized labor everywhere was on the march in the latter part of the decade. In June 1937, the United Leatherworkers Association struck the Union Tannery located at Valley and North Lee streets in Cumberland. One of the last tanneries in the area, this firm was already a marginal operation. The strike only added to the company's woes, and it came as no surprise when the firm closed its doors permanently. Another strike in June 1937 by bartenders and restaurant workers shut down many of Cumberland's downtown eating establishments for weeks, as well as a few other such businesses outside the city. Workers walked out at the Union Mining Company brickyards in Mount Savage in March 1938. Another walkout the same month against the Lashley and Anderson Bus Lines, successor to the Potomac Edison system, crippled both county and city of Cumberland transit. Even the anti-union Cumberland city government experienced labor troubles when municipal employees attempted to organize in the summer of 1938. Not until October 1941, however, did these employees feel strong enough to press their demands upon the city. At that time, a strike of workers in the city's water and street departments, which lasted more than a month, finally forced the city government to establish a labor policy covering wages and working conditions, although it refused to sign an official contract with the union. All in all, the period of the late 1930s was one of great labor agitation in Allegany County. While the unions won many well-deserved victories, organization attempts also forced several firms out of business. Because of their financial condition, however, some of those industries, such as the Union Tanning Company, would have collapsed soon anyway. Labor's efforts merely hastened their demise.[29]

The labor agitation of the 1930s only added to the already

bleak picture throughout Allegany County. Many residents remained jobless, even with the government work-relief projects in the area employing thousands. Between March 1938 and June 1941, for example, an average of 2,530 county residents, 8.7 percent of the number employed, worked on WPA projects. In fact, the highest relief expenditures within the state of Maryland in the late 1930s were in Allegany County; from October 1, 1935, to September 30, 1936, 14.7 percent of all Maryland relief money was spent here. In the period from October 1, 1939, to September 30, 1940, these expenditures in the county finally peaked at $389,873, which did not even include the sums spent on federal work-relief projects. Nevertheless, people seemed somehow to survive. Neighbors helped out the less fortunate, often sharing food and fuel. Grocers and merchants extended credit far beyond normal limits to regular customers. Companies spread out the work to keep as many as possible employed at least part-time. Some Westernport families even fed the homeless men riding the freight trains when they came begging for a meal. Of course, few people had extra money to spend. This scarcity of cash hurt the retail business in the county, forcing many small establishments to close. Service industries, particularly those dependent on orders from the mining companies, such as small foundries and machine shops, also collapsed in large numbers. Another victim of the Depression was the entertainment business. Booming in the 1920s in a properous economy when people had money to spend, entertainment in Allegany County had lost both its diversity and its resilience by the late 1930s.[30]

Many of the pleasures of the 1920s had disappeared a decade later. The Dreyer Boat Company, which suffered considerable damage in the floods of March and May, collapsed early in 1924. Its boat, the *Olympic,* never again would ply the waters of the Potomac from Riverside Park to Dreyer's Beach. Swimming in the Potomac River or Georges Creek was becoming unpleasant by the 1930s. Celanese, Kelly-Springfield, and the West Virginia Pulp and Paper Company now added their wastes to the untreated sewage from countless upstream municipalities. Georges Creek, polluted by mine drainage and municipal sewage, added its dirty water to the Potomac at Westernport. The great river had become an open sewer. Swimming was now hazardous to health. Even ice skating ended, because the warm water dumped into the river by industry prevented it from freezing in winter. Narrows Park, where county residents had spent so many pleasant summer afternoons, was a Depression victim, abandoned in the early 1930s. Sports also suffered from declining attendance. Boxing fell on hard times, and the once-proud Cumberland Colts dropped out of the Middle Atlantic League. Even the movies were in trouble by 1932. Cumberland's Belvidere, a firetrap with a narrow, rickety wooden staircase to the balcony, had closed in the late 1920s. The Empire and Capitol theaters followed shortly thereafter. One new theater, the Embassy on Baltimore Street, opened in 1931, but it found business marginal in the depths of the Depression. Frostburg's Opera House burned to a shell in 1936 in a spectacular fire of such intensity that even the copper roof melted. Cumberland's remaining theaters, as well as movie houses in Frostburg, Lonaconing, and Westernport, kept going by reducing prices, sometimes as low as ten cents for a second-run double feature plus short subjects. Those with money could hear the big bands, such as Benny Goodman's Orchestra, which still came to Allegany County. Many of them played at the Crystal Ballroom on Route 40 near Allegany Grove. Here, couples could dance away their evenings in a room with a huge crystal ball suspended from the ceiling. People with no money in their pockets, however, generally stayed home, obtaining their entertainment from the radio practically free. Frostburg had begun the first regular radio broadcasts in Allegany County in 1925 with a locally owned station in the Abramson Building on Main Street. Cumberland received its first radio station, WKBG, on March 18, 1928. This station, owned by the Cumberland *Daily News,* disappeared by the 1930s, but a more substantial one, WTBO, filled the gap. Radio's impact on the local area was evident when a number of people fled to the nearby mountains during Orson Welles's famous Halloween broadcast of *The War of the Worlds* in 1938. The Cumberland

Daily News itself disappeared on October 2, 1938, when the Cumberland *Evening Times* took over its operation. There is no question that the county's public entertainment business was in a steep decline by the mid-1930s. People had less money to spend in the Depression years and the radio had become increasingly popular, both factors contributing to the ebb. In this area public entertainment would never again approach the popularity it enjoyed during the prosperous days of the 1920s.[31]

Allegany County's economy in the 1920s had been healthy. The secret of its well-being at that time lay in its diversification. Many small industries, a bustling entertainment and sports business, and numerous service industries had combined with the giants of the county, namely West Virginia Pulp and Paper, the railroads, Kelly-Springfield, and Celanese, to bring extraordinary stability and prosperity to the area and its citizens. By 1940, something serious and permanent had occurred; Allegany County had lost its economic diversity. A combination of obsolescence, natural disasters, labor trouble, and financial problems caused by the Depression had killed many small industries and one large one, the N&G Taylor Company. Retail and entertainment businesses disappeared, or at best, declined from their earlier prestige. Nothing replaced these losses during the Depression decade. The formerly active Cumberland Chamber of Commerce could not raise money in a period of hard times, but even had it been able to do so, not many industries in the United States were in an expansionist mood in the 1930s.

Although few people perceived it at the time, Allegany County's economy by 1940 had become largely dependent on three large manufacturing concerns, Kelly-Springfield with 900 employees, Celanese with 8,660 employees, and the West Virginia Pulp and Paper Company with 1,390 employees. These three firms accounted for 83.4 percent of all the workers in the county employed in manufacturing businesses. The transportation industry also had thousands of county residents on its payroll. Now the area faced a new threat: if something serious happened to any of the big four employers economic disaster would result. Not enough job opportunities existed to absorb such a shock, as Celanese had done in the 1920s when the Georges Creek mining region fell on hard times. By 1940, Allegany County's economy rested on a very shaky foundation. A state study in 1941, referring to Allegany County, found that:

> Future prospects of improved economic conditions in the Area do not appear particularly promising unless existing manufacturing industries expand or other new manufacturing industries are attracted to the Area by the local supply of good coal, good transportation facilities, . . . an ample labor force and excellent living conditions.

The report continued:

> Without some appreciable further increase in manufacturing in the Area there is little probability of the Service Industries regaining the loss which resulted from decline of the Coal Industry and the generally depressed economic conditions which existed during a large part of the past decade.

Unfortunately, the leadership of both Allegany County and the city of Cumberland refused to face these problems. Despite the decline of the mining industry, Georges Creek area businessmen and politicians, a potent county power, could neither comprehend nor improve the region's basic economic difficulties. In Cumberland, the politicians and downtown businessmen simply refused to admit the city's—and the county's—real problems. Instead they found a convenient scapegoat in organized labor. Cumberland's city officials spent their time trying to "solve" economic difficulties by passing ordinances restricting picketing. The courts declared these restrictions unconstitutional. The county's leaders were so busy resisting change that they could see no real solutions to the problems that faced the area.[32]

In spite of the lack of leadership, Allegany County gradually emerged from the Depression. By 1941, the United States was preparing for war, and industry nationwide seemed to fully recover. Throughout 1941, local industry revived as war orders began pouring in. Employment rose. The county's economy appeared to be healthy again. This well-being, however, was an illusion created by the tremendous needs of World War II. The area's problems still lay beneath the surface, ready to emerge once the demands of the world conflict disappeared.

Long before the Japanese surprise attack against the United States Pacific fleet at Pearl Harbor on December 7, 1941, Allegany County had begun to feel the impact of world events. As early as March 1939, Cumberland Council Number 586 of the Knights of Columbus had begun a campaign to combat any "subversive influences" which might be found in the local area. A fascist-oriented, anti-Semitic organization, the Blueshirts of America, had formed a local chapter in 1938 with the slogan, "100 percent American," but, fortunately, it found few adherents. As the world situation worsened and the United States drew closer to being involved, activity increased. In August 1940, the FBI warned county residents to notify their local office of subversive actions or movements that could hamper the growing national defense program. By the spring of 1941, Allegany County had organized a local chapter of the "Bundles for Britain" program. The Western Maryland Industrial Union Council passed a resolution in August 1941 supporting President Roosevelt's decision to increase American aid to Great Britain. Cumberland WPA officials made plans to rip up more trolley car tracks for use in the defense program. Army recruiting grew more intense, and county men between the ages of twenty-one and thirty-six lined up to register for the draft. By the fall of 1941, the majority of local residents expected that the United States would soon be actively involved in World War II.[33]

People still recall where they were on December 7, 1941, when they heard the news of the Japanese attack on Pearl Harbor. Workers at Celanese virtually halted production while they attempted to hear the latest bulletins. People all over the county that fateful afternoon and evening gathered around radios for news of the bombing. War had finally come to the United States. Strongly condemning the attack, the Cumberland *Evening Times* urged its readers to prepare for war and do their part, adding that "It is exactly the same as if the bombs which fell on Hawaii had fallen on Cumberland. . . ." The area quickly responded to the crisis. Cities and towns of the county prepared for blackouts, fearing air raids in those first weeks of tension after Pearl Harbor. The Baltimore and Ohio Railroad, Kelly-Springfield, Celanese, and Potomac Edison increased security forces to prevent sabotage efforts by enemy agents. Cumberland placed its water supply under twenty-four hour guard. In early January 1942, the city experienced its first blackout.[34]

The wartime experience of county residents differed little from that of others throughout the United States. People turned to the radio constantly to hear the latest war news. Many consumer items became impossible to obtain. For example, women's nylon stockings disappeared and were replaced by a poor substitute, rayon. Rationing of all kinds of items, including canned goods, meat, and shoes, soon arrived. A vast government bureaucracy was created to dole out valued ration books to people nationwide. One could only purchase tires with a hard-to-obtain certificate from the local ration board. The government froze automobile purchases. New cars became a memory, although a number of people, anticipating the freeze, had hurriedly bought up new automobiles in 1942. Even used cars became extremely scarce as people held on to whatever automobiles they already had. Gasoline rationing soon altered the traveling habits of county citizens. A, B, C, and a myriad of other ration stickers cluttered automobile windshields, and people guarded gasoline ration stamps ferociously. We must remember, however, that most towns were still self-sufficient during the war years. People survived quite well even though the family automobile remained in the garage much of the time. Nevertheless, they probably complained more about meat and gasoline rationing than restrictions on other items. And, of course, black market gasoline soon appeared. If one knew the dealer, particularly in rural areas, then an extra tank of gasoline might occasionally be available. Several back-road stations in neighboring Bedford County, Pennsylvania, dispensed auto fuel illegally. Tires, like gasoline, could be found if one knew the right person. Retail stores saw that regular customers received the first opportunity to purchase scarce goods when a shipment arrived. Some people, anticipating rationing, had simply stocked up on enough canned goods to last for the duration of the war.[35]

While many county residents complained about rationing or found ways to evade the law, they also did their part to support the war effort. Thousands of young men and women from Allegany County volunteered for the armed services or were drafted. Some did not return, dying in the mud of the Italian campaign, in the hedgerows of France, or on steamy, disease-ridden islands in the Pacific. Others returned physically or emotionally crippled. Those who remained behind participated in other ways. Some residents joined the Ground Observer Corps, which established posts in several locations for reporting enemy aircraft. One particular outpost, 24-B, was situated on West Mechanic Street in Frostburg on land donated by Mrs. Blanche Price. Its record brought it an award for outstanding service at the end of the war. Others cooperated by buying either war bonds or defense stamps, a certain accumulation of which could be used to purchase bonds. Still others took part in various forms of volunteer work. People contributed to scrap-iron and other drives conducted periodically in the county. The labor unions pledged not to strike during the war, and most unions honored their patriotic commitment. Only wildcat strikes at firms such as Kelly-Springfield and the Cumberland Steel Company marred labor's excellent record, and these were short in duration. There was, however, an unfortunate exception to this record; the Georges Creek miners took part in a wartime strike ordered by the United Mine Workers, led by John L. Lewis, in 1943. This walkout crippled coal production in Allegany County. Many local people felt it was unpatriotic for the miners to strike for higher wages and fringe benefits while others sacrificed their lives in the armed services. The coal walkout tarnished the reputation of the United Mine Workers in particular and of all labor in general.[36]

One of the county's cities was singled out in 1945 when the United States Maritime Commission named a 10,700-ton cargo ship built by the Bethlehem-Fairfield Shipyards in Baltimore the U.S.S. *Frostburg Victory.* The commission apparently chose the name because Frostburg was "a typical main street American town with an interesting historical background." On Saturday, January 20, 1945, Mrs. Catherine Skidmore, wife of Frostburg Mayor Marshall C. Skidmore, surrounded by prominent local citizens, christened the ship, soon to serve the United States war effort. It is an interesting footnote that the ship's keel had been laid by W. O. Peterson, formerly from Eckhart, and the engineering work completed by Louis Young, once a Consolidation Coal Company engineer and a resident of Frostburg.[37]

Allegany County's industry boomed again during the war years as it strained to meet the many orders generated by the world conflict. Because Cumberland was a major railroad center, the tremendous upsurge in rail movements of war goods and troops spurred employment of local residents in the area's transportation systems. Freight traffic increased rapidly on the Baltimore and Ohio and the Western Maryland railroads. Even the Pennsylvania Railroad branch line to Altoona hauled more freight than usual during the war. As a result of gas rationing, people again turned to the train for transportation and passenger runs were once more filled to capacity. War demands also stimulated a temporary revival of the Georges Creek coalfields, where production again exceeded two million tons annually.[38]

Many of the area's industries converted their facilities to the manufacture of wartime supplies. As early as October 1940, the Celanese plant at Amcelle had begun producing Fortisan, a strong type of yarn used primarily in making parachutes. The war also increased the demand for other cellulose acetate products. Employment soared at Amcelle, eventually climbing over thirteen thousand, the highest it had ever been at the local textile facility. Celanese, in cooperation with the United States International Alcohol Company, began the experimental production of synthetic rubber in early 1943. This new five-million-dollar operation created butadiene, the major ingredient of Buna S, synthetic rubber. Celanese participated only in this intermediary stage of manufacturing synthetic rubber, however, and never produced the finished material. Kelly-Springfield also responded to wartime needs. When the Japanese advances in the Pacific and Southeast Asia cut off supplies of crude rubber in December 1941, all rubber stocks in the United States were frozen. Kelly-Springfield could no longer manufacture tires. The company, however, had already begun talks with the government about the possibility of making high-explosive artillery shells. The firm's officers planned for this conversion and acquired the necessary tools and machinery. Soon the local plant was mass-producing high-explosive, eight-inch shells. Shortly after the United States entered the war, the Army Ordnance Department leased the local factory. New machines arrived; supervisors and workmen studied the operations of other ordnance plants. Before long Kelly-Springfield was manufacturing great quantities of fifty-caliber, armor-piercing machine gun cartridges. In 1943, part of the plant was reconverted to produce tires again for the war effort. This change necessitated an expansion of the local factory. By 1945, Kelly-Springfield was making tires completely from synthetic materials. Between 1943 and 1945, the company spent eight million dollars to expand and modernize the Cumberland plant.[39]

World War II also brought a new industry to the area. In 1942, the United States Army acquired a 425-acre tract in Mineral County, West Virginia, just across the Potomac River opposite Pinto, Maryland. The Kelly-Springfield Tire Company built the Allegany Ordnance Plant, known as "Pinto Site," and began producing 50-caliber ammunition there. Soon, however, the property was needed for rocket development and was made available to the Office of Scientific Research and Development. George Washington University operated the local facility for the government, conducting major research in rocket technology and in the development of new weapons, including the bazooka, aircraft rockets, recoilless mortars, mine clearing devices, and Jet-Assisted Take-Off devices, known as JATO's. This new industry would play a major role in Allegany County's economy in the postwar years.[40]

Wartime demands on the economy created a tremendous upsurge in local employment. Workers labored long workweeks and many overtime hours. Paychecks bulged, and with consumer goods in short supply, much of the money went into government bonds or bank accounts, saved for the day when the war would end and desired items would be available again. With so many of its citizens in the armed forces, the area was hard pressed to find enough labor to meet employment needs. The Emergency War Manpower Commission saw that key industries such as Celanese, Kelly-Springfield, and the National Jet Company, a manufacturer of precision tools and drills, had the manpower they required. Nevertheless, by 1944, Kelly-Springfield needed employees so desperately to produce heavy-duty truck tires that it sought to have former workers furloughed from military service. Eventually, 150 Celanese employees were temporarily transferred to the tire firm to relieve its shortage. Of course, war production would have been crippled had not thousands of local women taken positions in local industry, replacing men in the armed services and doing a superb job on assembly lines, formerly male territory. At one point, the Baltimore and Ohio Railroad imported two hundred Mexican workers for its track gangs.[41]

By 1945, people in Allegany County confidently awaited the end of the conflict as United States troops rolled into a devastated Germany and bottled up the Japanese in their home islands. Although Japan was not yet defeated, the area held a mild celebration in May 1945 when President Harry S. Truman announced the end of the war in the European theater. Bars and public schools closed as did most stores. Churches held special thanksgiving services. It was nothing, however, compared with the jubilation when word of the Japanese surrender arrived. Crowds thronged the main streets of all the cities and towns of the county, exploding firecrackers, pounding on drums and dishpans, and singing "God Bless America" to mark the end of World War II. A swing band played far into the night in south Cumberland, while on Baltimore Street a large gathering battered a huge effigy of a Japanese. Stores and restaurants throughout the area closed.[42]

County residents, elated over the war's end, waited anxiously for an end to rationing and the return to a normal life style. Local business and industrial leaders confidently expected prosperity to continue.[43] Few realized that the boom of the war years had been temporary. County economic problems that had emerged in the 1930s were still unsolved; lurking near the surface, they would arise again. The years of the great decline would soon begin.

CHAPTER XII NOTES

1. James W. Bishop, *The Glass Industry of Allegany County, Maryland* (Cumberland, Md.: Commercial Press Printing Company, 1968), pp. 9, 50-51, 74-80, 83, 86.

2. Interview with Thomas B. Finan III, Aug. 18, 1975 (hereafter cited as Finan Interview); and Cumberland *Evening Times*, July 30, 1937.

3. Katherine A. Harvey, *Best Dressed Miners: Life and Labor in the Maryland Coal Region, 1835-1910* (Ithaca: Cornell University Press, 1969), pp. 367-69 (hereafter cited as Harvey, *Best Dressed Miners*); Henry A. Grine, *Preliminary Economic Studies of the Western Allegany County Area* ("Allegany County, Maryland: Economic Conditions"; Annapolis: Maryland State Planning Commission, 1941), p. 11 (hereafter cited as Grine, *Preliminary Economic Studies*); and interview with James G. Conway, Sept. 16, 1975.

4. Grine, *Preliminary Economic Studies*, p. 11; and Harvey, *Best Dressed Miners*, pp. 365-66.

5. Interview with William L. Wilson, Aug. 18, 1975 (hereafter cited as Wilson Interview); and Edmund S. Burke, *A Message to the Employes of the Kelly-Springfield Tire Co.* (Cumberland: Kelly-Springfield Tire Co., 1936).

6. Ibid.

7. Interview with Mrs. Frank Birmingham, Miss Mary M. Birmingham, and Miss Virginia Birmingham, Aug. 20, 1975 (hereafter cited as Birmingham Interview); and Cumberland *Evening Times*, Oct. 12, 1937.

8. *The Official Guide of the Railways, January, 1937* (New York: National Railway Publication Company, 1937), pp. 365-79, 407-8; Cumberland *Daily News*, May 4, 1929; and Cumberland *Evening Times*, Aug. 14, 1942.

9. *Frostburg Sesquicentennial Souvenir Book* (Frostburg, Md.: The Frostburg Sesquicentennial Committee, 1962), no page number (hereafter cited as *Frostburg Sesquicentennial Book*); Cumberland *Daily News*, Nov. 17, 1927; and Cumberland *Evening Times*, May 15 and 16, 1932.

10. *Cumberland Sesquicentennial Souvenir Program and History*

(Cumberland, Md.: The Cumberland Sesquicentennial Committee, 1937), pp. 24, 78 (hereafter cited as *Cumberland Sesquicentennial History*).

11. Ibid., p. 79; Cumberland *Evening Times,* April 16, 1933, Feb. 1 and 11, March 10, and April 28, 1941, and Nov. 10, 1944.

12. Interview with William L. Wilson, Nov. 12, 1975 (hereafter cited as Second Wilson Interview); and *Twenty-Fourth Annual Report of the Bank Commissioner of the State of Maryland to His Excellency, Albert C. Ritchie, Governor: February 10, 1934* (Annapolis: no publisher given, 1934), pp. 18-19 (hereafter cited as *Twenty-Fourth Annual Report of the Bank Commissioner*).

13. *Twenty-Fourth Annual Report of the Bank Commissioner,* p. 12; Memorandum, Charles R. Georgius to William L. Wilson, State Bank Commissioner, Oct. 22, 1975: Enclosed are copies of several pages from the *Maryland Bank Register* which give information about Allegany County banks (hereafter cited as Georgius-Wilson Memorandum); Cumberland *Daily News,* Oct. 27, 1931; *Twenty-Fifth Annual Report of the Bank Commissioner of the State of Maryland to His Excellency, Harry W. Nice, Governor: February 10, 1935* (Annapolis: no publisher given, 1935), p. 11 (hereafter cited as *Twenty-Fifth Annual Report of the Bank Commissioner*); *Frostburg Sesquicentennial Book,* no page number; Second Wilson Interview; interview with Ralph M. Race and Matthew Skidmore, July 30, 1975 (hereafter cited as Race-Skidmore Interview); interview with Fred Morton, Oct. 7, 1975 (hereafter cited as Morton Interview); and interview with Mr. and Mrs. Harry I. Stegmaier, Aug. 20, 1975 (hereafter cited as Stegmaier Interview).

14. Cumberland *Daily News,* Jan. 12, 1922, and July 14, 1928; *Westvaco News Letter,* April-May 1969; interview with Mrs. Frances D. Greaves, Oct. 23, 1975 (hereafter cited as Greaves Interview); Harold Blancke, *Celanese Corporation of America: The Founders and the Early Years* (New York: The Newcomen Society in North America, 1952), p. 14; and United States, Army Corps of Engineers, *Definite Project Report on Local Flood Protection for Cumberland, Md. & Ridgeley, W. Va.* (Washington: United States Government Printing Office, 1945), p. 9.

15. United States, Department of the Interior, *The Floods of March, 1936,* part 3, *Potomac, James and Upper Ohio Rivers* (Washington: United States Government Printing Office, 1937), pp. 8-10, 32, 34, 43, 58, 75, 97, 103 (hereafter cited as U.S. Department of the Interior, *The Floods,* part 3); Cumberland *Evening Times,* March 17 and 19, 1936; Birmingham Interview; Stegmaier Interview; and Race-Skidmore Interview.

16. Cumberland *Evening Times,* April 26, 1936, April 7 and July 27, 1939, and Dec. 3, 1940.

17. William E. Leuchtenburg, *Franklin D. Roosevelt and the New Deal, 1932-1940* (New York: Harper & Row, Publishers, 1963), pp.

46-47 (hereafter cited as Leuchtenburg, *FDR and the New Deal*); and William J. Kelley, *Brewing in Maryland from Colonial Times to the Present* (Baltimore: John D. Lucas Printing Company, 1965), p. 664.

18. Cumberland *Evening Times,* April 1 and July 30, 1934, Sept. 2, 6, and 26 and Oct. 4, 1935, Aug. 16, 1938, April 5 and Nov. 30, 1940, and Dec. 15, 1942; Greaves Interview; Grine, *Preliminary Economic Studies,* p. 31; interview with James Klippstein and Alvin H. Ternent, Oct. 1, 1975 (hereafter cited as Klippstein-Ternent Interview); interview with Matthew Skidmore, Fred Morton, and the Reverend George Wehler, Oct. 7, 1975 (hereafter cited as Skidmore-Morton-Wehler Interview); Second Wilson Interview; and Stegmaier Interview.

19. Cumberland *Evening Times,* May 8, 1936, Aug. 18, 1938, and June 18, July 13 and 15, 1939.

20. David A. Shannon, *Twentieth Century America: The United States Since the 1890's* (Chicago: Rand McNally & Company, 1963), p. 360 (hereafter cited as Shannon, *Twentieth Century America*); and Leuchtenburg, *FDR and the New Deal,* pp. 150-51.

21. Shannon, *Twentieth Century America,* pp. 361-62; and Cumberland *Evening Times,* Aug. 31, 1936.

22. Cumberland *Evening Times,* Aug. 24 and 26 and Sept. 1 and 3, 1936, and Feb. 14 and Aug. 1, 1937.

23. Interview with William E. Crooks, Nov. 5, 1975 (hereafter cited as Crooks Interview); and Cumberland *Evening Times,* Nov. 11, 1936.

24. Cumberland *Evening Times,* Nov. 11, 12, 13, 14, and 17, 1936; and Birmingham Interview.

25. Cumberland *Evening Times,* Nov. 27, 28, and 29, 1936; interview with Edgar M. Lewis, Dec. 10, 1975 (hereafter cited as Lewis Interview); Finan Interview; and Wilson Interview.

26. Cumberland *Evening Times,* Dec. 4, 1936, and Sept. 5, 1939; and Court Docket, Allegany County, Maryland, January and April Terms, 1937.

27. Letter from Leslie L. Helmer to James W. Bishop, November 1975 (hereafter cited as Helmer-Bishop Letter); and William Manchester, *The Glory and the Dream: A Narrative History of America, 1932-1972,* Vol. I (Boston: Little, Brown and Company, 1973), pp. 192-94.

28. Cumberland *Evening Times,* Jan. 4, 5, and 13 and Feb. 8, 1936, and July 18, 1937; interview with Anne Everline, Dec. 30, 1974; and Helmer-Bishop Letter.

29. Cumberland *Evening Times,* June 17, 28, and 29, and Nov. 24 and 26, 1937, March 6 and 13, and Aug. 27, 1938, Nov. 2 and 6, and Dec. 14, 1939, and Oct. 26, Nov. 9, and Dec. 5, 1941; Helmer-Bishop Letter; and Minutes of Board of Directors Meeting, Cumberland, Md., Chamber of Commerce, April 18, 1940, in Minute Book of the Cumberland Chamber of Commerce, May 1936 to January 1941.

30. Grine, *Preliminary Economic Studies,* pp. 11, 31-35; Morton Interview; Birmingham Interview; Stegmaier Interview; and Greaves Interview.

31. Cumberland *Daily News,* May 30, 1924, March 17 and 19, 1928, and March 20, 1929; Birmingham Interview; Stegmaier Interview; interview with Herman J. Miller, Oct. 15, 1975; *Frostburg Sesquicentennial Book,* no page number; and *Cumberland Sesquicentennial History,* p. 48.

32. Grine, *Preliminary Economic Studies,* pp. 5, 11, 26; and Cumberland *Evening Times,* Aug. 16, 1937.

33. Cumberland *Evening Times,* Sept. 30, 1938, March 20, 1939, May 26 and Aug. 4, 1940, and May 18, Aug. 5, and Oct. 21, 1941.

34. Ibid., Dec. 8 and 9, 1941, and Jan. 3, 1942; Birmingham Interview; Stegmaier Interview; Race-Skidmore Interview; Second Wilson Interview; and Skidmore-Morton-Wehler Interview.

35. Stegmaier Interview; Birmingham Interview; Skidmore-Morton-Wehler Interview; Morton Interview; and Greaves Interview.

36. Greaves Interview; *Frostburg Sesquicentennial Book,* no page number; Cumberland *Evening Times,* Jan. 16 and Sept. 13 and 28, 1942, June 1, 3, and 27, and Nov. 4, 6, 8, 11, 14, 18, 19, and 20, 1943, and April 5, July 28, and Nov. 14, 1944; and Harvey, *Best Dressed Miners,* p. 366.

37. *Historical Sketch of Frostburg, Maryland: A Brief History of Frostburg compiled at request of the Bethlehem-Fairfield Shipyards, Inc., in connection with the launching and christening of the SS Frostburg Victory in Baltimore, Saturday, January 20, 1945* (Frostburg: The Fidelity Savings Bank, 1945), no page numbers.

38. Harvey, *Best Dressed Miners,* p. 369.

39. Crooks Interview; Cumberland *Evening Times,* Oct. 6, 1940, Feb. 9, 1943, and May 23 and Aug. 3, 1945; *From Armorubber to Armor-Piercing Bullets* (Cumberland: Kelly-Springfield Engineering Company, no date), no page numbers; and *Thirty-Fifth Anniversary: Kelly-Springfield Cumberland Plant* (Cumberland: Kelly-Springfield Tire Company, 1955), no page numbers.

40. *History of Allegany Ballistics Laboratory,* pp. 1-2; a short summary of the history of the Allegany Ballistics Laboratory, enclosed in memorandum from M. Paul Thompson, Allegany Ballistics Laboratory, to author, December 1975.

41. Cumberland *Evening Times,* April 9, 1943, and June 3, Aug. 20 and 21, and Sept. 10, 1944.

42. Ibid., May 8 and Aug. 15, 1945; and Greaves Interview.

43. Cumberland *Evening Times,* Aug. 17, 1945.

XIII

THE GREAT DECLINE

The hopes of the citizens of Allegany County for a postwar revival were soon dashed. During the Great Depression, the county had lost its economic diversity, becoming almost completely dependent on a few large industries, an unhealthy situation. Wartime demands on these big concerns had boosted employment and raised false optimism for the future. In the postwar era the continued loss of smaller companies, the nearly total termination of coal mining, and the cutbacks at some of the larger industries would deal a devastating blow to the area. Even the construction of a major glass plant in the 1950s and new employment opportunities at the Allegany Ballistics Laboratory could not rectify the economic damage. In fact, blows to these two new businesses would make the predicament even worse by the 1970s. In 1949, over 10,000 workers would be jobless, creating a sobering 23 percent unemployment rate. A great exodus ensued as thousands left the region to seek opportunities elsewhere. Despite the loss of population, over 5,000 would remain without work in 1961, a 12.7 percent rate of unemployment. Throughout the 1960s, the percentage would hover in double figures, climbing rapidly upward again during the deep recession of the 1970s. The thirty years between World War II and the 1970s were the period of the great decline for the area. The Allegany County of the mid-1970s would be quite different from the Allegany County of the 1920s boom era.[1]

Some of the county's older industries completely disappeared between 1945 and 1975. The once prosperous hand-blown glass business had shrunk to only one plant after World War II. Begun in the 1930s, the Cumberland Glass

Company continued to produce hundreds of different types of glassware at the firm's location in one of the old buildings of the former Clark Distilling Company in LaVale. But as had befallen other glass companies on previous occasions, fire struck the Cumberland Glass Company. In the early morning of September 25, 1956, six volunteer fire companies battled an intense blaze that gutted the firm's facilities. The owners decided to relocate rather than rebuild the destroyed plant. By 1957, the Cumberland Glass Company was again in production, using the abandoned repair shop of the former Cumberland and Pennsylvania Railroad in Mount Savage. The company had been forced to start from scratch, which involved building furnaces and annealing ovens. However, after twenty-nine years of operation, the Cumberland Glass Company finally closed its doors for good on July 29, 1961, because of a scarcity of skilled glassmen. Unfortunately, glassmaking had become a dying art. Allegany County's handblown glass industry had reached a permanent end. Only cutting and engraving of manufactured glass remained.[2]

The brewing industry, located in Cumberland, survived longer than did glassmaking. In 1958, the Queen City Brewing Company purchased the entire stock of the Cumberland Brewing Company, the city's oldest brewery. Queen City continued to use the Cumberland Brewing Company plant, however, until 1969, making Old Export Beer and Gamecock Ale. Eventually the plant, with a capacity of 200,000 barrels per year, was shut down. The Queen City Brewing Company stayed in business into the 1970s, producing Old German Beer and Tudor Ale for the A&P supermarket chain, and later, American Beer. By the 1970s, small breweries throughout the United States came under increasing pressure as a result of inflation. Costs of raw materials rose precipitously. Competition from the larger, nationwide brewing companies drove the small firms out of business. The Queen City Brewing Company, with an annual capacity of 250,000 barrels, proved no exception. In the fall of 1974, company president William L. Wilson asked workers at the local brewery to take a 10 percent wage cut. When they refused, Wilson, with a buyer at hand in the Iron City Brewing Company of Pittsburgh, closed the firm and sold the formula and the right to produce Old German Beer to the Pittsburgh concern. Demolition crews soon leveled the huge red-brick brewery along Wills Creek, with its tall yellow smokestack. By the fall of 1975, little remained of the former Queen City Brewing Company plant, which had been a Cumberland landmark for decades.[3]

The Georges Creek coalfields had revived briefly during World War II because of wartime demands for fuel. Termination of the world conflict forced the industry to confront reality. More expensive Georges Creek coal simply could not compete with the cheaper product from the enormous West Virginia and Pennsylvania fields. Moreover, demand for coal decreased throughout the United States after the war as industries and residential users increasingly turned to oil and natural gas for fuel. Railroad conversion from steam engines to diesels contributed immeasurably to the falling demand. Several postwar strikes in the Georges Creek mining region did not help the depressed industry. Many companies, on the verge of financial collapse, simply disappeared, particularly after the 1949-1950 work cutback ordered by John L. Lewis in an attempt to stabilize employment in the bituminous coal industry. The Consolidation Coal Company, aware that the Georges Creek fields were finished, had already sold its Maryland property before the war ended. On March 1, 1944, William E. Jenkins and William S. Jenkins of Frostburg began operating all former Consolidation properties, having purchased them for a fraction of their former value. The Western Maryland Railway absorbed the Consolidation-owned Cumberland and Pennsylvania Railroad. In 1952, the George's Creek Coal Company, chartered in 1835, went out of business. Eventually all deep mining in the region ceased. Employment fell precipitously, from 2,049 in 1948 to about 350 in 1966.[4]

By the late 1960s, production of coal in the Georges Creek region had again reached over half a million tons a year. However, surface mining, popularly called strip mining, had replaced deep mining as the method of production. Surface mining, highly mechanized and employing but a fraction of the people needed by the deep mining industry, had begun in the Georges Creek fields during World War II. In its early stages this method, unencumbered by environmental legislation, had torn away foliage and topsoil, leaving ugly, deep scars upon the landscape. Several laws passed by the Maryland legislature in the 1960s and 1970s, partially through the lobbying efforts of the Citizens Coalition on Surface Mining, remedied the abuse of the environment by requiring mining firms to restore the landscape to its original contours and replant worked areas. Most of these miners were responsible men who, after passage of the legislation, worked hard to repair environmental damage caused by their operations. A few, however, gave the whole industry a bad name by their "environment-be-damned" attitude. Nevertheless, in the light of the energy crisis of the 1970s, it had become obvious to most local people that the Georges Creek coal deposits were a definite economic asset to the county. Careful surface mining of these deposits could provide employment for area citizens, and perhaps effect the return of a semblance of prosperity to the Georges Creek valley. Coal production might one day again become a prime factor in restoring economic health to Allegany County.[5]

As smaller industries such as glassmaking and brewing disappeared in the thirty-year period after World War II, the area came to rely more and more heavily on the larger industries for employment and economic stability. One of the healthiest of these firms was the Kelly-Springfield Tire Company. The main reason for its prosperity lay in the tremendous, ever-growing number of automobiles and trucks which inundated the postwar United States, creating an enormous demand for tires. Following the war, Kelly-Springfield poured millions of dollars into expansion and modernization of the local plant. As the postwar era progressed, the company spread its sales worldwide, marketing tires in seventy-one foreign nations. Demand for tires led to construction during the 1960s of new plants in Tyler, Texas; Freeport, Illinois; and Fayetteville, North Carolina. The firm did not neglect the local facility. Between 1964 and 1971, Kelly-Springfield invested over twenty-five million dollars in improving the Cumberland plant. Not only did the company produce its own brand-name tires locally but it also manufactured tire lines for discount chain stores, department stores, automotive and farm equipment supply firms, and the Sun Oil Company. Kelly-Springfield was one of the biggest employers in Allegany County by the mid-1970s, with over 3,100 people working at the factory, corporate headquarters, truck terminal, retail store, and the huge distribution center warehouse area at Mexico Farms east of Cumberland. Moreover, in 1974, the company paid out $44 million in wages, $3.6 million for utilities and supplies, $3.7 million for fuel oil, and almost $800,000 in city and county taxes, which together totaled over $50 million being poured into the local economy. Nevertheless, by the mid-1970s, Kelly-Springfield itself suffered from the recession of the Nixon-Ford years. Skyrocketing inflation made prices for raw materials almost prohibitive. At the same time, the company also had to convert two coal-burning boilers to fuel oil to meet Maryland standards for clean air, as well as provide other environmental protection devices. Despite these problems, the company had a huge capital investment in its local plant, in addition to an experienced work force with a low turnover rate. After a stagnant period in the early 1970s, when the company claimed that waste, absenteeism, and high labor costs were making the plant's future uncertain, the firm renewed its investment in the Cumberland factory. In 1974, Kelly-Springfield spent an additional $2.1 million for modernization and environmental protection. The company also wanted to reconvert its boilers to burn local coal, which in view of soaring oil prices would produce significant savings and make the plant more competitive with similar facilities. Unfortunately, although local coal met federal environmental standards, it did not conform to Maryland guidelines. The state agreed to waive its standards for Kelly-Springfield on account of the company's promise to install electrostatic precipitators, which would stop most air pollution. Maryland, however, could not change its standards without the approval of the federal Environmental Protection Agency even though local coal met the latter's guidelines. Soon the entire proposal became bogged down in the seemingly endless red tape of the federal bureaucracy. But despite these problems, Kelly-Springfield remained one of the healthiest and most economically important of Allegany County's industries in the mid-1970s.[6]

Another major employer in the postwar era, as well as one of the most prosperous industrial concerns in Allegany County, was the huge West Virginia Pulp and Paper Company complex at Luke. Its main product was fine-grade paper, such as printing and cover paper, which was used throughout the United States by many book and periodical publishers, including *National Geographic* magazine and *World Book Encyclopedia.* By 1973, the company was turning out over 312,000 tons of high-grade paper annually. This enormous production had been made possible by large postwar capital expenditures for new machines and more modern facilities. In 1960, the firm installed two new wide, high-speed paper machines which tripled the plant's output. That same year, the company also completed a new 81,000-square-foot warehouse for finished products. Other new additions included a new woodyard across the Potomac River in West Virginia in 1961, a lime kiln in 1966, an oil storage tank [building], and new boilers. Moreover, long before environmental protection became popular, the company had recognized the pollution problem at Luke. The first electrostatic precipitator was installed at the mill in 1951. By the 1960s, control programs were in full swing, ahead of the federal laws which would force companies to deal with these problems. Wet scrubbers, recovery tanks, and more electrostatic precipitators, some of the latter 99.9 percent effective in reducing particulate matter, were constructed. Most openings into the Potomac River, once discharging all kinds of waste, were closed up. In 1967, the company built a quarter-million-dollar Black Liquor Oxidation Unit, which reduced the odor from the mill about one-third, although it did not completely eliminate the disagreeable smell. By the 1970s, the firm had invested well over twenty million dollars for pollution abatement equipment at Luke, culminating in a massive 600-foot stack, costing $3.3 million, to reduce sulphur dioxide levels of the emissions

The enormous paper products mill of the West Virginia Pulp and Paper Company, later Westvaco Corporation, at Luke, Maryland, remained one of Allegany County's healthiest industries when this photograph was taken in 1974. Courtesy Westvaco Corporation

from all power and recovery boilers. The Potomac River was now cleaner and the once barren hillside behind the mill again green with vegetation. This kind of investment was possible only because the Luke paper mill was one of the largest in the United States, part of what had become an enormous worldwide company, renamed Westvaco Corporation in 1969 to "better reflect diversified company operations."[7]

The Luke mill remained one of the largest employers in Allegany County during the postwar era, just as it had even during the dark days of the 1930s. Employment hovered close to 2,000 in the mid-1950s, rose to 2,300 in 1969 as production expanded, and then dropped to about 1,900 in 1974. Between 1959 and 1974, wages and benefits paid by the company more than doubled, rising from $13 million to $29.1 million, thereby providing a major stimulant to a generally depressed county economy. Perhaps most important from an employment standpoint was the fact that 60 percent of the employees came from the tri-towns of Luke, Westernport, and Piedmont, with another 20 percent to 30 percent coming from the Georges Creek area. Job opportunities in this region were few after the almost complete collapse of the coal industry; the Westvaco Corporation partially filled this employment vacuum.[8]

Westvaco was a unique company in one respect, retaining a spirit of concern for its workers and for nearby communities that had all but disappeared in modern America. In addition to good wages, the firm's employees received life, accidental death, and dismemberment insurance, a pension plan, and many other benefits, all paid for by the company. Employees who contined their education received 90 percent tutition refunds. In 1973, Westvaco inaugurated college scholarships for the children of mill employees. Its concern could also be seen in its involvement with Luke and other nearby communities. In the mid-1950s, the firm sold its company housing to the occupants. The mill continued to provide heat and filtered water to much of the town of Luke for a minimal charge. Westvaco also underwrote the bonds for construction in 1960 of a tertiary waste treatment plant at Westernport which handled sewage for several local towns as well as the mill itself. After it was built, the company paid 96 percent of all costs of the plant, run by the Upper Potomac River Commission, including operating expenses. All in all, Westvaco was not only a major employer, but also a positive community asset for Allegany County in the postwar era.[9]

While Kelly-Springfield and Westvaco fared quite well in the decades following World War II, another industry, upon which the county economy heavily depended, did not have the same success. The Celanese Corporation's Amcelle plant underwent major changes following the war. Production demands in the years from 1940 to 1945 had taken a heavy toll of the machinery, much of which had also become obsolete in the light of technological improvements in the textile industry. Within a few months of the war's end, the Celanese Corporation embarked upon a major modernization program at Amcelle. Five million dollars' worth of equipment was scrapped and replaced by new machinery. This investment, plus other improvements, cost the company approximately twenty million dollars. While the changes took place, production was maintained fairly well, although some disruptions did occur. Then, as the improvement program neared completion, a major depression struck the United States textile industry. Massive layoffs at Amcelle resulted, contributing a great deal to Allegany County's 23 percent unemployment rate in 1949. Production picked up again in the early 1950s. However, Celanese decided by that time to cut out many of its peripheral operations, which had been instituted in the 1920s when other companies were not yet equipped to handle cellulose acetate yarn. Now that its customers possessed this ability, the firm decided to phase out those processes itself. In the spring of 1952, the dyeing and finishing department at Amcelle closed down as the company gradually withdrew from actual fabric production. Weaving and knitting were relocated to other plants before being discontinued. A plant in Bishop, Texas, took over chemical production. Celco in Narrows, Virginia, and Celriver in Rock Hill, South Carolina, part of a major corporate expansion program, took over the manufacture of cellulose acetate flake. Many buildings at Amcelle were torn down as these operations were removed.

This company move to become strictly a producer of basic products, along with modernization and more efficient production methods, resulted in a drastic decrease in jobs. Employment, which had reached 13,000 during World War II, fell to 10,560 in 1948, 5,036 by 1950, and a low of 3,055 by 1955. With its loss of economic diversity, the area was unable to absorb many of the unemployed in new jobs. A large number of those who could not find work went on the unemployment rolls. Others simply abandoned the region, migrating to Baltimore, Detroit, and other industrial cities.[10]

After the major changes effected during the decade following World War II, the situation stabilized at Amcelle from the mid-1950s until the early 1970s. The company itself expanded rapidly, building new plants throughout the United States and in foreign countries, eventually becoming by the 1970s a truly multinational corporation. New products such as Arnel triacetate were introduced at the local factory. Modernization of the solvent recovery system was completed in 1971. The next year, a gas-fired power plant replaced the old coal-fired one. In 1974, construction of a modern facility to produce Cytrel, a cellulose-based tobacco supplement, was begun. Then "the roof caved in" at Amcelle. Difficulties in obtaining raw materials forced production cuts and cost the company customers. Next, the market for colored yarn, a major product, collapsed. In late 1974, the firm began substantial layoffs of production and white-collar personnel alike, dropping employment below the 1,000 mark. All colored yarn production was phased out, leaving the local plant to produce only acetate and Arnel filament yarns and the new Cytrel. As the production process for the latter was automated and required few workers, even a possibly bright future for the tobacco supplement held out little hope for major employment in the future. Between 1945 and 1975, the number of workers at Celanese in Cumberland had fallen from 13,000 to below 1,000. Allegany County simply could not completely rebound from the loss of so many jobs at one of its largest industries during the three decades following World War II.[11]

Part of the slack in the economy caused by Amcelle work

force reductions was taken up by a new major employer in the county, Allegany Ballistics Laboratory. Actually, the industry could not be considered completely new as it merely succeeded the Office of Scientific Research and Development in operating the laboratory developed at "Pinto Site" during World War II. As previously mentioned, this facility had been renamed Allegany Ballistics Laboratory in 1943. After the war, the U.S. Navy Bureau of Ordnance took over the plant and transferred management and operations to the Hercules Powder Company, a defense contractor that had worked on rocket development during World War II. The two decades of the cold war which followed proved to be the halcyon days for the defense industry in the United States. Allegany Ballistics Laboratory prospered as defense contracts poured in for rocket and missile development, a basically new form of warfare. The local facility first developed rocket propellants, including solid fuel in various forms, as well as the motors themselves for the missiles. Double-base propellant rocket motors produced at ABL found use in the Nike anti-aircraft missile; the Honest John, an early U.S. Army artillery rocket; the U.S. Navy's Terrier anti-aircraft missile; the Talos long-range anti-aircraft rocket; a number of naval antisubmarine missiles; and the Air Force Snark, a long-range predecessor of the Intercontinental Ballistic Missile, or ICBM. Research for the infant space program led to the development of a lightweight, strong, filament-wound material called Spiralloy, as well as a method for casting propellant into firing chambers. These advances were put to good use in creating the second stage of a sophisticated ICBM, the Navy's submarine-launched Polaris missile. The latter necessitated a major effort as the United States rushed to stay ahead of the Soviet Union in the missile race. In 1963, Allegany Ballistics Laboratory began work on what may have been its most difficult project, the first and second stages of the Sprint, an antiballistic missile, referred to as the ABM, which was designed to knock enemy missiles from the air. The nature of its mission required high acceleration and involved trajectory problems. ABL met the challenge. Besides military contracts, the plant developed the Deacon rocket in the early days of the space program and later the Vanguard rocket motor for future space thrusts. All of this activity required teams of skilled chemists, engineers, mathematicians, and other technical personnel, as well as production workers, to experiment with and produce the motors and propellants. The county enjoyed an influx of well-paid, skilled professionals as a result. Moreover, the defense contractor provided jobs for many local residents. At its height, Allegany Ballistics Laboratory employed approximately 3,300 people. Most workers came from Allegany County, although the plant was located across the river in Mineral County, West Virginia. Expansion occurred with the construction in the 1960s of Plant Two, the new facility specifically designed to produce composite propellants and tactical rocket motors for the company, now renamed Hercules, Incorporated. The huge complex now occupied over 1,600 acres and included a new office building.

By the 1970s, however, the defense industry in the United States was depressed, as budgets came under closer scrutiny and Congress balked at passing massive appropriations for the military, particularly in the field of research and development of new weaponry. As Allegany Ballistics Laboratory defense contracts fell off, the company turned its expertise to other fields of endeavor, such as environmental research. In this area, it developed systems for desalinization of seawater, purification of ship waste waters, waste reclamation, and the use of Spiralloy in an experimental wind energy system for the National Aeronautics and Space Administration. ABL also offered the services of its computer to development and management personnel. The Testing and Analysis Division applied its knowledge, using techniques developed in rocket manufacture, to other business and industrial concerns, helping with planning and problem-solving. Allegany Ballistics Laboratory even began running tests for the automobile and tire industry with a fleet of test cars. Nevertheless, all of the diversification could not begin to make up for the absence of defense contracts on the scale of cold-war era spending. By 1975, employment had declined to less than 600, a major drop from the all-time high of 3,300. But ABL possessed excellent revival potential in an increasingly technological society because of the firm's technical nature and its pool of skilled professional personnel. Only the future would tell whether a new age of development and prosperity lay on the horizon for Allegany Ballistics Laboratory. Possibilities seemed good, however, that it would be a major factor in the future economic health of western Maryland.[12]

The county's economy, reeling from unemployment, received a large boost in the mid-1950s when a major industry, the Pittsburgh Plate Glass Company, decided to locate a plant near Cumberland. The civic effort to obtain the company rivaled the earlier campaign to attract Kelly-Springfield. This recruitment proved that the old spirit was not yet dead, and showed what could be accomplished if the business, labor, and political leaders put forth a cooperative effort. In the summer of 1952, the Cumberland Chamber of Commerce, aware of the area's need for new employment, formed an industrial promotion committee. Energetic Albert H. Hargreaves, named director of industrial development by the chamber of commerce, set out to learn whether any glass companies would be interested in the glass sand available in the area. The Pittsburgh Plate Glass Company responded in the affirmative, as it was looking for a new plant site at the time. In September 1953, the chamber of commerce acquired options on several hundred acres of land along the Potomac River at North Branch for possible use by the company. In the meantime, community leaders started studying the company's needs and making provisions to meet them should the firm decide to locate near Cumberland. William C. Walsh, acting as local legal counsel for the company, worked tirelessly with area officials to solve any problems that arose. The Allegany County Commissioners, in cooperation with the State Roads Department, promised to construct a new highway from Cumberland to the site. The Baltimore and Ohio and the Western Maryland railroads offered their assistance in luring the new company to Allegany County. City officials in Cumberland guaranteed waterline extensions and a sewage treatment plant to clean up the Potomac River. Potomac Edison and Columbia Gas agreed to supply needed amounts of electricity and natural gas. Pittsburgh Plate estimated it would require, for example, three million cubic feet of gas daily. Local labor leaders gave assurances that skilled workers were available in ample supply for both construction and then operation of the proposed plant. Edmund S. Burke, of Kelly-Springfield, and R. Finley Thompson, plant manager at Amcelle, told the glass company that area labor was as good as any it would find in some other location, if not better. Impressed by the civic effort, the ready availability of good water, rail transportation, fuel, glass sand, and labor, and Cumberland's proximity to southeastern markets, Pittsburgh Plate Glass decided in March 1954 to build an enormous, ultramodern glass plant at North Branch, costing approximately thirty-four million dollars. It was to be the largest expenditure on a single project in the company's seventy-one year history. The proposed facility would incorporate all of the latest technological improvements in the field to produce plate glass of precision optical quality.[13]

Building of the large complex led to a construction industry boom, as over 2,500 skilled laborers were needed for the project. Through 1955 and into 1956, work proceeded on the three-fourths-mile-long plant, which would become the most modern plate glass operation in the United States at the time of its completion. On June 24, 1956, company officials dedicated the nearly finished Cumberland facility. Production of rough plate glass soon began, although for a short time it had to be shipped to other locations for grinding, polishing, and finishing. After the installation of a unique turn grinding and polishing unit which operated on both sides of the glass simultaneously, Cumberland Works Seven of Pittsburgh Plate Glass began turning out a plate glass product superior to anything else then available. With the plant's production capacity of approximately fifty million square feet of polished glass annually, plate glass soon flowed from Cumberland to the furniture, mirror, construction, and automotive industries. Despite a high degree of mechanization, the local establishment employed nearly 800 people, giving a much needed boost to Allegany County. In 1963, the firm decided to build another plant, one-third mile long, in Cumberland, side by side with the existing one. The new facility would manufacture glass by the revolutionary "float" process, developed in Great Britain during the late 1950s. This method of glass production, which involved holding a ribbon of molten glass at high temperatures on a bath of liquid tin before cooling, cut costs 30 percent. The finished glass possessed uniform thickness and bright, fire-polished surfaces which eliminated the need for grinding and polishing. One of the reasons the company decided to locate the new operation at Cumberland was the receptiveness of local labor leaders to the highly mechanized process after the union at the Ford City, Pennsylvania, plant had opposed its installation. Robert M. Hainsfurther, a PPG vice-president, stated the company decision succinctly:

> When you take this community attitude, add to it an employee group that has demonstrated its ability and devotion, a labor leadership that is far-sighted, good transportation, available land and a ready supply of raw materials, you begin to see why it makes good sense to put this new facility in Cumberland.

Construction of the new building again stimulated the local economy, and once in operation, the plant required an additional 100 workers as well. By mid-1972, almost all of the glass produced by the company was manufactured by the new float glass process. Then, the recession of the Nixon-Ford years brought disaster to Pittsburgh Plate Glass as it did to many other area industries. Competition from cheap foreign glass, overexpansion by the company, now diversified and renamed PPG Industries, and the deep depression of the automotive and construction industries, both large consumers of glass, forced massive production cutbacks at the Cumberland facility. Employment at one point fell below seventy as the plant barely remained open. In early 1976, a ray of hope appeared as the company recalled several hundred employees to begin production of bronzed glass. Nevertheless, the loss of jobs at PPG Industries in the 1970s only contributed a bit more to a seriously depressed Allegany County economy.[14]

On the positive side of both the economic and the educational picture in Allegany County in the postwar years was the development of two major institutions of higher learning, Frostburg State College and Allegany Community College.

Frostburg State College was not a new institution, strictly speaking, having evolved from State Normal School No. 2 in Frostburg, which had a two-year program for training elementary school teachers. In 1931, the Maryland General Assembly made a three-year course of study the minimum requirement for elementary school teachers. Accordingly, State Normal School No. 2 lengthened its program. On September 1, 1934, the school became a four-year college, offering the degree of Bachelor of Science in elementary education, the first terminal degree program at the institution. Under the new system, emphasis was placed on the liberal arts in the first two years of study, and credits were transferable to other colleges. Moreover, the thrust of the school was changing from training to education, representing a new philosophy. The newly named Frostburg State Teachers College struggled to stay alive, however. Enrollments dropped so low following World War II that the state considered abandoning the institution. Only superhuman efforts by President Lillian Compton and the faculty, supported by many leading citizens of Frostburg, saved the school.

Enrollments began to rise in the 1950s, programs improved, and a more qualified faculty was acquired. By the early 1960s, another important change was gradually taking place. More and more students were coming to the college from the Washington-Baltimore area. Student enrollment reached 1,600 in 1963. These students proved to be more liberal than the conservative student body from the local area. New faculty members from outside were also arriving. Soon both were challenging the reactionary administration of President R. Bowen Hardesty, an ex-superintendent of schools in neighboring Garrett County. An example of his thinking came when he and state superintendent of schools, Dr. Thomas G. Pullen, organized a lobbying effort to prevent the college from becoming a part of the University of Maryland, arguing it would mean a take-over by that institution. What they really feared was loss of their personal power and control. One local newspaper commented that "The real losers are the people of Western Maryland and their children. . . ." The situation deteriorated rapidly. Four faculty members were dismissed for nonacademic reasons. Students demonstrated against an administration that refused to change with the times. Frostburg State College's accreditation from the Middle States Association was in doubt. In June 1963, as a result of state reorganization of higher education, a board of trustees was appointed for the state college system. Local attorney William L. Wilson of Cumberland, a brewery president and political power, was elected chairman of the board. The state of affairs at Frostburg reached crisis proportions in the fall of 1963. The administration could no longer control the institution. The faculty, the American Association of University Professors, and the student body all demanded an investigation of the college. The board of trustees held a number of meetings at the Fort Cumberland Hotel. Under pressure from the board and having lost the respect of nearly everyone at the school, President Hardesty resigned "for reasons of health." While the board of trustees searched for a successor, Dr. Rudolph S. Bremen of Frostburg's Foreign Language Department served as acting president. He proceeded to keep things in turmoil. Possessed of an inquisitive personality better suited to a secret agent than to a college president, Dr. Bremen was soon conducting electronic surveillance of faculty telephone conversations. A spyglass in his office augmented his repertoire. The situation became so bad that the Middle States Association placed the college on probation and threatened it with loss of accreditation. Fortunately, the board of trustees, after some careful searching, found a new president. In the fall of 1965, Dr. John Morey of Hamilton College in New York assumed control of Frostburg State College.[15]

Under Morey's presidency and particularly that of his successor, Dr. Nelson P. Guild, also of Hamilton College, who became president in 1968, the institution began to grow physically, academically, and in enrollment. Extensive new building programs led to massive physical expansion at Frostburg State College. By the 1970s, new classroom buildings were being augmented by a new dining hall, three new high-rise dormitories, and a beautiful new student union, the Lane Center. By 1976, a new, large, ultramodern library was completed, and construction crews were putting together an enormous physical education and sports complex. Frostburg State College advanced rapidly in other ways. Presidents Morey and Guild revamped the administration, bringing in energetic people with new attitudes and modern training. The faculty grew in number and intellectual stature. Some faculty members received national recognition for their books, articles, and professional papers. The academic program improved and expanded. Innovative courses appeared on the scene. Graduate programs were begun, including a master's degree course in management, which offered increased educational opportunities to local businessmen. By 1976, the student body exceeded 3,000. Frostburg was rapidly becoming a college town. As a result of the presence of the institution, the city enjoyed a prosperity rare in the area. Moreover, Frostburg State had become more than just an educational institution. With a full-time payroll of over five hundred people in 1976, the college had become one of the county's major employers. Plays, planetarium and art shows, and the appearances of nationally famous speakers on campus, plus many other events, made the school a major cultural center of Allegany County. By 1976, in a little over a decade, the college had grown from a divided, strife-torn institution into one of the area's greatest assets. Unfortunately, its continued growth became clouded by the low priority given the state colleges by Governor Marvin Mandel and the state legislature. Frostburg State College deserved assistance, as it remained in 1976 the only four-year public institution of higher learning west of Baltimore County, and provided a definite educational service for western Maryland residents. Yet, by 1975-1976, the institution, although a state college, received less than half of its support from the state. If the governor and the legislators continued to cut back funds for the college, Allegany County might find itself with another depressed industry on its hands.[16]

By the 1960s, Allegany County had acquired another institution of higher education, Allegany Community College, located near Cumberland, which first opened its doors in 1961. The junior college was the creation of the Allegany County

Board of Education headed by Dr. Ralph Webster. This agency, supported by the county commissioners, felt strongly that Allegany County needed a community college to provide two years of higher education at a reasonable cost to local residents, who could live inexpensively at home while continuing their learning. The first year of existence was hectic. Dr. Robert S. Zimmer was quickly hired to serve as the first president of an institution whose entire staff numbered three administrators, three full-time, and seven part-time faculty members. Moreover, a building had to be found to house the infant college. Fortunately, the old Carver School, a twelve-year school for blacks located on Frederick Street in Cumberland, was available, having been abandoned after the integration of Allegany County schools in the 1950s. Workmen quickly renovated the structure, creating a gymnasium, student lounge, bookstore, library, classrooms, biology and chemistry laboratories, and administrative offices. Allegany Community College opened on August 25, 1961, and classes began on September 25, with thirty-nine full-time and sixty-three part-time students enrolled. After initial problems were overcome, the college began to expand. In June 1965, the Middle States Association granted accreditation to the local institution, now growing so rapidly that the old Carver School was becoming overcrowded. In 1965, plans were under way for construction of a new campus on a 370-acre site just east of Cumberland on Willowbrook Road. Ground was broken in July 1968, and a modern complex, perhaps the most beautiful community college in Maryland, began to rise from what had once been a peaceful cornfield. In September 1969, Allegany Community College began classes at its new site, which was formally dedicated in November. In 1970, the institution took control of the countywide adult education program, which served well over one thousand residents at ten instructional centers in the county. Demand for career-oriented courses of instruction led to development of a diversified curriculum, including programs in such fields as dental hygiene, nursing, law enforcement, and forestry. In January 1975, a new Careers Center opened on the Willowbrook Road campus. By 1975-1976, Allegany Community College had become a major influence in the county, employing 167 full-time instructors, administrators, secretaries, and custodians to serve 1,083 full-time and 576 part-time students. Moreover, innovative teaching techniques, an Audio-Visual Department which included a modern television studio, and a data processing center indicated a fresh approach to higher education. Plays, sports events, and sponsorship of speakers and other cultural programs at Allegany Community College also presented many recreational and educational opportunities for local residents. By 1976, the institution, under the leadership of President W. Ardell Haines, had become a strong asset in serving both the educational and the community service needs of Allegany County. Moreover, its future seemed very bright in view of the growing role of community colleges in the national educational system.[17]

In addition to Allegany Community College, a new Vocational-Technical Center at Cresaptown provided instruction and job training in skills and careers for high school students who did not wish to pursue a college education. The Vocational-Technical Center prepared its students for rewarding careers in many mechanical and industrial fields. This new center, numerous elementary and secondary schools, with the two colleges, gave Allegany County an excellent system of education.

As many large industries suffered uncertainty and decline, important changes were also taking place in what had formerly been one of the county's biggest employers, transportation. The time following World War II became the golden era of the automobile and the highway. As the years passed, automobile registration in Allegany County soared. By 1952, there were 24,791 vehicles registered. The number climbed to 33,238 by 1960, despite a general population decline. Everyone wanted his private family car. There can be no question that the automobile was a convenience. It gave people mobility, being available whenever one wanted to go shopping, to places of entertainment, or just about anywhere else. People no longer thought much about using the family car to travel to another town twenty or thirty miles away, a journey once undertaken only after serious consideration.[18]

Freed from dependence on public transportation and able to move about whenever they pleased, people began leaving the crowded urban areas. After World War II, suburbs proliferated. The Bedford Road area was built up. By the early 1950s, the once beautiful LaVale farmland had been transformed into a major suburban tract, and this growth continued throughout the 1960s and 1970s. Soon Route 220 south of Cumberland was also dotted with housing developments, first in Bowling Green, and later in the huge tract at Bel Air, south of Cresaptown. On Haystack Mountain near Cumberland a planned community called Sunset View grew up in the 1950s, and after construction of the new Sacred Heart Hospital and Bishop Walsh High School in the 1960s, another elite residential area arose nearby. Braddock Estates near Frostburg and the Horse Rock Development, a Westvaco project on the hills near Westernport, were also built during this period. By the 1960s, developers were also erecting shopping centers, mainly in the areas surrounding Cumberland. There were three in LaVale: Searstown, LaVale Plaza, and LaVale Center; Weston's on Bedford Road; and Grant City on the Industrial Boulevard in South Cumberland. The Tri-Towns Shopping Center served Westernport, Luke, and the lower Georges Creek valley. Not to be outdone, Frostburg acquired its own shopping center in the 1970s on the eastern edge of town. At about the same time, developers attempted to construct a large shopping mall on Vocke Road in the LaVale district. This plan would complete the encirclement of the pleasant Coverwood section by highways and shopping centers. Residents battled the developers before the LaVale zoning board. Eventually the board ruled in favor of the developers. The county was faced with more destruction of residential areas in the name of progress, and perhaps another white elephant as well. Many who equated shopping centers with economic growth and supported the helter-skelter spread of these multi-business complexes refused to face in the 1970s the fact that the region could support only so many of these facilities. During the severe recession of the seventies, two major chain stores went bankrupt. Weston's department store was the first to go out of business, leaving in its wake on Bedford Road a massive vacant building and a huge empty parking lot. Then in early 1976, the Grant Company announced the closing of all its stores nationwide. The two Grant stores in the area, one in LaVale and the other in south Cumberland, now stood empty. Obviously, putting up more shopping centers was not the answer. Another effect of highway development was the ugliness near road junctions and shopping sites along busy thoroughfares. By the 1970s, the proliferation of motels, filling stations, and fast-food chains had turned some once-beautiful rural sections into neon nightmares.

As the automobile stimulated suburban development and shopping centers, it drove people from the older, settled areas of the county. Just as residents moved to new living locations, they also abandoned old shopping habits. Because the automobile made it possible to travel to the new suburban shopping centers, the main street business establishments of the local towns began to suffer from lack of customers. One by one, merchants closed their doors in Westernport and Lonaconing, leaving behind empty, run-down buildings. Frostburg's business district survived largely because of the trade generated by a growing Frostburg State College. Cumberland was not so lucky. While many downtown stores managed to survive the exodus to shopping centers, others, such as Rosenbaum's department store, which closed in the early 1970s, did not weather the economic storm. At times during that period, Baltimore Street looked deserted. One of the reasons people avoided the stores in downtown Cumberland was the traffic problem. The large number of automobiles clogging Cumberland's narrow streets made any trip a tedious, frustrating venture.[19]

As people increasingly turned to the automobile for transportation, they demanded new and better roads. Much of Route 40 east of Cumberland was rebuilt and widened in the 1950s and early 1960s. Highway improvements really moved forward during the sixties and seventies. The culmination of the highway boom came with the construction in the 1960s of a massive bridge over the city of Cumberland in an attempt to relieve downtown congestion and move through-

Baltimore Street, Cumberland, in the 1940s. Urban renewal would change much of its face in the 1960s and 1970s.
Courtesy Growden Collection, Allegany County Historical Society

traffic, as well as automobiles to and from the downtown area, with some degree of efficiency. The crosstown bridge was just the first step in the construction of Route 48, the National Freeway, which was designed to connect Cumberland with Morgantown, West Virginia, and the West, and to relieve the glut of traffic on overcrowded Route 40, bypassing bottlenecks such as LaVale and Frostburg. As the National Freeway neared completion in 1976, highway advocates, including most local industries, demanded a new freeway to link Cumberland with Interstate 70 at Hancock to the east. The new highway appeared unnecessary to many people, as it would save only about five minutes in driving time between Cumberland and Hancock, while inflated construction costs would be enormous. Moreover, many proponents of the freeway forgot that as more and more highways were constructed, the costs of road maintenance put an enormous strain on the taxpayer's pocketbook. Finally, those who equated freeways with progress did not realize that road construction was robbing Allegany County of one of its major assets, its natural mountain beauty. On the other hand, industrial and labor leaders alike believed that the area's economic future rested on the building of a Cumberland-Hancock freeway. Potential industry, which would ship by highway, and trucking firms needed a road that would eliminate the steep grades over the mountains. The freeway link would no doubt be a factor in attracting new industry. However, in the mid-1970s, the route's future remained uncertain.

From one vantage point, the growth of the county road system, as well as the suburbs and shopping centers, proved a boon to the local economy in the decades following World War II. Local construction firms flourished as they created the suburban houses, the shopping centers, and the new service industries that dotted the roadsides. All of this activity provided employment for many skilled craftsmen in the building trades. Jobs created by the highway and the automobile kept unemployment from worsening in the postwar years. Moreover, construction activity poured money into the local economy in the form of wages and money spent for supplies purchased from local firms. In this respect, the automobile and its offshoots were a positive influence in Allegany County.

The area's, as well as the nation's, dependence upon the automobile had been called into question by the 1970s. A fuel crisis during the winter of 1974 proved the point. A strike of independent truckers, generated by rising fuel costs, halted most deliveries of gasoline to Allegany County for one week. People waited in line for hours at the limited number of filling stations lucky enough to have gasoline. Business, shopping, and travel were paralyzed. Public transit was available in some areas, but people simply refused to use it. Even after the crisis ended, the energy problem remained. Inflated fuel costs consumed more and more of the buyer's purchasing power each year. Moreover, a freeway designed and built for high-speed travel at enormous cost to the taxpayer was of questionable benefit when a maximum speed limit of fifty-five miles per hour had been imposed. The simple fact remained that the family automobile wasted ever-decreasing supplies of energy. It was an inefficient method of moving people. By the 1970s, most of the freight and supply shipments to the county were handled by truck. Yet, trucks devoured large amounts of fuel, driving up retail prices for the consumer. Railroads could haul the same amount of freight for one-fourth of the energy used by trucks. Still, because of uncertain service, shippers and industries, as well as passengers, had abandoned the railroads by the 1970s. Both the Baltimore and Ohio and the Western Maryland tore down their freight stations in Cumberland. The energy crisis would bring important changes to the style of life in Allegany County in the decades to come. What form this transformation would take no one could accurately foretell.[20]

The new patterns in transportation had their effect on the railroads, once a mainstay of the local economy. The diesel locomotive completely replaced the steam locomotive by the mid-1950s, and because the new engine required less maintenance, jobs were lost. Road crews were cut off as trains grew longer and, therefore, fewer in number. Moreover, where each steam locomotive had required a crew, one engineer could control several diesel locomotives by means of multiple hookups. Technological improvements in signal systems and yard operations eliminated other jobs, as did consolidation of facilities. For example, the Baltimore and Ohio Railroad had virtually deserted Keyser, West Virginia, as a major rail center by the late 1960s, resulting in furloughs for many Allegany County residents. Railroad operations in Mount Savage, once the primary shop town of the Cumberland and Pennsylvania Railroad, had disappeared much earlier; a fire in 1939 had destroyed many of the facilities. Then, when the Consolidation Coal Company pulled out of the area in 1944, it sold its subsidiary, the Cumberland and Pennsylvania Railroad, to the Western Maryland Railway, which immediately replaced Cumberland and Pennsylvania locomotives and equipment with its own and eliminated all repair operations at Mount Savage. The decline of the coal region also led to the abandonment of many of the ex-Cumberland and Pennsylvania Railroad lines. Branches came up as mines closed down. Then, on September 3, 1954, the Western Maryland relinquished the line to Eckhart, the State Line branch, and segments of the main line between Mount Savage Junction and Mount Savage and between Frostburg and Shaft. The Western Maryland continued to operate trains from Frostburg to Zihlman and Mount Savage to serve local refractories. The line from Westernport to Shaft also remained, and by the 1970s it hauled a considerable amount of coal from the surface mining operations in the Georges Creek valley. The Western Maryland Railway was absorbed by the Chessie system in the mid-1970s. In 1963, the Chessie system had been formed by a merger of the financially ailing Baltimore and Ohio and the prosperous Chesapeake and Ohio railroads. Because much Chessie system trackage paralleled that of the Western Maryland, Chessie planned to abandon Western Maryland tracks from Hancock to Cumberland, from Cumberland to Dawson, and from Frostburg west to Connellsville. The consolidation, including the elimination of shop and repair facilities in nearby Ridgeley, West Virginia, in early 1976, cost Allegany County some jobs. The area was left with only one railroad system, the Pennsylvania Railroad line to Altoona having been abandoned in the early 1970s.[21]

Fortunately for Allegany County, the Chessie system was a profitable railroad which still provided many employment opportunities for the local citizenry. Cumberland remained a major junction requiring classification facilities, including the Evitts Creek yard constructed in the 1950s by the Baltimore and Ohio. Most important, however, were the extensive diesel repair facilities housed in a large red brick building in south Cumberland. Locomotives from all over the Chessie system were sent to Cumberland for major overhauls, some being stripped to their frames and completely rebuilt. The Chessie system was one of Allegany County's foremost industries in the mid-1970s and one of the area's largest employers.

The impact of the automobile and the highway upon rail passenger service and public transportation in Allegany County was enormous in the decades following World War II. First to feel the crunch were the local trains, as people began using cars for short-distance travel. By the late 1950s, all local train service on the Baltimore and Ohio Railroad, except for the run between Parkersburg, West Virginia, and Cumberland, had been abandoned. The Western Maryland Railway, in the early 1950s, eliminated one of its Cumberland to Elkins, West Virginia, trains, as well as its Hagerstown to Cumberland run. The latter had provided the only public transportation available in some of the remote areas of eastern Allegany County. Declining patronage finally killed the Western Maryland's last passenger train in 1958, a Cumberland-to-Elkins two-car local, also serving McCoole, Westernport, and Luke. The Baltimore and Ohio's long-distance trains were also affected by declining patronage. Following World War II, the railroad attempted to improve service by such measures as new streamlined equipment for the Capitol Limited, the inauguration of a streamlined, all-coach Columbian on the Washington-Chicago route, and the addition of dome cars to both trains, as well as to the Shenandoah. Nothing could halt the decline. One by one, the trains came off in the 1950s and 1960s—the Cleveland Night Express, the Ambassador, and even first-class trains like the National Limited. On May 1, 1971, all rail passenger service to Allegany County ended when the Capitol Limited departed for Baltimore for the last

An era ends as the Baltimore and Ohio's Capitol Limited pauses at Cumberland's Queen City Station on its last westbound run, April 30, 1971. The station would disappear soon after the trains. Courtesy Growden Collection, Allegany County Historical Society

time. On that day, Amtrak, a federally subsidized corporation, took over most passenger operations in the United States. Allegany County's only long-distance public transportation for a time consisted of three daily Greyhound buses in each direction on the Pittsburgh-Baltimore route, which served Cumberland, Frostburg, and other Route 40 communities, and a few air commuter flights to Washington and Baltimore in the small planes of Nicholson Air Service. Allegheny Airlines had served Cumberland in the 1940s and 1950s, but insufficient numbers of passengers and uncertain weather conditions in the mountains, which sometimes made landing difficult, forced the curtailment of these flights. By the mid-1970s, Nicholson Air Service was slowly expanding its operations, giving the county some hope for better service in the future. Eventually, Amtrak reestablished service to Cumberland in the form of a run from Washington to Parkersburg, West Virginia, known locally as "Harley's Hornet" in deference to powerful Representative Harley Staggers of neighboring West Virginia, whose efforts had led to restoration of the trains. Representative Staggers even used his influence to have high-speed turbotrain equipment operated over the route for a time, but the line was unprofitable and service was finally cut back to a Washington-Cumberland train. However, Amtrak planned to begin operating a Washington-to-Cincinnati train through Cumberland in October 1976, and there was talk of restoring Cumberland-to-Pittsburgh service, perhaps by running Amtrak's Washington section of the Broadway Limited via Cumberland rather than through Harrisburg, Pennsylvania. Despite the hopes of regaining passenger rail service, there is little doubt that the absence of good public transportation to the metropolitan areas had been a negative factor in Allegany County's attempts to attract new industry.[22]

Other forms of public transportation in the county also ran into trouble. Bus lines operating from Cumberland to nearby communities gradually died. Cumberland's Queen City Bus Lines found itself in serious financial difficulties by the 1970s, as fewer and fewer people each year used its increasingly decrepit buses. So this time, some positive action was necessary in order to prevent the loss of all public transportation service. The county finally responded with the formation of the Allegany County Transit Authority. Aided by federal, state, and county funds, the authority purchased new buses and revamped schedules, establishing good, reliable service within Cumberland, and between Cumberland, local industries, Frostburg, Lonaconing, Westernport, Mount Savage, State Line, and Cresaptown. Although people still were not riding the buses in large numbers, at least the service was available, and the future appeared brighter with each year as a result of the energy crisis and the high cost of gasoline.

The automobile, along with another product of modern technology, television, also had a profound effect on social life in Allegany County. In the late 1940s and early 1950s, drive-in movie theaters appeared throughout the area—along Routes 40 and 220, along Winchester Road, and near south Cumberland along Oldtown Road. Television, however, had an even greater impact on local entertainment. At first, because of the county's rugged terrain, there were reception problems. Only WJAC, of Johnstown, Pennsylvania, could be picked up clearly by aerial reception. Cable television solved that difficulty. In May 1951, the Potomac Valley Television Company, located in Cumberland, was incorporated. By early 1952, cables had been extended to much of south Cumberland, and by late 1952, to Washington Street on Cumberland's west side and to the city's north end. By 1955, the cable reached all areas of Cumberland and Ridgeley, West Virginia, and line building was begun to outlying areas such as Cresaptown, Rawlings, Bedford Road, LaVale, Eckhart, Corriganville, Mount Savage, Ellerslie, and nearby West Virginia, all of these sections being serviced by the early 1960s. Two new companies were formed to reach other areas of the county, the Frostburg Cable Television Company to serve that city, and the Upper Potomac Valley Cable Television Company for the Westernport-Luke region. Soon cable service reached Georges Creek area towns through the facilities of the Jackson Cable Television Company. Potomac Valley Television's three channels expanded to five in April 1955 and to twelve in 1967. Cumberland viewers could now select from several Washington stations, as well as from Baltimore, Hagerstown, Altoona, Johnstown, and educational television broadcasts. After earlier abortive attempts, Potomac Valley Television began originating its own broadcasts in September 1973, including local news and sports events. By the 1970s, Frostburg Cable Television also offered twelve-channel service, including KDKA and WTAE, both of Pittsburgh, which were not available in Cumberland.[23]

The number of people subscribing to Potomac Valley Television service provides a good indication of the impact of cable television on the entertainment habits of local residents. In 1952, the company had 670 subscribers. This number rose to 11,538 by 1958, grew to 18,447 by 1969, and had soared to 23,148 by 1975. One by one the theaters in Cumberland, once a mainstay of county social life, shut down during the 1950s and 1960s—the Garden, the Embassy, the Liberty, the New, and the Maryland. Only the Strand remained, and this once-opulent showplace had deteriorated badly. In the early 1970s, it too closed its doors, leaving Cumberland with no movie theater. This vacuum was filled in 1974 with the opening of the new G. Ray Light Cinema in south Cumberland. The Center Theater in the Searstown Shopping Center was also easily accessible by automobile for county residents. Patronage from the rapidly growing numbers of students at Frostburg State College helped keep the Palace Theater in Frostburg from the same fate as Cumberland's movie houses. Smaller theaters in the Georges Creek towns also closed their doors in a losing battle with the television set. However, a new dual theater, the Tri-Towns Cinema One and Two, near Westernport, revived movie-going opportunities not only for residents of the tri-towns but for people of the Georges Creek region as well. Even many of the drive-in theaters, unable to attract customers, went out of business. Television also had its impact on radio, once a major source of entertainment. Sports programming and, especially, popular music were substituted for the old radio shows by the early 1950s on Cumberland's WTBO, WCUM, and WDYK, the latter replaced by another station, WUOK, by the 1970s. Music also dominated programming on Frostburg's WFRB, which began broadcasting in 1958 from a new facility atop Little Savage Mountain.[24]

Sports in Allegany County also underwent a transformation in the years following World War II. Professional athletics had disappeared completely by this time. High school sports, however, particularly football and basketball, remained popular. County rivalries involving Bruce High School in Westernport, Valley in Lonaconing, Beall in Frostburg, and Allegany, Fort Hill, and La Salle, later Bishop Walsh, all in Cumberland, sometimes were fierce. Enthusiasm and pride were especially high in 1975, when Fort Hill High School in Cumberland won the state football championship in its class. In addition, area residents were treated to superb basketball each March when the best Catholic high school teams in the East came to Cumberland for the Alhambra Catholic Invitational Tournament. Horse racing had been a popular sport in the area. Each year a two-week meet had been held at Fairgo, the half-mile track outside Cumberland. However, small racetracks were dying throughout the United States by the 1950s, and Fairgo proved no exception. In September 1961, a county tradition ended when the last races were run at the local track. Cumberland's racing dates were sold the next summer to other tracks when it became apparent that few horse owners wanted to make the long trek to Fairgo for a short meet. By the 1970s, one of the favorite spectator sports of the Georges Creek region—chicken fighting—had also begun to suffer from declining interest.

With all of the changes Allegany County was undergoing and all of the problems it faced in the postwar years, particularly the economic decline, there was a need for farsighted political leadership. Unfortunately, however, this quality was often lacking in those men chosen to govern the county. At that crucial time, both county and municipal governments often showed a reluctance to analyze and deal with the area's real difficulties. Instead, those with political responsibilities frequently took a conservative, "don't change anything" attitude, wasting time and energy looking for scapegoats such as organized labor or Communists to explain the regional problems. Perhaps these leaders simply reflected the attitudes of many local citizens who liked things as they were and refused to admit change was necessary. In fact, even when public officials tried to initiate progressive measures, citizens often blocked them, such as in the tumultuous fight over the city of Cumberland's attempt to fluoridate the water supply. This inability to confront the real challenges the area faced was a major contributing factor in Allegany County's post-World War II decline.

Of course, there were intelligent, progressive officials, but in this period they seemed to be the exception and not the rule. Some politicians from the local area made their marks in the world outside the county. J. Glenn Beall, Sr., of Frostburg served in the United States House of Representatives from 1943 to 1951, and in the United States Senate from 1952 to 1964. His son, J. Glenn Beall, Jr., followed in his father's footsteps, holding a seat in the House of Representatives from 1968 to 1970, and then becoming United States Senator from Maryland in 1970. Another local notable, Thomas B. Finan II, was Maryland's attorney general from 1960 to 1966, and after leaving that post, rose to the position of judge of the Maryland Court of Appeals, after narrowly missing the chance to be governor in 1966. At times, the Allegany County Commissioners worked energetically to realize important projects, such as acquiring the Pittsburgh Plate Glass plant and establishing Allegany Community College. But at other times, the county commission was dominated by conservatives who thwarted progressive elements in the community.

The city of Cumberland proved no exception to the picture of generally ineffective leadership. A particularly trying period for the city was the administration of Thomas F. Conlon, Jr., who served as mayor from 1966 to 1974. During this time it often appeared that city officials devoted more time to disagreements with each other than to the business at hand. Mayor Conlon, heavily supported by south Cumberland voters, was opposed from the outset by the city's political establishment. A maverick, who was sometimes a Democrat and at other times a Republican or an Independent, the mayor was frequently embroiled in controversy and personal disputes with council members. During his reign, city council meetings often became rancorous proceedings. Lively though this period was, real accomplishments, such as an improved police department, came slowly in the Conlon years.[25]

Another unfortunate chapter in Cumberland's recent history was its crusade against local Communists. This issue arose during the hysteria of the McCarthy era in the late 1940s and early 1950s. Actually, there were only about a dozen members of the Communist Party of America in Allegany County, most of whom openly admitted their affiliation and had never done anything that could be considered subversive. Under authority from Maryland's infamous Ober Law, an anti-Communist piece of legislation passed in 1949, the state police checked into the activities of the local party members but found nothing about which to be seriously alarmed. Once the courts declared the Ober Law unconstitutional on several grounds, the state police simply forgot about the local Communists. At this point, however, the city of Cumberland, prodded by the local chapter of the Veterans of Foreign Wars and by John J. Long, police and fire commissioner, entered the picture. An ordinance was drawn up which, declaring that

> The Communist Party is part of a world-wide conspiracy to overthrow the Government of the United States of America and constitutes a clear and present danger to the United States of America, to the State of Maryland, to the City of Cumberland, and to all loyal and patriotic citizens thereof, . . .

went on to discuss the probable infiltration of local government and the possible sabotage and destruction of industrial plants and municipal facilities. This piece of legislation attacked the problem by requiring all Communists to register with the police, prohibiting the distribution of Communist literature, and setting maximum penalties of a $100 fine and thirty days in jail for failure to comply. At a meeting of the city council on September 5, 1950, the law was passed following a shouting match between the Communists and the supporters of the act. One party member suggested that the city would better focus its attention on the discrimination against blacks in local restaurants. Another called it a "picayune, hysterical, peanut ordinance." Supporters far outnumbered opponents. Labor leaders, their unions often labeled as "Communist" by many people in the community, rose up to exhibit their patriotism by supporting the bill. Prominent citizens also lent their names to the hysteria. While Allegany County's economy collapsed, the city government and citizens of Cumberland wasted their time on a few Communists whom the Maryland State Police had already written off as constituting no present threat.

On September 16, 1950, city police arrested two Communists, William B. Coleman and Arthur M. Schusterman, who simply refused to register. On September 18, Police Magistrate Frank Perdew, openly hostile and ranting about sabotage, found them guilty and fined each $100. The two men immediately appealed the decision in Allegany County Circuit Court. In an opinion handed down on January 25, 1951, Associate Judges Patrick M. Schnauffer and George Henderson declared most of the ordinance unconstitutional, including the section requiring registration, as a violation of the Fifth Amendment to the United States Constitution. In the meantime, Local 1874 of the Textile Workers of America had proven their patriotic fervor by expelling Coleman and Schusterman from the union. The latter, pressured by the atmosphere of persecution, resigned from the Communist Party and all political activity. John J. Long continued his crusade by calling all area police chiefs together to coordinate activities. Despite the fanaticism of a few of the police chiefs, most of those at the meeting urged caution, demanding positive proof before labeling anyone a Communist. Their good sense and judgment put a damper on the witch hunt. The furor soon died down and the crusade against local Communists ended.[26]

Even when local political leaders attempted to move forward in the postwar era, the citizens often blocked their way. In 1947-1948, a commission was formed to propose changes in the city charter in order to provide Cumberland with better government. The chamber of commerce backed the idea. Many prominent citizens drawn from all segments of the community, including lawyers, labor leaders, and businessmen, served on the charter commission, and Thomas B. Finan II, the city attorney, acted as consultant. The commission opened all meetings to public scrutiny. Yeoman work finally produced a new city charter that dispensed with the commission form of government in favor of an efficient city manager-council system, which would also be less susceptible to favoritism and corruption. The people of Cumberland, unwilling to countenance change and devoted to "politics as usual," voted down the new charter.

Another instance of citizen resistance to change was Cumberland's attempt to fluoridate the local water supply as a step toward preventing tooth decay. The issue had come up during the early 1950s, but loud, persistent opposition from some groups frightened city administrations, which refused to push the proposal for a decade. Finally, on December 3, 1962, the mayor and city council issued an order for the city to fluoridate the water supply, the only negative vote coming from the commissioner of water and electric light, G. Ray Light, who claimed that it was forced medication. The opposition marshaled its forces. Several nasty city council meetings ensued, in which citizens attacked the mayor and the council members. Dr. Harold Malin, a local chiropractor, insisted that fluoridated water corroded pipes and caused chronic fluoride poisoning in children. A man from LaVale maintained that it caused people to have mongoloid babies. Another asserted that the medical profession, which "gave us Thalidomide [and] X-ray," now advocated fluoridation. A local physician, Dr. Samuel Jacobson, said of the opponents of fluoridation: "They have misinformed the people . . . they have used half-truths or no truths at all." The opposition finally succeeded in having the issue submitted to the people in a referendum. The local citizens, more impressed by the charges of the anti-fluoride group than by the evidence of dentists and doctors, voted overwhelmingly against fluoridation, 3,827 to 1,503, in May 1963. The Baltimore *Sun* commented: "In the tradition of home rule, or in this instance the freedom to have cavities, the people of Cumberland have taken their stand. . . ."[27]

Despite frequent resistance to new ideas by government

and citizenry alike, some necessary changes did take place in the postwar period. One example was Cumberland's flood control project. By the end of 1945, the Army Corps of Engineers had devised a definite plan for the city. Changes in the proposal and other problems caused some delay, but by March 1949, construction was under way. Throughout the next decade, work continued on this enormous undertaking, built with both federal and city funds. Since Ridgeley, West Virginia, could not finance its part of the project, Cumberland agreed to pay its neighbor's share as well as assume responsibility for maintaining and operating the works in Ridgeley once they were completed. The project required extensive changes, including the removal of one highway and one railroad bridge and the rebuilding of two railroad bridges as well as the Baltimore, Market, and Valley Street bridges in Cumberland. Baltimore and Ohio-Western Maryland railroad interchange tracks were relocated; the Wills Creek channel was modified and paved; the North Branch channel was widened, straightened, and deepened; levees and flood walls were erected; fifty Cumberland buildings and seventy Ridgeley structures were either abandoned or relocated; a new dam, 600 feet upstream on the north branch of the Potomac River, was constructed to replace the old C&O Canal dam; pumping stations were built; and the sewer and storm-water drainage facilities of both Cumberland and Ridgeley were modified. The entire project, finally completed in May 1959, cost $18.5 million, of which Cumberland contributed $2.9 million. The installation had dramatically altered the face of Cumberland along Wills Creek and the Potomac River. Together with the Savage River Dam in Garrett County, which went into operation in 1952, the new flood control system would prevent a recurrence of such devastating floods as the March 1936 disaster. There could be no question that flood control was an essential project, one of the area's positive accomplishments in the postwar period.[28]

Another important development, although it generated controversy, was the Cumberland Urban Renewal Project. In this as in other matters, the Cumberland Chamber of Commerce demonstrated that it was one of the progressive forces in the postwar period. Overall, the chamber of commerce supported many of the accomplishments of those decades, including flood control, better transportation, and the establishment of Allegany Community College and the Vocational-Technical School. Unfortunately, this organization often encountered opposition to its programs from some of the extremely conservative downtown Cumberland businessmen, who resisted change strenuously and sometimes hindered attempts by other businessmen to bring progressive development to the city and county. Nevertheless, the chamber of commerce, under Robert Petersen's leadership, attempted to move forward. Its support for the urban renewal project is indicative of its work for progressive development.

Cumberland needed urban renewal by the 1960s. Many downtown buildings were in a dilapidated state. The upper sections of some three- and four-story buildings had deteriorated deplorably. Walls were cracking and structures unsound, the floors actually pulling away from the walls. Establishments such as Murphy's and the Windsor Hotel at the corner of Baltimore and North George streets were in dangerous condition. Chunks of building materials tumbled frequently from the Monarch Foods warehouse bordering Baltimore Street and the Baltimore and Ohio Railroad tracks. Actually, urban renewal had been proposed after World War II, but many businessmen had resisted the suggestions set forth in the early plan, known as the Minter Plan. By the 1960s, however, it was evident that something had to be done. The loss of trade to the new shopping centers finally forced many downtown Cumberland businessmen to accept urban renewal before the downtown suffered complete economic and physical collapse. Their support was crucial if the project was to succeed. Mayor Earl D. Chaney's administration also energetically approved the idea. A Potomac Edison Company study of Cumberland's downtown area served as the basis for the project. Plans were laid to begin work in the George Street area first, as that section showed the greatest disrepair. On November 1, 1965, the United States Department of Housing and Urban Development approved the George Street Project, and the first contracts were signed on

December 15, 1965. The race was now on to make Cumberland's downtown competitive with the burgeoning shopping centers before it was too late. On February 22, 1971, the second part of the project for the rest of the downtown area received approval. Destruction of buildings proceeded in the late 1960s and into the 1970s, raising cries of opposition from many local residents who did not want to see the city they remembered from their childhood changed. Other groups, such as the Allegany County Preservation Society, tried to prevent buildings they considered historically significant from being torn down. In essence, the whole urban renewal undertaking was a compromise. The original plan, which proposed drastic changes, was constantly revised. Under Director of Urban Renewal Jerry Goodwin, the agency tried to save all buildings that were structurally sound and not needed for a public right-of-way. Plans to create a new street through the downtown, paralleling Baltimore Street to the south, were dropped because of the enormous dislocation it would cause.

By the 1970s, new buildings were rising from the rubble—a new Holiday Inn on George Street, a modern C&P Telephone Building on Liberty Street, and the major economic anchor for the downtown area, the enormous Gee Bee Department Store-A&P Supermarket complex where the Baltimore and Ohio Railroad freight station and lumber yards had once stood on George Street. A new road, Queen City Drive, partially circled the downtown area, cutting traffic congestion and improving access to the growing number of parking lots. Streets such as Mechanic Street were widened and other changes made. Four pleasant parklets, although criticized by some as a waste of money, greatly improved the appearance of the downtown area. In early 1976, ground was broken for a new municipal complex on Bedford and Frederick streets. A new post office and railroad station were begun where the Queen City Station, torn down in 1972, once stood. While many people criticized the project as extravagant or complained about the inconveniences caused by construction, the fact remained that the project was necessary, and when completed, would make Cumberland a more attractive city in which to live. Moreover, many downtown businessmen who at first had been reluctant to take part in planning, were by the 1970s enthusiastic about the results. Donald Pell, the new manager of Gee Bee, was one who encouraged Cumberland businessmen to become involved. By August 1975, the Urban Renewal Agency had spent almost $10.5 million of the approximately $14 million which had been appropriated. The effects of urban renewal were already evident in 1976 in the resurgence of the downtown area as more and more people returned to the city to shop.[29]

Perhaps county and municipal government in the postwar decades simply reflected the prevailing attitudes of the voters, who resisted progress and attempts to solve the region's problems. Battered by years of economic blows, residents of Allegany County developed pessimistic, negative attitudes in the years following World War II. This outlook was reflected in the reaction of many people, for example, toward attempts to lure new business to the area, an endeavor they doubted had any chance of success. What could this area offer industry? Yet these harbingers of gloom ignored the fact that Allegany County still possessed many of the positive attributes that had brought business here in past decades. Abundant water and coal–if the Environmental Protection Agency would allow the latter's use–were still present. Good rail transportation, becoming more important in light of the energy crisis, still existed. Moreover, the region possessed an abundance of skilled labor.

Another attitude which has retarded development in this area is a mental isolationism. Afraid of change, many people have attempted to preserve Allegany County as it has been in the past rather than allow it to move into the future. These isolationists were often complacent and proud that this region was spared many of the ailments of modern American society. It was certainly true that Allegany County was a pleasant place to live, free of the rampant crime, pollution, overcrowding, filth, and impersonality of the urban areas. It was also true, however, that some change was unquestionably necessary in order to solve the region's acute economic problems. Furthermore, pockets of rural poverty existed in the county. There were residents of the area living in squalor, their families crammed into rotting houses with no indoor plumbing. This problem was highlighted when President Lyndon B. Johnson visited the region in the 1960s during a tour of Appalachia. Its citizens could not be justifiably proud of their county as long as conditions such as these continued. Moreover, even the high quality of life here was meaningless if there was no economic opportunity. Between 1950 and 1960, Allegany County lost about 5,400 people when it should have had a natural increase of around 14,000 in population. Seen in this light, the emigration and the failure of the area to grow cost the county 19,000 people. Most important, the statistics indicated that those leaving were primarily between the ages of twenty and forty-four—the young, most energetic, most productive part of the population. Between 1950 and 1960, Allegany County lost 22 percent, or over one-fifth, of its people in this category. As a result, the population was not only declining, but on the average, growing older. This trend, prevalent throughout Appalachia as younger people left to seek jobs elsewhere, indicated serious problems. An example of the isolationist attitude was the reaction of some area residents to the possibility that the Miller Brewing Company might locate a major factory in Cumberland. These citizens questioned why, when the county had just rid itself of one brewery, it should want another one. This outlook, although certainly not shared by the majority of people, impeded any real progress.[30]

Rather than finding solutions to the region's problems, many critics concentrated instead on searching for scapegoats on whom to pin the blame for the economic decline. According to one popular myth, it was organized labor that, having driven industry from Allegany County, caused the blight. Some industries did close down in the 1930s, apparently as a result of labor demands. In fact, however, these firms would have folded whether there had been unions or not because of their precarious financial condition. In the postwar decades, there is no solid evidence that organized labor actually drove any major industry from Allegany County, although the possibility remains that large firms in one or two scattered cases may have curtailed expansion programs in the area in favor of non-unionized locations elsewhere. The unions cannot be blamed fairly for the region's problems, which were caused primarily by other economic factors, often national in scope. On the contrary, labor often cooperated with management, as in the cases when PPG Industries installed the float glass process and Kelly-Springfield made its drive to use local coal. A reputation of wildcat strikes may perhaps have had some influence on firms considering locating in the region, but this was not the primary cause of Allegany County's decline. On the other side of the coin, there were those who believed that local industry had attempted to keep new businesses from locating in the area in order to prevent competition for the labor supply and keep wages depressed. There is no more evidence to support this myth than there is for the first. Local business leaders, such as Robert Mercer of Kelly-Springfield and George Fisk of Celanese, worked in the 1970s to help the county attract new industry and diversify its economy. The search for scapegoats not only served no useful purpose but also increased tensions in that it pitted one group against another.

Finally, cooperative action has been hindered by regional and class divisions in the area. By the 1970s these schisms, some of them having roots as far back as the nineteenth century, had become ingrained tradition, engendering distrust between sections and between economic and social classes. Residents of the Georges Creek area, for instance, disliked and were suspicious of people in Cumberland, who in turn disdained their neighbors "from up the creek." Within Cumberland itself, an antagonism existed between residents of the south end of town and those from other areas of the city. There were racial tensions. Blacks in the county were finally expressing their frustration over subtle, and overt, discrimination and lack of job opportunities, particularly in Cumberland, which the local NAACP chapter characterized in 1975 as a racist city. Divisions between classes were also present, rich versus poor, business management versus labor, the highly educated versus those with less schooling. The *People's Guardian,* a county newspaper published weekly in Frostburg, played on these conflicts by supporting the common man against public officials and established institutions. The paper, published by John H. Martin until 1972, when he attempted to kill his wife, the printer, and himself, and subsequently put out by his son, relied on speculation and frequently distortion in its stories, but it was widely read and believed by local residents.[31]

By 1976, Allegany County was in deep trouble, brought on by the rapid economic decline of the post-World War II era and other factors such as public attitudes and intra-county divisions. The area's future seemed uncertain. Yet, certain trends had begun to appear which encouraged optimism. Politically, new leaders were emerging. The city governments of both Cumberland, with Perry Smith as mayor, and Frostburg, under Arthur Bond, and later, David Linn, were showing signs of new vitality. The current group of county commissioners, John J. Coyle, Arthur Bond, and Richard Mappin, had the advantage of working under Code Home Rule, which was approved by county voters in the 1974 election and which gave the commissioners more power to enact local legislation. Moreover, business leadership, dormant for so long, had begun to revive. Executives of the large industries in the county combined with merchants to deal with the region's serious economic problems. One of their main objectives was to change the mood of negativism so long prevalent in Allegany County. The PACE program, "Positive Attitudes Change Everything," established in 1975, was directed toward altering pessimistic thinking. The region possessed many natural and situational advantages which could be emphasized. It had an abundant water supply, cheap fuel, a skilled labor force, new highways, and good rail transportation, assets which could be stressed in recruiting industry. Most important, perhaps, Allegany County was a pleasant place in which to live and raise a family, blessed with beautiful mountain scenery, and free from the high crime rates, massive pollution, overcrowding, and other problems of urban areas. This factor would serve as an attraction to the kinds of business and industrial concerns employing large numbers of professional people, to whom living conditions were an important consideration. Many of the county's leaders were beginning to realize that the area held advantages for enticing such enterprises. Moreover, understanding the importance of diversification of the economy, they were trying to recruit a number of small industries. It was hoped that the area's natural assets and the new attitudes and energetic leadership of its people could bring the county back from the brink of disaster and the problems that beset it in the post-World War II era. Could Allegany County revive? In the mid-1970s, the future still remained uncertain. The answer lay with its people.

CHAPTER XIII NOTES

1. Maryland Department of Economic Development, *Fact Sheet on Appalachian Maryland: Garrett, Allegany and Washington Counties* (Annapolis: Maryland Department of Economic Development, 1962), p. 10 (hereafter cited as Maryland Department of Economic Development, *Fact Sheet*).

2. James W. Bishop, *The Glass Industry of Allegany County, Maryland* (Cumberland: Commercial Press Printing Company, 1968), pp. 77, 78, 86.

3. William J. Kelley, *Brewing in Maryland from Colonial Times to the Present* (Baltimore: John D. Lucas Printing Company, 1965), pp. 665-67; and interview with William L. Wilson, Aug. 18, 1975 (hereafter cited as Wilson Interview).

4. Katherine A. Harvey, *Best Dressed Miners: Life and Labor in the Maryland Coal Region, 1835-1910* (Ithaca: Cornell University Press, 1969), pp. 366-67, 369-70 (hereafter cited as Harvey, *Best Dressed Miners*); Cumberland *Evening Times,* March 2, 1944; and interview with Matthew Skidmore, Oct. 7, 1975 (hereafter cited as Skidmore Interview).

5. Harvey, *Best Dressed Miners,* pp. 370-71; and Skidmore Interview.

6. *Kelly-Springfield Today* (Cumberland Edition), September 1973, June 1975, and September 1975; Kelly-Springfield Tire Company news releases, Oct. 17, 1974, and March 6, 1975; Kelly-Springfield Tire Company News Bureau, *The Kelly-Springfield Tire Company: A Part of History* (Cumberland: Kelly-Springfield Tire Company News Bureau, no date); and interview with Jerry Hess, Kelly-Springfield Tire Company, Oct. 10, 1975.

7. Westvaco Fine Papers Division, *Progress on the Potomac* (Luke: Westvaco Fine Papers Division, no date) (hereafter cited as Westvaco Fine Papers Division, *Progress on the Potomac*); Public Relations De-

partment, Luke Mill, *Luke Mill Report* (Luke: Public Relations Department, Luke Mill, 1975) (hereafter cited as *Luke Mill Report*); Westvaco Corporation, Luke Mill, news release, June 1974 (hereafter cited as Westvaco News Release, June 1974); Public Relations Department, Luke Mill, *An Unofficial Historical Outline of Westvaco Corporation (Formerly West Virginia Pulp and Paper) and Its Luke Mill* (Luke: Public Relations Department, Luke Mill, July 1974) (hereafter cited as Public Relations Department, Luke Mill, *An Unofficial History*); and interview with William M. Thompson, Feb. 11, 1976 (hereafter cited as Thompson Interview).

8. *Luke Mill Report;* Westvaco News Release, June 1974; and Thompson Interview.

9. *Luke Mill Report;* Public Relations Department, Luke Mill, *An Unofficial History;* Westvaco Fine Papers Division, *Progress on the Potomac;* and Thompson Interview.

10. *Amcelle: First Link in a Global Chemical Chain* (Cumberland: Celanese Corporation of America, 1974), pp. 7-10, 12-13, 21 (hereafter cited as *Amcelle*); Harold Blancke, *Celanese Corporation of America: The Founders and the Early Years* (New York: The Newcomen Society in North America, 1952), pp. 18-20; Fred T. Small, *Factory and Home* (Cumberland: Celanese Corporation of America, 1949), pp. 6-12; Maryland Department of Economic Development, *Fact Sheet*, pp. 3, 5, 10; Ladislas Segoe *et al.*, *A Report Upon Population and Other Characteristics: Allegany County, Maryland* ("Comprehensive Master Plan Series"; no publication data given, 1961), pp. 9-10 (hereafter cited as Segoe, *A Report Upon Population*); interview with William E. Crooks, Nov. 5, 1975; and Maryland State Planning Commission, *Lonaconing: An Economic Survey* (Baltimore: Maryland State Planning Commission, 1956), pp. 12-13.

11. *Amcelle*, pp. 6-9, 13, 21.

12. *History of Allegany Ballistics Laboratory*, pp. 2-8; a short summary of the history of the Allegany Ballistics Laboratory, enclosed in memorandum from M. Paul Thompson, Allegany Ballistics Laboratory, to author, December 1975.

13. J. William Hunt, "Across the Desk," in the Cumberland *Sunday Times*, Aug. 29, 1954 (hereafter cited as Hunt); Pittsburgh Plate Glass Company, news releases, Oct. 28, 1953, March 17 and Aug. 23, 1954, and one undated; PPG Industries, *The Logical Giant: A History of PPG Industries, Inc.* (Pittsburgh: PPG Industries, no publication date), no page numbers (hereafter cited as PPG Industries, *The Logical Giant*); the Greater Cumberland Chamber of Commerce, *A Challenge for Today* (Cumberland: The Greater Cumberland Chamber of Commerce, 1975), p. 6; PPG File, Allegany County Economic Development Company (hereafter cited as PPG File); and Wilson Interview.

14. Pittsburgh Plate Glass Company, news releases, 1955 and 1956

(exact dates not given), and March 18, 1963; PPG Industries, *The Logical Giant: Pittsburgh Press,* March 18, 1963; and PPG File.

15. Mary Elizabeth H. VanNewkirk, "The Evolution of a College," *The FSC Journal of Mathematics Education,* No. 8 (1974): 6-11; Baltimore *Sun,* Oct. 28, 1963, and May 3, 1974; and interview with William L. Wilson, Feb. 1, 1976.

16. Interview with Nelson P. Guild, March 7, 1976.

17. Hunt, Nov. 19, 1961; Cumberland *Sunday Times,* Oct. 10, 1971; and *A Brief History of Allegany Community College,* enclosed in W. Ardell Haines to author, Oct. 15, 1975.

18. Ladislas Segoe *et al., A Report Upon the Major Highway Plan: Allegany County, Maryland* ("Comprehensive Master Plan Series"; no publication data given, 1965), pp. 5-6 (hereafter cited as Segoe, *A Report Upon the Major Highway Plan*).

19. Baltimore *Sun,* May 3, 1974; interview with Charles Nuzum, Aug. 22, 1975 (hereafter cited as Nuzum Interview); and interview with Mrs. Frances D. Greaves, Oct. 23, 1975.

20. Interview with F. Patrick Allender, Charles Bramble, Stanley Zorick, and Alva Lewis, Jan. 31, 1976; see also Segoe, *A Report Upon the Major Highway Plan.*

21. Harvey, *Best Dressed Miners,* p. 369.

22. For information on the decline of rail passenger service, see *The Official Guide of the Railways* (New York: National Railway Publication Company, 1945-1976). This book, which lists passenger train schedules, is published monthly.

23. Interview with Dan Folk, Feb. 2, 1976; and memorandum enclosed in Buford L. Saville, Potomac Valley Television Company, to author, Dec. 16, 1975.

24. Ibid.

25. For a description of Cumberland city government in the Conlon years, see Cumberland *Evening Times,* 1966-1974; and Hunt, Nov. 28, 1948, and Feb. 28, 1965.

26. New York *Times,* Aug. 16 and 21, 1949; Cumberland *Evening Times,* Sept. 16, 17, 18, 23, 25, and 29, 1950; Case No. 2717 Miscellaneous, Allegany County Circuit Court, Sept. 18, 1950; and Minutes of Cumberland City Council meeting, Sept. 5, 1950.

27. Minutes of Cumberland City Council meetings, Dec. 3, 8, and 17, 1962, Jan. 14 and 28, Feb. 4, and March 25, 1963; and Baltimore *Sun,* May 23, 1963.

28. United States Army Corps of Engineers, *Definite Project Report on Local Flood Protection for Cumberland, Md. & Ridgeley, W. Va.* (Washington: United States Government Printing Office, 1945); *Cumberland, Maryland-Ridgeley, West Virginia Flood Protection Project, 1949-1959* (no publication data or page numbers given); and Hunt, Nov. 28, 1954.

29. Interview with Jerry Goodwin, Sept. 10, 1975; maps of the

Cumberland Urban Renewal Agency; Cumberland *Evening Times,* Jan. 4 and 7, Feb. 4, and Dec. 3, 1963, and Dec. 15, 1965; and Nuzum Interview.

30. Segoe, *A Report Upon Population,* pp. 7, 9-10, 12, Tables 2 and 3.

31. Any issue of the *Guardian* will acquaint a perceptive reader with the type of stories which it prints; see also Criminal Trials No. 1387 and 1388, *State of Maryland* v. *John H. Martin,* Allegany County Circuit Court, March 13, 1973.

BIBLIOGRAPHY

A. Primary Materials

I. Government, Municipal, and Industrial Reports and Books

Allegany County, Alien Docket, U.R. No. 2.

Allegany County Court Docket, January and April Terms, 1937; State of Maryland at the Relation of William Boyd Coleman, Petitioner, v. Frank A. Perdew, Police Magistrate for the City of Cumberland, Case No. 2717 (18 September 1950); State of Maryland v. John H. Martin, Allegany County, Circuit Court, Cases 1387 and 1388 (13 March 1973).

Allegany County Land Records.

Boyds Cumberland City and Allegany County Directory, 1877-1878. Cumberland: Alleganian and Times Publishing Co., 1878.

A Brochure About LaVale, Maryland (no date).

Burke, Edmund S. *A Message to the Employes of the Kelly-Springfield Tire Company.* Cumberland: Kelly-Springfield Tire Company, 1936.

Compendium of the Enumeration of the Inhabitants and Statistics of the United States from the Returns of the Sixth Census. Washington: Department of State, 1841.

Courier Cumberland City Directory, 1888.

Cumberland, Maryland. *Minute Books of the Cumberland Chamber of Commerce,* 1916 to 1975.

Cumberland, Maryland. Minutes of the Cumberland City Council Meetings, 1920 to 1976.

Cumberland and Pennsylvania Railroad. *Side Track Record, 1927.*

Cumberland Sesquicentennial Souvenir Program and History. Cumberland: The Cumberland Sesquicentennial Committee, 1937.

Cumberland Urban Renewal Agency, Maps and Records.

Cummings, H. S., ed. *An Investigation of the Pollution and Sanitary Conditions of the Potomac Watershed.* Washington: Hygienic Laboratory, 1916.

Donaldson, James L. *Speech in the House of Delegates of Maryland on the Subject of the Allegany Election.* Baltimore: E. French and Co., 1814.

First Annual Report of the Maryland Bureau of Industrial Statistics. Baltimore: William J. C. Dulany Company, 1893.

Fourth Biennial Report of the Maryland Bureau of Industrial Statistics. Annapolis: C. H. Baughman and Company, 1892.

Fifth Annual Report of the Maryland Bureau of Industrial Statistics. Baltimore: King Brothers, 1897.

Seventeenth Annual Report of the Maryland Bureau of Industrial Statistics. Baltimore: Kohn and Pollack, Inc., 1908.

Eighteenth Annual Report of the Maryland Bureau of Industrial Statistics. Baltimore: George W. King Printing Co., 1910.

Nineteenth Annual Report of the Maryland Bureau of Industrial Statistics. Baltimore: Kohn and Pollack, Inc., 1911.

Twentieth Annual Report of the Maryland Bureau of Industrial Statistics. Baltimore: King Brothers, 1912.

Flexner, Abraham, and Bachman, Frank P. *Public Education in Maryland: A Report to the Maryland Educational Survey Commission.* New York: The General Education Board, 1916.

Frostburg Sesquicentennial Souvenir Book. Frostburg: The Frostburg Sesquicentennial Committee, 1962.

The George Mercer Papers. The Darlington Library, West Chester State College, West Chester, Pennsylvania.

Grine, Henry A. *Preliminary Economic Studies of the Western Allegany County Area.* Annapolis: Maryland State Planning Commission, 1941.

Historical-Biographical Sketch of Frostburg, Maryland, and Its Citizens. Frostburg: Mining Journal Publishing Co., 1912.

Historical Sketch of Frostburg, Maryland: A Brief History of Frostburg compiled at request of the Bethlehem-Fairfield Shipyards, Inc., in connection with the launching and christening of the SS Frostburg Victory in Baltimore, Saturday, January 20, 1945. Frostburg: The Fidelity Savings Bank, 1945.

Insurance Maps of Cumberland, Maryland. New York: Sanborn Map Company, 1921.

Insurance Maps of Frostburg, Maryland. New York: Sanborn Map Company, 1910.

The Johns Hopkins University Faculty. *Maryland: Its Resources, Industries and Institutions.* Baltimore: The Johns Hopkins University Press, 1893.

Kelly-Springfield Tire Company. News Releases, October 17, 1974, and March 6, 1975.

Maryland Department of Economic Development. *Fact Sheet on Appalachian Maryland: Garrett, Allegany and Washington Counties.* Annapolis: Maryland Department of Economic Development, 1962.

Maryland Genealogical Society. *Allegany County, Maryland, 1800 Census.* Baltimore: n.p.

Maryland State Planning Commission. *Lonaconing: An Economic Survey.* Baltimore: Maryland State Planning Commission, 1956.

The Official Guide of the Railways. New York: National Railway Publication Company, August 1922 to May 1971.

Parker H. N., ed. *The Potomac River Basin.* Washington: U.S. Geological Survey, Water Supply and Irrigation Paper, 1907.

Pittsburgh Plate Glass Company, News Releases, October 28, 1953; March 17 and 18, 1954; August 23, 1954; and several undated from 1955, 1956, and 1963.

Proceedings of the Executive Department: State of Maryland Executive Minutes, January 8, 1896-January 6, 1904. Annapolis: Hall of Records.

Public Relations Department, Luke Mill. *Luke Mill Report.* Luke, Md.: Public Relations Department, 1975.

Report of the George's Creek Coal and Iron Company. Baltimore: Privately published, 1839.

Segoe, Ladislas, and associates. "Comprehensive Master Plan Series." *A Report Upon Population and Other Characteristics: Allegany County, Maryland.* 1961.

———. "Comprehensive Master Plan Series." *A Report Upon Population and other Characteristics: Allegany County, Maryland.* 1965.

———. "Comprehensive Master Plan Series." *A Report Upon the Major Highway Plan: Allegany County, Maryland.* 1965.

Small, Fred T. *Factory and Home.* Cumberland: Celanese Corporation of America, 1949.

Twenty-Fourth Annual Report of the Bank Commissioner of the State of Maryland to His Excellency, Albert C. Ritchie, Governor: February 10, 1934. Annapolis: n.p., 1934.

Twenty-Fifth Annual Report of the Bank Commissioner of the State of Maryland to His Excellency, Harry W. Nice, Governor: February 10, 1935. Annapolis: n.p., 1935.

U.S. Army Corps of Engineers. *Definite Project Report on Local Flood Protection for Cumberland, Md. and Ridgeley, W.Va.* Washington: U.S. Government Printing Office, 1945.

U.S. Congressional Record, 55th Cong., 2nd session, 1898, Senate Document 90.

U.S. Department of Commerce. *United States Census, 1850–Allegany County.*

———. Bureau of the Census. *Ninth Census of the U.S.: 1870.* Washington: U.S. Government Printing Office, 1872.

———. ———. *Tenth Census of the U.S.: 1880.* Washington: U.S. Government Printing Office, 1883.

———. ———. *Twelfth Census of the U.S.: 1900.* Washington: U.S. Government Printing Office, 1902.

———. ———. *Thirteenth Census of the U.S.: 1910.* Washington: U.S. Government Printing Office, 1912.

———. ———. *Fourteenth Census of the U.S.: 1920.* Washington: U.S. Government Printing Office, 1921.

———. ———. *Seventeenth Decennial Census of the U.S.: Census of Population: 1950.* Vol. II: Characteristics of the Population. Part 20: Maryland. Washington: U.S. Government Printing Office, 1952.

———. ———. *Eighteenth Decennial Census of the U.S.: Census of Population: 1960.* Vol. I: Characteristics of the Population. Part 22: Maryland. Washington: U.S. Government Printing Office, 1963.

———. ———. *1970 Census of the Population: Detailed Characteristics of the Population: Maryland.* Washington: U.S. Government Printing Office, 1972.

———. ———. *County and City Data Book: 1972.* Washington: U.S. Government Printing Office, 1973.

U.S. Department of the Interior. *The Floods of March, 1936. Part 3: Potomac, James and Upper Ohio Rivers.* Washington: U.S. Government Printing Office, 1937.

U.S. Sanitary Commission. *Report, 1862.* Washington: U.S. Government Printing Office, 1862.

———. *Report, 1864.* Washington: U.S. Government Printing Office, 1864.

Washington, George. *The Journal of Major George Washington.* Williamsburg, Va.: The Institute of Early American History and Culture, 1959. Facsimile of the original edition, Williamsburg, 1754.

Westvaco Corporation, Luke Mill News Release, June 1974.

II. Interviews and Letters

Allender, F. Patrick; Bramble, Charles; Lewis, Alva; and Zorick, Stanley. Interview, 31 January 1976.

Baker, William F. Interview, 5 December 1975.

Birmingham, Mrs. Frank; Birmingham, Mary M.; and Birmingham, Virginia I. Interview, 20 August 1975.

Bishop, James W. Interview, 4 November 1975. Note to Harry Stegmaier, Jr., November 1975.

Conway, James G. Interview, 16 September 1975.

Crooks, William E. Interview, 5 November 1975.

Cutter, Elsie. Taped interview by David W. Vaughan, April 1975.

Duckson, Don W., Jr. Memorandum to John B. Wiseman, 20 February 1976.

Elias, James. Taped Interview by Ward Orem, April 1975.

Everline, Anne. Interview, 30 December 1974.

Finan, Thomas B., III. Interview, 18 August 1975.

Folk, Dan. Interview, 2 February 1976.

Georgius, Charles R. Memorandum to William L. Wilson, State Bank Commissioner, 22 October 1975.

Goodwin, Jerry. Interview, 10 September 1975.

Greaves, Frances D. Interview, 23 October 1975.

Guild, Nelson P. Interview, 7 March 1976.

Haines, W. Ardell. Memorandum to Harry Stegmaier, Jr., *A Brief History of Allegany Community College.* October 15, 1975.

Helmer, Leslie L. Letter to James W. Bishop, November 1975.

Hess, Jerry. Interview, 10 October 1975.

Klippstein, James, and Ternent, Alvin H. Interview, 1 October 1975.

Lewis, Edgar M. Interview, 10 December 1975.

Miller, Herman J. Interviews, 15 October 1975 and 30 October 1975.

Morton, Fred; Skidmore, Matthew; and Wehler, Rev. George. Interview 7 October 1975.

Nuzum, Charles R. Interview, 22 August 1975.

Race, Ralph M., and Skidmore, Matthew. Interview, 30 July 1975.

Rice, Mrs. Gladys. Interview, 10 October 1975.

Saville, Buford L. Memorandum to Harry Stegmaier, Jr., 16 December 1975.

Shannon, John W. Interview, 4 October 1975.

Simpson, Olive. Interview, 3 September 1975.

Stegmaier, Mr. and Mrs. Harry I. Interview, 20 August 1975.

Thompson, M. Paul. Memorandum to Harry Stegmaier, Jr., *History of Allegany Ballistics Laboratory.* December 1975.

Thompson, William M. Interview, 11 February 1976.

Wilson, William L. Interviews, 18 August 1975 and 12 November 1975.

III. Newspapers

The Advocate (Lonaconing), 1915.

Alleganian (Cumberland), 1838-1865.

Allegany Federalist (Cumberland), 1816.

Allegany Freeman (Cumberland), 1816.

Baltimore American, 1896, 1899.

Baltimore Sun, 1861, 1895, 1899, 1963, 1974.

Civilian (Cumberland), 1828-1833, 1840-1865, 1890-1896.
Cumberland Civilian and Telegraph, 1859-1870, 1880, 1882.
Cumberland Daily Alleganian, 1876-1878, 1902.
Cumberland Daily News, 1871-1938.
Cumberland Evening Times, 1899, 1908, 1909, 1911, 1917-1976.
Cumberland Miner's Journal, 1851-1859.
Cumberland Sunday Times, 1920-1976.
Cumberland Union, 1865-1866.
Democratic Alleganian (Cumberland), 1860.
Frostburg Gazette and Mining Record, 1858.
Frostburg Mining Journal, 1871-1876, 1881-1883, 1896, 1898, 1901.
George's Creek Press (Lonaconing), 1907.
Heritage Press (Cumberland), 1971-1972.
Heritage Review, 1973-1974.
Maryland Advocate (Cumberland), 1823-1838.
Maryland Gazette, October 9, 1755.
Mountain City Times (Cumberland), 1870-1871.
National Intelligencer (Washington), 1825.
New York Evening Post, 1860.
New York Gazette, October 25, 1775.
New York Times, 1949-1950.
Niles Register (Washington), 1836.
Phoenix Civilian (Cumberland), 1833-1840.
Piedmont Herald, 1894.
Pittsburgh Press, March 18, 1963.
Telegraph (Cumberland), 1851-1859.
True Union (Frostburg), 1862.
Union (Cumberland), 1862-1866.
Valley Times (Lonaconing), 1879.

B. Secondary Materials

I. Government, Municipal and Industrial Reports

Aaron, Tim. *A History of the Cumberland and Pennsylvania Railroad.* Graduate paper, Frostburg State College, 1975.

Allegany County Federation of Women's Clubs. Cumberland: n.p., 1925.

Amcelle: First Link in a Global Chain. Cumberland: Celanese Corporation, 1974.

Burkey, Fr. Blaine. *"Als ich in Cumberland war . . .": Capuchin Franciscan Memories of 100 Years in Cumberland, 1875-1975.* Capuchin Franciscan Order, 1975.

Carney, Charles. "The History of Mt. Savage." Unpublished paper prepared for the Maryland Cooperative Extension Service, 1967.

Carraway, Angela. "The Chesapeake and Ohio Canal in the Early 1870's." Unpublished paper, Frostburg State College, 1975.

Cumberland and Pennsylvania Railroad Company. "Ninety-two Years of Transportation Progress." Cumberland: n.p., 1937.

Davis, Agnes M., and Butler, Sally Cutter. *History of Midland, Maryland.* Privately published, 1975.

Dowling, Nellie. "The Story of Westernport." Unpublished paper, Westernport Public Library, n.d.

Fairbanks, W. L. *The Manufacturing Industry of Maryland.* Baltimore: Maryland Development Bureau, 1932.

———. *A Statistical Analysis of the Population of Maryland.* Baltimore: Maryland Development Bureau, 1931.

——— and Hamill, W. S. *The Coal Mining Industry in Maryland.* Baltimore: Maryland Development Bureau, 1932.

Fox, William Lloyd, and Walsh, Richard, eds. *Maryland: A History, 1632-1974.* Baltimore: Maryland Historical Society, 1974.

From Armorubber to Armor-Piercing Bullets. Cumberland: Kelly-Springfield Engineering Company, n.d.

Frostburg Sesquicentennial Souvenir Book. Frostburg: The Frostburg Sesquicentennial Committee, 1962.

The Greater Cumberland Chamber of Commerce. *A Challenge for Today.* Cumberland: The Greater Cumberland Chamber of Commerce, 1975.

Greaves, Frances D. "Westernport Information." Typescript, 1975.

Harris, F. Paul. "Historical Sketch of Barton." 1932.

The Kelly-Springfield Tire Company: A Part of History. Cumberland: Kelly-Springfield Tire Company News Bureau, n.d.

Kelly-Springfield Today (Cumberland Edition). September 1973, June 1975, and September 1975.

Luke Mill, Public Relations Department. *An Unofficial Historical Outline of Westvaco Corporation.* Luke, Md.: Public Relations Department, 1974.

Maps of the Cumberland Urban Renewal Agency.

Masterson, Thomas D. "The Formation of a Progressive: Early Career of David J. Lewis of Maryland." M.A. Thesis, Georgetown University, 1969.

McCoy, Nellie H. "History of Westernport." Typescript, n.d.

Porter, J. Marshall. Essay submitted for "I Remember When" Contest, 1976.

PPG File, Allegany County Development Company.

PPG Industries. *The Logical Giant: A History of PPG Industries, Inc.* Pittsburgh: PPG Industries, n.d.

Reinhart, Scott. "The History of Frostburg Movie Theaters." Unpublished paper, Frostburg State College, 1972.

Richards, William M. "An Experiment in Industrial Feudalism at Lonaconing, Maryland, 1837-1860." M.A. Thesis, University of Maryland, 1950.

St. Patrick's Church, Mt. Savage, Maryland: Special Centennial Issue, 1873-1973. St. Patrick's Centennial Committee, 1973.

Thirty-Fifth Anniversary: Kelly-Springfield Cumberland Plant, 1920-1955. Cumberland: Kelly-Springfield Tire Company, 1955.

Town of Luke, Maryland: 50th Anniversary of Incorporation, 1922 through 1972. Luke: Privately published, 1972.

VanNewkirk, Mary Elizabeth H. "The Origins of Frostburg State College." Unpublished paper, Frostburg State College, 1975.

Walsh, Mary G. "Thomas Beall of Samuel, 1744-1823. Backward, Turn Backward!" in *Fort Cumberland Bicentennial, 1755-1955.* Cumberland: Fort Cumberland Bicentennial Committee, 1955.

Weatherholt, F. Allan, Sr. "A Tribute to Honorable David J. Lewis." Unpublished paper, Cumberland, Md., 1975.

Weeks, Thekla Fundenberg. *Oakland Centennial History, 1849-1949.* Oakland, Md.: Oakland Centennial Commission, Inc., 1949.

Westvaco Fine Papers Division. *Progress on the Potomac.* Luke: Westvaco Fine Papers Division, n.d.

Westvaco News Letter, April-May, 1969.

White, Frank F. *The Governors of Maryland, 1777-1970.* Annapolis: The Hall of Records Commission, 1970.

Williams, Gertrude. "A History of Education in Allegany County, Maryland, 1798-1900." M.A. Thesis, University of Maryland, 1936.

Willison, Hilleary F. "History of the Pioneer Settlers of Flintstone, District #3, and Their Descendants." Unpublished typescript, 1910.

Yankelevitz, Florence. Essay submitted for "I Remember When" Contest, 1976.

II. Books

Abbe, Cleveland, Jr. *The Physiography of Allegany County.* Baltimore: The Johns Hopkins Press, 1900.

Allen, Frederick Lewis. *Only Yesterday.* New York: Bantam Books, 1959. Reprint of the 1931 edition.

American Anti-Slavery Almanac for 1840. New York and Boston: American Anti-Slavery Society.

Bailey, Kenneth P. *The Ohio Company of Virginia.* Glendale, Calif.: The Arthur H. Clark Company, 1939.

Baldwin, Leland D. *Whiskey Rebels: The Story of a Frontier Uprising.* Pittsburgh: University of Pittsburgh Press, 1968.

Beebe, Lucius, and Clegg, Charles. *The Trains We Rode,* Vol. I. Berkeley, Calif.: Howell-North Books, 1965.

Besley, F. W. *The Forests of Allegany County.* Baltimore: State Board of Forestry, 1912.

Bishop, James W. *The Glass Industry of Allegany County, Maryland.* Cumberland: Commercial Press Printing Company, 1968.

Blancke, Harold. *Celanese Corporation of America: The Founders and the Early Years.* New York: The Newcomen Society in North America, 1952.

Boatner, Mark M., III. *Encyclopedia of the American Revolution.* New York: David McKay Co., Inc., 1966.

Bowen, Ele. *Rambles in the Path of the Steam Horse.* Philadelphia: W. Bromwell & W. W. Smith, 1855.

Bowersox, Hixon T. *History of St. Paul's English Lutheran Church of Cumberland, Maryland.* Cumberland: Monarch Printing Company, 1944.

Brehger, Jeremy. *Strike!* Greenwich, Conn.: Fawcett Publications, 1974.

Bridenbaugh, Carl. *Myths and Realities: Societies of the Colonial South.* New York: Atheneum Press, 1971.

Brigham, Clarence. *History and Bibliography of American Newspapers, 1690-1820.* Worcester: American Antiquarian Society, 1947.

Brown, Jacob. *Miscellaneous Writings.* Cumberland: Miller, 1896.

Browne, William Hand, ed. *Archives of Maryland: The Correspondence of Governor Sharpe.* 3 vols. Baltimore: Maryland Historical Society, 1888-1895.

Calendar of Maryland State Papers: The Black Books. Baltimore: The Genealogical Company, 1967.

The Calvert Papers, Vol. 2, No. 34. Baltimore: Maryland Historical Society, 1894.

Clark, Thomas D. *Frontier America.* New York: Charles Scribner's Sons, 1959.

Cleland, Hugh. *George Washington in the Ohio Valley.* Pittsburgh: University of Pittsburgh Press, 1955.

Cunz, Dieter. *The Maryland Germans: A History.* Princeton: Princeton University Press, 1948.

Doctorow, E. L. *Ragtime.* New York: Random House, 1974-1975.

Dubin, Arthur D. *Some Classic Trains.* Milwaukee: Kalmbach Publishing Company, 1964.

Edgar, Lady. *A Colonial Governor in Maryland.* New York: Longmans, Green, and Co., 1912.

Fitzpatrick, John C., ed. *The Diaries of George Washington, 1748-1799.* 4 vols. Boston: Houghton Mifflin Company, 1971.

Flexner, James T. *George Washington: The Forge of Experience, 1732-1775.* Boston: Little, Brown & Co., 1965.

Gara, Larry. *The Liberty Line.* Lexington: University of Kentucky Press, 1967.

Gilmor, Harry. *Four Years in the Saddle.* New York: Harper Brothers, 1866.

Greene, Evarts B., and Harrington, Virginia D. *American Population Before the Federal Census of 1790.* Gloucester, Mass.: Peter Smith Press, 1966.

Gutheim, Frederick. *The Potomac.* New York: Rinehart and Co., 1949.

Harvey, Katherine A. *Best Dressed Miners: Life and Labor in the Maryland Coal Region, 1835-1910.* Ithaca: Cornell University Press, 1969.

Hungerford, Edward. *The Story of the Baltimore and Ohio Railroad, 1827-1927.* 2 vols. New York: G. P. Putnam's Sons, 1928.

Jacob, John J. *A Biographical Sketch of the Life of the Late Captain Michael Cresap.* Cincinnati: J. F. Uhlhorn, 1866.

James, Alfred P., and Stotz, Charles M. *Drums in the Forest.* Pittsburgh: Historical Society of Western Pennsylvania, 1958.

Johnson, Allen, and Malone, Dumas, eds. *The Dictionary of American Biography.* New York: Charles Scribner's Sons, 1931.

Johnson, B. F. *Men of Mark in Maryland.* Vols. III and IV. Baltimore: B. F. Johnson, Inc., 1911-1912.

Jordon, Philip. *The National Road.* Indianapolis: Bobbs-Merrill Company, 1948.

Kelley, William J. *Brewing in Maryland from Colonial Times to the Present.* Baltimore: John D. Lucas Printing Company, 1965.

Kent, Frank R. *The Story of Maryland Politics.* Baltimore: King Brothers, Inc., 1911.

Lambert, John R. *Arthur Pue Gorman.* Baton Rouge: Louisiana State University Press, 1953.

Land, Aubrey C. *The Dulanys of Maryland.* Baltimore: The Johns Hopkins Press, 1968.

Leuchtenburg, William E. *Franklin D. Roosevelt and the New Deal, 1932-1940.* New York: Harper & Row, Publishers, 1963.

Lowdermilk, Will H. *History of Cumberland.* Baltimore: Regional Publishing Company, 1971. Reprint of the 1878 edition.

Malone, Dumas. *Jefferson the Virginian.* Boston: Little, Brown & Co., 1948.

Manakee, Harold. *Maryland in the Civil War.* Baltimore: Maryland Historical Society, 1961.

Manchester, William. *The Glory and the Dream: A Narrative History of America, 1932-1972.* Vol. I. Boston: Little, Brown & Co., 1973.

Maryland in the World War, 1917-1919: Military and Naval Service Records. Baltimore: Maryland War Records Commission, 1933.

Maxwell, H. U., and Swisher, H. L. *History of Hampshire County.* Morgantown: A. B. Boughner, 1897.

McCardell, Lee. *Ill-Starred General: Braddock of the Coldstream Guards.* Pittsburgh: University of Pittsburgh Press, 1958.

McHaig, Ian, and Muhlenberg, Nicholas. *George's Creek.* Philadelphia: University of Pennsylvania Department of Landscape, Architecture and Regional Planning, 1966.

Merriam, C. Hart. "The Flora and Fauna: The Life Zones of Allegany County," *Maryland Geographical Survey: Allegany County.* Baltimore: The Johns Hopkins Press, 1900.

Mulkearn, Lois, ed. *The George Mercer Papers Relating to the Ohio Company of Virginia.* Pittsburgh: University of Pittsburgh Press, 1954.

Nye, Russel. *The Unembarrassed Muse.* New York: The Dial Press, 1970.

Parkman, Francis. *Montcalm and Wolfe.* New York: Collier Books, 1966.

Pearson, Michael. *The Revolutionary War.* New York: Capricorn Books, 1973.

Roy, Andrew. *History of Coal Mining in the United States.* Columbus: J. L. Trauger Printing Co., 1905.

———. *Recollections of a Prisoner of War.* Columbus: J. L. Trauger Printing Co., 1909.

Sanderlin, Walter S. *The Great National Project, A History of the Chesapeake and Ohio Canal.* Baltimore: Johns Hopkins Press, 1946.

Scharf, John T. *History of Western Maryland.* Philadelphia: L. H. Everts Company, 1882.

Searight, Thomas. *The Old Pike.* Uniontown: By the Author, 1894.

Shannon, David A. *Twentieth Century America: The United States Since the 1890's.* Chicago: Rand McNally & Company, 1963.

Stanton, Thomas J. *A Century of Growth, or the History of the Church in Western Maryland.* Baltimore: John Murphy Company, 1900.

Stover, John F. *American Railroads.* Chicago: University of Chicago Press, 1961.

Thomas, James W., and Williams, T. J. C. *History of Allegany County, Maryland*. Philadelphia: L. R. Titsworth & Company, 1923.

Two Hundred Years. Washington, D.C.: U.S. News and World Report Books, 1973.

Wade, Richard C. *The Urban Frontier.* Chicago: University of Chicago Press, 1972.

Wainwright, Nicholas. *George Croghan: Wilderness Diplomat.* Chapel Hill, N.C.: University of North Carolina Press, 1959.

Wallace, Lew. *An Autobiography*. New York: Harper Brothers, n.d.

III. Journal Articles

Crooks, James B. "Review of *Best Dressed Miners,*" by Katherine A. Harvey. *Maryland Historical Magazine* 66 (Spring 1971): 82-83.

Harvey, Katherine A. "Building a Frontier Ironworks: Problems of Transport and Supply, 1837-1840." *Maryland Historical Magazine* 70 (Summer 1975): 149-66.

Jones, Mary H. "The Fairfax Stone." *State of West Virginia* 39 (January 1976).

Kelly, Tom. " 'Seducer' Murdered: Girl's Brother Held." *The Washingtonian Magazine* 7 (November 1971): 80-82, 125-27.

Lowitt, Richard, ed. "Frostburg 1882: German Strikers vs. German Strikebreakers." Society for the History of the Germans in Maryland: *Twenty-eighth Report* (1953): 72-78.

Stegmaier, Mark Joseph. "The Kidnapping of Generals Crook and Kelley by the McNeill Rangers." *West Virginia History* 29 (October 1967): 13-47.

VanNewkirk, Mary Elizabeth H. "The Evolution of a College." *The FSC Journal of Mathematics Education* No. 8 (1974): 6-12.

———. "Frostburg After Hours, Recreation: 1871-1877." *Journal of the Alleghenies* 9 (1973):21-27.

INDEX

Book printed on Westvaco paper

ALLEGANY C

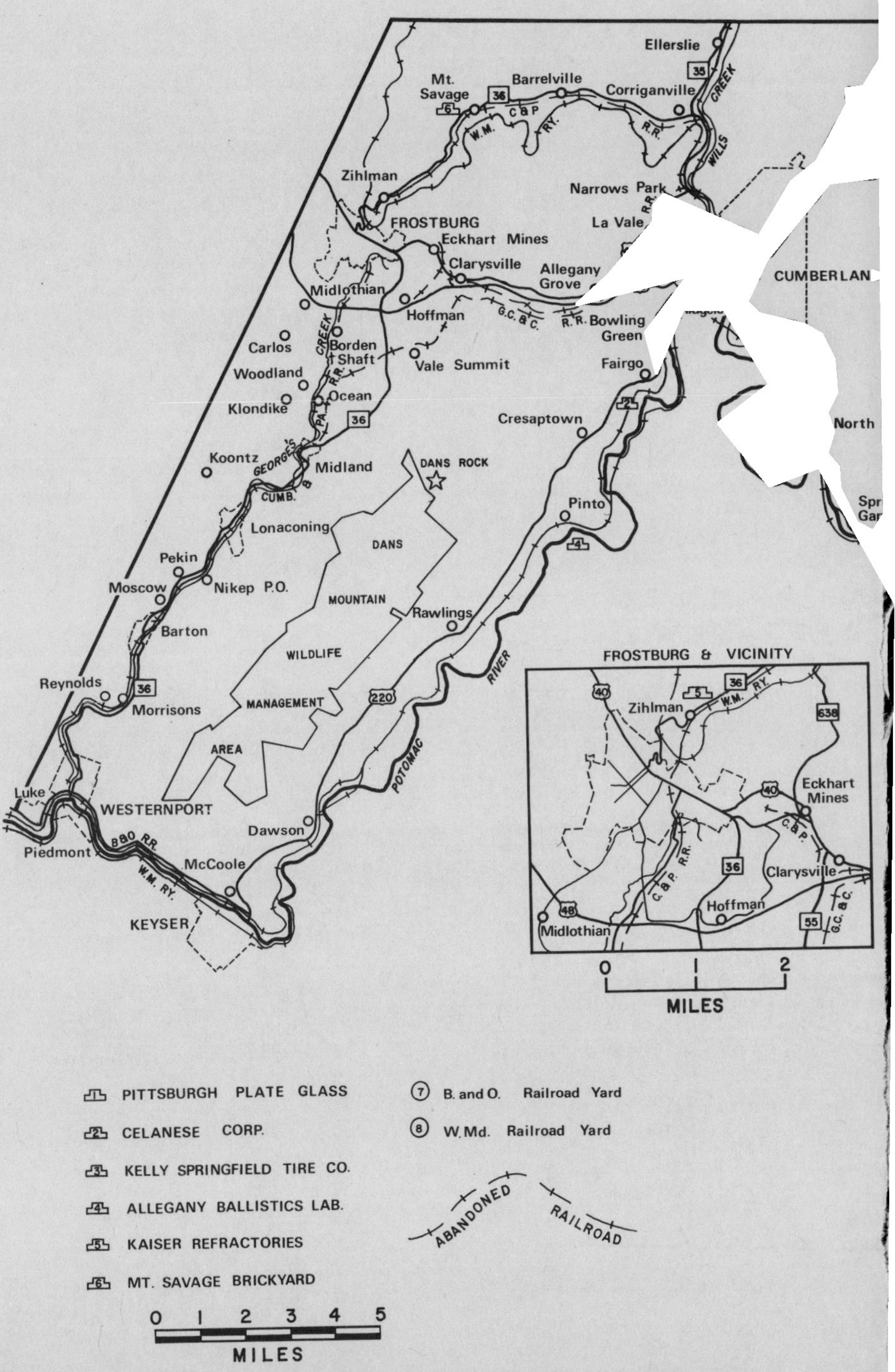

Ellerslie
Mt. Savage
Barrelville
Corriganville
C & P R.R.
W.M. RY.
WILLS CREEK
Zihlman
Narrows Park
FROSTBURG
La Vale
Eckhart Mines
Clarysville
Allegany Grove
CUMBERLAN
Midlothian
Hoffman
G.C. & C. R.R.
Bowling Green
Carlos
Borden Shaft
Vale Summit
Woodland
Fairgo
Klondike
Ocean
Cresaptown
North
GEORGES CREEK
Koontz
Midland
DANS ROCK
CUMB. & PA. R.R.
Pinto
Lonaconing
DANS MOUNTAIN WILDLIFE MANAGEMENT AREA
Pekin
Moscow
Nikep P.O.
Rawlings
Barton
Reynolds
Morrisons
POTOMAC RIVER
Luke
WESTERNPORT
Piedmont
B & O RR.
W.M. RY.
Dawson
McCoole
KEYSER
FROSTBURG & VICINITY
0 1 2 MILES
PITTSBURGH PLATE GLASS
CELANESE CORP.
KELLY SPRINGFIELD TIRE CO.
ALLEGANY BALLISTICS LAB.
KAISER REFRACTORIES
MT. SAVAGE BRICKYARD
B. and O. Railroad Yard
W. Md. Railroad Yard
ABANDONED RAILROAD
0 1 2 3 4 5 MILES